Yesterday's Soldiers

European Military
Professionalism
in South America,
1890–1940

Frederick M. Nunn

Yesterday's Soldiers

University of Nebraska Press
Lincoln & London

The paper in this book meets the guidelines for
permanence and durability of the Committee on
Production Guidelines for Book Longevity of the
Council on Library Resources.

Library of Congress Cataloging in Publication Data

Nunn, Frederick M., 1937-
Yesterday's soldiers.

Includes bibliographical references and index.
1. Sociology, Military — South America.   2. Military
art and science — South America — History.
3. Europe — Military relations — South America.
4. South America — Military relations — Europe.   I. Title
UA612.N86   306'.27'098   82-6961
ISBN 0-8032-3305-1   AACR2

For Susan & Jessica

Contents

ix   Preface

1   Introduction

PART ONE   CHAPTER ONE
13   The South American
Setting: 1890–1914

CHAPTER TWO
43   The South American
Military Tradition:
Preprofessional Armies

CHAPTER THREE
70   European Military
Professionalism: Its
Champions & Critics

CHAPTER FOUR
99   Missions & Missionaries:
The Meeting of Minds

PART TWO   CHAPTER FIVE
157   The South American
Setting: 1919–1940

CHAPTER SIX
182   Missions & Missionaries:
Professionalism
in a New Setting

CHAPTER SEVEN
222   European Military
Professionalism between
the Wars: Tradition
in a New Setting

CHAPTER EIGHT
249   South American Military
Professionalism between
the Wars: The Origins of
Professional Militarism

287   Postscript

297   Notes

351   Index

Preface

Some years ago I set about to study Chilean civil-military relations between the civil war of 1891 and the presidential election of 1938. I did not know then that one day I would use this same chronological framework for a somewhat more ambitious project. In *Chilean Politics, 1920–1931: The Honorable Mission of the Armed Forces* (Albuquerque: University of New Mexico Press, 1970), I discussed in detail the earliest example in South America of military-political action based on a professional ethos. In several articles published in scholarly journals I elaborated on Chilean civil-military relations, soon concluding that what I was discussing should be dealt with as *military-civilian* relations. A generous grant from the Henry L. and Grace Doherty Charitable Foundation made possible the bulk of my early published work on Chile.

As *Chilean Politics, 1920–1931* went to press, the American Philosophical Society funded preliminary research on French and German military missions in South America. The work I did in 1969 made it clear to me that Argentines, Brazilians, and Peruvians experienced the same kind of professionalization that Emil Körner had begun in Chile in 1886. In several essays published during the 1970s I treated this process as a continental phenomenon in comparative terms, one that led to comparable results vis-à-vis professional relations with civilian society and its institutions. I concluded tentatively that European-trained South Americans would think and write, and perceive themselves, as had their mentors. I therefore decided to press further in the study of the subject, examining the thought and self-perception of South American army officers during the era of European military professional hegemony. All told, this era extends from 1886, when Körner began his work in Santiago, to 1940, when French officers ended theirs in Rio de Janeiro and Lima. Research on comparative aspects led me to the conclusion that 1890 was a more suitable date to begin the present study, for by that date Körner was in place, and soon political decisions were made that facilitated the professionalization process elsewhere.

In the interim I sent to the publisher *The Military in Chilean History: Essays on Civil-Military Relations, 1810–1973* (Albuquerque: University of New Mexico Press, 1976). The writing of that book wove together many of the threads spun over the preceding years. I saw finally that Chilean officer-corps thought and self-perception simply had not changed all that measurably between 1920 and 1970. The passage of a half-century, and all the events that filled those fifty years, had changed faces, names, and some specifics, but the military mind remained essentially the same. If Chile's sister states shared the professional experience, might not the ideals and values of the officer corps be comparable as well? If Chilean military ideology changed little during an apparently tumultuous fifty-year period, might not the same hold true for the Argentine, Brazilian, and Peruvian officer corps? Was South American military professionalism really comparable over the years to that of the European powers?

The answer to each question is, of course, yes. But the half-century involved here is not that between 1920 and 1970, rather that between 1890 and 1940. Although I am convinced that South American military professionalism was in essence the same in the 1970s as it was in the 1920s, I choose to argue for the earlier period here. Suffice it to say at this point that I think the argument can be made for the later period, and convincingly so. Herein I propose to demonstrate that despite the passage of five decades, officer-corps (officer-*class* may indeed be more appropriate for the earlier years) thought and self-perception changed but little. These are the very essence of military professionalism, the state or condition of being professional in the dictionary sense. Professionalism could not have existed without the collective wisdom, opinions, and perceptions—or lore, as I have called it on occasion—that constitute thought on state, nation, and society, and the self-perceptions of the nature and role of the officer and his army.

The Joint Committee on Latin American Studies of the American Council of Learned Societies and the Social Science Research Council very kindly provided me with a fellowship in 1977–1978 to complete the research for this book. I was thus able to complete and compare findings for Argentina, Brazil, Chile, and Peru made on research trips to South American archives and libraries in 1962, 1969, 1972, and 1975 with those gleaned from poring over French and German military literature in the British Library. There I found that my preliminary conclusions were correct. South Americans very early in this century began to ape the Europeans in all ways. Soon thereafter they responded to domestic reality in ways comparable to European officers. They began to think like Frenchmen and Germans, and to perceive themselves in the same way. This obviously made life very frustrating for them, for not even Argentina at its most sophisticated was as advanced socially, politically, economically, or culturally as France or Germany. The pages that follow describe and interpret this frustration in terms of a grand confrontation between grim reality and wishful thinking. A small grant from the Portland State University Foundation assisted me in the study of growing U.S. military interest in South America in the National Archives, Washington D.C.

This book, then, is one that developed over a number of years. It is a book based somewhat on progression from the specific to the general and back to the specific on a grander scale; from a limited chronological frame to a more extensive but still specifically defined one; from a national to an international scope. Without the aid, at critical junctures, of the institutions mentioned above, this would have been an impossible task. I thank them again for their generosity.

There are individuals who also merit my gratitude. Unfortunately I cannot list them all, for it would be an extensive list indeed. Edwin Lieuwen of the University of New Mexico, who set me to work on Chilean civil-military relations some years ago, merits my gratitude once again. Thomas M. Davies, Jr., of San Diego State University, Michael C. Meyer of the University of Arizona, William L. Sherman of the University of Nebraska, and Joan Connelly Ullman of the University of Washington have patiently listened to my discourses on the subject over the years. So has Professor Robert A. Hayes of Texas Tech University, whose answers to several questions on Brazil proved helpful. Professors Anthony Bryan of the University of Rhode Island and Paul J. Vanderwood of San Diego State University were kind enough to advise me on Mexican archival sources at a time when I contemplated an in-depth investigation of pre-Revolutionary plans to modernize further the Mexican army. Professors Michael F. Reardon and Franklin C. West, my colleagues at Portland State University, rendered advice frequently on French and German military-civilian relations.

In South America the directors and the staffs at army libraries and archives in Argentina, Brazil, Chile, Colombia, and Peru were extremely helpful. Chief among these is Gonzalo Mendoza Aylwin, director of the Biblioteca del Estado Mayor del Ejército de Chile in Santiago. He has been generous with time and effort, and has on many an occasion opened his office and home to me. Without his friendship and assistance most of my initial work would have been difficult.

The Biblioteca del Círculo Militar in Buenos Aires, the Biblioteca do Exército in Rio de Janeiro, and the Centro de Estudios Histórico-Militares in Lima provided most of the archival, official, and secondary sources utilized in these pages on Argentina, Brazil, and Peru. To their personnel I owe much. In Mexico I spent some profitable time in the Archivo Particular Bernardo Reyes, where I was graciously allowed to read the correspondence and works of General Reyes. Although I do not dwell at length on Mexico or Colombia in the work at hand, these materials lent perspective to my thinking on the topic. In Bogotá I was able to use collections in the Defense Ministry Library and in the Biblioteca Tomás Rueda Vargas of the Escuela Superior de Guerra. Like don Gonzalo Mendoza in Santiago, General (r.) Juan Enrique Guglialmelli in Buenos Aires and Major (r.) Víctor Villanueva in Lima have exchanged frank views and offered advice on occasion. To these individuals and institutions, and to numerous Argentine, Brazilian, Chilean, and Peruvian officers, both active and retired, and many civilians who have allowed me access to their collections or counsel, and who have invited me to lecture in their universities, I am very grateful.

The months I spent in London during 1977–1978 were all the more pleasant and productive owing to the staff of the British Library, especially the North Library Gallery of the British Museum. What more can I say to such people, except "Thank you very much indeed," especially to the stalwarts of the Gallery who trundled the stacks of dusty journals and monographs to me day after day. Dr. Harold Blakemore, secretary of the University of London's Institute of Latin American Studies, was most gracious during my time in London. He and his colleagues made me welcome and, by inviting me to share my ideas in lectures, discussion, and seminars, gave me the benefit of their own wisdom.

No author with a family can fail to owe them much, especially during long months of writing. Love, encouragement, support, assistance, understanding, and advice were plentiful at all times from my wife and colleague, Susan C. Karant-Nunn. My daughters Marianna and Jessica were helpful in so many ways. My parents were, as always, most encouraging, and my in-laws were more than hospitable during the summer months of 1979 when I completed research for the second portion of this work in Washington.

No university professor ever had a more competent group of secretaries and assistants over the years than I. On this occasion I want to thank Joni Marie U. Johnson, who prepared the final version of this manuscript. Her knowledge of modern history and her considerable abilities as grammarian and typist blended splendidly.

All translations from French, German, Portugese, and Spanish have been made with the idea of rendering material into proper English while retaining as much of the flavor of the original as possible. I have freely improved on existing translations where I thought it appropriate. Many share in the various phases of this work's elaboration, including that editor and critic par excellence, Lysander Kemp, but I alone am responsible for errors of fact it may contain.

"Remember that amidst the ruins of hierarchies that were, there will be no end to the need for social discipline, for respect, for abnegation—and that the army will always be the best, if not the only, school in which you can learn these virtues."

Hubert Lyautey, "Du Rôle social de l'officier" (1891)

"Party politics subverts hierarchy, menaces the unity of the Fatherland, and endangers the existence of the nation, [thus] exacerbating rivalries and heightening civil discord."

Revista Militar Brasileira (January-December, 1937)

Introduction

Military-civilian relations has been an integral part of Latin American history from the conquests and occupations of the sixteenth century to the institutional *golpes de estado* of the 1960s and 1970s. Empires built by fighting men, frontiers expanded by adventurers, republics created by ambitious soldier-statesmen, new nations dominated by their lieutenants and defended by career officers, and governments guided by officer-politicians—each of these is Latin American reality.

For the past two decades historians have been systematically examining military-civilian relations (usually preferring to call them *civil-military* relations) of the area in general terms, more specifically on a country-by-country comparative basis. In the case of both general, theoretical works and case studies they have achieved various degrees of success. They have been enlightening, to say the least. Scholars from the disciplines of political science and sociology have also contributed solid works to the literature of this subject.

Scholars have paid a modicum of attention to the nature of the professional officer corps in Latin America from various points of view, especially from that of the increasing tendency of truly professional (i.e., educated, career-oriented, specialized) officers to involve themselves in the political and economic developmental processes of the post-World War II years. The base point for these studies, especially the policy-oriented ones, is the war, when the United States began to prepare South American officers and supply South American armies. By the time of the war, U.S. influence on the Caribbean and Central American armies was an established fact. Early sources that deal with pre-1940 military organizations tend to focus on political involvement, but in some of the literature there is mention of the European influences on the formation of modern South American officer corps.

There had been a formal European military presence in South America for fifty years and more before the United States took over the training and supply responsibilities (and liabilities). From 1886 forward, Chile, then Argentina, Peru, and finally Brazil contracted with European officers to professionalize their armies from top to bottom. Bolivia, too, had a German mission prior to World War I. Ecuador, Colombia, Uruguay, Paraguay, and even Venezuela had contacts with European armies or with Europeanized Argentines and Chileans.

The contacts were significant far beyond the bounds of military science, the armaments trade, and geopolitics, for the latter were merely superficial aspects of the professionalization process. South American contact with the army of France or Germany was far more significant in terms of professional orientation. During the half-century preceding 1940, South Americans learned to think like their European mentors and to perceive themselves in the same way. By 1940, military professionalism already showed signs of becoming professional militarism—the propensity and willingness to apply solutions based on a military ethos to social, economic, and political problems.

This book emphasizes the military side of military-civilian relations. The military's relationships with the civilian world were based on professional ideals and values expressed in the thought and self-perceptions (a kind of lore built up over the decades) written down by officers for the consumption of their fellows and, occasionally and selectively, for the public. The primary vehicle for this was, throughout the 1890–1940 era, the professional journal, the *boletines, memoriales* and *revistas* of South America, the *revues* and *Blätter* of Europe.

In their journals, and in monographs, newspaper articles, pamphlets, collected speeches, and memoirs, French and

German officers expressed their thought on various issues. Their pupils emulated them. Soon after the arrival of Germans in Chile (1886), and Argentina (1899), and of the French in Peru (1896) and Brazil (1919), South Americans began to write on themes identical to those treated in European circles. Politics, nationalism, social problems, obligatory military service, education, international relations, the social role of the officer in peacetime, and the army's collective, "civilizing mission" dominated officer-class thought and self-perception not strictly bound to technical aspects of military life. In quick order South Americans in their academies and staff schools absorbed the teachings, assumed the mentality, and aped the attitudes of Europeans. Training *in situ* gave to elite clusters of officers the opportunity to witness military-civilian relations in the two military powers of the European continent. Those who went as observers between 1914 and 1918 had similiar, if strictly wartime, experiences. From 1919 to 1940 South Americans studied the adjustments Germans had to make, and saw first hand the plight of disgruntled French officers. Denied legal continuance of German mission training, Argentines and Chileans (and Bolivians) clung to the past or adjusted their German traditions to newly-successful French doctrines. Brazilians and Peruvians enjoyed (up to a point) the presence of the victors in lecture halls, on drill fields, and on maneuvers.

Military journals form the bulk of the documentation for the following chapters. In their pages can be found the thought and self-perception from which comes the essence of modern-day professional militarism. There are two principal themes prevalent in the literature: scholastic and slavish reliance on precedent and prior authority, and determination to assume a universal role. In the case of the latter, the wide-ranging mission of the profession was based largely on traditional ideas transmitted through the education and training process. South Americans have always related to the past. What Fritz K. Ringer recently wrote concerning European higher education and the "idealized past" it may have represented in the late nineteenth century is true as well for military education: "Obviously the traditions and values

transmitted by higher education can conflict with the contemporary hierarchy of social norms and customs."[1] For the
teachers of the present were the pupils of yesteryear.

Military education has always been based on tradition, conformity, and inbreeding of ideas and attitudes. By the same
token, the officer corps in Germany and South America historically share large numbers of "military families," and
South American armies still are marked by the presence of
these families. In pre-World War II France the majority of
graduates of the École Polytechnique traditionally went into
the army. Thus adherence to traditional norms and reverence
for the past, conformity and institutional inbreeding, were
characteristic of early twentieth-century military organizations. If we had no other sources to indicate this, we would
know it from military literature.

The past proved attractive to officers, so preferable to the
present that they invoked it often. In the "good old days" society was stable, politics was minimal or under control, officers
had few(er) economic worries, all citizens were patriots, and
the entire population respected the army. If only the army were
allowed to play its universal role, that of defender, civilizer,
shaper of manhood, uniter of citizens, and bulwark of order and
decency, then all might be well again. Innovation, tampering with
tradition, was tolerable only under extraordinary circumstances
or in technological matters. A consistently uncomfortable relationship with the present was made more acceptable by clinging
as much as possible to tradition and by preparing, as much as
resources would allow, for the future.

That which is offered in the preceding two paragraphs constitutes a set of valid observations on military professionalism
in, say, 1900, 1910, 1920, 1930, or 1940. Only gradually over
that period did emphasis shift from past and present to present and future.

I have come to these conclusions by interpreting officer-class
thought and self-perception in comparative perspective.In
order to do this, I have examined the South American sociopolitical and economic setting twice, for the years from 1890
to 1914 and again for those from 1919 to 1940.

In the first part, devoted to the pre-1914 years, I have provided a description of both nineteenth-century South American military tradition and European military professionalism. This is followed by a narrative treatment of the process by which Europeans, at times behaving like zealous missionaries, brought their military professionalism to South America and an analysis of the ideals and values soon professed by South Americans. In the second part I have attempted to show how the role of the United States began as a reactive process in the face of continued European activity, notable South American shifts in sentiment, and the advent of war in Europe for the second time in a generation. Following this I have demonstrated how, despite adjustments after the Great War and during the Great Depression, European military professionalism retained much of its essence, then how South American thought and self-perception compared so consistently with, and evoked, that essence. In definition and comparison, South American military professionalism was based on European models throughout this entire period. In a brief postscript I have raised the question of whether or not it still is.

This book obviously does not deal with "military history" per se. There may not be much here to draw the attention of military buffs or of those interested in technology, tactics, and strategy, although they may find the information on military missions interesting. Nor is this book, strictly speaking, an "intellectual biography" or a "morphology of ideas." It is an exposition and interpretation of the long-term expression of what are in essence the very same views and role definition.

I have kept in mind Quentin Skinner's caveat of 1969 that one must beware the "crediting of an author with a meaning he could not have intended to convey, since that meaning was not available to him."[2] When I use terms like development and modernization I do so either in a broad sense or in a sense consistent with the meaning of the period under discussion. Contrasts inherent in the juxtaposition of Western Europe and South America between 1890 and 1914 make this difficult at times, but I have striven for consistency. Some terms—integration, nationalism, patriotism, discipline—are just not that much different in officer-corps usage, so there seems to be no danger of anachronistic definition or usage on my part. The stridently didactic purpose of much of the documentation I have utilized renders it obvious, I think, that ideas conveyed therein were indeed meant for contemporaries, and this precludes any danger of ascribing or imparting values other than those intended. In all cases where there is a question of interpretation I have attempted to provide alternative views.

The South American countries to which French and German officers went in the pre-1914 years were truly behind the times. Retarded social and economic development tempered their exotic appeal to some Europeans, yet stimulated others more used to primitive and alien environments. Superficial resemblances to Western Europe forms did not fool the French and Germans who attempted to bring military organizations up to modern standards. An unevenness in overall development made their job difficult. So did the woeful state of at least three of South America's armies, Argentina's, Brazil's, and Peru's. Even the twice-victorious Chilean forces were in dire need of assistance. South Americans forged their military tradition in battle during independence, and the political turbulence of ensuing decades did not provide environments compatible with orderly progress. Not even in relatively quiescent imperial Brazil, where many of Latin America's problems did not manifest themselves, did the army benefit from internal stability.

The Europeans were products of centuries of tradition but less than a century of outright professionalism; however, they were true professionals by the time South America called them. They were a subsection of society, a specialized and elite group. To some they were a dangerous and malevolent association of individuals. They brought their tradition, their ideals and values, their professional thought and self-perception with them, martial missionaries responding to the call.

A juxtaposition of official military literature indicates this. In their very first published efforts South Americans proved they had absorbed readily the teachings of the masters. The somewhat mystical and necessarily hierarchical qualities so characteristic of nineteenth-century officers, their distinct distrust of politics and liberal democracy, their fear of organized pacifism, their fervent desire to fulfill some kind of peacetime role, and their abject belief in war as inevitable and somehow beneficial all came through in unadulterated form. European military professionalism had crossed the Atlantic Ocean every bit as successfully as it had the Pacific to Japan, far more successfully than it had crossed the Bosporus.

World War I imposed a recess. Germany's defeat meant that Argentines, Chileans, and Brazilians had to adjust to a new order. Peruvians merely reestablished their ties with France. All became more concerned than before the war with politics and governments, the nature of the state, and the theoretical aspects of democracy. Once professional and intellectual associations had been reestablished—in the case of Argentina and Chile, they had been maintained by a steadfast Germanophilia—it was not long before the officers again displayed their European orientation. Former themes like obligatory service, the social function of officers, and antinationalism continued to be important, but now, even more than before, they blurred and fused with attitudes toward politics. The eccentric twists and turns of South American political systems were responsible for this.

During the 1920s the United States showed only the slightest interest in participating in the professionalization of South American armies. A wariness of stepping too far afield, "isolationism," and some unpleasant experiences in the circum-Caribbean delayed any commitment for years. So did die-hard Francophiles and Germanophiles in the southern continent. In Argentina and Chile, the United States had little military prestige. In Brazil and Peru, where naval missions operated, there were only glimmers of interest in military ties with the United States. Little came of all this until the late 1930s, despite the fact that French officers continually alienated politicians and more than a few officers. Documentary evidence suggests only a grudging awareness on the part of the United States from about 1910 forward that military missions were a significant adjunct to diplomatic relations and commercial advantages. This awareness grew in scope, so that by 1935 the United States thought seriously of sending missions to countries where some interest was discernible. But French- and German-style professionalism prevailed into the Second World War.

Meanwhile, for all the obvious advances in military science, tactics, strategy, and technology, for all the stress on mobility, mobilization, and military-civilian defense coordination, the mentality of European and Europeanized army officers remained the same. They still directed their thoughts toward the problems of state, nation, and society. Military-civilian relations had the same characteristics under the Weimar flag as they had under Prussian banners. French officers still complained about the Republic and lamented their eternal plights. French monarchists and French and German corporatists saw little of value in parliamentary democracy. During the 1930s, when extremes in thought were prevalent, officers still perceived themselves as purveyors of civilization, as indispensable upholders of patriotic values.

Official literature of South American officer corps during the 1919–1940 period showed the same dependence on European inspiration it had shown before 1914. But by 1940 South Americans were as truly representative of traditional European military professionalism as were the French and Germans. They eloquently exceeded their idols in championing the various causes espoused since the close of the nineteenth century.

The rigidity with which South American officers maintained their stand vis-à-vis the civilian world between 1919 and 1940 and their dogged adherence to tradition made them representative of an idealized past, a past that never was. Because they chose to identify only selectively with their pre-professional heritage, they transferred some of their identification to a European past, one that their mentors had written and spoken about nostalgically. The (idealized) past was gone forever, they knew, but they could affect the present—and perhaps the future. As the 1930s wore on, South Americans, ever mindful of what was happening in Europe, of the impending clash between authoritarian extremes and the apparent structural weaknesses of European and South American democratic systems, would continue to suffer from social upheaval, political instability, and economic weakness. These officers were intellectually indebted to Europeans and their own nationals who represented pre-World War I military professional archetypes. These were yesterday's soldiers.

One

"From many an ancient river,
From many a palmy plain,
They call us to deliver
Their land from error's chain."

"From Greenland's Icy Mountains,"
missionary hymn,
Reginald Heber (1819)

"The tropics are not so much
exotic as out of date. It's not
the vegetation which
confirms that you are 'really
there', but certain trifling
architectural details and the
hint of a way of life which
would suggest that you had
gone backwards in time
rather than forwards across
a great part of the earth's
surface."

Claude Lévi-Strauss,
Tristes Tropiques (1955)

CHAPTER ONE

The South American
Setting: 1890–1914

The quarter-century preceding the outbreak of World War I was one of constant tension in European military-civilian relations. The same era was one in which the genesis of the military-civilian relationship characteristic of contemporary South America took place. Tensions evident in France and Germany became contributory to attitudes expressed toward state, nation, and society by army officers, then by the officers they trained in Argentina, Brazil, Chile, and Peru. Owing to this, the profession of arms in these countries bears an indelible Gallic and Teutonic stamp from the beginnings of professionalism onward.

Latin America was particularly susceptible to foreign influences at the close of the nineteenth century. To the north the United States, its domestic frontiers "closed" by expansion in a literal sense, both intellectually and figuratively by Turner's dicta of 1892, had begun to export influence and capital to Mexico and the circum-Caribbean.[1] Further south, the impact of Yankee "expansionism" would not be felt until the United States emerged from the Great War a creditor nation, yet the psychological trauma of the 1898 victory over Spain, the wresting of Panama from helpless Colombia, and the rise of the northern republic as a hemispheric power did cause concerns like those articulated by José Enrique Rodó in his *Ariel* and by Manuel Ugarte in *El destino de un continente*.[2]

It was not yet time for the United States to supplant Western Europe as the prime exogenous contributor to South America beyond the Caribbean littoral of cultural, financial, material, and political influences. Aside from the Iberian-Mediterranean countries, Britain, France and Germany constituted the primary sources of capital, intellectual inspiration, consumer goods, and models for governmental organization for the four countries emphasized in the following pages. It is not surprising that France and Germany were also looked upon as sources of military inspiration and expertise by countries seeking to defend themselves from neighbors and by leaders seeking to insulate government and politics from men in uniform and vice versa.

The armies of Argentina, Brazil, and Peru had not developed formally apace with civic institutions.[3] Chile's armed forces, owing to Chile's maritime tradition and military necessities, probably had. Military-civilian relations were most harmonious in South America where civilian institutions were based on a political and economic policy consensus. Conversely, where consensus was lacking or where a gap existed between civilian and military institutional development (or where a gap existed between political theory, form, and practice), relations were disharmonious. Even in Chile, where the development of the military profession was at a relatively advanced state by the end of the century, the effectiveness of the political system proved illusory, and this provoked ruptures in the traditional military-civilian relationship: subservience to civilian direction and control.

This last statement might apply as well to France, for great strains on the traditional relationship were constantly evident there. From the publication of "Du Rôle social de l'officier"[4] in 1891 through the Dreyfus Affair to the scandal of *les fiches*,[5] politics and military affairs collided and overlapped, to the mutual consternation of civilians and officers.

There is much evidence that German army officers were perpetually alarmed by the policies of the Social Democrats, by the challenges to the authority of king and empire. "*Mit Gott, für König und Vaterland*" (with God, for king and fatherland) was no meaningless motto, however quaint it may sound today. If Lyautey's social role set officers apart from the rest of society (at least psychologically), the spirit of *Rittertum* (knighthood) imbued members of the Prussian officer corps with apparently unique characteristics.[6] Politics and professionalism became standard themes in South American military literature, most vividly in the writings read or produced by those who studied under French and German instructors.

The susceptibility of South America to European military influences was very much a symptom of the times. Barraged by European institutions and importations of all sorts, many military leaders and statesmen in South America saw Germans as the epitome of what professional military men should be. Some looked to France in the same way—especially once "the war to end all wars" had ended. When South American officers had been given a taste, however brief or diluted, of French or German military professionalism, it became impossible to convince them that they had had enough—and folly to try until the late 1930s.

In the South American milieu of the 1890–1940 half-century, the implantation of European-style military professionalism led to the beginnings of militarism. The main support for this hypothesis is the nature of the environment in which professional military values began to determine relations with the civilian sector of society and with the polity.

Military professionalism is to professional militarism as belief is to doctrine, theory, to practice. The second depends on the first. Corporateness, expertise, and service—the Huntingtonian concept of professionalism—became the basis of proposed solutions to social "problems," internal development, and governmental organization.[7] European professional values and ideals would become the basis for political action in South America. However tenuously at first, these links were forged before 1914, then tempered during the inter-war years.

What distinguished pre-World War II South America and Europe in this vein was not so much the difference in professional military attitudes; indeed, they were all too comparable, and so, with some exceptions, was the behavior of military organizations. The distinction lay in the resistance of civilian institutions of the French Third Republic and of the German Empire, then the Weimar Republic and Third Reich, to military political action and the widespread concurrence among members of the officer classes that political action was detrimental to the best interests of the profession and to the purposes of national defense.

Professional militarism took root, so to speak, in the soil of the Argentine pampas in the Peruvian Andes, in Chile's central valley and desert north, and out on the Brazilian frontier. Following independence the Iberian legacy of corporatism, the lofty state of the military caste as codified in *Las siete partidas*, and the martial experience of the campaigns precluded military subservience to civilian leadership in most of South America. Recent scholarship indicates that independence is indeed the correct breaking-point in Latin American military-civilian relations, not the era of military reform in the eighteenth century as previously suspected.[8] This would indicate an even more convincing conformity, for the Napoleonic period, coincidental with Latin American independence, is the European breaking-point.

The ground was fertile in South America as well because of the great disparity between theory and practice in republican politics. Republican government in South America was by no means synonymous with democracy. The majority did not rule; the majority did not even participate in the decision-making process, in the selection of representatives at any level. Therefore little attention was given to the bulk of the population. In South America this meant that peasants, workers, former slaves, poor immigrants—the socioeconomic, ethnic, occupational lower strata—were outside the pale of participatory democracy and politics.

Superficiality in political form was accompanied by a modernization limited in various ways to the elite of society, the major urban areas, and only a few portions of the economy—an uneven, uncoordinated blending of tradition with change. This, in turn, became compounded in Brazil and Peru by distance, topography, climatological variations, linguistic barriers, and racial distinctions. Any or all of these (as in the case of Peru) hindered attempts to devise programs and schemes to improve education and the transportation and communications infrastructures or to involve the state in so-

cial services. Even in Argentina and Chile, the more Europeanized countries, distance, tradition, ideological dog-
matism, and regionalism inhibited the realization of
aspirations. A legacy of mutual distrust among the four countries further influenced the ability of governments to satisfy
both spoken demands and unspoken needs.

By 1914 there was a clear delineation between things military and civilian in the thinking and writing of army officers.
Increasingly each year a conviction of superiority, moral, intellectual, and otherwise, began to dominate thought and
self-perception. What makes this all the more significant is
that those who observed most keenly their profession and
their *patria*, the most outspoken and articulate officers, were
those destined as well for staff duty and command positions:
the elite of an elitist profession in elitist societies. In a way
they were collectively a mirror image of their European
mentors.

Although they aspired to be, the South American republics
were no more the mirror images of France or Germany than
they were of Spain and Portugal. Culturally they were far
more divided, and not solely along ethnic, racial, or linguistic
lines. Fredrick Pike's observations on the lingering of the "*dos
repúblicas*" culture(s) in Spanish America constitute a perceptive appraisal of what might also be called "Athenian democracy—modern style."[9]

The privileged-advanced-involved sector of society was
more aware of European culture than it was of the cultural
attributes of its own surroundings. Art, music, literature—
these were derivative of European patterns. Readers preferred
imported works or national products inspired by European
masters to those based on truly national themes. The significance of Rodó and Ugarte, then, takes on a new light, for they
did revolt against the absolute penetration of their culture by
non-Hispanic invaders. The South American elite found itself
in the pre-1914 years buffeted both by an Hispanista revival
and by an attraction to the latest styles, trends, and ideas of
Paris, Berlin, and London.

Gone forever were the days of the nomadic gaucho, described artistically and nostalgically by José Hernández.[10] In

his stead, Argentine *estancieros* employed gauchesque fence-menders, outriders, and ranch hands to tend their herds, and immigrant peasants to work in the fields and tend flocks. In Brazil the abolition of slavery and the rise of the capitalized, export-oriented coffee and rubber economies resulted in boom towns in the Amazon Basin—an opera house in Manaus—and urbanization of the south, as well as creating a wage-labor rural and urban working class. State political machines ran the nation's politics. The arguments of Euclydes Da Cunha notwithstanding, Brazil's elite saw their cultural future tied to the city.[11] Chilean *rotos* left the *fundos* of the central valley for docks, nitrate pits, and copper mines, and as they did the Basque-Castillian aristocracy began to lose its grip on the political machinery. Chilean leaders boasted of being the English of South America.[12] To the mining centers, down to the coastal plantations—agribusiness in sedentary form—and to Lima, Trujillo, and Arequipa came *cholos* and Indians from the Peruvian sierra. The Peru of Ricardo Palma became that of Manuel González Prada, then that of José Carlos Mariátegui.[13] Save for politically expedient sops and campaign rhetoric, Peruvian leaders turned their backs on their indigenous heritage. It was a Connecticut intellectual who took credit for uncovering Machu Picchu, a London consortium that guaranteed Peruvian fiscal solvency.

Despite such changes, many of which were bound to occur anyway with foreign capitalization and resultant economic expansion, certain patterns remained. For although some leaders made conscious efforts to preclude the spread of egalitarianism as a fundamental of republican, democratic government, they did stimulate and participate in the Europeanization of the elite and its activities. It was from the elite, it goes without saying, that the most effective opposition to both egalitarianism and Europeanization came. This maintained the conflict of ideas within the ruling groups. Despite the trappings of elected, representative government, economic diversification, market economies, and social change, the essential social patterns of the past remained. In their works, Fernand Braudel and Emmanuel Le Roy Ladurie of the *Annales* school have noted the retention of traits and elements of cultures over a long period of time.[14] Latin America as a whole and South America in particular, during the period in question, testify to the validity of the concept of *longue durée.*

The emergence of the bureaucratic state—or a facsimile thereof—in Argentina, Brazil, Chile, and Peru did little to destroy the patrimonial statist doctrines of the past.[15] Power and authority, supposedly delegated by the people in a democratic polity, were in reality derived from tenure, from occupying positions of power and authority. Despite rules and regulations, codes and statutes to the contrary, patronage, influence, connections, and the various aspects of *compadrazgo* remained critical. The patron-client social relationship, therefore, simply became at once modernized, sanctioned, and protected by legislation. This made a mockery of theoretical and practical democracy alike.

An infusion of social doctrines popular in nineteenth-century Europe contributed further to the dichotomy of theory and practice associated with Latin America democracy before World War I. A blend of Darwinian, Spencerian, and Comtean ideas reinforced elitism and patrimonialism, giving them a rational, objective, and legitimate luster. Marxian ideas, it goes without saying, did not appeal to the privileged, but spread gradually among the disenfranchised and barely organized laboring classes. There was little of substance between the extremes because the nominally middle groups espoused the same theories of social and cultural elitism their aristocratic brethren did.

No longer can the importation of foreign capital by Latin American countries seriously be seen as the fundamental part of the process leading to liberal democracy. Late in the past century and early in this one, European (and some U.S.) investment reinforced the grip of the past on Argentina, Brazil, Chile, and Peru. Foreign capital allowed goverments to undertake mild social programs and impressive public works without altering taxing systems or encouraging internal capcapitalization. The state neither taxed domestic capital heavily nor redistributed income. Material progress was indeed tied to outside influences. Those members of the elite who protested the alteration of their status quo, who warned that capitalism, individualism, and materialism (and theirs was a natural curiosity about the association of these with Protestantism) would destroy the spiritual and moral values that they cherished and that reinforced their privileged position, did so in a nationalist spirit. They defended *argentinidad*, *chilenidad*, and *peruanidad.* There was no less nationalism in Brazil; the true nature of Brazil had already been scrutinized—as the empire fell—but would need more reexamination after the Great War.

Debate went on within the ruling classes. Opposition to the system of government, as opposed to opposition to specific administrations, was diffuse and poorly articulated. Occasional outbursts within the elites concerning division of power, state or national sovereignty, the size of the electorate, or the ruination of the *patria* by foreigners meant little, really, with regard to cession of political power to middle or lower strata. Much of "the challenge to the old order" was of an intra-elite nature, and any plans for real change seldom went beyond rhetoric.

The very things usually associated with change—modernization, development, and reform—did as much to maintain tradition, even to reinforce it, as they did to break it down. The resilience and flexibility of the civilian elite in Latin America is indeed a major influence on the modern historical record of that region.

Prior to World War I each of the countries dealt with herein had two faces. Throughout the social order a patina of modernity struck the eye first, but on closer examination the reality became clear. The latest in Paris and London fashions clothed the affluent; modern tools were used in some of the mines, but hand labor prevailed in most. Cities teemed with both commerce and crime. Ports were jammed with ships loading wheat, meat, nitrates, copper, sugar, rubber, and coffee; peasants toiled long hours on land they did not own or, worse, land their forebears had owned and lost. Elite conspicuous consumption at home and abroad contrasted sharply with poverty and lack of opportunity. Democratic government was subject, in its every manifestation, to decidedly non-democratic influence.

In such an ambience German and French officers began the professionalization of South Americans. Products of their environment and heredity, South American military men were far more susceptible to foreign influences than their civilian counterparts, for the influences came in steady, controlled doses at academy, school and college, on manuevers—and in courses in France and Germany, if one were qualified (and lucky) enough to be sent across the ocean for additional training.

The South American officer found himself, on reflecting, a part of the changing scene, one of the Europeanized, modernized elite, with most of the same material values. But the nationalistic orientation of officer training also made him particularly aware of the telluric values of his country. He found himself a part of the present and a builder of the future, yet a bulwark of historical tradition and order. He saw himself *as a part of*, yet *apart from*, the society surrounding him; as a neutral in politics yet intimately involved at times in unsavory political matters. The ways in which officers coped with these circumstances were based on their thought and self-perception.

Briefly, South American officers saw themselves as defenders of both hierarchy and egalitarianism, for military organizations are by definition hierarchical, yet promotion should be based on merit and equality of opportunity. Statements—and there are many to be cited in the pages to follow—that the army was the most democratic sector of society neither contradicted nor rendered hypocritical others that praised hierarchy. Officers also saw themselves as a mass vanguard of material development as well as being protectors of spiritual and moral values associated with the past. Here as well, such positions were reconciled within the limited parameters of military thought and officer-class self-perception. Officers were worldly, spoke German and French (rarely with fluency), but defended indigenous culture as *nacional*. The officer was a leader, but of the people; the army was the *pueblo*, *la nación en armas, o povo fardado.* Its mission became one of defense and civilization, of protection and improvement. In fine, the army was to its leaders the bridge uniting past and present, material and spiritual, peasants and workers, professionals and oligarchs; the unifying agent of state, nation, and society, of America and Europe, of democratic theory and reality. The army was perfect, or ought to be.

Such thoughts and self-perceptions were the result, obviously, of both foreign and domestic influences. The latter can be classified as civilian and military, the civilian influences being those of the national environment, and the military influences those of the residue of post-independence military experience and tradition. But the foreign influences were solely military, the end results of the transmission of military culture from the Old World to the New.

Colmar Freiherr von der Goltz published the first edition of *Das Volk in Waffen* in 1883.[16] Based largely on ideas derived from Clausewitz's classic *Vom Kriege*, Goltz's work maintained traditional German military thought and adapted it to his present. Should the modern nation defend itself with a mass conscription army led by professional officers, or should professionals lead a small specialized force of career mercenary fighters, was his main question. Eight years after Goltz wrote, Captain Hubert Lyautey anonymously published "Du Rôle social de l'officier," itself somewhat derivative, in its praise for the career of arms, of Alfred de Vigny's *Servitude et grandeurs militaires.*[17] Lyautey's question for the present generation of officers was: Did the corps have more than a strictly defined professional role; did it have a social and educational role to carry out within the framework of obligatory military service?

From Europe, then, came food for thought for the advocates of specialization, obligatory service, and the army's civic function. Controversies over the themes and questions raged in Argentina, Brazil, Chile, and Peru. Soon other concerns of French and Germans found their way into the South American military as well.

Revolutionary upheaval, followed by the industrial revolution, the expansion of commerce, and the liberal political movements of mid-century had separated Europe from the past—extricated it from what Le Roy Ladurie called *l'histoire immobile*, motionless history. If one accepts (if only for the sake of argument) the concept of *longue durée*, one is struck by the fact that Latin America had but a touch of the West's nineteenth-century experience. It becomes possible, therefore, to see the ramifications of a figurative dose of one variation of European institutional modernity ingested by backward South American countries.

By 1890 *Junkertum* was no longer synonymous with *Rittertum*, nor nobility with the officer class.[18] The armies of the German Empire's constituent kingdoms were led by officer corps with large numbers of non-aristocratic members. Many of these strove to be more aristocratic than the nobility itself; others did not. Then it became necessary, early in the twentieth century, to officially ban political activity by army officers, a ban unnecessary in previous decades. Modern warfare, especially from the Franco-Prussian War onward, meant more specialization, technological expertise, special education. Logistics, transport, and supply became important as never before, owing to the fear of protracted conflict. Engineers took on a new significance, even though the cavalry still ranked highest in prestige. As war became modern, so did its practitioners. Society and politics changed as well. It might still be difficult for non-Prussians to achieve high rank in the emperor's own army, and well nigh impossible for Roman Catholics, much less Jews, to enter schools and then join regiments anywhere in the empire, but the social composition of the officer class did change. German would-be aristocrats in uniform found themselves in social limbo, and this rubbed off on their protégés. The effects of World War I, then the expansion of the officer corps preceding World War II, destroyed forever the aristocratic officer caste in Germany, but it did not break down the corps' elitist nature.

When Lyautey published his eyebrow-raising essay of 1891, the French officer corps, indeed the entire army, had undergone nearly twenty years of remodelling in an unsuccessful attempt to make it as modern and efficient as that of the German Empire.[19] The war of 1870–71 not only had destroyed the army's credibility, it had forced the creation of the Third Republic. Young noblemen with no affinity or aptitude for republican politics found a refuge in military life. For the French nobility the officer corps was a godsend. In the main, Catholic noble officers were repelled by the secular state and society. Not all French officers were Catholics, of course; there were Protestants, many of them, Masons and loyal republicans; and there were a handful of Jews. The Alsatian Jew Alfred Dreyfus's 1894 conviction for treason showed clearly the structural weaknesses of republican military-civilian relations, the durability of a strong anti-Semitic tone, continued fear of Germany, and an inability on the part of the army to insulate itself from civilian meddling, as well as the vulnerable position of officers who were Catholic. Encouraged by Catholic social action movements[20] and the publication of *Rerum Novarum* in 1891, and discouraged by political meddling and infighting, some Catholic officers—more than a few were monarchists as well—opted for the colonial army.

Lyautey, "the monarchist who created an empire for the Republic," was given no choice; he was shipped out to Tonkin in 1891. In contrast to the garrison life of the metropolitan officer, colonials in Indo-China and Africa found challenge, adventure, danger, more rapid promotion, and more opportunities to put theory into practice. They also found ample opportunity to innovate and show their initiative while their colleagues and former classmates grumbled and suffered through *l'affaire Dreyfus* and had to read Zola's strong words. Then the keeping of *fiches* on officer's religious and fraternal affiliations was exposed. During all this the colonial army became the laboratory for Lyautey's ideas. He codified these for France's new *outre-mer,* or "overseas" holdings in 1900 in a second major essay, "Du Rôle colonial de l'armée."[21]

Many, but not all, of the German officers who served in Argentina and Chile were Catholics. Most were commoners and were not Prussians. The majority of French who served in Peru and later in Brazil were veterans of the colonial army. A few were nobles. All were Roman Catholic. The experiences of these men, based on social position and service, as well as professional expertise, were transmitted to America.

It ought to be noted, for the sake of perspective, that French and German missions, cadres, and individual officers appeared prominently in other countries during these years, making the South American experience but a chapter of a larger story. Turkey, Japan, and the Balkans were scenes of intense competition for influence between those who wore the kepi and those who affected the *Pickelhaube*, the spiked helmet. Significant as the South American chapter was, it was not singular. Germans prepared Japan for foreign military adventures and conquest and for government influence by military leaders.[22] Germans brought fresh ideas to the moribund Ottoman Empire and provided an atmosphere for the maturation of the Young Turks.[23] French officers developed the governmental transportation, communications, and distribution infrastructures of African and Asian colonies-cum-nations. If, as Felix Gilbert proposed, the European era ended with World War I, it did not do so until the exportation of its military ethos as well as other aspects of its cultural heritage and institutional tradition had occurred.[24] Military aspects of the European era lived on in South America amidst the social, economic, and political realities of the present century.

Before assessing the materials and the craftsmen of the professionalization process and the qualities of military professionalism in both South America and Europe, it remains to provide a native setting appropriate to the introduction of exotic influences. Between the closing months of 1889 and of 1891 four major events occurred that significantly affected the professionalization of South America's major armies. First in order of long-term sociopolitical significance was the revolt of 1890 in Argentina.

Late in July 1890 some disgruntled Argentine professionals, a few declassé aristocrats, and others who simply were on the outside of political circles and wanted in, formed a political organization called the Unión Cívica de la Juventud.[25] Led by Leandro Alem, a lawyer of modest means and member of a family close to the infamous caudillo Juan Manuel de Rosas, the Unión Cívica attempted to overthrow the administration of President Miguel Juárez Celman. Corruption, speculation, foreign penetration, urbanization, and economic expansion had characterized Argentina since 1870, and Buenos Aires had become more European than Argentine. The foreign-born population, the working classes, and much of the urban middle groups were without political voice.

The Unión Cívica, soon to become the Unión Cívica Radical, then the Partido Radical, at once launched the modern era and exposed the superficiality and corruption of pre-World War I Argentina's *bella época.* The revolt of 1890 failed, but not because the rebels had not tried hard. Barricades, exchanges of gunfire, oratory and rhetoric jolted *porteños.* All Argentines took notice when Juárez yielded to pressure and resigned. Not for eight years did political life return to normal. Despite economic recession and revolts in 1893 and 1895, the political prestidigitation of the "Córdoba clique" of oligarchs kept them in power. In 1898 the clique's strong man, General Julio Argentino Roca, returned to the Casa Rosada for six more years. Roca was a former war minister, had led the desert campaigns of 1878–79, and had been president from 1880 to 1886. During his second presidency a Germano-Argentine military link reached its zenith under the watchful eye of Roca's own war minister, General Pablo Riccheri. German officers had been instructing and training Argentine officers since 1890, and the officer corps as a whole had stood firm with the ruling class, despite the tumult of 1890 and 1894. This early political involvement would soon lead to an Argentine variation on the theme of French Catholic-Masonic rivalries.

Roca—a figure comparable to his contemporary Theodore Roosevelt and the Colombian president Rafael Reyes as man of action and dramatic figure—championed the cause of military modernization at precisely the time the Argentine political system faced its severest challenge. As Riccheri took office, and as steps were being taken to insulate the officer class from intrigue and create the machinery for an obligatory military service system, the Radical party, now under the leadership of Alem's enigmatic nephew, Hipólito Yrigoyen, was carrying on a militant propaganda and boycott campaign. Other dissident parties, notably the Socialists, participated in elections, but with little success. Yrigoyen did not succeed in organizing the Radicals into a national machine until 1910, at which point it was clear that Argentina's oligarchic leadership, concentrated in the National Autonomist (Conservative) party, was favorably disposed toward electoral reform. In Argentina, as in much of Latin America, the rush to modernize political systems took the form of broader suffrage, a proportional representation system, and legitimacy for opposition parties. Depending on the vantage point of the observer, proportional balloting and party politics—trappings of modern democracy—appeared ways to both coopt dissidents and broaden the political base.

There had been advocates of electoral reform in Argentina since the early 1890s. Carlos Pellegrini, successor to the disgraced Juárez Celman, had favored a larger electorate, but the hard-liners of the elite hung on through the second Roca term, and it took another Radical-army revolt in 1905 to convince them they had less to fear from reform than from their own stubborn resistance to change.

Roque Saenz Peña[26] became president in 1910 as the result of another fraudulent election and another boycott by non-organized Radicals. A diplomat, a distinguished volunteer and Peruvian war hero in the War of the Pacific against Chile, and son of a former president, don Roque was also one of the few South Americans thought highly of by United States observers. He urged passage of electoral reform legislation.

His election year was also the centennial of Argentina's independence. It was a centennial year for many Latin American countries, and Buenos Aires was no exception to the rule of *fiestas nacionales*. Argentines were treated to an elegant display, as representatives of European and American countries came to the River Plate metropolis to share in the pomp and pageantry. Baron von der Goltz was there and filed a glowing report of German accomplishments. Georges Clemenceau was there too. A young Chilean captain who had trained with Germans in Santiago and Charlottenburg, one Bartolomé Blanche Espejo, rode brilliantly in a equitation competition the Argentines were expected to sweep. Argentine soldiers marched in parade after parade. But the majority of the country's citizens still could not vote for their leaders in one of the continent's most advanced countries.

Two years later, at Saenz Peña's urging, congress passed the measures collectively known as the Saenz Peña Laws. Males eighteen years of age and older gained the vote; balloting was made secret and obligatory; a proportional representation system was introduced for legislative elections. Known as the "two-thirds rule," it assured the winning party two-thirds of the seats, and the next highest party received the remainder. Voter registration also meant an improved military conscription list; universal male suffrage, then, was tantamount to obligatory military service. Saenz Peña died in 1912; two years later, Europe went to war; two years after that, Hipólito Yrigoyen, *El Peludo*,[27] won the presidency he had coveted for so long. In the interim the Radicals dominated provincial and legislative elections.

Argentina was a nation of 8,000,000 people (double the figure of 1895) by 1914. Agriculture now amounted to nearly 60 percent of exports as opposed to pastoral products with 40 percent (compared to 30 percent and 65 percent respectively in 1895). Immigration provided 200,000 new Argentines a year by the late 1880s and in some years between 1905 and 1914. That year 53 percent of the population was urban, as opposed to 37 percent in 1895. Argentina had changed socially, economically, and politically; so had military-civilian relations.

Just eight months before the Unión Cívica first exhorted soldiers to build barricades in the street of Buenos Aires, a group of army officers toppled the Empire of Brazil and sent the infirm Braganza emperor, Pedro II, into exile.[28] Their action was a result of intensive interaction of Republican politicians, civilians, and officers under the influence of Comtean Positivism (ironically pacifistic and anti-militaristic), as well as angry monarchists and some pro-slavery aristocrats who blamed the royal family for abolition. The leader of this political revolution was Marshal Deodoro da Fonseca, no enemy of monarchy, but a man who had been persuaded to defend army interests against those who would use the institution politically and prevent officers from voicing opinions. Fonseca showed little talent as a political leader and resigned the presidency of the fledgling republic in 1891, but not until he had proclaimed the new political system and decreed its constitution, Brazil's first charter since the imperial constitution of 1824.

"The Old Republic," as Brazil's first essay in popular sovereignty is called, lasted until 1930. Along its road to oblivion the armed forces, most importantly the army, became enmeshed in civic affairs. The creating and dismantling of the Old Republic would probably have been impossible without military involvement.

Between 1889 and 1914 Brazilian politics was dominated by a powerful combine of state leaders representing the interests of São Paulo and Minas Gerais. These two southern states were populous, economically dynamic areas and had become increasingly significant as centers of political influence in the late stages of the empire. Coffee, transportation, banking, agriculture, and light manufacturing had shifted economic power from the northeast during the second half of the nineteenth century. Creation of the Old Republic was as much the political recognition of this shift as was the oligarchically-granted Saenz Peña legislation the recognition of change in Argentina.

Not that either should be mistaken for the product of widespread democratic egalitarianism; few Brazilians seriously believed emancipated slaves were capable of sophisticated political participation; few believed, as did Cunha, writing in *Os Sertões*, that the true Brazil lay among the *sertanejos*, out on the frontier, and not along the coast. The inability of Marshal Deodoro or his rival-successor, Marshal Floriano Peixoto, to satisfy the Paulista and Mineiro leaders resulted in evacuation of the presidential office by the military in 1894.

The Old Republic survived the next five years because regionalist revolts in the northeast—the subject of Cunha's book—and in the far south, where *gaúchos* from Rio Grande do Sul renewed traditional hostility to Rio de Janeiro's control, failed to topple the goverment of President Prudente de Morães. Financial chaos, the legacy of world recession in the early 1890s, abated, and confidence in the economy grew. The navy ceased to be uncooperative with the federal government when the generals left politics in 1894. As Brazil entered the twentieth century the country was comparatively peaceful, in the midst of rubber and coffee booms, in the process of resolving its border disputes with Bolivia, and growing in continental and hemispheric prestige. Brazil, in fact, was the first South American country to be accorded an embassy in Washington, the first to have one of its citizens named cardinal.

Paulistas and Mineiros controlled the presidency—delegates, really, of their state Republican party machines—until 1910. Morães and his successors Manuel de Campos Salles (1898–1902) were Paulistas. So was Francisco de Rodrigues Alves (1902–5). Affonso Penna (1906–10) was a Mineiro. When he took office Brazil was once again on the gold standard and Foreign Minister Rio Branco had successfully negotiated Brazil's boundary settlements. By the time he died in office, Rio de Janeiro was a city of over eight hundred thousand and had undergone a needed facelifting. Health conditions arising from endemic yellow fever, frequent outbreaks of malaria, and widespread pulmonary ailments were improved. Yellow fever plague, and smallpox no longer posed perpetual threats. Opposition to mandatory smallpox vaccinations in 1904 (which involved army officers influenced by Positivist propaganda)[29] had withered. The 1904 revolt probably put an end to *positivista* dreams of a Comtean republic. Urban renewal projects cleared away some crowded quarters in Rio, and avenues were widened and beautified. Foreigners no longer wrote of the dreadful, inhuman conditions among the lower classes of one of the world's most beautifully situated cities, either because they did not witness them or because they were awed by civic improvements that complemented the natural setting.

Nonetheless, Brazil had its problems, and these did not go unnoticed by army officers. One of Brazil's increasingly serious problems was that of regionalism. Imperial rule had united Brazilians under a hereditary head of state, theoretically above the partisan issues of Conservatives and Liberals, northeasterners, and southerners. The Republic, Positivist designs notwithstanding, was a contradiction to this, a reaction against the past. The Paulista-Mineiro axis was the mechanism. Only Rio Grande do Sul posed an effective challenge during these years. In 1910 Marshal Hermes da Fonseca, nephew of the Republic's first chief executive, won the presidency as candidate of the *gaúcho* political machine and its allies. By the time he left office and war broke out in Europe, it became clear that sovereignty rested in the states and their political cliques—and this meant principally São Paulo and Minas Gerais—not in the nation, certainly not in the people. Brazil was politically less than the sum of its parts.

The army confronted this actively, for it too was less than the sum of its parts. A few German-trained officers resented the fact that the *Força Pública* of São Paulo had a French military mission while the army had nothing of the kind. Hermes da Fonseca was a Germanophile; he and other officers had urged a formal military training arrangement, but the government, dominated by Paulista and Mineiro interests, had no intention of creating a powerful federal army they might possibly not be able to control as firmly as they did politics. Georges Clemenceau commented pithily on the national *army* and state *armies* when he visited Brazil in 1910.[30] Little wonder that when the irascible Hermes ran for the presidency his opponent, the famed statesman Rui Barbosa, formally campaigned on a platform of anti-militarism. In 1914 Brazil's army had a cadre of middle-rank officers who had received additional training in Germany, but the São Paulo constabulary-army was better paid, better equipped, and better armed. Professional officers were, to say the least, disgruntled. Civil-military strife did little to assuage them.

The economic boom enjoyed by entrepreneurs, planters, merchants, and foreigners (a distinct economic elite) continued until the war. There the growth pattern ended, for

Brazil's wealth was based on the exportation of coffee, rubber, and other agricultural products. In 1910 Brazil produced 90 percent of the world's rubber and 75 percent of its coffee, the price of the latter already supported by valorization. Encouraged by Brazilian recruiting agents, over a half-million immigrants, Portuguese, Italian, Spanish, German, and others, came to Brazil between 1910 and the beginning of the war.

The war damaged the coffee market temporarily and competition continued to hurt it. By 1921 Brazilian rubber amounted to a mere 10 percent of the world's needs and the price had tumbled from 34¢ a pound in 1910 to 6¢ a pound in 1921. The population of Brazil in 1890 was nearly 14,000,000; at the turn of the century it was 17,000,000. A total of nearly 3.5 million immigrants had arrived in the country between 1870 and World War I, and the population was roughly 26,000,000. By the end of the war Rio had four million inhabitants. The majority still lived in rural areas until a decade after the war began. It is at about that time that the military-civilian relationship altered its course dramatically and with it that of the Old Republic.

To the west, across the vast, unexploited interior of Brazil and across the prairies and hill country of Argentina, over on the Pacific coast two other countries entered the twentieth century in notable fashion. Chile and Peru had been enemies since independence, their enmity a blend of commercial rivalry, nationalism, territorial conflict, and simple mutual distrust. Twice in the nineteenth century (1837–39 and 1879–84) they had gone to war. Both times Peru had been saddled with Bolivia as an ally, and both times Peru had been defeated. Chile's two triumphs were as much due to the weakness of her Andean foes as they were to her own strengths. In the War of the Pacific, concluded only in 1884 by peace accords, Chile had taken the provinces of Tacna and Arica from Peru and Antofagasta from Bolivia. Chile's national territory increased by a third. Exploitation of copper and nitrate deposits fueled her inflationary economy but brought a modicum of national prosperity, limited to those linked to transportation, extractive industry, commerce, shipping, large-scale agriculture, and light manufacturing. For this reason alone, military-civilian relations west of the Andean crests were more tense and determinative of national policy than they were on the Atlantic coast.

At the time Radical supporters and soldiers were in the streets of Buenos Aires and Marshal Deodoro was trying to consolidate his grip on the Brazilian government, Chilean President José Manuel Balmaceda and the national congress were locked in a constitutional struggle over fiscal authority.[31] The struggle went further than just that. Balmaceda was a political throwback who resembled the mid-century autocrat-modernizer President Manuel Montt (1851–61) in his desire to develop the country materially but administer it rigorously. He also resembled Diego Portales, the master mind of Chile's 1830–39 politicoeconomic emergence from post-independence chaos and Peru's shadow. In short, Balmaceda represented both a past and a future he preferred. His present was a tragic one.

On New Year's Day, 1891, congressional leaders revolted against him. Charging that Balmaceda had usurped power and violated the constitution (by declaring one-twelfth of the 1890 budget in effect for each month of 1891 after congress had failed to appropriate funds to run the government), they steamed north from Valparaíso with the support of the naval high command. They then began their operations against the central government from a base in the northern nitrate region, where they could control exports and imposts. In control of Chile's principal source of income, they were soon able to squeeze the loyalists and their army economically.

But not without force and much bloodshed. The genius behind the rebels' military strategy was not found among those officers who had opted for the congressional side. Good men and true, most of these officers were steeped in the military science of the past or were recent volunteers to whom politics and economic issues were prime motivations. The man who planned and administered the coup de grâce to the strong executive system of Chilean national administration (or, say Balmaceda's detractors, to flagrant, abusive demagoguery) was the German Colonel Emil Körner. Körner had arrived in Chile in 1886, under contract to the Chilean government to instruct and organize only. By 1891 Chile had a staff school, the Academia de Guerra, patterned after Prussia's Kriegsakademie.

Körner's and the congress' victory in 1891, achieved at great cost to the country, ushered in the dichotomous military-civilian relationship of the Parliamentary Republic. From 1891 until the writing of a new constitution—some insist until the new document was put into use, to be presidentially ignored by General Carlos Ibáñez del Campo between 1927 and 1931—parliament governed and executives either went along or suffered, bridled, and sometimes simply gave way. Patterned stylistically after the British system, the Chilean system resembled more closely the French polity under the Third Republic, except that in Chile the president was less of a figurehead.

He was beholden to parliamentary cliques and coteries. There obviously was no unifying, stabilizing, non-partisan monarch. Powers retained by the president under the constitution were subjected to severe restrictions. Cabinet ministers were subjected to frequent interpelations and cabinets to votes of no confidence. Executive-legislative relations were perpetually, soon "traditionally," tense. Politics became baroque and Byzantine at the same time, and the Chilean population at large was the loser. For although serious socioeconomic issues were discussed, little was ever done about them; although most political leaders supported the non-involvement of the state in economic affairs, their laissez-faire principles faltered when it came to assistance to the nitrate industry. Those who spoke most cogently for social reform projects, labor legislation, low-cost housing for workers, and the like were those who most avidly supported parliamentary politics, coalitions, and confusion. On the right, those influenced by Social Christian ideas imported from France spoke for state involvement but were by no means interested in political democracy; they were split into a socialist, statist wing and another devoted to parliamentary procedure and little else of substance. Vociferous, they were also impotent.

Thus Chileans knew what the problems were. The press, literary circles, and parliamentary debates were free from controls. Strikes and demonstrations by barely organized labor (with no legal status) met with repression. Troops were used in the mining districts of the north, the central valley, and the south on occasion after occasion to break the heads of protesting miners whose working and living conditions were horrendous. The attitude of some army officers—though not particularly sensitive to labor demands for obvious ideological reasons—was that of professional officers: their men should not be used as policemen. Coincidentally, Argentines and Brazilians (the latter until 1888 frequently ordered to pursue escaping slaves) shared these beliefs. Peruvians, as will be shown, resented having to force Indians and peasants into military service.

Meanwhile the system rumbled on under control of the declining Basque-Castilian aristocracy. Chile's nineteenth-century ruling class had lost cohesion, vitality, and ability. Cohesion had been in decline since foreigners and mine owners had joined the land-business oligarchy of the central valley. Vitality was a result of the political schisms of the second half of the century; aristocratic outlooks did not alter, but their transformation into ideology and concentrated political action became difficult.

A changing Chile had destroyed the monopoly on ability and talent previously enjoyed by the aristocrats. A bourgeoisie emerged in the last forty years of the century, with social ideas only slightly less exclusivistic than those of the aristocracy, but with political ideas that coincided with those of the aristocratic *fronde* that resented the direction of all national affairs by the centralized, executive-dominated regime.[32] They especially disliked leaders such as Montt and Balmaceda. The Chilean middle sector, then, hardly presented a unified or defined political alternative to the class that supplied most of the leaders. Between 1896 and 1910 a president who was the son of a former president turned over the sash of office to his cousin and brother-in-law, who in turn passed it to another president's son.[33] By then there had been several instances of military grumbling about political and governmental failure to act on social and economic questions. Disgruntled officers clearly expressed views that the state ought to do something more than merely exist.

During these same years the Prussianization process begun by Körner in 1886 had transformed the officer class into a poor but proud copy of the Prussian officer corps. Mostly from modest origins, the Chileans became aspirants to elite status in an elitist society still dominated by a decaying aristocracy. They found themselves the latest word in modernity in a superficially modern country. They were respected (for the deeds of their nineteenth-century predecessors), yet they were manipulated politically, at no time with graver consequences than during the 1915–20 presidency of Juan Luis Sanfuentes Andonáegui.

Chilean population grew from barely 2,000,000 in 1880 to over 3,000,000 inhabitants by century's end; Santiago was a city of 225,000 inhabitants by 1900, and one of slightly over 400,000 by the end of World War I. Immigration was a factor, though less than in Argentina or Brazil. The most significant features of Chilean population figures are those concerned with demographic shift. Acquisition of territory in the 1880s, then the collapse of the nitrate market during World War I, created two concentrated shifts of population, first up to the nitrate fields, than back to the center of the country or to cities. There was also a middle-group opportunity-seeking movement to provincial towns during these years. By the 1920s over half the population lived in towns of over 2,000. Nearly a quarter of all Chileans lived in the Santiago-Valparaíso area. Urbanized and rootless, many were ripe for demagoguery.

Up the coast in Peru, a French mission had been molding an officer corps and general staff, conducting maneuvers and cartographical expeditions, and inculcating developmentalist ideas since 1896. President Nicolás de Piérola, an engineer-builder-politician-entrepreneur, brought the French to Peru in the hopes that the army could be rebuilt and officers reformed.[34] His dreams were only partially realized.

Between the outbreak of the war with Chile in 1879 and the prevention of fiscal collapse by the Peruvian Corporation of London in 1890, Peru had eight presidents. Between 1890, when Colonel Remigio Morales Bermúdez[35] won election to the executive office, and the outbreak of the European conflict Peru had eleven presidents, a somewhat better average than in the 1879–90 years. At no time during these decades was there a harmonious military-civilian relationship. At no time were civilian institutions safe from military meddling.

In economic decline after the collapse or outright loss of revenue-producing mineral properties, Peruvian leaders, at the urging of Michael and W. R. Grace, resorted to arrangements in 1886, 1889, and 1890 with a London-based banking consortium, the Peruvian Corporation. By virtue of agreements ratified in 1890, "La Peruvian" gained control of the railroads and the steamer line on Lake Titicaca, free use of ports for the importation of equipment, and monopoly control of the guano industry, such as it was. The consortium also had a lien on customs receipts. In return for these concessions the bankers assumed responsibility for Peru's debts. Peru probably was lucky, so devastated was her economy, so bleak her political prospects, so backward her society, and so primitive her institutional infrastructure.

Piérola (who on leaving office would become principal owner of "La Colmena" (The Beehive), a construction company involved in large-scale paving, clearing, and construction projects in central Lima, one of which, Avenida Nicolás Piérola, bears his name, between 1899 and 1910) assumed the presidency for the second time in September 1895. He is one of the few chief executives to serve a full term of office in Peru's independent history. Perhaps his greatest achievement was to arrange a pact between the Civilista party and his own Democrats—a pact that gave him the presidency and that endured until 1903. By the time he retired to business life in 1899, the French mission had begun its work with éclat under Colonel Paul Clément.

It was with dedication and high hopes that the French—all veterans of colonial service—produced their 1897–98 report to the president outlining Peru's needs for internal development as a prerequisite to national defense.[36] Peru's needs were at once simple and complex. The country had few all-weather roads, an insufficient rail system, and no telecommunications outside Lima. The majority of the population was illiterate and could not even speak fluently the official language of the country—a problem the French well understood.[37] Aside from the oasis-dotted coastal desert, the terrain was tortuous; communications with the Andes, where most of the indigenous population, arable land, and mineral and natural wealth were located, were primitive and seasonal. Altitude problems added to the transportation and communications difficulties. Many *costeños* became violently ill with *soroche* (mountain sickness) when they went to Cajamarca, Ayacucho, Arequipa, and Cuzco, not to mention Puno.[38] In ways Peru resembled Brazil; still largely unexploited, cursed with hostile terrain, it was somewhat less than its constituent parts, yet it attempted to be somewhat more.

Peru, then, needed integration and development. It needed a modernized, educated society capable of contributing to economic change. As in Argentina, Brazil, and Chile, there was debate over just where Peru's future lay. Was Peru European or Andean—a modern version of an ancient civilization? One of the great questions asked in Peru was, what should be done about the Indian?[39] Late in the nineteenth century this question was raised by the firebrand Manuel González Prada. A century later, attempts to answer it still lead only to frustration, failure, shame.

Amidst the hectic politics of the pre-war years, Peruvian army officers ventured some answers. Few listened to these intrepid types. About equally divided between the Civilistas—representatives of the political and economic interests of the Lima oligarchy and its allies—and the Democrats—the Piérola-led party of provincial and coastal business interests—Peru's electorate was defrauded most of the time. The Democrats attempted to mobilize small merchants and professionals, but the Civilistas were able to hold them off. There simply was no major political, social, or economic breakthrough in Peru.

Don Nicolás was short and energetic, like Roca and Fonseca a man of action, perhaps more pragmatic, tractable, and likable than they, but no less convinced of the need for a strong army. He prolonged his inter-coalition, quasi-class struggle against the Civilistas with the succession in 1899 of Eduardo López de Romaña, and the Democrat congress showed its democratic spirit by expanding suffrage to allow all literate males to vote and by obliging them to register for conscription as well. Peru, like Argentina, thus tied civil rights to military service.

Civilistas José Pardo (son of President José Pardo, 1872–76) and Augusto B. Leguía filled the presidential office until 1912. Pardo the autocrat modestly championed the cause of state-supported education, and during his 1904–8 administration Cerro de Pasco Corporation entered the Peruvian economic scene. Leguía, the provincial arrivée, was a failure as president and the Civilistas were unable to retain control of the executive branch in 1912. If the recitation of failure (aside from the achievements of Piérola), during decades of tumult and calm alike, appears as an augury of military-civilian tension, it should. Whether Democrats or Civilistas were in power, little was done to attack Peru's recognized social problems. Expansion of rubber harvesting, cotton and sugar cultivation, and the coming of Cerro were not so much achievements as they were fortuitous occurrences. The land still exuded misery as an archaic reality.

Democrat Guillermo Billinghurst won the election of 1912. A Balmacedesque figure, he attempted to legislate landlords into a more dependent position (vis-à-vis the state) and made demagogic appeals to highland peasants, *montaña* rubber gatherers, and coastal workers. He had the audacity to agree with Roger Casement's accusations of brutality in the Amazon rubber forests. A military revolt ousted him in February 1914. In the *golpe* the young lieutenant Luis María Sánchez Cerro, a *cholo* of obscure origin, burst upon the political scene, to retire only with his assassination in 1933; in his footsteps calmly came Lieutenant Colonel Oscar Benvides, scion of a distinguished family, who served as interim president, 1914–15, and again as chief of state, 1933–39. Sánchez Serro the *cholo* malcontent and Benavides the urbane Civilista-professional officer symbolized the extremes of the officer class in its formative years and the extremes of Peru's social structure as well.

By 1914 the Peruvian economy was stronger than at any time since the War of the Pacific. Copper, cotton, sugar, rubber, and even a little guano contributed to the bulk of export revenues. Politics was less concerned with action than with the achieving and holding of power, and disruptive issues were at least confined to elite circles. The country was quiet. There were nearly 3,800,000 Peruvians in 1900, nearly 5,000,000 in 1920. Of these, 40 percent were Indians, 30 percent mixed, and 30 percent of European descent. Lima had grown from 110,000 inhabitants in 1890 to 200,000 by 1920. That same year Cuzco had a population of 100,000, Trujillo 65,000 and Arequipa 125,000. Only 8.4 percent of Peruvians lived in towns of over 10,000, as compared to 27.1 percent of Argentines, 21.8 percent of Chileans, and 10.9 percent of Brazilians. With only a modicum of economic development (international trade did jump 800 percent between 1900 and 1920), a politically inarticulate population, and a stratified society Peru had barely entered the twentieth century. In comparison with Argentina, Brazil, and Chile, Peru was an anachronism. This bothered many army officers as much as did their slowly declining share of the budget (even if expenditures in *soles* grew).

As French and Germans toiled in South America or worked with South American pupils in Europe, South American officers became more conscious of their own country, of the countries around them, and of the world across the Atlantic. The interlacing of military-civilian relations now assumed new dimensions as many South Americans (including, to a far lesser degree, the Bolivians)[40] did not like what they saw about them at home and idealized what they saw in, or heard about, Europe. They absorbed the thought and self-perception of their instructors. Steeped in professional lore and beguiled by thoughts of military grandeur, Europeanized officers, often called *afrancesados* or *germanófilos* by their contemporaries, began to take themselves very seriously. And why not? They had come a long way since 1890.

"The ancients declared that a commander should possess four qualities: first, intelligence; second, strength; third, good natural prudence; fourth, loyalty."

Alfonso el sabio, *Las siete partidas*, 2ª Partida, XXII, i.

"To the Europeans, South America is a man with a mustache, a guitar and a gun."

Gabriel García Márquez, "No One Writes to the Colonel" (1961)

CHAPTER TWO

The South American Military Tradition: Preprofessional Armies

By the time the French and German officers arrived in South America, European officers had served for years in the Ottoman Empire and Japan, launching Turks and Japanese, as noted, toward military modernity. The success with which European military professionalism was transmitted can be assessed in two ways. Obviously the Japanese learned some of their lessons well, for their artillery and infantry performed well against the Russians in 1904–6. Still, it would be less than candid to say Japanese successes were strictly the result of Jacob Clemens Meckel's teachings or emulation of great general staff techniques. The Russian Empire was a military shambles, and its navy was no less a pathetic imitation of a modern fighting unit than its army. The fact remains, however, that Japan owed much in the way of organization, techniques, tactics, and strategy, though not spirit, tradition, and post-Meiji fervor, to the Europeans.

The Ottoman Empire stands as an example of little reward for much effort. The work of Goltz Pasha and the Liman von Sanders mission did not achieve their purposes.[1] True, the Turks under Abdul Hamid II did ally with the Central Powers in their time of need; German foreign policy followed military missions in other cases, too. This alliance, however, proved worthless in the military sense, about as worthless as, say, Peru's nineteenth-century ties with Bolivia. But there were some results anent the inculcation of a military ethos. The Young Turk movement, arguably in its inception a medical corps movement, was in the greater sense a result of frustrated professionals seeing themselves out of step with the state, nation, and society about them. Political action and the rise of the military caste, modern-style, in post-1900 Turkey and Japan— "neo-Janizaries" and "neo-samurai"—came as results of European values superimposed on exotic (to Europe) reality.

Reality in South America included both commitment to the martial spirit and the need for national defense. On their arrival in Buenos Aires and Santiago, Lima and Rio de Janeiro, the French and Germans found raw material, its quality variable and its availability not always guaranteed. Existing military organizations presented challenges, and not all South Americans welcomed their new mentors.

Argentines trace their military institutional history as far back as 1810, when the Escuela de Matemáticas in Buenos Aires trained some engineers to lead 2,400 veteran militiamen, and see their martial heritage beginning with the expulsion of the British invasion force of 1806 by creole militiamen led by Juan Lavalleja. Military education was not even sporadic during most of the nineteenth century, not even codified until 1864, when President Bartolomé Mitre attempted to arrange for cadets at the Escuela de Artes y Oficios to study at St. Cyr. His successor, Domingo Sarmiento, founded the Colegio Militar in 1869 and ordered the procurement of foreign instructors.[2] Aside from these good intentions there was little action, and until 1880 provincial militias were more significant than the national army—a portent of army compatibility with strong, centralized government in Argentina (and elsewhere).

Several events and some national issues of import encouraged Argentine leaders of the post-Rosas era to undertake the modernization of the army. The 1864–70 war with Paraguay, in which Argentina, Brazil, and Uruguay struggled for six years to defeat the "South American Prussia" (some might prefer Macedon), convinced both Mitre and Sarmiento that Argentina needed to assure its new-found integrity and sovereignty. Coordination of the war effort was difficult; cooperation among the provinces was tenuous.[3] Paraguay proved a resolute little country, and Brazil was not the most amiable of allies.

Over the nineteenth century the presence of Brazil as a rival on the Atlantic and in the River Plate basin also indicated a need for national defense; indeed, the Argentine-Brazilian rivalry is a dominant theme in the entire history of military professionalization on the Atlantic coast of South America. During the 1829–52 Rosas era (and even earlier) the two powers had clashed repeatedly over influence in the Banda Oriental. This Argentine-Brazilian rivalry is merely an extension of the older Luso-Hispanic conflict over access to the La Plata estuary and the Paraná River route to the continental hinterland. Until the commencement of hostilities between Chile and the Andean allies in 1879, the latter hoped for Argentine participation on their side. But the long-standing dispute between Buenos Aires and Santiago over Argentine-claimed, Chilean-settled Patagonia came to an end. Satisfied with the acquisition of territory via peaceful means, Argentina did not go to war, and a southern frontier opened for expansion in the Río Negro–Río Colorado areas.

But not before "the conquest of the desert." When President Nicolás Avellaneda selected General Julio A. Roca to succeed Dr. Adolfo Alsina as war minister in 1878, the government's policy toward the few remaining indigenous hostiles in the south changed radically. Alsina had relied on frontier garrisons, treaties, and patrols along the Río Negro line, features that made this aspect of Argentine expansion comparable with that of the United States prior to 1876 and the Little Big Horn debacle. General Roca had commanded a garrison in southern Córdoba province and was experienced in Indian fighting; he immediately pressed for an offensive sweep south, and the rest is history.[4] By the end of 1879 the Río Negro line was pacified and communications with Patagonia by land assured. Within a year, Roca was president and the army had a champion in office. The desert campaign (concentrated efforts in the Chaco, along the northern Andean frontier and Patagonia, had been undertaken since 1870) proved the value of a federal army superior to provincial militias.

In 1875 the army received roughly 18 percent of the national budget, in 1880 just over 41 percent, thereafter just under 14 percent until 1895, and under 10 percent of budgetary expenditures until 1914.[5] Actual peso amounts increased every year, despite percentage variations, and amounted to roughly one-third of education expenditures. At the end of the century the army had 1,600 officers and 6,000 men, and in 1914 1,800 officers and 22,000 men; obligatory military service made the difference in size.[6] Roca introduced general staff organization in 1884, during his first presidency, although the staff system had functioned in rudimentary fashion since 1861; the Escuela Superior de Guerra, founded in 1900, provided the talent for staff service. Both necessary ingredients of a modern military organization became functional realities only after the arrival of German officers in 1899.

Between Mitre's and Sarmiento's "era of good intentions" and the promulgation of obligatory service, general staff regulations, and codes lay a good deal of slow, hard work by Argentines and Germans alike. The troubled history of the Colegio Militar (Palermo), later named Colegio Militar San Martín, ceased only under Sarmiento, for Mitre's plan to send cadets to St. Cyr was shelved when the war with Paraguay broke out. Sarmiento's decree of September 7, 1868, and subsequent legislation in October, then still another decree in 1870, finally got the Colegio Militar on firm ground, at least organizationally and fiscally. Three years later one Captain Otto Rose took up his duties as artillery instructor.[7]

In the last decades of the century Argentine cadets studied in their three years at the Colegio, mathematics, military history and geography, military law, cartography, languages, tactics, marksmanship, and fencing. There was little pure or applied science in the curriculum. Three cadets graduated in 1873, no more than thirteen a year for the next decade, thirty-five in 1884, and no more than 159 in any year until 1915.[8] Until the arrival of the Germans, graduation from the Colegio was not a prerequisite for a commission. Manuals were Spanish translations of French works or original Spanish works in use since mid-century. Admission to the Colegio was open to healthy, literate males between the ages of fourteen and eighteen. Three years of study led to the rank of sub-lieutenant and five to the initial rank of second lieutenant until 1884, when the top-ranking students in each "promoción" were accorded that rank on graduation. In 1888 the government incorporated the national guard into the army, giving Argentina a poorly-trained and roughly-equipped reserve force on paper of 65,000 men ranging in age from seventeen to fifty years.[9] Eleven years later great changes took place.

The failure of Argentina to develop a military organization commensurate with its political system ought to be seen in terms of the development of that system. Until 1852 Argentina was a collection of provinces, a loose federation beholden to the strong man of Buenos Aires province, Juan Manuel de Rosas. Then, after his fall and exile, the federal system established by the Constitution of 1853 allowed provinces to retain their own armies as militias. National defense had been associated only temporarily with foreign threats or adventures. Despite the fact that both Mitre and Sarmiento were aware of the need for a national army, it took a military man as president (Roca, 1880–86) and the formal establishment of a sovereign federal government to place the national army in a position at least theoretically superior to that of gaucho- and peasant-manned militia units.

Roca's first presidency, during which he established the so-called *unicato*—presidential domination of the executive branch—set the stage for the suppression of the old federalism and the erection of provincially-dominated centralism under executives beholden to specific provincial political interests. This was the arrangement that dominated Argentine government and politics until the triumph of the Radicals in 1916. Roca's policy of arming his army well and of imitating the staff system for organizational and planning purposes did more than place the army in a theoretically superior position; these measures gave him the power to exert his will over recalcitrant provincial bosses and opposition politicians. By the 1890s the army had become a political creature, subject to the whims of the chief executive. Roca's return to the Casa Rosada in 1898 provided a second stage in the emergence of the modern Argentine army as a political interest group.

Between the Roca presidencies the army became involved actively in politics. The revolt of June 26–29, 1890, involving Leandro Alem, the Radicals, and General Manuel J. Campos, then the 1893–94 mutiny in Corrientes, were symptomatic of the times and alarming enough to persuade Roca and his right-hand man General Pablo Riccheri to seek German assistance in the professionalization, and removal from partisan politics, of the army.

So did the example directly west of the Andes, where, by 1900, Roca and Riccheri thought Chileans were planning war. If the association of national defense consciousness and strong, centralized government with strong, efficient military organization is valid (it is a tenet of South American military ideology today), Chile stands as an example of advanced military status in the nineteenth century. For Chilean leaders were ever wary both of their northern Andean neighbors and of Argentina to the east.

War created and maintained the Republic of Chile. Chileans fought for their own independence and Peru's. They fought Indians in the south; they fought each other in the 1820s, and while Conservative party leader General Joaquín Prieto and his *éminence gris*, Diego Portales, fashioned the political system that dominated Chile until 1891, they fought Peruvians and Bolivians. They fought them twice: between 1836 and 1839, again between 1879 and 1884, when simultaneously their southern forces finally pacified the warlike Araucanians. Chile, like Argentina, increased its national territory and protected it with armed force.

There had been a military school of sorts in Chile since 1817. It functioned intermittently between the ouster of Supreme Director Bernardo O'Higgins in 1823 and the triumph of the Prieto-led Conservatives seven years later. Portales reopened the Escuela and put it on a sound footing financially. The government reversed policies of earlier years and recruited only from members of known Conservative or nonpartisan families. By the end of the decade the professional officer class was an armed extension of the Basque-Castilian aristocracy. As this oligarchy began to show signs of strain, there were examples of conspiracy and political activity by officers (1851, 1859), but on both occasions it was civilians who initiated conspiracies.[10] A further buffer between the army and exponents of partisan issues was the presence of a militia, forerunner of the national police, that had responsibility for routine maintenance of internal order.

Like the Brazilians and Peruvians, Chilean military historians routinely see their subject as continuous, dating from colonial times (sometimes even pre-colonial). The fusion of Araucanian and Spaniard, aborigine and Iberian, defender and conqueror, created a "race of warriors," they argue.[11] This is not the case with their Argentine counterparts; it is comparable to Peruvian and Brazilian military historiography, in which lip service to aboriginal contributions to institutional development has been paid.[12] Where resistance by civilized aborigines was either organized or protracted, the South Americans have seen fit to absorb that resistance as part of their self-justification and martial spirit. What civilian writers of all genres see as quaint and folkloric, or decadent and inferior, Chileans, Brazilians, and Peruvians in uniform have noted as a sign of national vitality and strength—on paper, at least.

Chile emerged from the War of the Pacific as the leading power on the Pacific Coast of South America. By the time Argentina had violently subdued its Indian inhabitants and was still resolving its internal controversy over the relationship of capital city to province and nation, Chile had defeated Bolivia and Peru and occupied the City of the Kings, once Spain's proudest South American city. In the euphoria of victory Chilean leaders were not blind, however. The army had a wealth of tradition, whether contrived of the stuff that went into Alonso de Ercilla y Zúñiga's *La araucana*[13] or fashioned from the less than thrilling reality of Maipú and Lircay, Yungay, Chorrillos and Miraflores, or the Araucanian campaigns. There is no question as to the backlog of experience drawn upon by Chilean commanders, whether forcing their way north toward Lima or pushing back the Indians along the southern frontier. The discipline of the army was outwardly solid; its links to the ruling elite were still intact, even if strained by the infusion of new blood during the War of the Pacific, when so many officers lost their lives.

Therefore, President Domingo Santa María, at the urging of high-ranking officers, instructed Guillermo Matta, head of Chile's diplomatic mission in Germany, to seek out a qualified instructor. Flushed with their foreign victories at sea, on the desert, and in the foothills of the Andes, yet mindful of obvious shortcomings in organization, materiel, and morale, Chileans turned to the victors of Sedan and conquerors of Paris, those masters of modern warfare collectively known as the Prussian Army. Chile thus set the standard to which her neighbors would march toward military modernity in the decades to come. Only in the case of Peru would foreign instructors have comparable authority and influence over a South American army. Nowhere would they have the direct command functions they would have in Chile.

Matta found his man, or thought he had. Jacob Clemens Meckel came with high recommendations, but he chose to go to Japan instead. He became a legend there.[14] The second name on Matta's short list was that of Captain Emil Körner, a Saxon commoner who had served with distinction in the Franco-Prussian War. An agreement was made and a contract drawn up; a new era began. Emil Körner would become a legend in Chile.

Chile had nearly 25,000 men under arms, equipped for the most part with outdated French and German rifles and Krupp field pieces, when the war with Peru and Bolivia ended. A sharp reduction in size followed, so that when Körner arrived there were no more than 6,000 men in uniform and a militia of perhaps 6,000 more.[15] The army received no more than 10 percent of the federal budget. The Escuela Militar, on solid ground since the 1830s, produced about fifty junior lieutenants a year; there were not a thousand qualified officers, and though many had leadership experience from the recent war, they had little formal training. Those who had graduated from the Escuela studied tactics and strategy, military history, basic physics and chemistry, mathematics, and technical subjects of a military nature. Chileans were better fighters than theoreticians. Most of the younger officers looked forward to the arrival of this unknown Saxon captain; many of their superiors were skeptical of his ability to improve an army that had defeated Peru and Bolivia.

Four years before some Argentine officers conspired with Leandro Alem's "Civic Union of Youth," then, Körner inaugurated the first courses in Chile's Academia de Guerra. Chile was clearly the military leader of the entire continent. The kind of difficulties that retarded development of a national, professional army in Argentina were no longer inhibitive to a coordinated Chilean military or defense policy when Körner took up his duties. For the time being the political system was stable. There was little pressure from outside the ruling class for systemic change. No provincial clique contested for power with the energy of the "Córdoba Clique" in Argentina; no provincial militia rivaled the national army.

Both countries undertook military professionalization because of the awareness of potential threats to national security. Both had triumphed in recent wars and had put a finish to aboriginal foes within national boundaries. In Argentina there may have been more of a sense of political expediency, i.e., a necessity to do something in order to preclude military-political involvements despite the presence of Roca as champion. Military involvement in the incidents of the 1890s lends some weight to such a hypothesis. In Chile the political interests of the army officer corps were determined by the 1891 civil war, then by the inculcation of Prussian values from the bottom of the officer corps up. Obviously by 1890 there were rifts within the corps of both countries, or there would not have been collusion in the Radical-inspired movements of the 1890s in Buenos Aires and Corrientes nor a division of sentiment in the 1891 revolt against Balmaceda across the cordillera. From the beginning, therefore, civilian political issues of some magnitude influenced the process of professionalization in Germany's client states. This was equally true in the French client states, Peru and Brazil, diplomatic and military rivals, respectively, of Chile and Argentina.

Peru smarted from its war losses of the 1880s. For the second time in barely a half-century, Peru had fallen to Chile, her Bolivian alliances had done her no good, and her prospects for the future had dimmed. The government was discredited and the army and navy reduced to pathetic imitations of defense forces. The introspective and pessimistic nature of Peruvian social and political thought stems, in part, directly from the country's collapse in 1879–80, the occupation of Lima by Chilean forces, and the victor's demands solemnized in the 1883 Treaty of Ancón. The loss of Tacna, Arica, and Tarapacá deprived Peru of rich copper and nitrate deposits that might have contributed to economic growth. The Tacna-Arica dispute was not settled until 1929 (and festers on, owing to Bolivian-Chilean-Peruvian disputes over access for the Bolivians to the sea). Tacna-Arica was to Chile and Peru—and Bolivia also—what Alsace-Lorraine was to France and Germany, for a quarter of a century concomitantly, then for a decade beyond World War I. Of the four countries considered in these pages, Peru had the least to work with in the effort to create a modern army.

It is difficult to take seriously Peruvian tracing of their military history to pre-Columbian times, but Peruvians do just that: to an alleged training school near Cuzco for *Incanato* nobles. From that point forward, peninsulars and creoles dominate official histories. Education of Euro-Peruvians for military service dates from the eighteenth century, when creole militia officers were supposed to study mathematics if they expected to serve in artillery units.[16] Spaniards routinely studied mathematics for artillery service (from 1715 on in Barcelona), and there were courses from 1764 on in Havana, making Viceroy Amat's urging of mathematics on creole aspirants seem less prejudicial or out of line than one might think.[17] Military education in the national period began in 1823 with a short-lived academy opened by President José María Riva Agüero, where theory was heavily emphasized; then again in 1826 with the founding of the Colegio Militar Andrés de Santa Cruz, located in an abandoned convent in the San Felipe district of Lima.[18] In 1830 President Agustín Gamarra decreed the opening of the Escuela Militar. The Escuela lasted for four years, then closed from 1834 to 1851. All of these were located in Lima proper; none had adequate funding. Riva Agüero's administration did not last long enough to provide any kind of continuity, nor did that of Santa Cruz. The Escuela Militar de Chorrillos dated from a decree of January 7, 1850, emitted by President Ramón Castilla, Peru's mid-century soldier-politician. Marshal Castilla wanted the existing facilities (such as they were) removed from the political life of the capital, so he moved military education in toto from a building on Calle Espíritu Santo to the summer barracks in rural (now suburban) Chorrillos, south of the capital on a bluff near the sea. It successively recessed in 1854, functioned again from 1859 to 1867 (despite the 1862–66 conflict with Spain), then recessed during the War of the Pacific. By that time most of the three-year program's courses were held in Lima again, where cadets studied mathematics, geography, languages, drill exercises, and marksmanship. Piérola began the reform program with the hiring of French instructors and the relocation of the school in Chorrillos—still outside the city, but beginning to blend with suburban Miraflores.

When he did so, military training in Peru was in a sorry state. The on again, off again post-war programs, which included a course for non-commissioned officers inaugurated by President Andrés Cáceres in 1888, were held in antiquated barracks. Navy and army cadets shared classes, and the turnover of instructors was rapid, owing to political interference. An estimated four hundred students attended these classes, many of which existed on paper only; funding was undependable and facilities were obviously primitive. Military presidents—Gamarra, Castilla, Cáceres—had made most of the plans. Gamarra even hired a German, one Major Karl Pauli, to teach in Peru and publicly advocated civics classes for conscripts. Civilian politicians—the Civilistas, then Piérola—showed more interest in proper finance, facilities, and faculty. They saw education as a means of weaning men in uniform from political aspirations.

When the reform program began, the Peruvian army had

distinctive racial characteristics. All the troops were Indians or *cholos*. The vast majority of officers were Euro-Peruvians, still known as creoles, and they came from Lima or the other, smaller, urban centers. *Clases* (non-coms) were of peasant stock, *cholos*, and a few Indians. Some took courses with officer cadets, and these *clases*—or *niños*, as they were called condescendingly—were highly regarded for their valor in the war with Chile. From the beginning of Peru's modern era, the officer class in Peru has included men from throughout the country of both European and mixed origin, giving rise to the ceaseless claims that the army is the "nation in microcosm."[19] The historical ability of non-commissioned officers, representative of the lower classes and racially mixed, to rise to officer status, though rarely to high rank, is more pronounced throughout the national period in Peru than in Argentina, Brazil, or Chile (or, for that matter, Bolivia). Indeed, some sources allude to *cabitos* (from *cabo*, corporal) moving into the officer class from the 1820s forward.[20] At the close of the century the army was equipped with Winchester rifles, Krupp or Schneider-Creuzot field pieces, and, as one astute observer noted, "some bayonets that were functional."[21]

The War of the Pacific had done greater damage to military education schemes, for the Lima-Chorrillos area was the scene of battles and occupation between 1880 and 1883. Thus, even before Piérola took action, Gamarra and others had seen clearly the formulation of defense policy and isolation of the army from politics as one and the same process. Peruvian officialdom's first French mentor put it tersely: "As soon as the Chileans left, army leaders realized that professional preparation, the training of officers and non-commissioned officers, was the first step toward the reconstitution of the exhausted and nearly defenseless national organism."[22] Post-1884 war ministers Colonels Javier de Osma and Justiniano Borgoño had urged the funding and staffing of military schools, but political conflict and economic limitations simply precluded action until Piérola's ascendence in the 1890s.

Peru had maintained approximately 5,500 men under arms prior to the war, and kept a 6,000-man peacetime force afterwards. On paper 4,250 were volunteer career soldiers and 1,750 were conscripts or one-year enlistees.[23] Until the arrival of Paul Clément, Peru's was decidedly a paper army.

Only with the reestablishment of internal order would continued support for a professional officer corps be forthcoming. In the 1890s, binding of the army to maintenance of stability, therefore, was a necessity, but not a foregone conclusion. The forging of the Civilista-Democrat coalition by Piérola, and its duration until 1908, then the rise of Leguía, proved critical to harmonious military-civilian relations. Inculcation of French colonial military theory only drew the first *afrancesados* away from ruling forces, however, for during the first decade of this century junior officers began to see their country in a decidedly different way than did most of their superiors.

Meanwhile, far across the continent, the Brazilian army had toppled a monarchy, created a republic, helped promulgate a constitution, and lost its credibility on internal battlefields and in the political arena—all within a decade. Victorious years before against Paraguay, Brazilians had shared the gains of victory with their erstwhile Argentine allies. Inept politically, they now shared the ignominy of political ineptitude with their confreres from Peru. Traditionally removed from politics, until the 1880s, at least, they had a past characterized by respectability similar to that of the Chileans.

The very vastness of Brazil and the continuation of the Brazilian monarchy after independence conspired to inhibit a political army. Titled officers were but a uniformed nobility in the best tradition of nineteenth-century Europe. The national army was really little more than a collection of provincial units, recruited, staffed, and trained apart. Until the Paraguayan War, Brazil had never mobilized on a large scale, and it showed. Local landowners had bands of fighting men, private armies that could put the nationals to shame.

Independence, moreover, did not even provide the army with either a glorious tradition or the makings of one in order to justify its importance or existence. Separation from a weakened Portugal was achieved in 1822 with minimal violence: a few skirmishes with recalcitrant pro-Portuguese units of the colonial forces and Lord Cochrane's investiture of Salvador da Bahia. When Emperor Pedro I attempted to hold the Cisplatine Province (Brazil's name for Uruguay) in 1826–27—neither the first nor the last unfortunate involvement in that country—he used German, and even some Irish, mercenaries, not his Brazilian troops. This was a blow to the latter's pride, alienated them from the monarch, and contributed to his downfall in 1831. Separatist movements during the 1831–40 regency and following the restoration of the monarchy did little to either endear Pedro II to the army or provide the latter with prestige or influence. Not until 1864 and a new Platine–Paraná Basin imbroglio was national defense seriously considered on a grand scale, and only then did anything resembling a "military point of view" exist in Brazil. As with the Chileans, victorious Brazilian officers would use victory to justify improvement of their lot.

Prince Regent João (João VI, 1816–22) founded an "Académia Real Militar" in Rio de Janeiro in 1810 for the purpose of improving organization and ordnance.[24] The Académia functioned intermittently throughout the Dominion period and into Pedro I's reign. Ideally the Académia availed qualified young men of a six-year course: two years of preparatory and four of professional training, expanded to eight years in 1815. Poor funding, the uncertain situation of the Regency period, and regional revolts precluded the early post-independence emergence of a true officer class.[25] During these years Brazil had more in common with Argentina and Peru than with Chile.

In 1852 an infantry and cavalry training center opened in Pôrto Alegre, capital of Rio Grande do Sul, where separatist sentiment ran strong. Chartered in 1851, it specialized in the two branches of training only, lending a *gaúcho* touch to foot and horse soldiers. Three years later the Académia Militar San Pedro opened its doors, and the Escola de Aplicação in Rio for advanced training of officers also opened. In another three years Rio boasted the Escola Central Militar and a preparatory school as well.[26] However much activity there appears to have been at mid-century, officer training was not standardized, nor even considered all that necessary. Classes were irregular, schedules were highly flexible, and no cohesive corps of graduates emerged from military schools.

During the War of the Triple Alliance several training centers turned out officers rapidly in Pôrto Alegre, Rio, and Fortaleza. After the war, officer training continued in haphazard fashion, with schools in Rio—a preparatory school in Realengo and the Escola Militar in Praia Vermelha—and a school at Rio Pardo in Rio Grande do Sul. By the time the empire fell in 1889 the majority of officers had come either out of the Paraguayan War or from the institutions in Pôrto Alegre or Realengo–Praia Vermelha. Early in this century, at the prodding of career officers like Hermes da Fonseca, there still were programs designated as Escolas de Aplicação for artillery and engineers and artillery and infantry, and a general military course and staff training in Rio Grande do Sul, as well as a staff school, the Escola de Estado Maior do Exército, and the Praia Vermelha center in Rio. On the eve of World War I, Praia Vermelha was Brazil's best-equipped and best-funded military educational institution.

Regionalism was still a factor. Each state had its own *colónia* at Praia Vermelha, composed either of alumni of the state military preparatory schools or of those who entered the cadet corps from civilian *colégios*. The Escola reflected state political issues as well as state loyalties. There were frequent suspensions of classes, such as one during the 1904–5 mutiny caused by the involvement of cadets in protest against compulsory smallpox vaccination.[27] Compounding political and regional influences on the formation of a military mentality was the lack of a highly specialized professional curriculum. An inordinate amount of time (as compared to that allotted in Argentina, Chile and Peru) was given over to pure science, political and social thought, and philosophy. If the impact of Positivism—attributed to the proselytizing tendencies of Lieutenant Colonel Benjamin Constant Botelho de Magalhães, a mathematics instructor at Praia Vermelha, and subsequently first war minister of the Republic—has been exaggerated, the effect of loosely structured liberal arts courses and the lack of strictly professional courses on politically- and regionally-minded cadets should not be dismissed. Benjamin even questioned the true vocation of most cadets, alleging that many entered the officer corps, as others entered the clergy, in order to gain a free education and a secure career.[28]

An army that numbered 16,000 men and officers in 1865 grew quickly to 67,000 by 1866 but contracted sharply afterward. It was no more capable of sustaining a protracted campaign than it had been during the war with Paraguay. The army barely kept pace with changes in doctrine, strategy, and tactics. In the wake of confrontation in the South American heartland the army found itself in an ironic situation: the victors were forgotten. Pedro, no friend of the military, did not yield to the arguments of generals nor to those of the army's champion, Luis Alves de Lima e Silva, Duke of Caxias, that the empire needed an army capable of defending it at any time. Brazil's most significant military figure of the past century, Caxias held the country together during the 1831–40 regency. He was an able war minister (1855–57, 1861, and 1875–76), was in the field during the Paraguayan war, and carried the army's case to Pedro. He was also a noble, close to the emperor and only informally speaking a professional army officer. He may have been the army's champion, but he was also the emperor's man. Between 1870 and his death in 1880 the army was buffeted by the rough and troubled politics of the late Empire.[29] Caxias did much to protect the institution but did little to satisfy those who wanted to professionalize the officer corps along European lines.

From 1880 to 1889 the army became embroiled in a series of political questions, as Liberals maneuvered with their military link, Viscount Pelotas, and Conservatives countered with theirs, Marshal Fonseca. Abolition, Republicanism, Positivism, the upgrading of military capabilities, and the dignity, inviolability, and professional nature of the institutions, as well as regional issues, were subjects of cadet discussions. In the 1880s some Brazilian officers may have seen a political stance similar to that of their Spanish American brethren as necessary to the cause of modernization. The Brazilians searched for an identity. Their role as founders of the Republic did not result in a political stance, nor did it result in rewards commensurate with what officers thought was their due. It merely perpetuated the *questão militar:* just how politically involved could military men be? Before the fall of the Empire the question centered on the right to speak out on political, social, and economic questions. With the Empire's demise, active officers were excluded from elective office, but the armed forces exercised the *podor moderador,* formerly the emperor's moderative power of intervention. Thus the military did gain a sense of collective legitimacy for a stance; corporate self-interest—already evident in Marshal Deodoro's 1889 defiance of the Emperor—was existent,[30] but there was little substance to it.

A good part of the officer corps in 1889 was composed of non-aristocrats and there was a sizable "military family" contingent. A few officers were of Negro origin. Spread thin, assigned duties in the interior military colonies, and denied a modern system of rail transport comparable to that in rival Argentina (a product of economic expansion more than of military planning based on the lessons of the Franco-Prussian War), the army was armed with French Comblain rifles and Krupp artillery pieces. Outdated Portuguese field manuals remained in use until 1913. Cadets specialized in branch training (when they could get it) and learned little of the other branches of the service. Attempts to centralize training were shunted aside, as was the obligatory service code, first introduced in 1874. Recruits were of Negro and mixed background, and 70 percent were illiterate. As one specialist wrote, what came of all this were "isolated efforts, lost opportunities, measures that did not reach the point of execution. On the other hand, the intellectual level of the corps improved, they…were still heterogenous, composed of educated or scientific[ally-educated] officers and uneducated doltish [ones]."[31] Such was the institution that had toppled an empire.

Military modernization in Brazil came only during the Republican era, and only after the army had been persuaded to retire from active participation in politics. Entrapped for five years (1889–94) and humbled by the disastrous 1896–97 Canudos campaigns, the army emerged less than lustrous from its "chest to chest" confrontation with civilian political life.[32] What Benjamin Constant and his activist cadre had hoped for—a quick thrust against the Empire and a retirement to the barracks—had ended up as a disaster. Early in this century, years before the arrival of the French, Marshal Hermes began the groundwork on which the likes of Maurice Gamelin and Charles Huntzinger would try to build a modern officer corps. When they did, the Brazilian army numbered nearly 30,000 men. The rise from 16,000 to 67,000 in 1865–66 was followed by reductions to 19,000 in 1871, 15,000 in 1880, and 13,000 in 1889—the low point in many ways for officers and emperor alike, and the point where the state *forças públicas* became more powerful than the national army.[33] From 1889 forward, the army had only one way to go, but it was a long, slow climb up.

In the last decade of the nineteenth century, the armed forces of Argentina, Brazil, Chile, and Peru confronted politics in different ways, but the confrontations resulted in comparable reactions. Each of the armies had undergone the rudiments of professionalization; each had officers in important staff or command positions who understood, at least, the need for modernization of equipment. In three of the armies there was a core of junior officers who already considered themselves either underprivileged or superior to their commanders, or both. Only in Peru was there no clear rift within the officer corps during the first decade of this century. Each army had its champion—or soon would have.

Argentines, whether sympathetic to the newborn Radical party or not, knew that Julio Roca believed in a modern well-equipped, and well-trained fighting force. With the passing of the Empire, Brazilian officers found that their champion, Marshal Deodoro, could do little in the chaos following Pedro's abdication. Benjamin Constant attempted to initiate a reform scheme while he was in the war ministry, but failed. After the establishment of civilian rule in 1894 and the Canudos disasters of 1896–97, the army was reduced to observer status and shown to be a white elephant, and not until the outspoken Marshal Hermes took up the cause could the damage be repaired.

When the dust settled following the Chilean Civil War of 1891, Emil Körner found himself in a superb position to carry out Prussianization. Balmacedista officers were purged from the rolls, and those who had received commissions in 1891 were kept on with Körner-trained junior grades and the older veterans of the War of the Pacific. The officer corps was a divided lot: Germanophile juniors, grizzled veterans of the Peruvian campaign, and the 1891 volunteers. This division and the fact that the army's most articulate champion was a foreigner (albeit very popular in Chile) influenced the development of military-civilian relations as much as domestic tribulations in Argentina and Brazil influenced development there. The 1890s, as noted, proved salutary to the modernization of Peru's officer corps and its army. Fiscal health, the multi-racial composition of officialdom, the abilities of Piérola, and the coming of Colonel Clément precluded the early development of divisions within the nascent officer corps.

It is clear that civil conflict has had much to do historically with political action by South American men in uniform. Not until what have been called the "institutional golpes" of the 1960s and 1970s has civil conflict resulted in widespread military-imposed-and-administered alternatives with long-range goals in mind. Early in this century, just as the modern, professional armies took form, officers were as vulnerable to outside influences as were the governments they served. Thus the Civic Union of Youth and its spawn, the Radical party, made inroads into the Argentine officer corps precisely as professionalization got under way. The experiences of the 1890s induced Brazilian officers to realize just what the results of political activity could be. The crisis of 1891 in Chile and the ensuing parliamentary system did the same for Chilean officers. In Peru the great differences between the words and the actions of political leaders led to the strikingly early and sophisticated elaboration of an army officers' "point of view."

None of the armies discussed here, with the qualified exception of Chile's, had a consistent tradition of professional preparation by 1890. This may have retarded the ability to seize an initiative in the 1890s—provided anyone had been inclined to do so. Economic growth in Argentina and Peru and the dramatic nature of political revolutions in Brazil and Chile may have conspired to temporarily strengthen civilian political leadership. Hence there may be a cause-and-effect link between moderation in the civilian sector—moderate economic growth, moderate expansion of the elite and of the politically articulate population, moderate social change brought about by wider distribution of economic opportunity—and moderation of the military profession's thinking. One of the points to be raised in the chapters to follow concerns the point at which a military point of view can indeed be discerned. That is to say, or ask, when is it apparent and negative anent civilian attitudes toward the political system, the nature of the economy, and social problems?

Obviously something resembling a military point of view can be discerned at any time in these countries about the middle of the nineteenth century: efficient government and proper training and equipping of the armed forces. But as long as no one involved them in anything but the traditional responsibilities of national defense, officers did not menace the essence of things political; participation was on partisan and personal, not professional, grounds. But when the Brazilians were ordered out of barracks and posts to supervise the capture and return of escaped slaves (after having seen the fighting capabilities of ex-slaves in the 1864–70 war), or to smash the Canudos rebels; when Peruvians and Chileans struggled to make soldiers out of illiterate *cholos*, Indians, and *rotos* (after having witnessed troop training methods in France and Germany); and when Argentines were subjected to the manipulations of post-Roca political leaders, then the shaping of a formal, defined ethos did take place. In sum, the establishment of professional officer corps in South American based on European models and the incessant aping of those models led officers to adopt beliefs and value systems that differed from those of the society about them. This would not have happened without specialized training and resultant expertise, a defined defense role, and professional attitudes based on internal regulation, norms, and practices that set armies apart from civilian sectors.

It is clear that Argentina, Brazil, Chile, and Peru adopted European military systems for two prime reasons based on necessity and a third reason based on desire. The prime reasons were to isolate the army and insure civilian control of government. Argentine and Peruvian, and later Brazilian, leaders saw the need to mollify officers, to co-opt them, and to keep them happy and occupied in the barracks. Activity there, on the parade ground, and on study trips would allow civilians a free hand to run national affairs. This was particularly attractive when the allure of foreign capital and the expansion of extractive industries, agriculture, stock raising, and mining opened a new era. Chilean leaders saw less need for isolating the army and navy from politics, though the issue would come to the fore well into the professionalization process. In Chile the prime reason for modernization was the desire to maintain defense capabilities. In Argentina, Brazil, and Peru this was of some importance as well.

A glance at the map of South America gives visual evidence of defense concerns. South America has been a geopolitician's paradise and a source of international conflict since colonial times. Leaving aside details of the frontier, squabbles involving Spain and Portugal, it is sufficient to repeat that Argentine-Brazilian rivalries derive from colonial disputes in the Platine and Paraná basins. Paraguay, Uruguay, and much of modern Bolivia were under the jurisdiction of Buenos Aires in the late eighteenth century; their independence from *porteño* control was a jolt to the new Argentine government. Brazil's interests in the upper Paraná, Uruguay, and Paraguay basins, and the occupation of Uruguay (known as the Cisplatine Province from 1816 to 1827) was an early sign of geopolitical rivalry in the area. Argentine and Brazilian policy since the last decade of the nineteenth century hinges on power politics in the Platine-Paraná zone, access to the Platine heartland, and a power balance on the Atlantic coast. Historically it stands to reason that what impedes the armed forces from fulfilling the dictates of their policies cannot be tolerated.

America's Alsace-Lorraine was merely the late-nineteenth-century, temporary resolution of a similar power rivalry on the Pacific coast. Like the War of the Triple Alliance, the War of the Pacific was partially the result of colonial-era issues colliding with mutual antipathy, fear, and distrust. Chile was a breakaway extremity of the Viceroyalty of Peru, and maintained its independence and expanded its territory by force of arms. As with Argentina and Brazil, Pacific coast military policy hinged on maritime and territorial power conflicts and continued tenuous relations compounded by the mediterranean status of Bolivia.

By the end of the century, as Robert Burr has noted, there was a functional balance-of-power relationship in South America.[34] Indeed, Theodore Mannequin helped point out the European qualities of South America power politics as early as 1866, politics based on the territorial interests of Argentina, Brazil, Chile, and Peru, on Argentina's imperialistic nature, on Atlantic-Pacific trade rivalries, on Brazil's "disputed conquests" achieved by treaty, and on the emergence of the (as yet informal) Brazil-Chile and Argentina-Peru axes.[35] If diplomacy was highly derivative of European international relations, it should not seem odd that defense policy was equally derivative. This derivation, in conjunction with the characteristics of indigenous society, politics, economics, and culture, produced a Europeanized military caste in a quasi-Europeanized setting. Hopes that this would result in a Europeanized military-civilian relationship, albeit an idealized one, were high, doubtless, but they had the substance of misguided wishful thinking and nothing more. In South America, a wedge between military and civilian institutions was being driven into place.

By the 1890s the Europeans were barely aware of South American military activity. They knew of the Triple Alliance and the war that bore its name, and of the War of the Pacific too. They could follow the upheavals of 1889, 1890, and 1891 in Brazil, Argentina, and Chile with great interest. News of London's financial coup in Lima traveled far, rapidly. Although Germans were aware of Körner's work in Chile, they were far more interested in Colmar von der Goltz's in Turkey, building his "bridge between Central Europe and Asia" (Moltke was less than enthusiastic), and Meckel's work in Japan. They were far more concerned with Germany's latest colonial ventures in Togo, Kamerun, Tankganyika, and Southwest Africa. Germans were hardly enthusiastic about the abilities of Latins to absorb military expertise. Bernhardi, author of "the book that caused the war," observed tersely that, after all, being an amalgam of Gothic and Mediterranean, they were inferior to racially pure Germans.[36]

Likewise the French, even after Clément arrived in Peru, became more deeply interested in imperial adventures in Indo-China, Madagascar, and North Africa, ventures of greater import to military-civilian relations and international affairs. The French appeared to be proof of Guglielmo Ferrero's comment of 1898 that "French colonial policy signifies that the age of great military undertakings is now ever past in Europe. It therefore strives to perpetuate the glory of arms in Asia and Africa."[37] Appearances are ever deceiving. It was too soon, perhaps, for reflection on the presence of Europeans in South America, too soon, probably, to ascertain just what this could mean beyond extrapolation from conclusions like that made in 1903 by Paul Jaillet: "It is totally logical that the role of the army will not be the same as long as the colonies-to-be are situated in different climates and latitudes."[38]

At the beginning of the age of professionalization in South America, the French and Germans had large armies composed of volunteers and career soldiers. In 1889 the French army numbered nearly 490,000, and Germany had slightly fewer, just under 470,000. Both could count on 2,000,000 men in case of mobilization for war. France regularly had a larger number of men under arms until the end of the century. Her defense-oriented doctrines and colonial theories appealed to Peruvians. Just as obviously the Prussian offense-oriented order of battle and doctrine were a great attraction to more aggressive-minded Argentines and Chileans.[39] The advantages of small fighting forces led by professional officers expressed in *Das Volk in Waffen* were obvious to all South Americans, for none of the four continental powers could ever hope to put in the field an army comparable to that of France or Germany.

Whereas the Germans who went abroad were innocents when it came to politics, French officers were attuned to political life Republican-style. Their Latin pupils reflected these peculiarities, more so when social distinctions in the French and German officer corps became significant and when German politics became enmeshed in social questions early in this century. By that time South Americans could respond both to Bugeaud's declaration of 1832 to the Chamber of Deputies that "French bayonets only thirst for the blood of the stranger…in the sense that they only desire to fight against the enemies of France, but they also are always ready to fight the factions,"[40] and to Goltz's dictum of 1899: "States which are weak from a military point of view, and which are surrounded by stronger neighbors invite war, and if they neglect their military organizations from false motives, they court this danger by their own supineness."[41]

Troubled armies, those in need of refurbishing, resuscitation, or discipline, looked to armies that had proved themselves capable and resilient—but that were no less conscious of their associations with state, nation, and society. What little interest the Europeans had in their clients-to-be can be found in the pages of professional journals, and consists primarily of news items and correspondence from America.

Chile, since it was the first South American country to adopt a European military system, received the most regular coverage. Körner's plans to send outstanding Chilean cadets to study at the Kriegsakademie and the previous year's military parade in Santiago received notice early in 1890 in Germany's major military journal, *Militär Wochenblatt*,[42] and in 1892 the *Revue Militaire de l'Étranger* noted for its French readers that Körner's congressional forces had utilized Krupp artillery in their victory over Balmaceda.[43] The article drew attention also to the mobility of the rebel forces as contrasted to the lack of mobility on the part of the loyalists. Firepower, strategic control of both the nitrate provinces and the sea, and the lack of adequate land transportation to facilitate a loyalist campaign in the north figured in the news from the Pacific. The German counterpart of the *Revue Militaire de l'Étranger*, the *International Revue über die Gesammten Armeen und Flotten*, revealed with pride the accomplishments of the Körner mission as of the mid-1890s. Chilean officers, the dispatch noted, were better disciplined than any South American counterparts; they were hardworking and conscientious. Discipline, broken in 1891, had been restored by the Saxon "missionary," but Chilean officers, though warmly appreciated and universally praised by civilians, "still had a long way to go before achieving the social standing enjoyed by Germans."[44] *Neue Militärische Blätter* carried a strictly professional appraisal of Körner's wartime feats.[45]

Despite her upheaval, commercial significance, and strategic position anent Brazil, Argentina drew slightly less attention than Chile. In a *Militär Wochenblatt* essay of 1890, the writer claimed that a real revolution would have occurred if the army had not remained loyal to the government, perhaps giving more credit to the Civic Union of Youth than was its due. The army's "unity, concentration, and discipline" had saved Argentina from anarchy.[46] The theme of the military as balanced against upheaval was a constant in German literature. The next appearance of news from Argentina in the pages of the *Wochenblatt*, nearly a decade later, was a mere snippet of news about the duties of Colonel Alfred Arent, new director of the Escuela Superior de Guerra, and about German and French officers serving in other South American countries.[47] Interest in the Latin world was slow building until after the turn of the century. Brazil fared more poorly, Peru not at all, prior to 1900. A brief note in the *Revue Militaire de l'Étranger* gave some statistics on the Brazilian Army in 1890.

Such was the extent of officially-published knowledge of the armies of South America's leading countries at the dawn of the age of professionalization. Traveler's accounts, newspaper coverage, and the like provided military men with most of their information on South America. Classified materials, it must be supposed, were little better in content and sophistication. With the turn of the century, though, the quantity and quality of coverage improved, for by then not only was there more interest and contact, but the great enterprise of the German and French "martial missionaries" had begun in Argentina, Chile, and Peru. Brazil as well soon showed signs of interest in establishing ties with the Kaiser's army. South America, then, came face to face with European military professionalism. That professionalism is the subject of the following chapter.

"Every special calling of life, if it
is to be followed with success,
requires peculiar qualifications of
understanding and soul."

Carl Maria von Clausewitz,
On War (1832)

"Prusso-German militarism...has
become not only a state within a
state, but actually a state above a
state."

Karl Liebknecht,
Militarism and Anti-Militarism
(1907)

CHAPTER THREE

European Military Professionalism: Its Champions & Critics

Even though both Europe and South America were at peace between 1890 and 1914, there was no widespread belief that the war to end all wars had been fought. The Roman maxim attributed to Vegetius, *si vides pacem, para bellum* (if you care for peace, prepare for war),[1] appears as a theme in military or pro-military literature of all countries throughout the period. Only extremists like the German Social Democrat Karl Liebknecht argued against the maintenance of some kind of army. Jean Jaurès, the French Socialist, may have opposed the professional qualities of a standing army but clearly saw the need for a defense force in the time of emergency. His compatriots the Dreyfusards, and even Emilé Zola, did not seriously question the advisability of national defense; they were shocked and motivated to act on behalf of Dreyfus because of the sociopolitical implications of intra-army conflict and civilian involvement, not because they wanted to abolish the army. The Masonic-Catholic controversy a decade later became similarly a pretext for attacks on the perversion of military authority. Very few Europeans, then, and most of them extremists, were wholeheartedly committed to eliminating the armed forces.

Across the ocean, where civilian euphoria accompanied professionalization, the situation was analogous, albeit with some differences. Crises, war scares, mobilizations, and exchanges of notes between chancelleries led to a greater amount of favorable public opinion on military build-ups than was the case in Europe. Free from the dynastic snare of continental power politics (within which problems were solved as well as created), Argentina, Brazil, Chile, and Peru were still trying to solve lingering border problems, still probing their own hinterlands, still achieving nation-state status. Extremist political forces had not yet reached an organizational status enabling them to mount sophisticated anti-militarist campaigns. South American army officers were not of such homogeneous origins, training, and experience that they could form an "interest group."

As the French and German officer corps began to show the strain of modernization, owing to expansion and the inclusion of a greater proportion of bourgeoise talent, so did their South American counterparts. The ideas that South Americans of modest origin absorbed were those of upper-class or would-be upper-class French and Germans, committed professionals, who strove to maintain their ideals and values against modern-day social, economic, cultural, and political pressures from without. Resistance to change is one of the hallmarks of the European professional army corps prior to 1914, yet advocacy of change is one of the hallmarks of pre-war South American military thought and self-perception. This is not contradictory at all.

Concomitant expression of similar or identical ideas in different milieux may encourage contrasting actions based on those ideas, with consequently differing results. The acceptance of certain ideals and values by South American officers by no means removed them from their environment, but it made them more keenly aware of the differences between military and civilian life. A diploma from the École Superieure de Guerre or the Kriegsakademie did not mold Peruvians or Chileans, Brazilians or Argentines, into Europeans; but it did distinguish them from their fellow officers and citizens. Long-term contact with training officers added immeasurably to the professional world-view of a Benavides, an Ibáñez, a Fonseca and an Uriburu, in South America.

The alarm with which French and German officers viewed politics and politicians was not diluted in transit across the equator, over the Andes, and through the Strait of Magellan. Likewise, the principles of national defense were intact on arrival in South America. Obligatory military service was a constant. South American diplomacy was still based very much on European balance-of-power theories.[2] Security and defense capabilities, international relations and foreign policy, politics and national service, all were integrated phenomena in Europe, phenomena of great importance and under the constant scrutiny of officers and their staffs. Two of the components of modern military professionalism—expertise and a sense of service to state, nation, and society—were thus as inseparable in South America as they were in Europe.

French and German army officers hardly were removed from politics, for the internal affairs of the nineteenth century, as well as international conflict, bound them to their government and its policies. Ties between army and state chafed both parties at times, especially when partisan politics became the modus operandi of parliaments and cabinets in the late part of the century. A number of contemporary standard sources, civilian and military, portrayed military-civilian relationships, and these merit citation in order to lend perspective to the military-civilian *Zeitgeist* of the entire 1890–1914 years as portrayed consistently by officers in their professional journals.

By the end of the century, political parties played a steadily increasing role in the representative system of decision-making affairs of the state and all the processes that made the system function. At the same time, the armies of both France and Germany "retained most completely...the features which the old absolutist systems had stamped upon them."[3] By that, Gaetano Mosca meant simply that in the face of change and in confronting democracy, however limited, armies remained authoritarian and elitist. Germans could purchase commissions until World War I; German regiments nevertheless did not have to accept officers, and still voted on their acceptability. Discipline was rigid in both the German and French armies (although numerous sources portray French discipline as lax). To the French, politics was a bewildering process that defied rules of order, unity, and duty; politics went against an officer's self-perception of the corps as "bureaucratic nobility, combining the orderliness and conscientiousness of the civil service employee with the chivalrous spirit and the high sense of honor that were traditional to the high born."

Officers, whether noble or—each year more and more—commoners, therefore found themselves between two worlds and torn between branches and sectors of society. Pareto's simplistic juxtaposition of Machiavelli's lions and foxes, of Sparta and Athens, hence of absolutism and republicanism, might support the position that the officer class represented two faces of a coin: patrimonial authority, tradition, and force; bureaucratic authority, innovation, and reason.[4] Moreover, his hypothesis (however fraught with exceptions) of pluto-democracy—the synthesis of plutocracy and democracy in which the *rentier* class is exploited both by the speculators and the laboring classes—would further establish the officer class as representative of *the* alternative to an unholy plutocratic-democratic alliance.

Both Mosca and Pareto saw clearly the changes wrought in Europe by the blending socioeconomic development and political experimentation prevalent since 1789, certainly after 1848, and vividly in France from 1871 forward. They, the former specifically, the latter by implication, placed the officer class in a tenuous position. Guglielmo Ferrero called the German officer class a "caste," the French a bellicose people whose "public passion for military glory was responsible for colonial ventures." "The decline of militarism," he wrote with customary lack of foresight, "is everywhere connected with the rise of the bourgeois class....Hence in those countries where this class is in power war loses any romantic character of political glory." The Germans thus formed a caste, the French were bureaucrats. Stilted observations, yet not without substance. Ferrero's Francophobia blinded him to the fact of German ambition in Europe (and overseas).[5] His belief in the pacifism of the middle sectors was misplaced, but this noting of the caste/bureaucratic aspect of officer classes lends additional support to the "dilemma thesis" anent the sociopolitical outlook of the late-nineteenth-century officer corps. Of the two European armies looked to by South America, it is the French that experienced the most intense political pressures, both in favor of military strength and against it.

John Steward Ambler recently made the point that the French Army had never formed a caste such as the *Junkertum* but was instead a mix of men promoted from the ranks and graduates of the military institutes. By the end of the century, graduates of St. Cyr and the Polytechnique prevailed. This was because young aristocrats and members of monarchist families, almost all of them Catholic, were discouraged from joining many Republican institutions and therefore sought a kind of refuge in the uniform. With the eclipse of the nobility as a politically potent estate and socially distinguished class, noble surnames on the officer's roster declined rapidly. Thus there was a social isolation and insulation of the officer class from certain unpleasant, ungentlemanly aspects of civilian, social, political, and economic life.

The Republic denied political rights to its officers, and professionals frowned on colleagues who consorted with politicians or activists. Ambler has emphasized the hostility of the officer class (as typical rather than monolithic) toward Republicanism. He noted three chief contributors to officer-class hostility: the conservative, Catholic background of many officers and the conservative, middle-class *rentier* background of others; the clash of the so-called traditional values—honor, fidelity, sacrifice, service—with the values ascribed to the middle class at large—security, comfort, thrift, material wealth; and the obvious everyday differences between the military and the civilian way of life.[6] This last involved the differing opinions on the use of force; clashing views of international relations; glaringly opposing views on individual vs. group, hierarchy vs. equality, and discipline vs. debate; nationalism; and the autonomy of the military institution. In his *Lettres du Tonkin et de Madagascar*, Lyautey dubbed the Republic living evidence of "incompetent, unstable and irresponsible parliamentarism."

"It is a challenge to good sense," he wrote in 1897, "this regime where almost the entire executive has passed into the hands of a parliament issuing from universal suffrage: people who do not know the first word of governmental affairs and who last only three years. And that being the only effective government, at the mercy of which are ministers, bureaux, established corps of public servants, professionals of all categories!—no fixed, stable element independent of popular caprice."[7] Those words, written in 1897, soon echoed in South America, and continued to do so decades later.

Whatever the extent to which Lyautey's perception of the polity may apply to the officer class as a whole, that class was by its very nature committed to a government and political system that could provide order and was inclined, indeed sworn, to neutrality in partisan struggles. In short, *la grande muette*, as Vigny called it, could be at a grudging stalemate with the Republic by default and, as Gorce would have it, be "a social milieu in which the changing times are mirrored."[8] The numerous crises of the pre-1914 years caused varying degrees of friction, but they did not impose the army on the state or vice versa in a political sense. The perpetual shifting of cabinet ministers playing the game of musical portfolios that was parliamentarism—nineteen governments and sixteen war ministers from 1870 to 1888, eighteen more governments by 1897: thirty seven cabinets in all—did not disrupt seriously the inner workings of the military institution. Politics delayed and frustrated, bewildered and bothered, but did not destroy the army.

As the Republic matured, relations mellowed. The de facto colonial empire and the revelation of *l'affaire Dreyfus* and of General André's *fiches* ultimately reduced the mutual hostilities of Republicans and Monarchists within the ranks of the officer corps. Georges Clemenceau proved a moderating influence, as did the fact that in contrast to earlier years there was less Catholic-Protestant strife within the officer corps, less of a conservative and monarchist tinge to army leadership. By World War I, Gorce claimed, the high command was better organized than the government. Joffre, a Mason, but no staunch anticlerical, assumed the post of chief of the general staff, putting to an end one kind of traditional discrimination.[9] .

"Uneasy," then, would be an appropriate word to describe the relations of officers and politicians in France. The military-civilian relationship was indeed a tenuous one, and although mutual suspicion did ease, it did so only slowly, owing more to the eventual durability of Republican institutions than to their acceptability to men in uniform. Moderation of feelings was as much the outcome of non-interference as it was of wholesale conversion on the part of civilian and military men alike. The fact that publicly-expressed opinions indicate reasonable consistency shows again just how steadfast military men have always been in their thinking on non-professional issues.

Indeed, well before the decades under examination here, standards had been set publicly. Marshal Bugeaud had drawn the line between "divisive" civilians and "unifying" military in an address to the Chamber on February 1, 1832. In still another Chamber speech he had attacked the press bluntly: "the greatest despotism we have yet lived under." Then came Vigny's classic *Servitude et grandeurs militaires*, in which he portrayed romantically the peacetime position of the army vis-à-vis the state: "blind and dumb," "a body searching in vain for its own soul," little more than a degraded "constabulary."[10] Vigny decried the using of the army by political factions in power for the purpose of maintaining internal order. He considered this a corrupting influence that exposed the army to attack from all sides.

Little changed over the decades—from the military standpoint, that is. In the age of Dreyfus, the army was still subject to attacks, but now it counterattacked as well. Urbain Gouhier, a stern critic of both the Monarchist cause and the army, claimed that Socialism and Catholicism-Monarchism menaced the Republic because of the pervasive secularism and materialism of state and society. The army "under the control of the Church," and riddled with Action Française sympathizers, was a menace to all France because it had made a mockery of justice (in the Dreyfus case), was outside of Parliament's control, and, moreover, ruined the lives of countless young men who were forced to spend time in obligatory military service.[11] Gouhier did not think a standing army served France well at all, rather the army was a parasite, immune to governmental controls. Retired Captain Gaston Moch countered Gouhier's arguments in his own book,

L'Armée d'une démocratie, published by the same house. Moch believed that conscripts brought a civic spirit to the barracks, then returned to civilian life with a healthy, martial spirit. He argued as strongly for the merits of obligatory service as Gouhier had argued against them. To Moch the army and democracy were not mutually exclusive, because they reinforced each other. Another contemporary of Moch and Gouhier wrote that obligatory service was to the army what universal manhood suffrage was to the Republic: indispensable and inseparable.[12]

Owing to conscription, the line between civilian and military once drawn by Bugeaud and Vigny became blurred socially. The schemes of the Socialist Jaurès blurred it further just three years before the Great War. Discrepancies in salaries, however, tended to create an alternative focus for military criticism of civilian affairs and institutions, of politics and politicians. Poverty, assumed by some to be a military virtue, was often blamed on legislators who did not support the army's budget requests. Bismarck's term "splendid misery" (and decades later Gorce's "gilded poverty") signified that military values and ideals reaped less than modest rewards from the state, from the Republic, from democracy. Paul Gabillard went so far as to claim that junior officers on routine assignments earned less than common laborers.[13] This is an argument that has been reiterated ad nauseam on both sides of the Atlantic.

French officers believed that their institution was linked to the civilian world but unique, that it represented consistency in an age of transition, and that it was quite vulnerable to pressure from without. Popular sovereignty, party politics, and Darwinian theories, one general believed, caused people to question too much of the past and the present. This put a strain on military-civilian relations, for the military, he thought, should not be subject to question. He believed, as did the Germans Clausewitz and Goltz, that "politics and the army are by definition two terms permanently united"; that military power was linked to national prestige; that the Republic was a rational approach to politics, devoid of personalism, as was the army.[14] The good general argued consistently, if not convincingly, for recognition by civilians of their and the army's mutual interests.

Young Captain Lyautey was not so optimistic, of course, and it may have been his anonymous essay of 1891 that prompted said general to take pen in hand. Lyautey blamed the Republic and its divisive politics for the dilettantism of France's youth. Rather than defy the political system he had sworn to defend, he devoted his first venture into print to a definition of what the army's role ought to be in remedying the negative influences of Republicanism. The essay of 1891 was pivotal, for it provoked a good deal of thought on obligatory service and the potential of the army as an educative and informative force.

In the midst of the Dreyfus snarl an obscure lieutenant colonel named Henri Jougla transmuted Lyautey's championship of army values into a riposte directed to all "outsiders" who attacked the army. To criticize the army, he believed, marked one as a traitor, a "sans patrie." "To demilitarize France is to de-Christianize France," he wrote.[15] At this time both the French and German officer corps equated anti-militarism with international movements; these were of a Socialist and Marxist nature, abhorrent to military professionals, for they denied the essence of nationalism. Many French officers had become convinced over the years that the most effective government and most valuable army could be found in the colonies, where "it is absolutely necessary to have civil and military authority together."[16] Authority there blended with initiative, discipline with independence of action, tradition with innovation, and administration with organization, all of which produced a military *mission civilizatrice.* Overseas the military felt much freer in its movements than in Metropolitan France. Subordination to civilian authorities and strict application of governmental directives simply were not the rule in Morocco, Senegal, and Madagascar as they were in Paris, Metz, or Strasbourg. Could it be that the French revived the validity of the old adage, *obedezco pero no cumplo,* ascribed to Habsburg administrators of centuries gone by?

Lyautey, as usual, put it better than anyone else. Just a few years after Paul Clément began his work in Peru, Lyautey wrote: "In the colonies improvisation is the rule, and where decisiveness is a daily requirement, the rule that outweighs all others is, 'The right man in the right place.'" To the French, then, military-civilian fusion was a prerequisite to effective government under extraordinary (non-European) conditions. Initiative, responsibility, common sense, interpretation of rules: were not these also necessary for civilian leaders as well as officers? Were not colonists soldiers of a type, were not soldiers colonists and administrators? "Vainly," wrote Lyautey, "one seeks a demarcation."[17] Of course Morocco, Senegal, and Madagascar were not Paris, Metz, or Strasbourg. Metropolitan France sought no military-civilian fusion, nor would the maturing Republic need such an arrangement until extraordinary conditions obtained in the form of a wartime military government. It was then, significantly, that the colonial army provided much of the leadership.

German officers had deep-seated political concerns, though they did not vent them as much, owing to their rigid identification with monarchism and the empire. They traced their heritage back to the medieval *Ritter*, the Teutonic knights, and *Junkertum*. They and many of their civilian brethren venerated the martial spirit, Germany's military successes, and war as the creating and sustaining forces of Prussia and the German Empire.

Germany remained overwhelmingly monarchist during the late nineteenth century as France became, once again, a Republic. Thus tradition, the crown, and history had different, more consistent connotations for German officers. They believed that military service, in Treitschke's melodramatic words, "brings home to the simple man, more directly than any other institution can do, the realization that the state is one and that he himself is part of the whole." Veterans' associations extended this effect to the fullest.[18] Germans subscribed to variations of a belief held by French colonial and metropolitan officers: that the army was the integrator of citizens, all sons of the same fatherland. In Treitschke's essay "The Constitution of the Army" in *Politics*,[19] the ponderous Prussophile saw the people and the army as one with the state; *Volk-Staat-Heer* were inseparable. The Prussian army was the nation in arms— "das Volk in Waffen"—and the finest embodiment of national characteristics and values.[20] In Prussia, at least, state and army had historical reasons to be mutually supportive, since one could not have been created or sustained without the other. "Gentlemen," as Helmut von Moltke had put it, addressing the Prussian Reichstag back in 1868, "when has there ever been amongst us any question of distinction between army and people?"[21]

Despite this apparent communion of spirit and mission, neither the monarchy nor the army won every political battle. The war ministry, then in the 1880s the military cabinet, struggled constantly with the Reichstag over men, manpower, budget control, and promotions policy. After the turn of the century, Social Democrats in the Reichstag made things difficult for the army whenever they could. No one expressed officer corps hostility toward them in better form than Lieutenant Emil Dangelmaier in a *Neue Militärische Blätter* essay of June 1898. In "Der Zeitgeist, die Gegenwart und das Heer," he attacked international socialism. "[It] is common throughout the world," he wrote, "and it is extremely active." But there was hope, for Germany had ceased to be an absolutist monarchy. The empire was democratic; democracy, though, must not lead to a breakdown of discipline or authority in the military and society, or provoke national "moral decay." Democracy must not be manipulated by a vociferous minority (Social Democrats), allowing the minority to prevail over the rights of the majority. To the Social Democrats' attacks against what they called the "Moloch of militarism," Dangelmaier replied: "Without discipline, no army; without the army, no state."[22] Politics, soon to become the bane of the South American professional officers, was just as disgusting to German monarchists.

The Kaiser barred his officers from voicing political opinions and reserve officers from expressing opinions favorable to any political system but monarchy. Even though Germans did not have to experience a change of political system as the French did—and as did Brazilians after them—or a marked shift within the system as in Chile and Argentina, changing times did affect the Germans and influence their attitudes toward politics and the state.

By 1914 one-half of the higher echelons of the officer class (from colonel up) were non-nobles; as late as 1865 over 80 percent of those echelons had been of noble birth. But the growth of the bourgeoisie provided an excess of fit, educated young men, and these sought a career in uniform if they did not have an attractive post awaiting them in civilian life. The proportional growth of the middle sectors everywhere, of course, created situations in which more and more officers had common (if distinguished and comfortable) origins. Gordon Craig has pointed out that commoners were as much elitist when they donned a uniform as were their "betters."[23] Nobility of character became a military hallmark. The army's role as "barrier against upheaval" could be exercised (for good reason) by members of the upward-aspiring classes. To be accepted as a regimental officer a non-noble had to distinguish himself as a professional, of course, but also as a conservative, a gentleman, and a defender of the monarchy, as well as a champion of the army's interests. Tradition, continuity, elitism, and militarism thus prevailed beyond the confines of *Junkertum* by the time Germany showcased its military expertise in South America, and Argentines, Brazilians, Chileans, and Bolivians began showing up in Berlin.

The most widely read piece of European military literature in Germany's South American sphere of influence was Goltz's *Das Volk in Waffen*. The military-civilian relationship most favored by South Americans, whether French- or German-trained, is described in its pages. This book was to the traditional military role definition what Lyautey's "Du Rôle social" would be to the internally oriented role definition in existence by 1914.

Widely read by Germans as well as others, Goltz believed that national cultural levels went hand in glove with superior defense capacity: the more powerful a country's army, the higher its cultural level. There was no excuse for a country's government not to support its defense force to the utmost of its capability. Mutual distrust among peoples of the world (i.e., Europe, to Goltz), meant that armies had to exist. But national defense ought not sap a nation (*Volk*) of its vitality.

"The enigma to be solved in the present state of affairs is how to produce a complete fusion of the military and the social and industrial life of the people, so that the former may impede the latter as little as possible, and so that, on the other hand, the full wealth of the resources of the latter may be evidenced by the healthy condition of the former."[24] To Goltz, citizen and soldier were one and the same: "man and soldier are convertible terms."[25]

If Goltz saw the army—the mass army—as the binding agent of citizenry and state, Friedrich von Bernhardi saw the army as the most perfect expression of the state. In his outrageous *Kriegsbuch* of 1902, often called "the book that caused the war" or "the most remarkable political indiscretion of modern times,"[26] he asserted that the state should use the army to reassure realization of its aims. "The great aims which must sway the policy of the government should correspond with the requirements of the nation, with its need of development and with its political interests....The most important duty of the state consists in increasing the intellectual and moral forces of its citizens to the utmost."

"Politically a nation cannot stand still. It must either rise to greatness or decline politically and morally."[27] Proper political leadership meant military superiority and expansion. Citizen and state, fused through the army, provided the vehicle for the Clausewitzian fusion of domestic and foreign policies. Bernhardi's chauvinism—by no means atypical of his generation or his nation—did not fall on deaf ears in Argentina or Chile, where military and political leaders saw their own lands as sharing a regional destiny akin to that of Germany.

Moreover, Bernhardi had little good to say for democracy as a political system per se. It was too individualistic and fractious. It made individuals easy prey for demagogues, ambitious politicians, and those who would manipulate for their own ends. Democracy allowed certain "transcendent" values to be questioned: nationalism and patriotism, hierarchy, community, religion, discipline, and service to the state. Democracy meant that the press could be free. Echoing Bugeaud's words of nearly seven decades before, the bumptious Bernhardi averred, "The press should be made to serve the political and cultural aspirations of Germany."[28] Incitant to Europeans, Treitschke's, Bernhardi's, and Goltz's works made sense to ambitious South American militarists because they justified the existence and improvement of military organizations. To paraphrase Treitschke on Frenchmen, it is not hard to imagine a Chilean officer telling his men: "Each dragoon who knocks a Peruvian on the head does more for the Chilean cause than the finest political brain that ever wielded a trenchant pen."[29] Controversy swirled about the relationship of the army and the polity, the state, the nation; opinions clashed as to whom should be assigned the role of leaders and to whom that of followers. Politicians emerge from German and French military literature as, at best, necessary evils.

Much of the political interest shown by members of the officer class originated in concerns over the obligatory military service laws. Bound to states, as armies were, they served as agents of national mobilization in a greater sense. Dependent on obligatory service as they were, they also were vulnerable to shifts and currents of public opinion on the value of universal training. In the decade-and-a-half preceding World War I, particularly, challenges arose to the hitherto accepted (if grudgingly) practice of requiring citizens to render military service for a fixed period. Obligatory service, German- and French-style, met with little opposition in South America, although it came in for the same kind of officer-class scrutiny that Europeans accorded it.

To writers like Treitschke (the son of an army officer, after all), who glorified the state above all else, military service was both an obligation and a privilege, for it "brought home," as noted, to the masses the true meaning of the state. It bound citizens together. Treitschke, of course, emphasized that obligatory military service assured citizens of their *right* to bear arms.[30] Others, like Captain K. Isenburg and anonymous writers using variations on "Einem alten Offizier," believed that obligatory service was the best method of inculcating discipline, morals, patriotism, and personal hygiene—in short, civilization and culture—in the common man.[31] Some were convinced that a "psychological approach," so useful in other endeavors (and in Germany based most probably on the wide-spread popularity of *Lebensphilosophie*, which encouraged sensitivity to environmental and emotional experiences), would maintain morale at a peak and was necessary if military training was to succeed.[32]

Even Goltz, however sympathetic he may have been to the old ways, reluctantly justified obligatory service in terms of the civilization of the male populace as well as national defense. Obligatory service was necessary in order to involve the entire nation in war—a natural state that Goltz saw as the product of nationalism, rivalries, selfishness, and disputes. Obligatory service was democratic, he believed, for it affected all classes; it distributed "the burden equally," as opposed to earlier conscription programs that weighed "with varying degrees of hardship upon the lower classes."[33] Goltz ought not to be mistaken for a devotee of the "civilizing mission," however.

Bernhardi the bombastic also saw obligatory service as the agent binding the common man to the state (as tradition bound the officer class to the crown), much as did Treitschke. Germany's predestined role as "leader of humanity" could be assured through obligatory service, for it "humanized and nationalized the common people." "It teaches men to use body and mind energetically; it awakens in them the sense of order and teaches them discipline and resolution; it strengthens and steels them for the battle of life." Bernhardi based his argument on the conviction that Germany's schools, so riddled as he believed them to be with individualism and libertarianism, had failed to prepare German youth for patriotic citizenship.[34] The army was not only a binding agent and an instrument of foreign policy, it was a nation-building device.

Even in Germany, where the traditional role found its greatest expression, officers, civilian militants, and Prussophiles viewed the army as a sociopolitical entity too. Military might assured German greatness, the crown and the officer corps mutually reinforced each other; obligatory service or reserve status enveloped all German males, in theory, regardless of class. The army bound together *Heer, Volk* and *Staat.*

Much the same can be said about South America's other model, with Lyautey's thesis being the most cogent (but not sole) 1890–1914 expression of the civilizing, harmonizing, nationalizing function of barracks life. Like his German counterparts, Lyautey stressed that male citizens of all classes passed through the ranks, or at least were supposed to, according to the law. Officers, he believed, needed to do a better job with their men, needed to be teachers and friends if military service was to serve its purpose. He wanted military service to be a "field of social action," not a brutal, servile *corvée*. He wanted "the flower of the military schools" to spend careers "forming men rather than being constantly preoccupied with the requirements for the general staff insignia—*le bouton de mandarin*."[35] In sum, Lyautey and other Frenchmen saw that the prime, not the ancillary, role of obligatory service was that of educator of youth, molder of character, shaper of citizens.[36] This was the majority opinion—in print—throughout the quarter-century preceding 1914.

It was not all that easy, of course. Though the laws varied as to length of service from as many as five years to as few as one, few youths ever spent a full term in uniform.

Prior to the Great War, wrote one of France's future heroes, roughly a quarter-million young men each year passed from "life in field, factory or office to a monotonous existence in barracks." Members of the clergy were usually exempted, and others, like university graduates with jobs, married men, and teachers, were also exempted. The monotonous existence varied so much in length and the laws changed so frequently that continuity existed only in the methods of training. Frenchmen were liable for active and reserve status until the age of forty, but their experience in the barracks might have been limited to as little as six months. Still, even a perceptive man like Charles de Gaulle would view the service as a beneficial (if tedious) experience. Long-termers helped the conscripts learn their drill; if indeed the conscript became only an "anonymous cog in a gigantic collective machine,"[37] at least he was being trained by "conscientious and devoted" officers.

Some pre-1914 writers were more specific about the merits of military service. A. Garçon of the Polytechnique believed that military service ought to be merely the capstone of a program of military education in the schools, for military training per se contributed to education and reinforced patriotism, morals, dignity, and discipline. Civic education was necessary to maintain national freedom and liberties, military education to maintain national honor, even France's existence. Henri Iung, like Lyautey, favored a heavy dose of civics taught in the barracks. Officers were superior teachers, he thought, because they could *command* the respect and attention of their troops. Moreover, he believed that obligatory service and military education should both be prerequisites to bureaucratic posts and public office.[38] Early in this century, Georges Duruy and Captain Couderc de Fonlongue were strong advocates of the officer's role of friend, mentor, and guide. "The function of the officer, as I see it, is an apostleship," wrote the former in comparing the officer class to the priesthood. "The army is a filter through which pass the generations; the country gives it its young; it makes men and citizens of them, thanks to the officers whose competence and devotion, communal respect and sympathy, guide their every act." Couderc de Fonlongue maintained the stress on psychological approaches to the training of troops and inculcation of the proper virtues,[39] a clear reflection of the attraction of the newly popularized social science of the age.

Peculiar to France at this time was the religious question with its military ramifications. Within the officer class it was serious enough, but it also was important when linked to military service. It was one of Lyautey's concerns, and it continued to worry Roman Catholics. If the army and the *Patrie* were bound together—as they were across the Rhine (Alsace and Lorraine in German hands notwithstanding)—was the army thus bound to a secular *Patrie*? If so, what would be the effect on Catholic conscripts? Abbé Lucas Championnière, Père Didon, and Père Caruel, S.J., insisted that military service and Christianity were complementary. The Abbé, an activist in the Catholic Workers' Organization, was concerned that seminarians liable for military service in the 1890s would like their vocation.[40] Père Didon was an outright militant; France needed both religion and military zeal, and could assure it through both schools and barracks, in order to protect itself from Germany and "other sources." Between the lines of course, lie the specters of Lutheranism, Calvinism, and Anglicanism.

Père Caruel echoed Père Didon: "The army, we say to you, *is the living image of the fatherland.* Young men, it is necessary to support it." Caruel called the army the "supreme hope" of the fatherland, it's "visible force." That universities should provide military education, these clerics all agreed. The army, added Caruel, "was neither monarchist nor Republican, neither Catholic nor Protestant; it was French and it made full citizens of French men."[41] The Lyauteys of the *soutain* thus strove to defend their own interest.

As in Germany, voices could be heard in France that extolled the democratic nature of the military as well as of the officer class. Arguments for the former fared better in French theory, perhaps, but certainly no better in practice. Gaston Moch wrote that the length of military service ought to be increased and the requirements enforced, for they not only assured a steady supply of soldiers but also produced "disciplined patriots." Germans, Russians, and French were, after all, the most patriotic of Europeans; Scandinavians, the British, and Americans, including Canadians, were not, because—how could one but notice?—they had no universal military training system. Democracy required service from all, support from all, participation by all; military service provided this support.[42] In his widely-read works, Lieutenant Marcel Demongeot concurred, but elaborated on the subject of democracy by casting it in an institutional mold. Demongeot explained "military democracy" by stressing the mutual dependence of army personnel. Officers relied on sub-officers to carry out numerous assignments, and the latter depended on the former for direction. The troops were necessary, for obvious reasons, and they in turn were dependent on the sub-officers and their commanders for education and training in "the school of national and social energy."[43] Such views had more than passing significance.

Demongeot's definition of democracy was set in terms of an organic state within which the intradependent army was one part of the organism. Order and hierarchy were necessary for the protection of the rights of all. Officers had an educative mission; civilians had one too. The civilian population was most perfectly democratic within peer groups, associations, corporations, or guilds. The army functioned in the same way: within each rank the officers and non-commissioned officers were equal, and the conscripts, owing to their temporary status, were equal to each other because they were, after all, citizens of France.[44] Obviously influenced by Lyautey and Catholic social thinkers of the day, Demongeot saw democracy through "corporativist" eyes and viewed the army as the proper expression of national power and prestige: "France is a complete moral entity. To be a good Frenchmen is not just loving one part of France, but loving all of France. To be a good citizen is not just doing part of your duty, but doing all of it."[45] Doing one's duty involved something more than drill and practice to French officers.

Captain Bernard Serrigny assessed the technical ramifications of obligatory service in his own publication advocating "barracks education." Small, long-term or career armies, he believed, could militarize France, turn the *Patrie* into a garrison; short-term obligatory conscription was better.[46] He warned Frenchmen of Goltz's alternative to *la nation armée*, the small, permanent, highly-trained force, referring to it as a "collective Moloch."[47] Obligatory service, then, prepared and educated citizen-soldiers and kept France from becoming a modern Macedon.

Democracy, patriotism, character, morals, liberty, equality, and fraternity were both results and benefactors of vigilant professional officialdom and obligatory service. In words that were being spoken coincidentally in South America, another Frenchman tied obligatory service to universal male suffrage, both being the privileges of citizens of a democracy; he called the army a "marvelous school of democracy."[48] At this time— a year before World War I—Frenchmen attended their "school" for three years and were liable for twenty-five years' additional reserve service.

Karl Liebknecht claimed that he knew Prussian militarism for what it was, and there were strong anti-militarists in France as well. Not all Frenchmen believed in institutionalized conscription. Gazing at the whole of Europe, Ferrero, as mentioned, had accused the French of embarking on the imperial way because warfare was suitable neither to continental affairs nor to Republicanism as a governmental form. He had little use for conscription schemes, for he thought they did not really turn citizens into fighters. Volunteer armies were more easily controlled but consisted of "willing militarists."

France's most significant critic of the military was, of course, Jean Jaurès, the Socialist and pacifist whose views of society and politics were not, oddly enough, altogether unlike those of the military's defender, Marcel Demongeot, in their emphasis on unity and corporativist structure. Socialism, Jaurès thought, would encourage men and officers to behave more like brothers than like fathers and sons. The new army he proposed would not weaken France's military power nor diminish her prestige, it would continue the role of the officer as educator. Jaurès's militia-like *armée nouvelle* would have a small cadre of officers, a large number of training officers and instructors. Training would consist of six months of active duty and thirteen years of liability for maneuvers lasting from ten to twenty-one days annually. Pre-military education would begin at the age of ten years and reserve liability would last throughout active duty at twenty until retirement from the territorial reserve at the age of forty-five.[49] Above all, the role of Jaurès's model army would be defensive. Nothing ever came of his proposal, needless to say.

Obligatory service, then, the "life blood of armies," the "symbiotic integrator of citizen, army, and state," "the price of citizenship," was a controversial and complex subject in pre-war Europe. So it was elsewhere. Soon after war broke out, the American Colonel Leonard Wood would put it to his own fellow citizens, looking as he was to probable United States involvement. He thought it was "murder not to provide the wherewithall for universal military training."[50] Young men must be prepared for war, lest they be thrown into battle too quickly. By this time, obligatory service had become a subject of widespread thought in South America.

The years of peace between 1871 and 1914 did not preclude rivalries and the hostile feelings between Frenchmen and Germans. Military thought indicated that European officers believed mutual antipathy and international conflict were constants and that periods of peace were intervals in a historical continuum. South Americans who learned their tradecraft from Europeans would also adopt European concepts of national defense and priorities for national security.

Opinions on national defense, when not rendered in discussions of education and training, or of the varying roles of the officer, appeared in essays of an even more technical nature or those dealing with international affairs. They also appeared in comparative studies of preparedness, military service, and the situation of the officer. Lieutenant Haffemeyer's 1902 article in the *Journal des Sciences Militaires* is illustrative of highly technical discussions devoted to issues of a sociopolitical nature.

In this essay, the egalitarian-minded Haffemeyer compared the social standing of French, German, and Russian officers. The French, he concluded, were far more useful in peacetime because more of them came from the bourgoisie; they were, therefore, closer to the people. The French army was more democratic, in harmony with society and the Republic. The German and Russian officer corps were, for the most part, aristocratic, therefore removed from the bulk of the population. He thought this might make it difficult for Germans and Russians to lead their citizens in time of war. It ought to be noted that a previously-cited article published in 1901 was not so optimistic about *esprit de corps* among French officers and warned that France needed greater standardization of training at the Polytechnique and St. Cyr[51]—a point of some interest to officers of France's client-to-be, Brazil.

Over the years between 1871 and 1914 the French and Germans watched each other's armies carefully. Most studies of military strength in France òr Germany made note of the strength of rival powers in order to justify additional expenditures or new programs. Argentine, Brazilian, Chilean, and Peruvian works did the same. This makes it difficult to arrive at exact estimates of strength, for figures were often padded or altered in order to prove a point or substantiate an argument. All too often, comparative military strength is difficult to judge because data are gathered from comparable yet different sources.

In a 1938 Ph.D. thesis done at the University of Heidelberg, Richard Theiss estimated that the peacetime armies of France and Germany between 1890 and 1905 were fairly consistent in relation to each other, with France having slightly larger forces than Germany (489,000 to 470,000 in 1890; 595,000 to 558,000 in 1905).[52] Theiss, as one would expect, saw no drain of national strength by standing armies of this magnitude based on universal military training. At the turn of the century the standard estimates of Charles Jerram, generally consulted, if not accepted definitively, gave the Germans an edge in standing army, 526,000 to 517,000. This was, according to Jerram, in keeping with Germany's population edge.[53] N. W. Barnardston placed the German figure for 1900 at 580,000 men ready to take the field for combat and 3,215,000 in all categories.[54] Garçon, a decade later, gave Germany nearly 490,000 peacetime soldiers and a 1,565,000-man force easily mobilized, slightly lower than other sources.[55] Argentina supposedly had 76,000, Chile 12,000, Brazil 15,000, and Peru 5,000 peacetime soldiers and (respectively), 33,000, 30,000, 66,000 and 16,000 wartime troops. Questionable figures notwithstanding, the German clients surely appeared more capable of expanding geometrically the size of their armies in time of war.

Jerram considered France "ripe for military despotism," owing to its poor financial situation, the after-effects of the Dreyfus case and the apparent popularity of the Boulanger movement. Germany had no such problems and was, therefore, better prepared for war.[56] This was the prevailing view of international military experts, at least.

The Germans watched the French closely and warned their leaders in moderate tones that France's every military policy

was designed to gain the strategic advantage. They alter-
natively warned of and scoffed at French prowess and preparedness. The Germans viewed the French as comparatively
undisciplined, bent on revenge, politicized, convinced of the
rôle social, and haughty in demeanor. These views changed
little in the quarter-century prior to the war. Official fear (for
propaganda reasons) and professional disdain (for institutional reasons) characterized German views of the French.

Acceptance of war as an extension of politics and of the
military career as symbolic of German society and polity was
portrayed no better before World War I than in an *Internationale Revue* essay of 1890. Aphorisms used to justify war as
a facet of international relations formed the core of the discussions; sources used by the author to praise war embraced
all fields. "War is in itself a holy thing, a product of natural
law" (Martin Luther); "Man on earth must ever be in conflict" (Luther); "War is healthy for the race, just as necessary
as the movement of the wind which keeps the sea free from
its own stench" (Hegel); "Without war the world would fall
into decay and lose itself in materialism" (Moltke); "Law lives
through armies" (Seneca).[57] Out of context though they may
have been, these aphorisms provided officers with the ra-
tionale—philosophical, theological, practical, professional—
they needed to justify themselves. Clausewitz "lived," in no
source more vividly than in the works of Goltz.

War was natural, Goltz said, because of human nature; it
made necessary the permanent "fusion" of civilian and military interests. Goltz blamed civilians for resisting this fusion
because of their "lack of understanding." He singled out intellectuals, politicians, bureaucrats, and farmers (an odd combination) for their resistance to total preparation; he blamed
"the dandy" and "the moralist" for their lack of understanding. Goltz's argument for fusion is nowhere better stated than
in his discussion of defense and foreign threats. Moltke and
Clausewitz would have agreed, obviously. Moltke's own arguments for military strength had emphasized foreign threats
and the necessity of a permanent deterrent force to guarantee
peace on the continent.[58] Goltz thus perpetuated the teachings of the past, a most professional thing to do.

Poor defenseless Germany. General von Blume, in an essay of 1899, thought the empire was in mortal danger from within. Her neighbors were undependable, alliances fragile. Germany's traditional enemies were not yet capable of defeating her in concert, but they soon would be unless Germans took the necessary measures to rid the *Vaterland* of polluting influences. And what did von Blume see as polluting influences? Social Democrats, of course; night clubs, "which multiply like mushrooms," "where youth and workers waste their time and money listening to scantily clad singers"; and the bugbears of materialism, individualism, foreign ideas introduced by "workers of a foreign race" who spread pollution through intermarriage (i.e., Polish peasants in Saxony and Prussia), and rampant capitalism, which destroyed the fabric of society.[59] If not checked, these would destroy the basis of German military prowess, hence Germany herself.

Seven years later, Major Karl von Bruchhausen saw enemies all around—natural enemies as well as those created by jealousy and recent rivalries. The French were ambitious in Africa and elsewhere; they coveted Alsace and Lorraine. A conflict with France meant conflict with all of Germany's enemies, whether or not they were France's allies. France, he alleged, regularly increased her defense budget; Germany must follow suit to survive.[60]

Bernhardi in yet another "work that caused the war," this one brazenly entitled *Britain as Germany's Vassal*, assailed his own government for not recognizing the British threat to Germany's future. War was the only means of assuring security, eroded as it was by Britain's very existence. German superiority and Germany's destiny were pre-ordained. In Bernhardi's opinion Germany was *the* civilized nation of Europe and must spread civilization if "the leader of humanity" were to achieve her place among world leaders.[61] His racist views merit no elaboration here beyond noting that they were very much a part of his paranoid appeal to Germans to "defend" the *Volk* and to preserve its integrity.

To Germans, war was more than a historical reality; it was an entree to their "place in the sun." In lieu of a great fleet of commercial carriers, a colonial empire, geopolitically advantaged war, or war-making potential assured Germans of their ability to keep historical enemies, the Slavs and the French, at bay. Such chauvinism was diluted, but only selectively, when transmitted across the Atlantic to the nations of South America.

Despite Marshal MacMahon's professionally narrow-minded warning that "I shall remove from the promotion list any officer whose name I have read on the cover of a book,"[62] there was never a dearth of officer-authors in France to whom defense and security were just as significant as the *rôle social.* The disillusionment of defeat in 1870 did not dissuade officers from arguing for stronger defense capabilities to assure security and from inveighing against periodic slashing of defense budgets. It is not at all easy to evaluate French and German complaints that "the enemy is gaining the advantage," nor is it a simple task to confirm similar South American suspicions. What is obvious is that a military mentality practically predestined a vigilant advocacy of regular increments in defense expenditures based on what someone thought or wanted others to think the enemy was up to.

Most *fin de siècle* French defense specialists had read Goltz. They wavered between doctrines of offensive and defensive warfare, and shifted very slowly from a strategy based on the conduct of a brief war to that based mainly on a long campaign.[63] Some officers were concerned that colonial service, rather than preparing officers and men for war, turned them into pseudo-soldiers, providing them only with a "breeding ground for pronunciamientos." There was some doubt that the empire was a worthwhile enterprise. On the other hand, General de Trentinian, writing in 1911, was convinced that their incorporation into the metropolitan army would boost their prestige and at the same time show the metropolitans a thing or two. If, indeed, "the function created the organ," then the colonial officers were multi-talented leaders of men.[64] The role of the colonials during the Great War attested to their skills and their ability to improvise. Some officers warned that the corps no longer provided a solid bulwark for the defense of French interests as the German officer corps did. One of the reasons given repeatedly for this was that there were more and more middle-class Frenchmen in the officer corps.[65] These short-sighted writers ignored the increased numbers of non-aristocrats and non-nobles in the Kaiser's army. Heterogeneity in any form worried military men, whether they were Europeans or South Americans, in each decade dealt with in these pages.

France was not without her outspoken champions of national honor and prestige, though there was no one quite like Bernhardi to defend her. Captain Jibé stressed that the sole purpose of an army was to protect these qualities. Any other activities, such as politics or empire-building, should be disdained. Captain Spero, who claimed that Germany increased her peacetime military strength every year after 1890, also believed that his country's honor depended on a successful foreign policy, its pride on its war-making capacity, its existence on its army. Paul Fontin responded to Anglo-German tensions—the same tensions that Bernhardi sought to exacerbate—by arguing for greater coordination of military and naval tactics and strategy: joint planning.[66] Whereas Germans saw Franco-Russian connivance and British malice in continental diplomacy, Frenchmen like Fontin feared that an outbreak of hostilities between Anglo-Saxon and Teuton would involve France inevitably.

Perhaps Serrigny's was the most judicious estimate of what indeed France's defense needs were. His *Les Conséquences économiques et sociales de la prochaine guerre*[67] also had an influence on defense planning in South America, and later work by Serrigny also found an audience in Peru. Although he considered the "Volk in Waffen" a Moloch, he argued for a large standing army composed of short-term obligatory-service soldiers. He advocated a more demanding reserve obligation and was adamant on the need for better transportation and communications. He also urged the government to provide for military supervision of mobilization. Serrigny was arguing for a policy of total mobilization but for the retention of overall civilian controls over a population that, owing to obligatory service, had been thoroughly imbued with "preparedness."

The outbreak of war in 1914 confirmed to many wary, ambitious Germans and many self-conscious Frenchmen that defense had to be based on a close military-civilian coordination of both national resources and mobilization; that large standing armies were indeed necessary; that citizens had civic rights and as well an obligation to defend their country. Defense and security, politics and diplomacy, obligatory service and the forming of patriots, all brought citizen, army, and state together.

"In a time such as ours," reminisced Ferdinand Foch, "when people believe they can do without an ideal; cast away what they call abstract ideas; live on realism; rationalism; positivism; reduce everything to knowledge or to the use of one or more ingenious and casual devices—let us acknowledge it here—in such a time there is only one means of avoiding error, crime, disaster; of determining the conduct to be followed on a given occasion—but a safe means it is, and a fruitful one; this is the exclusive devotion to two abstract notions in the field of ethics: duty and discipline."[68] Foch summed up the pre-1914 philosophical orientation of the European professional officer in that captivatingly prolix statement.

Manifestly not all Europeans concurred with Foch, with Serrigny, Lyautey, and Père Didon, with Moltke, Baron von der Goltz, Bernhardi, and Bruchhausen. Jaurès clearly did not subscribe to the thesis that armies defended by attacking the enemy first. Victor Leuliette the pacifist decried pre-war patriotism and its pervasion of the teaching of history. He pleaded with teachers to point out to their students the misery, death, and suffering in war rather than the glory of victory; sheer luck in battles rather than the wisdom of military science; human qualities rather than "superhuman, heroic" ones. Children ought not to be encouraged to play with toy guns and tin soldiers. The heroes of science, arts, and peace merited more praise, and war should be treated as expensive

and destructive, as an abberation. He deplored the basis of a
"funny incident" (possibly apocryphal), described by a friend
who had heard it from a schoolmaster. Teacher: "What is patriotism?" Pupil: "Please, sir, killing Froggies" (i.e., Frenchmen).[69]

Peter Kropotkin's *La Guerre* circulated widely in France
from 1912 to 1914. His well-known argument—similar in
tone and detail to that of Liebknecht—that war "enriched the
privileged classes" and was the creature of capitalists, therefore to be avoided at all cost,[70] was popular among the working classes but meant little to Frenchmen when the Hun did
attack.

George Perres's *The War Traders* hit hard as well at capitalists, industrialists, politicians, and profiteers. War, Perres
claimed, was a menace to democracy and civilization. The
jobs, salaries, and pensions derived from the armaments industry lured mankind to its ultimate destruction.[71] Militarism, Charles Ogden claimed, was the chief reason women
still suffered oppression by males. War, militarism, and impe-
rialism made slaves of women, forced them to bear children
for service in the armies of nations, and kept them in an inferior status. Man the warrior did not care if war ever
ended.[72] Ogden's argument may appear overdrawn and dependent on stereotyped sex roles, but his citation of Bernhardi
as the epitome of the war-loving, domineering male was on
the mark.

The European war of 1914–18 involved the South American
client states across the Atlantic only slightly. Observers came
to France and Germany already imbued with the lore of their
mentors, convinced of the supreme necessity of standing armies, obligatory military service, and close military-state relations; certain that democratic forms of government were
essentially unstable and undependable in time of mobilization; monomaniacal in their belief that their neighbors conspired against them. For by 1914 South American military
tradition had been exposed to the military professionalism of
France and Germany described in this chapter.

"I am a man under authority,
having soldiers under me; and I
say to this man, 'Go,' and he
goeth; and to another, 'Come,' and
he cometh; and to my servant, 'Do
this,' and he doeth it."

Matthew 8:8–10, as rendered in
Ernest Psichari, *A Soldier's
Pilgrimage* (*Le Voyage du
Centurion*, 1917)

"Soldiers are like priests. At any
time in any situation we are 'on
the job.' Our rest can be cut short
by a blast of the bugle, [and] even
though in mufti our personality is
not changed."

Tobías Barros Ortiz, *Vigilia de
armas: Charlas sobre la vida
militar destinadas a un joven
teniente* (1920)

CHAPTER FOUR

Missions & Missionaries:
The Meeting of Minds

The civil war of 1891 interrupted don Emilio Körner's work brusquely, but he returned to it as if there were no break at all. Such was the ability of the man that he shifted easily from organizer and instructor to strategist and planner, then back to instructor, with consummate ease. The first of the significant military missionaries had been on the job five years when congress revolted against Balmaceda, and his career in Chile would last nearly twenty years more.

Körner came from Saxony. He was born in Wegwitz, October 10, 1846.[1] He received a diploma in humanities in Halle, and he had served in the army for twenty years before coming to Chile, as a volunteer in a Magdeburg regiment in 1866, then as a noncommissioned officer in 1867. The next year he received a second lieutenant's commission from the Hanover Military School, and in 1869 he entered the Artillery and Engineer's School in Berlin (Charlottenburg). He fought in France in 1870, in the battles of Worth and Sedan, winning the Iron Cross, Second Class. He returned to Charlottenburg in 1871. Four years later he made lieutenant, and in 1876 he graduated from the Kreigsakademie, third in his class behind Paul von Hindenburg and Clemens Meckel. He served in Italy, Spain, and Africa from 1877 to 1888, his only experience outside Europe before going to South America. In 1881 he was promoted to captain and given command of an artillery battery. Within a year he returned to Charlottenburg as an instructor of tactics, military history, and weapons science. He was a member of the Charlottenburg faculty when Matta offered him the Chile post.

Once it was clear Meckel preferred Japan to Chile, the offer became firmer. In the face of a Japanese offer to join Meckel that would have paid him more, not to mention the fringe benefits *muchas gangas*, in the words of General Jorge Boonen Rivera,[2] Körner agreed to 12,000 marks payable in Chilean gold in return for his services as instructor of artillery, infantry, cartography, military history, and tactics. He was given the title of sub-director of the Military School and the Chilean rank of lieutenant colonel—a normal jump in rank for a captain with nearly twenty years of service in Europe's finest army, and a nice arrangement for a forty-year-old Saxon commoner in the Prussian army with little chance for promotion. Körner's record was a good one, but he was, after all, of common birth, and had only four years to go in rank before being retired automatically. There is no mention of his qualities in German military literature of the times. He was one of many hard-working, capable officers. He was thorough, very ambitious, and adventuresome. He also had read up on Chile's military successes.

Slightly a year after he had agreed to serve in Chile, the long-hoped-for Academia de Guerra opened its doors. According to the government decree, the purpose of the Academia was "to elevate the level of technical and scientific instruction of army officers, in order that they be able, in case of war, to utilize the advantages of new methods of combat and modern armaments." In the four years before the civil war, Körner formulated the Academia's three-year curriculum, emphasizing those subjects that were taught in the Berlin Kriegsakademie as well as the École Supérieure de Guerre in Paris. Tactics, fortification, cartography, ballistics, military history, physics, mathematics or world history, general military science, and German constituted the first year of study. Those who survived it then took advanced courses in tactics, fortification, cartography, military science, history, geography and physics, chemistry, mathematics or history, and German. They studied topography and war games as well. The final year's curriculum was advanced war games, Chilean and South American military history and geography, hygiene, international law, staff service, a choice of mathematics or world history, and German. The academy enrolled its first students in 1887. Out of the first fifteen graduates, five went to Germany for additional studies. According to one participant in the Prussianization program, Körner had some assistance between 1886 and the civil war from a certain Major Betzhold and Captain Januskowski, both of whom came from Germany, the former to teach fortification and the latter to instruct cadets in fencing and gymnastics.[3]

All was not smooth for the German. Despite the rigorous training at the Academia, Körner lamented the state of the profession in Chile—especially the condition of the Escuela. In so doing he legitimized, in a sense, the complaints of members of the profession in decades to come, that the "government did not treat the army well." This complaint was heard perpetually in South America as well as in Europe. Körner bluntly said that the instructional budget was too low, that there was an "exaggerated economy" in maintenance, supplies, and books, and that the capacity of instructors in languages, sciences, and natural history was insufficient. As sub-director, one of his most serious criticisms was the organization of instruction itself. Although Chile did have a single, national military school, its curriculum was divided into special fields of concentration, producing an effect not unlike that that characterized Brazilian instructional programs (albeit to a greater degree, owing to the various institutions offering military education). Specialists who were trained apart with scant knowledge of the other arms or of combined operations were not good officers, Körner thought. Products of the same school, in contrast to Brazilian officers, Chileans were no better prepared to devise or carry out a multi-phased and combined military operation. Academia training could make up for some but not all of the Escuela's deficiencies. To cap it all, Körner recommended a revised examination schedule that would force cadets to maintain currency throughout the term and not simply during the days and weeks immediately preceding final examinations. What don Emilio wanted was an

Escuela that could provide the Academia with officers capable of assimilating high-level training.

As Chile approached the executive-legislative impasse of 1890–91, Körner was advocating a major shake-up of the Chilean military profession. He wanted the army to be an exact replica of the Prussian army, not only in appearance but in training, instructional methods, and strategic and tactical orientation. Never popular with Balmaceda, he objected to Balmaceda's alleged pro-navy attitude and was therefore distrusted by the beleaguered president and was separated from the service when the war broke out. He joined the congressionals as secretary to their "general staff." In effect, he masterminded their campaign.

The civil war of 1891 provides the sole example of a European mission officer actively participating in a South American armed conflict—unless the performance of Hans Kundt as mastermind of Bolivia's 1932 military thrust into the Chaco is considered. By 1932, of course, Kundt was no longer representative of either Germany or her army, though he did represent German commercial firms; thus his action was more the act of a mercenary. Körner reasoned that a congressional victory would permit him to create his replica. He was correct, but only so far, and in this context Körner's opinion of Balmaceda was comparable to that of Brazilian enthusiasts who saw Pedro II as a hindrance to their professional aspirations. Despite Germany's tacit support of the rebels, Wilhelm II allegedly rebuked him for breaking his oath of loyalty to a chief of state.

Following the war the officer corps went through a purge. Officers who had stood with the president and who had been accused of war crimes or violations of military or civil law were put on trial. The congressional commander-in-chief, Colonel Estanislao del Canto, a fervent Blamaceda baiter, was in charge of trials, and he saw to it that most of the accused were punished by being denied pensions and civil rights following separation from the service. Defenses based on "loyalty to the supreme commander-in-chief" were used to no avail. Canto also persuaded the new government of Admiral Jorge Montt (1891–96) to separate a number of other loyalist officers, against whom no charges had been made, enabling congressionals to move in or up in rank. Since the last phases of the war, Körner had been chief of the general staff, so that his role in selection and retention doubtless was of some consequence.

In 1892 he was back at the Academia, as well as heading the general staff. Two years later he returned to Europe— nearly a decade after he had decided to go to Chile. He went to Germany to supervise the manufacture of coastal artillery pieces and to hire a number of training officers to staff a full-fledged mission. He was back in Chile by October 1895, accompanied by thirty-six officers, most of them Germans. His gamble in 1891 had won him a solid grip on instructional, ordnance, and organizational aspects of the Chilean Army. It is no wonder that at this precise time Peruvians began to think very seriously about a training mission themselves.

Don Emilio brought with him one of the single largest European contingents ever to serve in South America. Partially renewed in 1897 (with twenty-seven lieutenants for garrison duty and instruction), the German mission had a profound effect at every level of organization and training.[4] Germans, aside from Körner and Wilhelm Ekdahl (actually a Swede by birth), receive little notice in official Chilean sources, for names do not normally appear in such materials.[5] They obviously have not figured in non-official sources, most of which are memoirs or studies of civil-military relations. Nevertheless, the Körner mission, like others in South America, does bear some examination, owing both to the extent of penetration of the institution and the type of assignment carried out. In Chile both were extensive.

Division General (as of 1895) Körner brought back to Chile one colonel (assimilated ranks are given), an Irishman named Gilbert O'Grady ("don Gilberto" to Chileans), whom he had recruited in Berlin. O'Grady taught courses on fortification along with Lieutenant Carl Sanders and Thilo, Graf von Brockderfallefeld. Lieutenant Colonel (soon Colonel) Ekdahl, a 1875 graduate of the Royal Military School of Stockholm, and an 1880 graduate of Sweden's War Academy, became director of the Academia. He had previously taught at the Equitation School in Sweden and was reputed to have been

military tutor to Prince Charles of Sweden. Major Felix Deinert and Lieutenant Werner Herzbruch were assigned to the
Technical Section. Major Henry Marcard and Captains Hans
Bertling, Erich Hermann, Robert Horm, and Friedrich Pirsher
took charge of the reorganized Escuelas de Clases for non-
commissioned officers. Major Friedrich von Rojister was assigned to the staff of Military Zone II (Santiago) and Major
Alexander von Joeden to Zone III (Concepción). Majors Edward Banza and Carl Zimmerman were on Ekdahl's staff at
the Academia. Majors Herman von Bieberstein and Alfred
Schönmeyer (another Swede) and Captain Günther von Below
taught at the Escuela. Captains Eugen von Fritszch, Fritz von
Wrangel, and Victor Lindholm (a Dane) were assigned to cavalry regiments. Major Friedrich Sipman worked with an engineers regiment in Antofagasta. Major Egon von Wulffen and
Captain Hugo Schnevoigt taught marksmanship. Majors
Friedrich Nunk, Alfred Kellermeister von der Lund, and Georg von Oven and Captain Friedrich von Erbert served with
infantry regiments. Majors Herman Haard and Ernst Roth
were posted to the armaments commission. Major Constantine von Alvensleven and Captains Hans, Graf von
Schulenburg, and Fritz Guttich were posted to artillery units.
Captain Wilhelm Bronsart von Schellendorf served under
Körner on the general staff. Captain Wilhelm Graf von
Königsmark trained the presidential cavalry escort. In sum,
the Körner mission had staff, command advisory, and instructional responsibilities; it penetrated the Academia, the Escuela, the Escuela de Clases; it supervised the training of
artillery, infantry, cavalry, and, to a lesser degree, engineers
officers. Germans supervised methods of fortification, trained
Chilean marksmen, and influenced the workings of the armaments commission. The Germans, the two Swedes, the Dane,
and the Irishman were ubiquitous, and with their assimilated
rank were privileged beyond their status in Europe. They
were more highly visible than any other mission of the era. If
less has been noted about their work—Körner having received
far more attention than any other member of the mission—it
is because they did their work quietly and efficiently, as models of the late-nineteenth-century German officer.[6]

With the arrival, assignment, and renewal of the German mission, Chileans began again to study in Europe. Between 1896 and 1902, twenty-three officers went to Germany, and between 1902 and 1905 another nineteen. The most notable of these officers, with rank and year of posting to Europe, were Major Pedro Pablo Dartnell Encina (1896); Captains Francisco Javier Díaz Valderrama, Carlos Fernández Pradel, Julio César Del Canto Toske, Washington Montero (1901), and Pedro Charpín Rival (1904); and Lieutenants Francisco Lagreze (1896), Manuel Bulnes (1901), José María Barceló Lira and Renato Valdez (1903), and Félix Urcullo (1904). All later made their mark in military-civilian relations, along with others who had studied in Germany prior to the civil war.

Of the latter, several names stand out. Lieutenant Colonel Tobías Barros Merino, a strong Germanophile, wrote a pamphlet entitled *La vida militar en alemania*, and Gustavo Walker Martínez published a provocative work entitled *Estudios militares*[7] based on his experiences in Germany. Major Juan Pablo Bennett Argandoña would serve as a division general in the 1924–25 Junta government. He also led a mission to El Salvador. Captain Ernesto Medina Franzani led a mission to Ecuador and rewrote that country's military code. F. J. Díaz became a prolific and long-lived author who was a staunch Germanophile long after it became passé. Barceló also was a prolific author, primarily of historical work. The Germanophiles became an officer corps elite very early, a kind of class within a class, and their continued presence had an increasing effect on subalterns.

Chileans who trained in Germany did so at the best institutions. Infantry officers attended Spandau marksmanship courses and took fencing and gymnastics courses in Berlin with Germans. Cavalry officers went to Hanover, artillery officers to Jüterbog. Engineers went to Charlottenburg, the alma mater of their German mentor. Others were assigned to cavalry and infantry regiments, transportation and machine gun units. The military mix of Chile and Germany was a thorough one by the end of the century, and became even more intense early in the new century.

At this time, according to Chilean sources, Chile had 6,000 men under arms, with a capability of equipping 100,000 in time of war. The army had been transformed, one officer wrote, "from a collection of fighting men with esprit de corps to an institution to which officer and men could feel proud to belong." It was divided into three zones, each garrisoned by a mixed brigade of artillery, cavalry, and engineers.[8]

From the beginning of his Chilean service Körner stressed the education (including classes in etiquette and conduct) of army officers as a prerequisite to success in the field. Chilean army officers were highly trained after 1886, and they also had a heavy dose, by contemporary standards, of general education, both in the Escuela and the Academia. Time spent in specialty courses in the Escuelas de Aplicación increased their technical skills. By 1900 the typical staff officer had four years at the Escuela, one to two of Aplicación, and three at the Academia. But education did not end there. Körner saw around him a population capable of supplying officers, well and good, but the recruits were something else.

Chile had no national military training requirement in the nineteenth century. In times of emergency Chileans were liable for service in uniform, and many held rank in the militia, but there was no formal, obligatory military service scheme. Körner's experience led him to see the army as an educational institution, and his followers would see it as a nation-building one, for most of those who arrived at the barracks were illiterate. Chile was not Germany, and Chile's educational system proved less accessible to those of modest and less than modest means. For this reason Körner encouraged primary education programs called "escuelas de tropas" in the army barracks. In the general staff section of the 1895–96 report (*Memoria*) of the war ministry to the Congress, Körner wrote somewhat optimistically of his educational achievements to date: "The role of these schools is quite important if the great number of individuals who arrive at the barracks without knowing even their abc's is taken into account."[9]

By 1897 Körner pressed for a resolution of salary inequities. Some junior officers received more pay than senior officers, and staff responsibilities were not yet taken into account.

Some field commanders (line officers) received more than military zone staff officers. So new was the German general staff system to Chilean military affairs that compensation for increased duties and responsibilities of staff officers had not been adjusted. Körner's argument, that authority and responsibility as well as rank be taken into account, was one that created some discussion in Germany as well, where changes in the relationships of rank to responsibility also were taking place.[10]

In the 1899 *Memoria* Körner's plan to streamline army administration appears for the first time. Chile's Teutonic general staff chief was in Europe again (February 7, 1898–May 9, 1901), but he filed his report prior to departure. What he wanted to do was to create a position called director general (i.e. a new commander in chief) directly responsible to the war minister. The director general would be advised by the general staff. Each branch of the army—artillery, cavalry, engineers, infantry plus instruction, supply communications, medical corps, shops and maintenance—would have a separate staff responsible to the commandant, then to the general staff and the director general.[11] He also proposed that the commandant of each branch be nominated by the director general and confirmed by the president.

As the century ended, Körner, from his office at general staff headquarters, presided over the reorganization of the officer corps, the rewriting of salary and promotion regulations, the restructuring of educational programs, and the beginnings of a military educational role in the barracks. In one sense he was the most powerful man in Chile. His professional prestige declined after 1906, but even on his retirement in 1910 Chileans still regarded him with a certain awe. His forthright sobriety, devotion to subordinates, and ability to get along with civilians lent luster to the army that fellow German Alfred Arent could not impart similarly east of the Andes.

Late in 1902 Körner returned to Germany to carry out a study of organizational and administrative reforms, ending nearly a decade's service as chief of the general staff. "To him we owe the high standard of discipline and morality found in the army," read the official report for 1903.[12] In 1904 he moved up in responsibility to the post of inspector general. At this time he and other high-ranking officers began to plan for the reorganization of the army in keeping with the changes he had observed while in Europe. One of the problems they saw was in the promotion system, which did not yet provide adequate numbers of men at the necessary ranks to make re-organization feasible. They also found fault with the 1900 obligatory military service law. Körner was alarmed that only the poorest of Chileans should bear the brunt of military service. As in Argentina and Peru, it was commonplace to claim exemption or purchase one's way out of the army, especially if one were well off or a student. Lower-class Chileans did not make good soldiers the way lower-class Germans did. Despite the 1900 law, military training and service did not, moreover, earn them or noncoms special privileges on returning to civilian life as did veteran status in Germany.[13] In Chile as elsewhere, however, well-off citizens who avoided military service were regarded as parasites.

There were other problems, most of them in the fields of recruitment and training. There were not enough second lieutenants to fill training positions needed for reorganization. There was an alarming number of desertions in the northern nitrate areas. Conscripts and volunteers sneaked off to work in the nitrate pits; when patrols were sent after them, workers would fight and strike to protect the erstwhile defenders of national sovereignty turned workingmen. Army life must have been extremely harsh for conscripts and volunteers to prefer the nitrate pits. Körner suggested a one-year training period for troops in the north and south of Chile, with southerners training in the north and vice versa. That way, he reasoned, when the army was called on to move against nitrate miners, friend would not have to take up arms against friend.[14] The conscription schemes employed in Chile never did please Körner.

The reforms of 1906 were a big disappointment as well. Most important, they affected the officer corps directly. Already conscious of the great discrepancy anent obligatory service, Chilean officers could now see just how imperfect was the imitation of the Prussian officer corps they had become, for in 1906 the army adopted an organizational scheme patterned after that of Germany. Although Körner had proposed a similar plan in 1899, he lived to rue the act. The reforms of 1906 cut back the authority of the inspector general and expanded those of divisional commanders; it decentralized control—a measure designed to accommodate Chile's "geografía loca." The general staff replaced various other agencies as a central planning board.[15] This ensured conflicts at each level of administration.

New units, created to more accurately portray a Prussian-style war machine, did not—and would not—have the necessary number of staff and line officers to carry out assignments. Junior officers with the proper training still clashed with senior officers who had more years of experience. Colonels still filled positions that called for qualified general officers according to rank and authority charts; lieutenant colonels still did the work of colonels, and on down to sublieutenant. "The year 1906, the first of the present organization of the army, has resulted in exceptionally unfortunate conditions," wrote Körner in the 1907 *Memoria*. Troops were busy fighting strikes in the nitrate fields and the coal and copper mines. Shuffling and revision of assignments caused instability and lack of continuity. "The lack of qualified officers prejudices in an extraordinary manner the job of the army," he stated in closing.[16] Politics and family connections, he reminded the government, were responsible for too many promotions and soft assignments. "The ease of jumping in rank predisposes the favored one to become restless in a short time, and if his aspirations to be promoted even further are not satisfied, his energy and enthusiasm diminish, no doubt justifiably."[17] Despite Körner's many successes, Chileans had some problems, just as Argentines, Brazilians and Peruvians did. Lack of prepared officers, civilian meddling, socioeconomic problems—all these conspired to hinder the "proper" progress and necessary improvement of European-trained South American armies.

As of 1909 the Chilean reforms of 1906 had not been implemented fully. Adopting a four-division system, moreover, extended the administrative expertise and material resources of the Chilean army too far.[18] The army's official line in 1910 was that "the present complement of army officers, in terms of numbers, does not correspond to the service's needs. In the last few years a number of units have been created in order to provide for the new organization of the army [but] the officer corps has not been augmented in corresponding proportions."[19] Furthermore, despite the 1906 reforms, promotions were still being administered according to "previous customs."

When don Emilio finally retired in June, problems were glaringly obvious, particularly so when seen from within. Already there were secret clubs, lodges, cabals, and organizations of discontented officers. Seen from the outside, however, the army was a showpiece. Officers from Ecuador studied at the Escuela and Chileans manned the Escuela Militar in Quito. Chile sent missions to Colombia and El Salvador. Second-generation Prussianization thus extended north to outflank the Franco-Peruvian experiment, even to penetrate Central America.[20] Chileans were active in El Salvador from 1903 to 1910: Captains Juan Pablo Bennett and Francisco Lagreze and Lieutenants Julio Salinas, Armando Llanos Calderón, and Carlos Ibáñez del Campo carried Körner's teachings there. The Ecuadorian Major Luis Cabrera wrote Ecuador's military code revisions of 1902 with the cooperation of Chilean Captains Ernesto Medina, Luis Bravo, and Julio Franzani. The next year Captain Estanislao García Huidobro and Lieutenants Arturo Montecinos and Luis Negrete went to Quito as instructors.[21]

In 1907 Colombia's president, Rafael Reyes, a figure cut from the same bolt as Marshal Hermes and Julio A. Roca, welcomed Captains Arturo Ahumada Bascuñán and Diego Guillén to Bogotá. Both Ahumada and Guillén had studied in Germany; they assumed command of Colombia's Escuela Militar. Two years later they were replaced by Majors Pedro Charpín Rival and Francisco Javier Díaz Valderrama, Chile's most prolific Germanophile. Charpín and Díaz founded Colombia's staff school and modeled it after the Academia de Guerra and the Kriegsakademie. Thirty-seven Colombians earned staff diplomas in 1910, quick work by anyone's standards. A third mission arrived in Bogotá in 1912, led by Colonel Washington Montero, assisted by Captains Pedro Vignola and Manuel Aguirre. That year Captain Carlos Sáez Morales went to Colombia for a two-year tour of duty.[22] A cluster of Prussianized Chileans and carriers of Prussianization had emerged by 1914 as the junior and middle-ranking elite of the Chilean army. Among others, Marmaduke Grove Vallejo (who carried calling cards inscribed "Marma Duque de Grove" to impress socially-conscious German officers while he served in Hanover), Bennett, Ahumada, Díaz, Blanche, Ibáñez (who preferred teaching in El Salvador to learning more in Germany), and Sáez Morales stood out by the time of World War I, and they would stand out further in the coming decade.

A full decade after Körner arrived in Chile, Captain Paul Clément came to Peru, the second of the military mission leaders. If Clément did not (and would never) have Körner's authority, he certainly had his enthusiasm and optimism. He had as much professional prestige and he was as tireless in his efforts; his career lasted, similarly, for decades.

"Don Pablo" arrived at the port of Callao on November 7, 1896. A captain in artillery, he had been selected personally by French War Minister Billot to head the mission requested by José F. Canevaro, the Peruvian minister to Paris. From the outset the Franco-Peruvian tie was more formally state-to-state than was the Germano-Chilean relationship, but the international implications were much the same. Clément received the rank of colonel in the Peruvian army and a salary of 18,000 francs. He was directly responsible to the war minister. Accompanying him were (Peruvian rank) Lieutenant Colonels Ernest Claude Perrot, Edouard Dogny, and Armand Pottin, Comte Vauvineux. Clément was mission leader and chief of staff. His responsibilities were overall planning of all training programs and personal supervision of artillery instruction. Perrot took over supervision of infantry training and Pottin assisted Clément with artillery. The Clément mission's charge was to provide technical training and practice, present lectures to officers of all ranks, direct exercises and maneuvers: to "give to the Peruvian army the best possible instruction."[23] The French had no command functions at the beginning of their tenure in Peru.

Clément was thirty-six when he signed up for duty in South America. Born in Sens-Yonne on March 18, 1860, he was an 1880 graduate of the École Polytechnique, where engineers and artillery cadets pursued their military training, and had attended the artillery and engineers school, from which he received a diploma in 1882; the cavalry school, with a diploma in 1886; and the École Supérieure de Guerre, from which he graduated in 1891. He had served with distinction as a lieutenant in Clermont-Ferrand, Douai, and Caron, as a captain in Besançon, and then in the geographic service in Algeria and Tunisia.

Dogny was an 1881 graduate of St. Cyr (where cavalry and infantry officers studied) and had served as a lieutenant in both Tunisia and Algeria, then in the Sudan and Haute Niger. As a captain he attended the Saumur Cavalry School. Perrot also was a graduate of St. Cyr, *promotion* of 1881, and had served in Algeria and Madagascar. The very popular and engaging Count Vauvineux, "El Conde," was born in Blois in 1862, was an 1883 Polytechnique graduate with service in Tunisia and with diplomas from Saumur in 1888 and from artillery and engineers in 1895. Dogny, Perrot, and Pottin all had extensive garrison duty in Metropolitan France in addition to their colonial service, and thus were well acquainted with conventional as well as non-conventional tactics, terrain, populations, and climates.[24] The French officers who came to Peru in 1896 were all in their thirties, all Catholic, and all sympathetic to the monarchist cause. Colonial service, and now foreign service, provided such officers with opportunities to realize more in their careers than could be theirs in Belfort, Douai, Lyon, and Aix-la-Chappelle. Partially renewed in 1902 (Clément and Dogny stayed on), this first French mission laboriously pursued the modernization of the Peruvian army. Within three years Clément and his aides had assessed the problems and provided proposals for solving them. Clément's 1898 report to President Piérola indicates just how much had been done and what tasks remained.

Unlike Körner's individual *Memoriales*, the Clément *Memorandum* was written in an optimistic tone. Its closing lines link army to citizenry in a common goal of progress and continuity. Clément was pleased with the government's response to army needs, for most of its measures were the result of proposals he and his mission had made. Despite Körner's overwhelming authority, he had more rivals and difficulties than did Clément.

In the 1898 document Clément noted that he and his men had made a careful study of Peru's frontier defense needs based on French fortifications and border defense policies.[25] They had made a review of the army's needs in terms of finance, organization, recruitment policy, and administrative and support services. Clément had asked for and received the authority to put military-civilian commissions to work on legislative projects. Each commission was under the direction of a Peruvian and included one French officer. They worked independently on separate and then joint proposals. Lieutenant Colonel Dogny served with Colonel Julio Jiménez, Major Enrique González, and two lawyers, Alfredo Gastón and Miguel de la Lama; Lieutenant Colonel Perrot served with Colonel Enrique Varela and lawyers Luis Reynal and Celso Zuleta. Vauvineux worked with Colonels Leoncio Lanfranco and Ricardo Cáceres and Major Alberto Panizo. The commissions focused on matters connected with the speciality of their French members.

The results of these loosely structured efforts were major, specific items of military legislation, all submitted to the war ministry in July 1898: a military legal code, an obligatory service law, an organizational and administrative code, a military territorial ordinance, a law defining peacetime military-civilian lines of authority in the provinces, a code defining the rights, obligations, and duties of officers, regulations for promotion, pay scales, and retirement, and a financial program. There is no portion of Peru's military legislation, internal regulation, or organization that does not bear the stamp of the commission's efforts.

Clément commented favorably on the promulgation of the obligatory military service law of December 17, 1898. This law gave the army the right to draft up to 1,750 men annually to complement a 4,250 permanent army. Clément stressed that volunteers made better soldiers and that the ideal would be for volunteers to re-enlist, reducing the number of new trainees for each year. He also placed great importance on strict definition of lines of authority during normal and emergency times. In the years to come, Peruvians would blur these lines increasingly, especially as national defense underwent redefinition. In the beginning, however, Peruvian military codes strictly reflected French ideas.

The *ley de suministros* (provisions and supply law) set down in no uncertain terms just what demands the army could make on civil authorities and citizens for necessary items. Such abuses of the past as commandeering—outright seizing and pillaging were more descriptive—could now be punished. The *ley de organización* established a peacetime structure of garrisons and the garrison army in toto, and its instructional function was to prepare for any contingency. In its paragraphs, French recognition of the regional nature of Peruvian military organization is vivid. Topography, climate, and infrastructural deficiencies made communications tenuous, at best, in peacetime; in time of war there had to be easily implemented instruction and mobilization at the departmental level if Peru were to withstand an invasion. For this reason the general staff replaced the Dirección General de Guerra (head office) as administrative and planning nerve center.

The *ley de justicia militar* proposed in 1898 was far more strict in the definition of exactly what fell under military jurisdiction and what was the responsibility of civilian courts. It was in a sense a modern version of the *fuero militar*, in that it protected military men (in theory) from a form of civilian meddling as well as protecting civilians from military abuses of privilege. Its administration was to be zonal, and the relationships between military commanders and local prefects at all levels were spelled out. This law also called for a national police force under civil jurisdiction, composed of former officers and soldiers under the executive branch of government.

The *ley de situación militar* defined service as active duty; *disponibilidad* (available, in reserve) for officers between assignments; indefinite leave or separation (sickness, punishment, resignation); and retirement, both permanent and temporary. It closed the officer corps to anyone who had not graduated from Chorrillos and fixed qualifications for promotion at all levels. This law also established (temporarily) a ceiling of thirty cadets in each year—*promoción*—at Chorrillos: 14 infantry and 8 each in artillery, engineers, and cavalry, in order to maintain a permanent roster of 493 active officers.[26] Such was the need for specificity in Peruvian military legislation. The work of the Clément mission was as much that of foundation and stabilization as of simple organization and modernization.

The work of the mixed commissions also resulted in regulations for each branch of the service and for an emphasis on education and training of "new officers" to implement the regulations from the bottom levels upward. The 1898 *Memorandum*, in its section on instruction, stressed discipline, routine, structure, and application of classroom lessons to exercises and maneuvers; individual as well as group attention to cadets, subalterns, students, and troops. Maneuvers, *viajes de estudios*, war games, and mapping expeditions held under the tutelage of the general staff should provide the participants with a better knowledge of the whole of Peru, "coasts, frontiers, and interior terrain," in order that they be prepared to defend it all. "Be it aggressive or defensive, the first theater of war will be that of frontier operations," was the way Clément put it. Garrison maneuvers taught tactics, he wrote, but maneuvers taught their use to one's advantage and how "to have a good eye." Perhaps Clément's most acute and far-reaching observation—one cited elsewhere—was that "Peru has not one topographic map, not even of the outskirts of the capital. It will be the army's responsibility to correct this fault and to provide a map to the nation."[27]

Starting from a point far below that of Körner in 1886, Clément had achieved much on paper in his first three years. At century's end Peru's army was nowhere near Chile's fighting capacity and its new doctrine was defense, not offensive; nature influenced this as much as European orientation. Chile's Academia had trained over a hundred staff officers by this time; Peru's Escuela Superior de Guerra was still in the planning stages. Chileans took Körner's emphasis on the education of illiterate soldiers seriously and would continue to do so, unaware perhaps that they were following the suggestions of Goltz. Peruvians took Clément's insistence on individual attention in instruction to heart, not yet knowing how much he and his fellow countrymen owed to Lyautey.

Peruvians thrived under French tutelage. A second mission arrived in 1902 (Vauvineux and Perrot had been replaced two years earlier), consisting of seven officers and three civilian employees (two physical education instructors and a veterinarian). A third group (some simply continued on the job) served from 1905 to 1910, and in 1911 seven new officers arrived. Two years later, ten additional officers came to Peru.[28] Between 1896 and World War I a total of thirty-one French officers taught in Lima and Chorrillos and a two-man navy mission served in Callao from 1910 to 1914.

Although, Clément remained in overall command of French activities in Peru (even in absentia, 1902–5), the 1902 contingent was administered by Colonel Edouard Dogny, director of the Escuela Militar until 1910. He was accompanied by Colonel René Chaumeton, an artillery instructor who also taught at the Escuela Superior, founded in 1904, and Colonel Felix D'André, who assisted Dogny, taught marksmanship, and also taught at the Escuela Superior. Also in the second French mission was Colonel Stanislaus Naulin, first director of the Escuela Superior, and Majors Pierre Berthon and Paul Beretron. The majors taught at both the Escuela Militar and the Escuela Superior. Major Georges Fievet also taught at the Escuela Militar.

Constituting the 1905 mission, in addition to Clément, as chief of staff, were Dogny as director of the Escuela Militar, D'André as chief of cavalry inspection, director of marksmanship courses, and briefly commandant of the military school, and Lieutenant Colonels Ferdinand Goubeaux, Jacques Romieux, Leoncio Larregaín (of obvious Basque origin), Paul Berthon, Louis Salatz, and Gaston Hébert. All these officers served as instructors at the Escuela Militar and the Escuela Superior and as directors or instructors of special courses for artillery, cavalry, engineers, and infantry. Major Emil Bourgueil commanded the brand-new veterinarians' school.

Six years later Clément returned to France and was succeeded by General Jean Calmel. Calmel commanded the engineers and served as army chief of staff. Colonel Hébert continued in Peru as director of the engineers' school. Colonel Henri Melot directed the Escuela Superior; Colonel Raymond Tisseyre directed the Escuela Militar (1911–12), as did Colonel Dutheil de la Rochère (1912–13). Colonel André Melot organized the medical corps and Colonel Paul Patart the administration. All these officers had direct control of instruction, active staff duties, or inspection posts. Lieutenant Colonel Pierre Dorroux was the new head of the veterinary service.

In 1913 the last pre-war mission came to Peru, the fifth since Clément's arrival seventeen years before. Dorroux the veterinarian continued on, and was joined by chief of mission General Marcel Desvoyes, who held the title director general and inspector. Colonel Samuel Bourget directed the Escuela Superior. Colonel Gaston Philbois was an inspector of administrative services. Lieutenant Colonel Edouard Paté commanded the Escuela Militar; Lieutenant Roger Baley de Langlade was cavalry and transportation inspector; Lieutenant Colonel Christian Termé was artillery inspector; Lieutenant Charles Cassamatia was inspector of engineers and the geographic service. Although the French were no longer in direct command of troops (outside the schools), they were able to penetrate deeply into instruction, administration, inspection, staff planning, and auxiliary services.[29] Officer education was designed to prepare the graduates of Chorrillos to be educators and civilizers of troops, and the graduates of the Escuela Superior to be high-level organizers, commanders, and planners.

The result in Peru by 1914 was a thoroughly *afrancesado* group of cadets and junior officers promoted to the rank of lieutenant colonel. The Escuela Superior was as direct a copy of the École Supérieure de Guerre as the Argentine Escuela Superior and the Chilean Academia de Guerra were copies of the Kriegsakademie.

The Peruvian Escuela Superior de Guerra offered its first classes in 1904. Official sources also emphasize that the early years were extremely difficult. Inadequate financing caused many complaints by the French, including the allegation that they were being overworked unnecessarily. Not until 1914 was a Peruvian placed in charge of the Escuela Superior: Colonels Naulin, Goubeaux, D'André, Melot, and Tisseyre and Lieutenant Colonel Bourget ran it except for several brief interludes. Only in 1914 did Peruvian Lieutenant Colonel Manuel María Ponce take command. Peruvians served until the French returned after the war; all Peruvian administration was by early Escuela Superior graduates: Ponce of the first *promoción* (1904–6), Lieutenant Colonel Isaac Zapater, also of the first *promoción*; Lieutenant Colonel Germán Yáñez of the third (1911–12); and Lieutenant Colonel Ernesto Montagne Markholtz, also of the third.[30] From the *promociones* of the pre-World War I years came several officers who later would assert themselves politically or become influential because of their contributions to professional journals: Oscar Benavides, Ponce, and Zapater of the first, Montagne and José R. Luna of the third, and Antonio Dianderas of the fourth (1913–14). From *promociones* of the post-war era came other activist writers and the founders of the Centro de Altos Estudios Militares.[31] A clearer case of historical continuity in South American military institutional development is hard to find.

One of the most important activities of the Escuela Superior was the annual *viaje de estudios*. Each year students would spend up to three months of their course in exploration and reconnaissance. Later (from 1936 on), the time would be spent mapping that which had been explored during the previous quarter-century. The French insisted that Peru could not defend itself unless it was thoroughly known and charted. Clément's cartographic lament of 1898 bore fruit. During the first ten years of the Escuela Superior the army explored and held maneuvers in the Andes or along a portion of the coast every year.[32] Escuela Superior graduates were more familiar with the climatological, logistical, topographical, and economic features of Peru than were their fellow citizens.

The Escuela Militar, officially dated from February 10, 1898, was no less a French creation, revived as it was after

Clément arrived. Twenty-five years after he had reopened it, General Clément wrote: "The Escuela Militar de Chorrillos is not just an institute where that virile vocation of national defense is imparted, but a sanctuary in which we profess a fervent cult of honor, the highest moral attribute of the perfect soldier."[33] The legislation proposed in the 1898 *Memorandum* had resulted in a program modeled after those of St. Cyr and the École Polytechnique combined. Even the noncommissioned and marksmanship courses took place at Chorrillos's facilities, lending much support to the practice of promoting outstanding noncoms to officer rank or officer cadet status. The first Clément mission, composed as it was of officers from the different branches, and the later French missions blended the civilized environment of Chorrillos with experiences distilled from St. Cyr and the Polytechnique, from the Fountainbleau artillery school, the Saumur cavalry school, and the École Supérieure de Guerre, and from colonial service in Africa. By 1910 a Peruvian, Colonel Emilio Sofer, was serving as Chorrillos commandant. Thereafter, Peruvians and French alternated until the war. As late as 1924 there was a French commandant. The first quarter-century of modern military education in Peru, then, was under close Gallic supervision and influence, and until World War II under the control of French-trained Peruvians.

According to one graduate of Chorrillos, the school was the equivalent of the University of San Marcos (in 1915 either hyperbolic wishful thinking or the damn of faint praise, depending on one's viewpoint), with far more time each year devoted to higher mathematics and technological courses and with a steady raising of entrance requirements.[34] Peruvian lieutenants were probably the equal of Chileans in terms of scientific and technical training, and superior to Argentines or Brazilians. Beyond that rank, much depended on specialty and experience. Surely, though, the overall result was essentially the same: a cadre of highly trained, motivated officers who aped their mentors and who absorbed their values.

But it was not all rosy for the Peruvians or the French. The 1898 obligatory service law malfunctioned. Financial resources necessitated periodic cutbacks in curriculum and the combining of courses; members of some *promociones* suffered for it. The 1910 mobilization undertaking, owing to a Bolivian, then an Ecuadorian, war scare, was chaotic.[35] New units existed on paper only, and there were not enough lieutenants—ever, it seems—to adequately carry out training exercises. Civilian secondary education came in for routine heavy criticism because it did not provide enough applicants qualified to meet Chorrillos entrance requirements; rote learning and neglect of empirical methods made for dull cadets. This, argued one officer, actually dragged the Escuela Militar down to the lowest level of Peruvian education.[36] Near the level of San Marcos, one wonders? Political meddling made for inconsistency and lack of administrative continuity in the high command. Nothing, believed this Peruvian, interrupted St. Cyr or the Polytechnique or the École Supérieure, and nothing should interfere with Chorrillos and its various institutes. Of course the very necessity of renovation, innovation, and reform provided for instability in the army.

The obligatory military service law underwent revision frequently, and rarely met with unanimous approval. The general staff system, adopted technically in 1896, likewise was altered to keep up with the times; so was the French-style 1910 promotions law. When the Escuela Superior opened in 1904, Peru also had spanking new administrative and arsenal systems and medical and veterinary services, as well as a professional journal, the *Boletín del Ministerio de Guerra y Marina*. The next year, the war ministry introduced another new conscription system based on regional administration, and in 1910 a new retirement law took effect.

Obligatory military service took in males from nineteen to fifty years of age. All were liable for up to three years of active duty save those who could delay or avoid it, depending on the annual needs of the army; the sum of 500 *soles* transferred one immediately to the first-line reserve. Exempted were the surviving sons of indigent widows, widowers with children under fourteen, postal workers, police officers, the physically disabled, the chronically ill, the clergy, and those in the navy. Students from nineteen to thirty years of age and members of the liberal professions all belonged immediately to the reserves. At age thirty-one they passed to the second reserve, and at age thirty-five to the national guard.[37] Quite typically, the pre-war conscription burden fell on the penniless, single males, the bulk of whom were *cholos* or Indians.

The image of the French was positive. Some of the older Peruvian officers grumbled perpetually about "too many changes," hardly unusual in South America at this time, but most officers and civilians favored the French. Pride, the desire for a link to Europe, fear of the Chileans and their "Araucanian hordes" reappearing in the streets of Lima— whatever the cause, reactions to the French were similar to those accorded the Germans in Chile. In this sense the Pacific coast republics contrast sharply with the Atlantic republics, where German training and Germans were a mixed blessing in the eyes of many.

Ernesto Montagne (the elder), who graduated from Chorrillos in 1905, was thoroughly *afrancesado*, although he looked in later life like an archetypal Prussian. Of the thirty members of his *promoción*, six became generals, and he proudly referred to his graduation class as the "promoción de los generales." The class of 1905 was the first full four-year course totally under French tutelage. Montagne graduated from the Escuela Superior in 1912, then went to Paris for additional study. He and his classmate in the 1913–14 École Supérieure session, Major José R. Luna, declared their spiritual adherence to the French army and people in a letter to *Le Figaro*, published August 25, 1914. Montagne had nothing but good things to say about the French. The same was true of Colonel Pedro Pablo Martínez. France, he believed, had sent her very best to Peru, and had made Peru's army into a smaller version of her own.[38] He cited several examples of press response to Clément and his officers, specifically praising Colonel Dogny and the French manner of imparting discipline, responsibility, morals, and dignity. Montagne and his colleagues all figured prominently in future military-civilian relationships.

Far to the southeast of Chorrillos and across the Andes from Santiago, Colonel Alfred Arent took up his duties in Buenos

Aires, the most important of thirty military missionaries to instruct and prepare Argentine officers prior to World War I. Arent had retired from the Prussian Army in 1899, and on August 13 of that year he signed a contract to head a mission to Argentina for the express purpose of reorganizing the Escuela Superior de Guerra, the moribund Argentine staff school. Classes began at the reorganized Escuela in May 1900 with forty-one students—nine majors, six lieutenant colonels, sixteen captains, and ten lieutenants.[39] According to one staff officer writing over a half-century later, the main reason for both the hiring of a German mission and the revival of the staff school was to provide Argentina with military leadership capable of countering Chile's recent gains and to prepare a staff for war with Chile—a possibility, thought many, from mid-1899 to late 1901.[40] President Roca and his war minister, Riccheri (who served as minister from July 1900 to October 1904), did not consider a French mission.

Arent's appointment, arranged by the Argentine chargé in Berlin, Ricardo Seeber, caused mixed feelings in Buenos Aires once the news reached America. Some officers saw no need for a German presence; mostly senior officers, no doubt, they feared for their prestige if subalterns were to receive advanced training. Some did not believe a German capable of dealing with Latins—ignoring, perhaps, what was going on to the west, but confirming Bernhardi unknowingly. Accompanying Arent were Lieutenant Colonel Rollo von Kornatski, professor of tactics and staff service; Major Bertram Schunk, professor of artillery; and Major Alphonse Diserre (a Swiss), professor of fortification. The Arent mission was not as readily identifiable as that of Clément in Peru or Körner's mission of 1895, for fewer Europeans came over and they did not stay as long as a group or individually. Arent directed the Escuela Superior from 1900 to 1906. Kornatski and Schunk were in Buenos Aires only two years. Diserre, the Swiss, stayed twenty years. In 1906 Hans von Below—brother of Günther, who had served briefly in Chile—came to Argentina for a four-year term. So did Friedrich von der Goltz, the Baron's son.

In his 1900 inaugural speech, Arent tried to allay the fears of his Argentine detractors by insisting that all Argentines were doing was what Frederick II himself had done when he sought assistance from France to upgrade his Prussian engineers and artillery a century and a half before. Other Germans served in instructional capacities at the Argentine Escuela Superior until 1914, and by the time they had returned to serve the fatherland Argentina's army had adopted much of Prussia's military system. Thus, although Arent was no Körner or Clément, either in the sense of long years of service or effect on the public, he and "don Rollo" (an extremely controversial individual in Germany as well as Argentina)[41] did their job well.

Riccheri's 1900 disavowal claiming Argentina would not ape any European military system notwithstanding, Argentine officers did appear quite Teutonic in the second decade of this century. What kept them from slavish imitation may have been the example unfolding before their eyes west of the Andes. Riccheri and others ridiculed the Chileans for doing everything they could to copy the Germans, including adopting the German (originally French) parade step, usually known as the "goose step." Indeed, one Argentine, probably Augusto Maligne, went so far as to call the Chileans fools and to wonder how much mud could be spattered on a rainy day by the crashing of boots by Körner's pupils and their men.[42]

But there were hard-core Germanophiles in Argentina, especially at the Escuela Superior. In 1906 Argentina began sending officers to Berlin for advanced study. The next year Argentina officially adopted the German war doctrine, which, coupled with assumed intentions in the diplomatic sphere (based on historical interest and the 1810 Buenos Aires declaration of independence), made Argentines look like potential aggressors. That same year the general staff transformed itself into the *gran estado mayor*—a creole *grosser Generalstab*—lending an additional touch of Germanophilia and aggressive luster to the Argentines. Still in 1907, new artillery, cavalry, and infantry manuals were translated from the German and published in Buenos Aires. Until this time, Escuela Superior graduates had been sent to Italy, Belgium, and France for advanced training in artillery and fortification, and some engineers had gone to France. All Escuela Superior graduates went to Germany if they ranked high enough in their class.[43] Riccheri's Belgian ties were cut.

Two Argentines stand out, representative of the pre- and post-Arent eras of Argentine military professionalization: Riccheri and José F. B. Uriburu. Riccheri was a second-generation Argentine, born in San Lázaro, Santa Fe, in August 1859 (he died in Buenos Aires in 1936).[44] He graduated from the Colegio Militar in 1879 with a second lieutenant's commission; four years later he was studying in Brussels at the École de Guerre. He visited Germany in 1884. Five years later, then again in 1892, he made trips to Europe to supervise the purchase of German weapons. By this time, the Argentine army had benefited from Roca's largesse of 1880–86, had suffered its first serious brush with politics, had adopted the staff system (without, as yet, a staff school), and was armed with German weaponry. Riccheri assumed a low profile as director of arsenals until Roca returned to the presidency in 1898, at which time he became chief of staff and went off to Europe yet again. When he returned in 1900, mission in tow, he rose to the war ministry. As independent as he was—and as determined to avoid imitation of the Germans—he plunged ahead with Prussianization.

His 1892 trip, following as it did the uprising of 1890 and subsequent attempts to subvert army discipline, most probably convinced him of the need to upgrade the profession; rumblings of war with Chile doubtless confirmed his conviction. Riccheri may even have been the pseudonymous Captain Johannes Dingskirchen, author of an 1892 treatise, written in Spanish and published in Buenos Aires, on the need for military modernization. The author claimed to be a veteran of the Franco-Prussian War and a guest at the 1892 maneuvers in Buenos Aires. His conclusions on Argentina's war-making potential provide an intriguing note of the times, although they had little apparent dissemination. What Argentines lacked in discipline, he wrote, they made up in valor. Colegio cadets appeared to be bright. Argentine troops were handsome men, and their dark skins displayed their Indian heritage. Uniforms were shabby and needed improvement. So did instruction at all levels. Argentina ought to emulate the finest army in the world to order to produce a capable fighting machine, and the best army in the world was Germany's. Instruction, equipment, better training—all these would keep politics out of the army, which was important given human nature and Argentina's "Spanish background."[45] Dingskirchen/Riccheri(?) was at least a realist.

Riccheri's greatest success, similar to feats achieved by Körner and Clément (i.e., Europeans), was the obligatory military service law, the *Ley Riccheri* (No. 4031, December 6, 1901). This law created a national conscription system and training centers throughout the country, such as the perpetually political Campo de Mayo, just outside the federal capital; organized the country into military districts; created national shooting clubs (a most Germanic importation); and organized training cadres and specialty schools.[46] Law 4031 was a direct response to Chile's alleged border violations, not a response to political pressures or subversion.

Riccheri returned to active service in 1904 when Roca left office. For a brief time he was commandant of the Colegio Militar, and he commanded Military Region II from 1905 to 1907. In 1910 he was promoted to division general, and when the war broke out he went to Europe as one of a number of South American observers. As he moved from the ministry back into the ranks and duty roster his hoped-for quasi-Germanic army had become an unadulterated copy of the Prussian army.

This happened because of the incurable Germanophilia of Riccheri's successor as professional strongman, José Félix Benito Uriburu. Uriburu was the nephew of former president José Evaristo Uriburu (1895–98). José Félix was born in 1868 and graduated from the Colegio twenty years later.[47] He was implicated in the 1890 revolt in Buenos Aires but was later reincorporated through his uncle's influence. He made first lieutenant in 1891 and became aide-de-camp to his uncle when the latter assumed the presidency in 1893. Four years later he was promoted to captain. In 1900 he was one of the first enrollees at the brand-new Escuela Superior. Two years later Major Uriburu went to Germany, where he served in an artillery unit for two years. Having moved from infantry to artillery as a staff officer, he transferred to the cavalry and took command of the escort attached to the Casa Rosada in 1904. Lieutenant Colonel Uriburu directed the Escuela Superior from 1907 to 1912. He traveled to Germany again in 1908 to gather information personally on German military education and made colonel the same year; in 1914 he was a division general, commanding Division I. After a stint as inspector general he retired in 1923, to emerge a few years later as a political figure.

During Uriburu's five years as head of the Escuela Superior he did his best to create a Kriegsakademie and an army molded in the German image from top to bottom. The Escuela, in the words of one contemporary, became a "perfect adaptation of that which is the Kriegsakademie." Instruction, organization, and discipline were easily as Prussian as they were in Chile's Academia. Uriburu even insisted that his aids be unswervingly "Germanic in bearing and public utterances."[48] Thus the Argentine variation on the theme of European military professionalization was as much a creole-induced phenomenon as it was an imposition by non-Latins. Those Germans contracted individually for service in speciality schools and the Escuela Superior knew that they had a strong, influential ally in José Félix Uriburu.

Alfred Arent was home in Germany in 1905, just when Radical-inspired revolts broke out in several provincial garrisons and just two years before Uriburu, the Argentine aristocrat, would begin refining what the German career officer had begun. The German published a little book in 1905 that reflected German attitudes of the times toward at least one of its South American client states. Arent's *Ein Land der Zukunft* is more a guide book for businessmen, travelers, and diplomats than it is a memoir of military service (although dedicated to Colmar von der Goltz). In the chapter "Heerwessen und Marine," though, Arent did set down his thoughts on Argentina's military future—apparently important for German businessmen as well as diplomats.[49] Like Dingskirchen /Riccheri(?) of some thirteen years before, Arent thought Argentines were fine physical specimens. The gaucho was a good horseman and, if not as good a rider as the Magyar or the Cossack, was their equal as a fighter. Until he and his aides had come to Buenos Aires, the officer corps had been at best of marginal quality, but German training had remedied that, Arent was convinced. Armament, discipline, equipment, organization, uniforms, and (he hoped) doctrine were German, therefore the best. The Germans had even dosed the Argentine cadets with etiquette and ballroom dancing lessons, making them into gentlemen and officers equal to Prussianized Chileans. Whatever their capabilities on the field of battle, Prussianized South Americans were good dancers and acquitted themselves well in social situations. Near the end of the book Arent mentioned an important principle of German militarism: political stability made for better military potential. Chile's army, he wrote, was a better army than Argentina's; all things being equal in regard to German training (which of course is debatable), the civilian situation determined the success or failure of the military—a most Prussian point of view.[50]

Much of the book deals with Argentina's potential as a trading partner, indicating the German interest in overseas expansion, the search for markets and sources of raw materials. Seeking what some now call an "informal empire," the German foreign office capitalized on the likes of Arent, Körner, and Kundt to further the interests of the likes of Krupp, Mauser, and I. G. Farben.[51] Perhaps not as skilled in trade as the British, though they claimed to be, or as noteworthy as the French for their diplomacy and cultural proximity, Germans made their move in South America by using their strongest selling point: achievements in military science.

Argentines were not immune to the difficulties confronted by their Chilean co-professionals. Budget stringency in 1904—the year Roca left the presidency—forced the Colegio Militar to close temporarily. The army combined the Colegio's staff and classes with those of the Escuela de Aplicación de Artillería e Ingenieros until funds were forthcoming for 1905. Such interruptions pleased no one. Another problem faced by Argentines early in this century was that of application of the 1901 obligatory military service law. Title I of the *Ley Riccheri* stated that all males twenty years of age and over owed twenty-five years of service liability to the state. Unless excused, all men would serve a six-month tour of duty at age twenty. One-fifth of those, chosen by lot, would serve an additional eighteen months. At either twenty years and six months or twenty-two years—depending on initial service—they entered the reserve, at age twenty-eight the national guard, and at age forty the territorial guard—in other words, the army, first- and second-line reserves, and home guard.[52] At first glance this law provided the country with a steady supply of fighting men and reserves for war, domestic crises, and maintenance of internal order, and it was a far more effective law (especially when tied to the Saenz Peña electoral reform legislation) than its 1895 predecessor. Nevertheless, it did not work.

Whereas Title I called all males to military service, Title XIV provided for a *tasa militar,* a military tax, whereby one could buy out of service for twelve pesos a year. The poverty-stricken, workers with dependents, and eldest sons of widowed mothers could also get out of service (as in most countries), as could clergymen, some students, physicians, and critical-need employees. But the provision for purchase of immunity from service permitted those with money to escape their national obligation. The *tasa* went to the coffers of the war ministry to be spent for equipment, but the burden of national defense became that of single males of modest or less than modest means. The "best and the brightest" did not fear conscription. This displeased officers who saw military service as a national unifier, an integrative institution, and those who envied the lifestyle of privileged Argentines.

There was an uneasiness about the Germano-Argentine relationship. Although Roca had arranged for a few advisors to serve in Argentina as early as Körner's appearance in Chile, many Argentines were never convinced—as Riccheri's comment would indicate—that foreigners ought to have much influence. The war scare with Chile caused some anti-German feelings to abate, but they revived soon after the turn of the century. When Arent arrived in Buenos Aires to take up his duties, it was with full knowledge that hostile civilians and officers awaited him (nothing unique by South American standards) and that his duties had been curtailed and the original size of his entourage pared, owing to political and press opposition. Arent was no Körner when it came to public relations. He did not get on well with Riccheri, he drew Roca's ire more than once, and his arrogance and tactlessness alienated many. He was perhaps too blatantly Prussian in his disdain for politicians, the press, underlings, political appointees in the officer corps, and untrained Argentine commanders.

Kornatski and Arent did not get along for personal as well as professional reasons, and Arent was induced to leave the country because of the quarrel.[53] The in-house squabble subjected the Germans to ridicule in the press, something the irascible don Alfredo would not have been forced to tolerate in Germany. Once Arent was recalled by command of Wilhelm II, never to return, the Escuela Superior settled into the pattern he had shaped for it, the officer class into its German mold. By the time Uriburu assumed command of the Escuela Superior, guided by his own statement that "the academy is not destined to supply incoherent knowledge; quite the contrary, it is expected that the instruction...be based on previously-accepted and well-assimilated principles,"[54] anti-German feelings had subsided. Such problems of course were present wherever a European mission appeared in South America.

A decade into this century the Germano-Argentine fusion was apparent. Argentines who were more Prussian than the Prussians themselves had assumed responsibility for its maintenance. The army had superficial trappings of modernity and professional aspirations that went deeper. Men like Uriburu, trained by Germans, were on the rise; they controlled promotions and assignments between 1908 and the war. Even after the war, Prussian-trained officers stood out at staff and command level and in instructional positions. The Prussian imprint on Argentine military civilian relations was clear.

The year 1910, as noted, brought Chileans and Argentines together, not on the battlefield, but on athletic fields, equestrian courses, and parade grounds. Baron von der Goltz came to Argentina for the independence centennial (and to visit his officer son, no doubt). In a solemn ceremony in Santiago, Division General Emil Körner retired from active duty in the Chilean army. This was Germany's high-water mark in South America, for Brazil, too, had her own Germanophiles.

Brazilian Germanophiles were officers of all grades who were drawn to the Prussian model for various reasons. German military progress was impressive to all who saw Prussian maneuvers. Monarchist officers (and there were still a few who lamented the passing of the Empire) yearned for an army-crown relationship, or the closest thing to it. Junior officers envied Argentines, Chileans, and the better paid, equipped, and armed São Paulo *força pública*, now under French tutelage.

Years before initial contacts resulted in agreements to bring German officers to Brazil and to send Brazilian officers to study in Germany (in both Prussia and Bavaria), Colonal Benjamin Constant, that "pride of our race and perfect distillation of our wisdom," had spoken out brashly for better treatment of the army.[55] Decrying the lack of professional expertise and the poor condition of arms and equipment, he held the government responsible for army discontent. He did not, however, plead a case for military professionalization similar to that going on elsewhere in South America. Benjamin wanted cadets and officers alike to be exposed to general education in order that they be better prepared to serve the nation. In fact, most of the officers in Benjamin's time were *bacharies*—degree-holders in science or philosophy, weak in strictly-defined military service. This may have been appealing to men like Benjamin because, like seminaries, the military schools were tuition-free until 1910. More than a few young men enrolled simply to get an education, with little idea of pursuing a military career. "Scientific, moral, and civil education," he said, "is far more important then military education."[56] The date of his statement was October 23, 1889; the audience, a group of Brazilian and Chilean army and navy officers; the occasion, a reception for the officers of the Chilean cruiser *Almirante Cochrane*, in Rio on a goodwill visit. The outspoken Colonel went unpunished for his re-marks—although they did cause a furor—for, just three weeks later, the Empire fell. Thereafter his remarks went unheeded in the midst of military-civilian political squabbling, intra-military feuding, and military loss of face in the Canudos campaigns.

Up in the Bahian *sertão*, Brazil's proud but outdated army was hard-pressed to squelch the rebellion of two hundred frontiersmen. Cunha called the abandoned Krupp cannons along the bloody trail to Canudos "Pyrrhic elephants."[57] As heirs of Caxias and Pelotas, of the glory of "A Retirada de Laguna," of Fonseca and Peixoto, officers had come out of the 1890s with mixed feelings. They had defended the Empire, then destroyed it; then they had saved the Republic, but had been made to look foolish doing it. Junior officers, wherever they had trained, were often fanatical in their self-perception and institutional loyalty.[58] Neglected by the Republican ad-ministrations from the mid-1890s on, the army stood its ground and did not question the Republic's legitimacy (not until the 1920s, at least). One officer described army life in terms reminiscent of Lyautey and his confreres. Estevão Leitão de Carvalho, a 1903 graduate of Praia Vermelha, wrote that from the 1890s through the first decade of this century many officers wanted to modernize the institution and model it after a European army. Some preferred the French system, and others saw the German army as the best to emulate. Most of their *chefes* wanted to affirm the army's value to the state: similar goals, different priorities.

Two things, he claimed, helped both groups to achieve par-tial success. Marshal Hermes organized field maneuvers in 1905, after a twenty-year hiatus. After witnessing the German maneuvers of 1908 he became convinced that Brazil badly needed advanced training—by Germans. He then persuaded Foreign Minister Rio Branco to make arrangements to send a number of Brazilian cadets and officers to Germany for fur-ther training. (Four had studied in Germany between 1906 and 1908.) Law No. 2050 of December 31, 1908, initiated the interchange. Soon an obligatory service law was on the books as well. The Germanophile Hermes was to Brazil what Roca,

Riccheri, and Uriburu were to Argentina, for Hermes had held posts both the civil and military equivalent of theirs. Rio Branco was willing to go along, for he did not want a French mission for the army as well as for the São Paulo militia. His purpose was simple; he wanted a cadre of German-trained Brazilians "to direct a renovation of the armed forces." But, partisan politics blocked Fonseca's and Rio Branco's plans. The German mission never arrived, providing a further embarassment and source of frustration to the officer corps. By 1912, though, thirty Brazilians had spent up to two years each in Germany; thus Brazil did have a cadre. There were twenty-two officers in Germany in 1912, including Lieutenant Bertholdo Klinger (1910–12), and twenty-eight sailed to Bremen in 1912. The army was by no means accorded a privileged status because of all this.

Far from it, especially when Hermes became president in 1910. Favorite of the Kaiser and military giant, he was no favorite of Brazilian civilians and he was a political pygmy. Junior officers fresh from Charlottenburg were scornful of their seniors, stale after Humaitá or Canudos. A number of the latter had performed poorly on maneuvers, and many would never forgive Hermes for favoring junior officers who had criticized them.[59] Rio Branco's diplomatic acumen resulted in Brazil's having no additional significant border problems and no pressing reasons for a national defense doctrine, a modern mobile army, or an obligatory military service system. The brief crisis with Bolivia—which resulted in the acquisition of Acre and caused Argentines to accuse Brazil of bellicose tendencies—emphasized the comparative ease with which Brazil could prevail over limitrophe states with undeveloped interiors and poor transportation and communications systems.[60] Finally, the state forces—and São Paulo's was still preeminent—assured internal stability. The road to military professionalism in Brazil was as tortuous as the trail to Canudos.

The Germanophiles led the way at the road's beginning. From the Rio garrison, where most of them served on returning from Germany, they moved into state garrisons. They maintained contacts with their fellows in Rio, constituting a network of captains and majors and the odd lieutenant, known as *a missão indigena*, the indigenous or domestic mission. This movement was the first evidence of "military centripetalism" since 1889 in the centrifugal sociopolitical milieu that was Brazil.

In 1913, with no objections from the high command, they began to publish a journal, little more than a tabloid at first, called *A Defeza Nacional*.[61] Lieutenant Leitão de Carvalho was on the editorial board, called collectively the Grupo Mantenedor, and so was Brazil's junior Germanophile, First Lieutenant Bertholdo Klinger, "o prussiano paulista." Of the dozen men in the Grupo Mantenedor, four had been sent to Germany. *A Defeza Nacional* made no bones about its purpose. Its editorial board decried the entrapment of the army in politics by civilians—and by Hermes too, now that he was president.

The army, the editors asserted, "was the only truly organized force in the midst of an amorphous mass of ferment—it exceeds its professional obligations at times to become...a decisive factor of political change or social stability." Officers in Argentina, Chile, and Peru may have concurred with *A Defeza Nacional*'s definition of what was an army, but they did not say so in an officially-sanctioned journal. Relatively early in their contacts with a European model, the Brazilians took a stand on social and political roles. The peculiar situation of the army—creator of the Republic, sensitive to the failings of their creature and anxious to improve their lot—was as responsible for this as was German orientation.

But it was German training that had given the Brazilians involved in *a missão indígena* a grasp of what defense and security meant. They cited interrelated reasons why Brazil needed a modern army: Brazil needed to defend against all external threats and she needed a centrally coordinated internal security force. Defense, therefore, was linked to internal security, and the army should be the source and guarantor of both. "Moreover, the army in a country like Brazil is not just the prime factor in sociopolitical transformation, nor the principal form of exterior defense; it has as well an educative and organizational function to perform on the masses of citizens."[62] This is simply a pre–World War I augury of the latter twentieth-century linkage of national security to socio-economic development. Like most such auguries, it is devoid of references to structural change.

What marks Brazil at this point in the professional development of its army is the fact that the "Young Turk" element, so clearly caught up in Germanophilia, was allowed to publish such editorial opinions. Brazilian officers, to be sure, were traditionally more outspoken, but they had refrained from being so for some time. In early issues of *A Defeza Nacional* there were frequent references to German military superiority, translations of articles by German officers, and photos of figures like Baron von der Goltz, ever the South American favorite. By the end of 1914 over seventy officers had agreed to write, edit, distribute, or serve as correspondents, and as Europe fell under the pall of war these military journalists focused on the war as a "lesson of history."[63]

The war found Brazil dependent on Germany in the institutional sense. Brazil's entry into the war broke psychological ties, of course, but changed neither the immediate attitudes of junior officers nor the outward appearance of the army. Armaments were exclusively German, another example of German trade "following the sword." Brazilians carried Mauser rifles and pistols and used Krupp 75 mm. and 105 mm. cannons. Not until well into the 1920s would French armaments replace German equipment, and then only after many complaints of French arm-twisting.[64] Until the very end of peace in 1914 *A Defeza Nacional* plumped for that elusive German mission, and even after the war Klinger and his close allies were wary of the French officers in Brazil. The journal also continued to tie defense and security to development in the sense that a small army defending a large country needed to modernize in order to do so, and to serve thereafter as a modernizing force in its own right.

Not until 1914 did Brazilians have anything resembling a general staff, a reserve system, or an administration based on modern organization concepts. The army's finances were poorly coordinated and recruitment was disorganized. Under constant revision, the conscription law barely served its purpose. Despite the influence of the Germanophiles, the old ways died slowly. During 1915 and 1916 a barrage of legislation provided at least a modern organizational structure on paper, one that French officers would use as a base for updating organization, administration, conscription, education, and training. But their task was not going to be easy, for by the end of the war Brazilian Germanophiles had achieved new stature as middle-ranking officers. This propelled them into the political arena in the last decade of the old Republic.

Germanophilia and Francophilia were easily discernible in South America when the Europeans went to war, even in remote Bolivia, where Hans Kundt was struggling against great odds to do something with that country's ragtag army.[65] European doctrine, training, philosophy—a European ethos—was dominant in the major military powers of South America, by extension even in Ecuador, Colombia, and El Salvador to the north. Missions, of course, assured this, but even where no missions toiled (e.g., in Brazil), European models were accepted. Internal and superficial realities of an institutional nature, and the political, social, and economic vicissitudes of the early twentieth century, made the process of professionalization a painful one for many South Americans. A great gap developed between political theory and practice, and soon between most things military and civilian, as South American officers began to assess traditional military concerns. Doing so, they began to define a professional role somewhat distinct from that of their mentors. As might be expected, evidence of role definition is firmer (not necessarily more plentiful) where missions were present. In each of the countries treated herein, evidence is conclusive: there was a meeting of minds.

Officer-class values clashed with civilian democratic practices throughout this period, beginning in South America the process of separation of things military from things civilian. The chief end result of obligatory service in Europe—national defense and the fulfillment of a social role—became the same in South America. But the social role loomed even more prominently because of the retardation of social development in Argentina, Brazil, Chile, and Peru. National unity, mobilization capabilities, and economic development were more difficult to achieve in South America, especially when obligatory military service schemes were based on regional and local conscription and training of troops. Social, economic, political, and cultural realities were even more inseparable from professionalism, if that be possible, than they were in Europe. The lines between classical, traditional, and developmental roles merged from the outset, but at no point did the majority of officers consider seriously anything close to true structural change. It is questionable whether they have in the decades since.

Military literature circulated primarily among members of the officer corps. It was no more widely read than professional literature of any other type of the day, but may well have provided subjects for more intense discussion owing to the state of the profession. Because of pressures on officers to conform (yet to be innovative) and to base their thought and action on established procedure and precedent (yet to project a bold and original image), and simply because of peer pressures to be aware of contemporary currents of thought in professional circles, the ideas expressed in house organs probably did have a greater effect than anything comparable emanating from civilian liberal professional organizations. The literature is notable for its lack of originality and its dependence on European sources. Aside from the fact that it provides for numerous allegations of plagiarism and repetition, this means that over the years military thought and self-perception remain essentially the same.

Officers in early twentieth-century South America reflected traditional European disdain for civilians, a reinforced hauteur, and a distinct wariness of liberal democracy. The tone of essays dealing with the values of the traditional professional officer varies, depending on the attendant level of hostility between the army and politicians, but the conclusions are in the main identical: army officers and their values were innately superior in most ways to civilians and theirs; and military structure and organization provided a more effective and orderly model of progress than did political systems based on egalitarianism and mass participation. The fusion of European values with pre-1914 South American realities is most evident in Chile and Peru, the two countries that tied themselves most firmly to European military professionalism through German and French military missions.

Goltz was to Chileans and Argentines what Lyautey was to Peruvians. With no hinterland to develop, no sociocultural problem of Peruvian magnitude, Chileans focused as much on national defense and preparedness as on the civilizing mission, but they did not begin to do so until they saw them as inseparable.

Indicative of the powerful influence of Goltzian military thought in Chile is the 1912 publication of *El problema militar de Chile* by Colonel Ernesto Medina Franzani, the first significant piece of Chilean professional literature. Besides being stylistically pleasing, sophisticated in its manipulation of quantitative data, and forceful in its plea for greater military expenditures, Medina's book is a Chilean *Das Volk in Waffen*, evincing the same ideals and values.

Colonel Medina was concerned by the state's apparent unwillingness to devote more financial resources to defense. He criticized the bureaucracy, especially the war ministry, for its inefficiency, and he advocated educational reforms to raise the moral level of the Chileans, for "the quality...and homogeneity of our people constitutes...a most precious raw material, whose conservation we must guard with the greatest attention."[66] He stressed the role or mission of the modern military organization, claiming that it was to maintain national integrity, "political, territorial, administrative and governmental," "to respond to, and to solve, international situations and problems," and "to intervene in [i.e., participate in the solution of] those problems that, directly or indirectly, affect the interests and the future of the republic."[67] His argument was close to that of Goltz, but his contemplated military role was more ominous vis-à-vis Chilean internal affairs, because of the failure of the Santiago government to address domestic problems.

Medina was by no means alone in his application of German military thought and priorities to the Chilean situation, thus fusing defense and development early on. In the years before and during the war, outspoken colleagues like Captains Alberto Muñoz Figueroa and Domingo Terán, Major Aníbal Riquelme, and General Manuel Moore Bravo expressed discontent with aspects of civilian guidance of national affairs, partisan political influence in the officer corps, political corruption, and Chile's anachronistic social structure. These essayists called upon the government to respond more adequately to all the army's needs, thus setting the tone the Chilean military thought in this century. They inculcated a feeling of "frustrated superiority" among army officers. Captain Muñoz pointed out that army training programs were superior to civilian primary education and that the officer was a superior teacher. Civic and moral education of lower-class Chileans was provided by men in uniform, he "lamented with pride." In what had by this time become a universal complaint, Captain Terán chided the government for allowing the obligatory military service scheme to become a farce by making it easy for young men of influence and means to find loopholes. He wrote that the army was more truly democratic than civilian society because professional success and advancement were based on ability rather than influence—a standard argument itself. The officers, he believed, were "morally superior to the civilians." General Moore decried the use of "connections with friends in high places" by some officers in order to obtain assignments, and he criticized the amount of politicking within the ranks. In a somewhat controversial essay, Major Riquelme attacked Chile's political system for its lack of cabinet continuity and parliamentary responsibility. He stated that the armed forces should be regularly consulted by the government on all matters of national policy.[68]

Chilean concerns with political stability and systemic continuity were natural results of the Parliamentary Republic experience. They also reflected German concerns over the plight of the officer class and the army as a whole in the changing political life of the Wilhelmian era. However static German politics may appear in comparison with those of Republican France, contemporary officers did perceive changes. If Chilean military literature is less than stunning in quantity, it is noteworthy in quality. Rigid discipline held Chileans back but did not diminish the depth of their thought and self-perception.

In Peru, military professionals early on seized the opportunity to proclaim themselves civilizers of their country and to claim a monopoly on this role.[69] As early as 1904 a then obscure lieutenant colonel raised the question of basic education for conscripts in a brief essay as significant to Peru as Lyautey's "Du Rôle social de l'officier" had been to France since 1891. Gabriel Velarde Álvarez (who twenty years later would be the chief of staff) admonished his colleagues to press for implementation of a decree dating from 1888 that established barracks schools for conscripts. This piegonholed decree had charged officers and noncoms with instilling a sense of patriotism and civic pride in the conscripts. The troops were supposed to receive regular instruction in history and government, reading and writing—but, as Velarde pointed out, nothing had been done to carry out this *misión civilizadora*. His prime example of the *misión* was not France, as might be expected, but Germany, for German victories in 1870 and 1871 had been won by educated soldiers, not ignorant brutes.

Since Peruvian soldiers came overwhelmingly from the Indian population, traditionally isolated from the main currents of national culture and policy, they could hardly be expected to have a stake in national service. "What more meritorious labor," he wrote, "than to transform the unfortunate helot into a civilized being, the miserable slave of tyranny and superstition into a free man, conscious of his rights and duties."[70] What more arduous task, one wonders, was there than contemplating the making of a modern army from human resources still steeped in antiquity and overwhelmingly distrustful of all those who sought to monopolize their lives? Between Velarde's essay of 1904 and the outbreak of war in Europe several other such articles appeared in the *Boletín del*

Ministerio de Guerra y Marina. These pieces all relied heavily on French sources in advocating the *misión civilizadora*.

The civic program discussed by Velarde still languished. J. C. Guerrero found this intolerable. "Let us educate the Indian," he wrote, "and we will have citizens; once we have citizens, then we will have a nation." Lieutenant A. Escalona continued in this vein, pleading for drill and instruction of Indian troops in the Quechua language—and for classes in which the officer class could learn Quechua in order to better communicate with the Indian. The experience of military life transmitted through the Quechua language (which dialect was not stipulated) would therefore integrate the Indian into the mainstream of national life.[71] Then Major David Fernandini published the first of three 1911 articles, doing for Peruvians essentially what Demongeot had done for Frenchmen.

Fernandini emphasized the importance of military life for the masses. His first two essays dealt in general terms with what he called a "wholesome barracks life experience." These arguments found support in Captain Nicanor Beúnza's "Servicio militar en el Perú," which sharply criticized the extant obligatory service law and its application. Beúnza cited a "brutalizing trinity of provincial governor, judge, and priest" with malfeasance and incompetence in administration and record-keeping. Indians had to be freed from the control of these exploiters before they could become useful citizens of Peru—through military service.[72] But the best of 1911 was yet to come.

Major Fernandini's third essay of the year dealt with the difficulties of inculcating patriotism and "love of country" in the conscripts, a recurrent French theme. He made no mention of the Peruvian army's inglorious historical record, but insisted that an appreciation of the country's history through study of its heroes was necessary for the soldier. He suggested that training officers stress the role of Túpac Amaru as precursor to independence in order that Indian and *cholo* identify with Peru's past—and present. Once the masses were thus imbued with love of country and patriotic verve, he was convinced, "we can say 'Banzai Peru!'"[73] Hyperbole aside, this was a legitimate reaction to a situation where the past might be dismal but where young officers had great hopes for their professional future.

Major Carlos Echazú was equally outspoken in "La disciplina militar." The major sought to impede civilian meddling in military affairs and, conversely, military involvement in anything but strictly professional questions. He juxtaposed democracy and authoritarianism, civil liberties and military discipline: "The officer may think what he wishes, but more than anything he must obey....Respect for civil liberties and freedom of speech, which society maintains by law, are replaced in the military by respect, blind obedience, and denial of the right to question authority or the actions of those in authority."[74] Abnegation, service to the fatherland, and sacrifice governed military life. Echazú's use of arguments advanced in French military literature helped to convince his fellows that their way was the more patriotic, organized, disciplined, productive, and progressive, and the drawing of the line between things military and civilian had begun.

Pre-war Argentine officers showed aggressive concern for both their national and their public image. One writer claimed in 1910 that Argentina lagged far behind Peru, Bolivia, Chile, and even little Uruguay in quality of modern weaponry. Artillery pieces, especially, were outdated. Argentines could be proud of their officer corps and of their army only as long as the obligatory service system continued to function. Owing to German training, the efforts of Roca and Riccheri, and a general feeling of good will on the part of the citizenry, he went on, the Argentine officer corps would very soon be composed entirely of Colegio Militar graduates. Indeed, all lieutenants commissioned since 1905 had graduated from the Colegio. German-style, the ranks were closed to nongraduates.

But the army was only at half-strength. Argentina needed 60,000 trained men to counter Brazilian "adventurism"; only 43,000 were available at any one time. Argentina should really have a total of 500,000 men in active and reserve categories in order to be prepared at all times to defend the *patria*, he averred. Military service (as if one needed reminding) bound the country together and civilized humble citizens who, if not for their time in the barracks, would remain illiterate and unhealthy.[75]

There were those who objected to what they considered excessive expenditures on modern armaments. One early writer referred to Riccheri as *el industrialista*, linking him by innuendo with the German officers and Krupp sales representatives who had made the army a "medium of exhibitionism"; the formal parades so beloved by officers and civilians alike were just "theatrical spectacles" and "Roman circuses requiring, during peacetime, many ruinous imports and during time of war leading to disorganization and defeat."[76] There were too many evasions of Law 4031; the privileged simply did not serve their country—a standard South American professional viewpoint by this time.

In Chile, wrote the same author, "they train soldiers, not gardeners." Argentine conscripts spent too much time as houseboys, butlers, gardeners, and strikers instead of working on drill field and firing range.[77] Chilean and Brazilian successes—what appeared to be successes, or what were held up as successes for propaganda purposes—prompted this writer to write exactly like a disgruntled European.

In 1900 the German Captain R. von Colditz recorded his critical view of Spain's and the United State's performance in 1898 in the widely-read *Revista del Club Militar*.[78] He wrote that mobilization had been slow and haphazard, most of the equipment was antiquated, and uniforms were not standardized; the United States was no military threat to a first-rate power, he concluded. Argentines could do better at all facets of warfare (especially health and sanitation conditions). The next year, forty-five Bolivians, led by a nephew of President José Pando, arrived to study in Buenos Aires. They had been hand-picked by a group of Argentine officers resident in La Paz.[79] For most of the next decade, articles on aspects of defense and affairs in borderland countries dominated the pages of Argentina's first military journal.

Centennial spirits, Göltz's visit, the novelty of German-style military pomp (if not with the Germans themselves), and widespread optimism about Argentina's economic potential led Lieutenant Colonel Maligne to wax euphoric about the country's future in the Southern Cone. The Germans had trained Argentines well, he wrote, but Argentines had retained their essential integrity; they avoided total *adoption* of German models. Maligne reasoned that if Argentina had copied German military systems totally, at the onset of a war "all things alien to Argentina would be whirled away by the *pampero*, and, as nothing indigenous would then remain whole beneath the foreign patina, there would be nothing."[80] But adaptation of German ways to pampa and littoral, had made Argentina ready to export her own expertise to Bolivia, Peru, Ecuador, Venezuela, and Colombia and enabled her to receive cadets and officers from those countries in the Colegio and the Escuela Superior. General José Rodríguez's "La Guerra" described the English as parasites, crass materialistic merchants who reaped profits while France and Germany suffered. (There was no later acknowledgement in Argentina of the role played by the British or Americans in the outcome of the war, save for routine notices.) France's debility was due to Socialist conspiracies. Prussia's and Germany's strength was due to tradition and military-civilian aristocratic fusion. "Germany," Rodríguez predicted, "will win because with her armies she manifests order, discipline, character, energy, abnegation—moral factors that tumble walls and annihilate any force arrayed against her will to triumph." Bloody though it was, war was a great civilizing force. Its results constituted positive gains for humanity. Wilhelm II came in for praise as "that genial chap, that knight who, with visor raised, throws down the steel gauntlet to all infamous and envious enemies of the grandeur of [the German] nation."[81] Bernhardi would have been so pleased. Selective adaptation of the German military system and retention of Argentine ways notwithstanding, *Rittertum* was alive and functional in the Argentine military mentality.

The Colegio Militar class photograph of 1914 shows all cadets wearing the *Pickelhaube* and German-cut uniforms. Benjamín Rattenbach, the officer-author-to-be, was among their number, a man whose ideas would influence promotions of cadets for half a century to come and more.[82] Two months prior to graduation, on October 19, 1914, Julio Roca died, ending an age that began in 1878 with the "Campaign of the Desert" and ended with the Prussianization of the Argentine officer corps. The same month, José F. Uriburu published "Socialismo y defensa nacional," one of the earliest South American military blasts against a specific political organization. To the prestigious General Uriburu, Socialists were anti-patriotic and pacifist. They were anti-nationalist and subversive. Their anti-militarism was destructive and immoral. Militarism, he believed, was no danger to humanity. To be sure, Mexican militarism—the civil war now in its fourth year— was chaotic, destructive. But real German militarism was a civilized and creative force. Obligatory service precluded professional praetorian and aggressive military adventurism; volunteer, improvised, and mercenary forces promoted war and slaughter.[83] Therefore, Argentina (despite spiked helmets, jackboots, and intimations of *Rittertum*) could not be considered a militaristic nation. Uriburu and his confreres had learned well the lessons of European military logic; they had absorbed fully the thought and self-perception of their training masters.

Brazilian officer corps thought and self-perception prior to the appearance of *A Defeza Nacional* in 1913 centered on the importance and positive contributions of obligatory service. Late development of European contacts precluded absorption of ideals and values in a degree comparable to Chile, Peru, or even Argentina. The official *Relatório* for 1907–8, for example, stated that conscription schemes had been "received with sympathy and general applause by the nation, especially by studious youth." Young Brazilian males "were happy to do their duty."[84] Officers could have suffered under no greater delusion. Law 1860 of January 4, 1908, was a vain effort on the part of the federal government and the national army chiefs to centralize conscription—in essence to "nationalize" military service—and to wrest military preeminence from the *forças públicas*, especially the French-trained São Paulo militia.

Prior to Law 1860, wrote Lieutenant Heitor d'Araújo Mello in May 1914, the army had been a long-term service organization of conscripts and volunteers, without an equitable draft system.[85] Reserves existed on paper, "without any military value," and the *forças públicas* were sufficient only to maintain internal order. D'Araújo Mello went further, defending and justifying the new law. All Europe save England had obligatory service systems, and this he believed (naïvely) assured an "armed peace." South America, unlike Great Britain and the United States, still had frontier conflicts, and Brazil faced potentially hostile neighbors. Therefore the anti-military arguments of civilian Anglophiles and Yankeephiles were of little value in Brazil.

There were too many ways to avoid one's national duty, asserted Dom Heitor. Connections, political influence, student deferments, and professional exemptions—all of these ate into the annual total of 40,000 conscripts necessary to man the army. Too many young men were thus denied the experience of serving a year in "the school of the nation." D'Araújo Mello made numerous allusions to Goltz as he lauded the army for its work in inculcating discipline, morals, patriotism, and a sense of responsibility (as well as stimulating interest in personal hygiene) among the conscripts.[86] He closed this professionally unoriginal yet significant-to-Brazil essay by pleading the army's case against the numerical superiority and better equipment of the state forces.

By the time D'Araújo Mello wrote, Bertholdo Klinger and Estevão Leitão de Carvalho and their comrades had launched *A Defeza Nacional*, Europe was at war, and the case for obligatory service, a large standing army, and a national mobilization plan could be made by more officers, more easily and in good taste. Before the war ended, Brazilians pulled even with Argentines, Chileans, and Peruvians in the production of literature indicating the presence of an ingrained military professionalism. On the arrival of the French mission headed by General Maurice Gamelin in 1919, Brazil became the fourth breeding-ground for professional militarism on the South American continent. On both sides of the continent and on both sides of the Atlantic Ocean, European military thought and self-perception dominated the profession. South Americans soon began to fancy themselves to be as relatively modern (in theory) and as superior (in practice) as their mentors.

They convinced themselves that they were their country's elite.

It is clear that their opinions of politics, international relations, obligatory service, and the role and situation of the officer class in society, however briefly or sporadically expressed, were identical to those of Europeans, and as similar to each others' as national differences would permit. Information on Ecuador, Colombia, Venezuela, Paraguay, and Uruguay, on the Germano-Bolivian tie established by Hans Kundt, and on the aspirations of Mexican officers like General Bernardo Reyes on the eve of the Mexican uprising of 1910 makes it equally clear that either France or Germany, not the United States, was the preferred model to be emulated. (Indeed, if Reyes had had his way, the Mexican Army in 1910–11 might have changed the course of the revolution.)[87] Not until midway between the world wars can one discern a U.S. military policy in the making anywhere in Latin America.

The quantity and quality of literature of a non-technical nature depended, of course, on a mix of extra-professional as well as professional variables. Depth of mission penetration, strength of contacts, the army's accumulated prestige or lack of it, the domestic political situation, and the strength of institutions all influenced just how aggressive, defensive, self-serving, or tentative military literature was and would be. Germany's defeat in 1918 did not diminish Argentine and Chilean (or Bolivian) reverence for the Wilhelmian military-civilian relationship; it bound them to a past, to an idealized past. France's victory enhanced the stature of her army, especially the colonials, whose Gallieni and Lyautey, among others, came home to Metropolitan France's rescue in her time of need. This was felicitous—at first—and it was enough to justify a French mission to Brazil—at first. From the end of the Great War to the outbreak of war in 1939, pre-World War I French and German military professionalism endured, certainly as vitally in South America as in the homelands.

If most South American officers were enthralled by their new connections and mentors, most of Europe's military leaders, like those of the United States, were by no means convinced of

South America's significance in other than commercial terms. They devoted only perfunctory attention to South America from the turn of the century until the Great War. Peru and Brazil still went barely noticed by Europeans; as before, Argentina and Chile stirred the most interest.

Activities of the French officers outside the frontiers of the empire were under the supervision of the Deuxième Bureau, that department of the army concerned with intelligence and foreign affairs. Owing to this, much of the material relating to missions became classified instantly. There is little detail on any aspect of the missions to Peru. A brief note of 1909 in the *Revue Militaire des Armées Étrangères*, on the latest renewal of the mission, reported that the French were in charge of educating 100 cadets and 700 non-commissioned officers a year at a place called Chorrillos and that Peru had a 4,000-man standing army.[88] Nothing appeared in detail on Clément's work.

The *Internationale Revue über Gesammten Armeen und Flotten* was likewise devoid of detailed information on Peru and France's work there. "As in Chile, so it is in Peru," was the *Internationale Revue's* 1901 penetrating conclusion on pending obligatory service legislation in Peru.[89] Another article of the same year estimated that Peru spent 30 percent of government revenues on its armed forces, Argentina 26 percent, Brazil 27 percent, and Chile 16 percent, figures not deemed exorbitant for the time because Germany, the editors claimed, spent 50 percent of national revenues on her armed forces.[90] A 1903 item asserted that the French mission was controlled by the Peruvian president (Candamo at this point), for its chief was directly responsibile to the executive-appointed war ministry—and equal in terms of protocol to the president's own aide-de-camp.[91] Beyond these notes, Peru remained *terra incognita* to the majority of French and German officers. The French paid far more attention to Africa, the Levant, and Asia than to South America. Germany paid more attention to Argentina and Chile.

Brazil fared no better, for there was no official mission to merit printing of the briefest of French or German news items. A few individual instructors brought by Marshal

Hermes rated no coverage. The *Internationale Revue* twice dismissed prevailing Brazilian conscription regulations as worthless in 1900, noting that Brazil's 15,000-man army commanded by 3,000 officers (an erroneous figure) posed a military threat to no one.[92] In July 1902 a brief item in the *Internationale Revue* informed readers that the general staff (an organization of record, not functional) planned a major cartographic effort to produce a national map of Brazil.[93] Like their neighbors to the far west, Brazilians lacked definite knowledge as to their national patrimony.

Shortly before the war, the French took more notice. In the longest essay devoted to Brazil since Europeans began their martial missionary efforts on the continent, *Revue Militaire* editors spoke generously of Brazil's "flexible" army organization, which "rendered the army sufficiently supple to permit the progressive afflux of citizens provided by obligatory service." In other words, there was no space problem in the enlisted or conscript ranks. The Brazilians lacked both a coordinated officer preparation and a nationwide recruitment policy. Their theoretical preparation of officers may possibly have been as good as that of the French, but the Brazilians were far behind in practical, technical preparation. Professionalization would not diminish Brazil's pacific inclinations; on the contrary, a prepared officers corps could be "a new guarantee of South American peace."[94]

Argentina and Chile received the bulk of German attention, as might be expected. The *Militär Wochenblatt* reported on affairs in Argentina and gave a reportorial nod to the other powers in the above-noted piece of 1899 entitled "Vier Fremde Militär Komissionen." "A French colonel" was in Peru, and another in Colombia. An officer or two were in Brazil, Mexico, and El Salvador. Germans were active in Argentina and Chile. The fact that the information was scant and that this hardly amounted to four "missions" did not deter the editors. An untitled item on Arent and Kornatski also appeared in 1908.[95] The war scare with Chile, hence the possibility of German trainees fighting German trainees, was the subject of a 1902 article. The *Wochenblatt*'s conclusion here was that Argentina was in an advantageous position geographically but that Chile was better off in terms of preparation and armaments owing to a longer experience with a German mission.[96] "The army and the navy are extremely popular with Argentines," was Goltz's conclusion in a notice on the centennial gala.[97]

Argentina received but one discreet pre-war notice in France's *Revue Militaire*. The *Ley Riccheri* appeared in translation sans comment in 1905.[98] This hardly constituted a breakthrough in military intelligence.

Germany's *Internationale Revue* covered Argentina more satisfactorily than any other journal. Roca and Riccheri's relationship was held responsible for the passage of military legislation and for the attraction of superior students to the Colegio in 1901.[99] Arent's difficulties also made the news. His Körneresque complaints about facilities, poor classroom preparation, poor application of the *Ley Riccheri*, and the ignorance and illiteracy of the troops found their way into print. Ten years later, an *Internationale Revue* essay prompted by centennial celebrations in Buenos Aires and Santiago had absolutely nothing good to say about the Arentless Argentine army.[100] Unless Germans were present, by inference, there could be little true military achievement.

German ambivalence and moderation, both so apparent in the case of "ungrateful" Argentina, did not apply to Chile, "that land between the Andes and the Pacific where one hears with pleasure 'the Prussia of South America.'"[101] The *Wochenblatt* spoke highly of the 1906 maneuvers (this despite the bumbling of recently-deployed junior officers and untrained seniors that marked most maneuvers held in South America at this juncture), and praised Körner as "the finest son the Fatherland could have."[102] Chile simply had the best army— "a miniature replica of Prussia's"—in Latin America, conceded one author. "The staff of the Escuela Militar," he went on, "enjoys the felicitous cooperation of the three B's: Bieberstein, [Günther von] Below, and Barceló."[103] The same editors of *Internationale Revue* who scorned Argentina in "Die Militärischen Machmittel der Staaten von Südamerika" began their assessment of the continental powers bluntly. "In South America the Chilean army is generally regarded as the best and most capable of making war."[104] Germans reacted to Argentina's policy of pursuing its own military modernization—Prussianization without the Prussians—like spurned lovers, but Chileans could do no wrong.

Civilians, French civilians at least, were not impressed with Brazil's military potential; they had an idea of what Germans had wrought in Chile and a somewhat less than objective view of what their own officers were doing up the coast in Peru. Georges Clemenceau toured the continent in 1910. He coolly appraised the Brazilian army as having "far too many coloreds in the ranks" but as being decently equipped, with well-trained officers. The São Paulo public force was superior to the army because of French instruction; the national army, "officered by men of fine public spirit...needs reorganizing." Clemenceau dismissed any possibility of Brazil's making war, allowing that the army was necessary only "because the public interest requires that military force be at the disposal of the government, capable of enforcing obedience to the law."[105]

"Le Tigre" thought Argentina had a suitable government, and he was impressed with the parliamentary actions he observed in congressional proceedings. He opined that Argentina as a federal system was as much an adoption of the U.S. system as continental parliamentarism was reminiscent of the British system. But, he warned, "here as elsewhere, politicians who are more or less the official mouthpieces of that vague concourse of general opinions we call the mind of the public may very easily mistake the ephemeral demands of a party for the permanent interest of the country." Perhaps Clemenceau had been listening to Argentine politicians who feared the growth of the Radical party.

Goltz's 1910 centennial visit prompted Clemenceau to admit the shrewdness of the German foreign ministry in sending officers to Argentina, for the Germans had done a fine job in modernizing the army. About the Chilean army Clemenceau had nothing to say. His visit to the Atlantic Coast did not allow him to judge either Körner's or Clément's achievements.

He did note, perceptively, that in Chile parliamentary coalitions amused themselves by "knocking over ministries like ninepins."[106]

Henri Lorin, in "Impressions du Chili: Les Chiliens et la France," written after a centennial visit, called the Chilean a "soldier by vocation," and drew attention to German influence in business and university communities as well as in the army. German officers had great prestige in Chile, wrote Lorin, owing to the Chileans' long-standing belief in the necessity of permanent military strength. "By virtue of regulation, organization, and uniforms the army is 'all German'; it is a fine military organism; one could not pay it greater homage than to state that various other South American countries, Colombia and Paraguay [Ecuador], have asked for [Chilean] missions for education of their own men."[107] Lorin made it clear that he believed military and commercial influence went hand in glove.

In the preface to the English version of Francisco García Calderón's *Latin America: Its Rise and Progress*, Raymond Poincaré drew attention to the Peruvian savant's wariness of outside stimuli in Latin America—German, Japanese, and American—and his call for French and Italian migration to counteract what he saw as Saxon and Asiatic hegemony. He concurred with García Calderón's praise of the French missions and Germanophobic pronouncements, and drew attention to his observations that the French had been able to remove the army from politics and vice versa and had given Peru an organization capable of maintaining internal order.[108]

And so, proud but frustrated, the officers of Argentina, Brazil, Chile, and Peru confronted the real war involving their mentors from 1914 to 1918. In countries where political theory and practice were far apart, where military legislation often was inapplicable, but where armies had been assigned important defense and security roles, officers were already turning their eyes to the civilian sector. They would continue to do so. South Americans began to think as they had been trained to think. By 1914, they had the same ideals, values, and political outlook as well as the conviction that they had a social role to play. However unacceptable their thought and self-perceptions may have appeared to civilians, officers were now a force to be reckoned with. The missionaries had done their job well.

Two

"The army is the most healthy
profession possible—naturally
I mean in a neutral country
like ours. The annual
maneuvers do one a world of
good, brace the system, clear
the blood."

Graham Greene, "Dream of
a Strange Land" (1963)

"In reality, parliamentarism as a
system of government resulted in
sterility. It came to nothing more
than interminable speeches on
partisan topics. Purposeful action
on problems of national progress
was not forthcoming.... Moreover,
formalities were not even observed
faithfully."

Carlos Ibáñez del Campo, in an
interview with Luis Correa Prieto
(1958)

CHAPTER FIVE

The South American
Setting: 1919–1940

When Hans von Seeckt wrote that "Mars lies dead," he meant that both the army he knew and war as he knew it were things of the past. World War I did not end war for all time, and Seeckt's army sprang anew from the fields of Prussia, Saxony, and Württemberg. To the west—now, indeed, west of the Rhine—France entered the post-war era triumphant. Frenchmen avenged the disgrace of 1870–1871 and regained Alsace-Lorraine. The Third Republic survived the war and so did the military-civilian relationships it had engendered. The German Empire, like Mars, lay dead; unlike the German martial tradition it would not be born again. Germany became a republic and stayed one until Adolf Hitler became both chancellor and president in 1934 on the death of Paul von Hindenburg. By that time, close ties between army and state had been reestablished.

Perduration of traditional military professionalism in the face of change wrought by war, economic vicissitudes, and political upheavals meant that the essence of officer-class thought and self-perception changed but little.[1] The examinations to follow of military literature make it clear that attitudes toward politics and society, security and development, and the assumption of a social role or civilizing mission were more constant than variable. They evoked the past as much as they responded to the present. Perhaps the Habsburg, Hohenzollern, and Romanov eagles had fallen, but the hawks lived on; Lyautey retired, but De Gaulle was just beginning his career.

The end of dynasties—and dynastic and diplomatic wars—did change Europe. The fall of the Romanovs ushered in the Russian Revolution, the political fruition of Marxism engineered by Lenin from the outside and by his minions from within. The breakup of the Habsburg Empire created an unstable central and southeastern Europe in mixed republican and monarchic form. Germany's defeat and the Kaiser's abdication were followed by the establishment of the Weimar constitutional regime, in which coalitions of parties and the chancellors beholden to them rose and fell before a dismayed populace and the prestigious figurehead, President Hindenburg.

Two decades later, Europe became a battlefield again. East of the Rhine, liberal parliamentary political forces proved brittle and ineffective everywhere but in Czechoslovakia. Corporatism, in its political guise referred to as fascism (after the Italian party), dominated in Italy and in Germany (not to mention Iberia) and was a force to be reckoned with elsewhere. Further to the east, Soviet Russia stabilized internally under Joseph Stalin and began to build up its army. Communism challenged fascism in much of Europe, where partisans of one or the other did not already hold power.

Between them the democratic parties struggled on. By 1939 only France on the continent (aside from Switzerland) could be considered a stable, functional democracy. In France, Communists and Fascists (Action Française) clashed with each other and attacked the Republic. The rupture of European institutional stability (such as it was) between 1914 and 1918, followed by the impositions of Versailles, had created a situation throughout Europe in which tradition was challenged wherever continuity was lacking and in which the professional military found itself again politicized, infiltrated, and manipulated. Oaths of allegiance notwithstanding, French officers were not unanimously well-disposed toward the Republic. They never had been. In the 1920s, many of them who wrote continued to describe democracy as chaotic, politics as corrupt, capitalism as base, and youth as materialistic, individualistic, and undisciplined. By the mid-1930s, the tone had not changed but had hardened and become more complex, for French officers faced a dilemma with foreign and domestic ramifications.

Clearly their arch enemy was Germany. Clearly Chancellor Hitler was doing all in his power to reconstruct the army and reshape the officer corps in a National Socialist image. That image, while disgusting to the French, represented a style of corporatism, a disciplined, hierarchical, nationalistic movement, that appealed to the anti-capitalist, anti-individualist, anti-egalitarian views of hard-line officers. Action Française, the *Croix de Feu,* and the *Cagoulle*—the French Fascists and the military cabals—made inroads into the corps: witness the ideological appeal of Marshal Pétain's Vichy government after the fall of France in June 1940. But fascism linked Frenchmen to Germans, and that was abhorrent to the majority.

France allied herself diplomatically and militarily with the Soviet Union; this was a traditional tie, with Germany ever the common foe. But the Soviet Union was an atheistic, materialistic state. The French officer corps viewed communism, almost any form of socialism, as the diametric opposite of military professionalism. Communists were blamed for rebellions in the Republic's colonial empire. French views of communism were long-standing and were shared by their German counterparts, but this did not draw them together. Instead, the French military men continued to consider themselves isolated from the rest of society and the polity that surrounded them, cut off ideologically and professionally from foreign "fellow professionals."

Despite the fact that the Third Reich allied itself with the Soviet Union in 1939, there was no doubt that Germany considered Russia a foe or that Nazis considered Communists an omnipresent danger. Since the 1920s, with the army as witness, whipping boy, and battleground, Nazis and Communists—Social Democrats, Spartacists, specific titles were of secondary importance—had contested for influence. Hitler's elevation to the chancellorship in 1933, and his assumption of presidential powers in 1934, just nineteen months later, then his blatant violations of treaty after treaty in asserting Germany's rights and "fulfilling her destiny," doomed both German democracy and communism for the Reich's duration.

The German army found itself nationalized yet controlled, privileged yet politically infiltrated, only one of several elite, militarized organizations.

With all this, the essence of traditional military professionalism was still discernible. Officers still wrote on the themes their pre-1914 predecessors had emphasized. The literature of French and Germans was comparable with regard to attitudes toward state, nation, and society throughout the 1919–39 era. Despite the external differences—the collapse of monarchy in Germany, the glaring structural weaknesses of the Weimar regime and the Republican's intense political activity, the subterfugal methods to keep the army functional made necessary by Versailles, the rise of the National Socialist German Worker's party and its cadre of psychopathic leaders—the German officer corps retained its heritage. Its members, especially those in senior positions, still found politics disruptive, factionalism destructive, and democracy dangerous. They remained convinced that military service made better citizens, that state and army should be bound together. They still considered themselves above the rest of society.

French officers did not have to deal with dramatic changes of regime in the interwar years; the Third Republic prevailed, strengthened perhaps by the experience of war. Precisely as Germans witnessed the torrent of Republican politics for the first time the French merely continued to find the Republic disorganized, inconsistent, and ungrateful. They grew more alarmed year by year at what they considered to be Great Britain's and America's "Anglo-Saxon hegemony." The British and their trans-Atlantic cousins were dominating French culture, they believed. They feared the pollution of Gallic culture by alien elements from across *La Manche* and from the Western Hemisphere. Nationalism, whether that of Seeckt from his desk at the *Truppenamt* or that expressed from the speaker's podium at the École Supérieure by Pétain's protégé, Charles de Gaulle, was more than ever an important theme of military literature. Franco-German enmity did nothing to reduce nationalism in the officer corps; it exacerbated it. It drove military men inward, made them regroup and seek solace within the corps, for they still saw society through jaundiced eyes. If French and Germans had been asked during the inter-war years to write in a third language on the theme "What the army means to state, nation, and society," their responses would, in the main, have been interchangeable.

This was true for Argentines, Brazilians, Chileans, and Peruvians. The similarities in views indicated in the pre-World War years did not evaporate between 1914 and 1918. The "Radical Era," the Old Republic, the Parliamentary Republic, and the awakening of Peruvians to find foreigners eager to invest, manage, and dominate—these all continued. By the time Marcelo T. Alvear broke with Yrigoyen and drew together the "Anti-Personalist" Radicals, Argentine officers were convinced that politics had invaded and infected the army. Some benefited through political connections, some did not. José F. Uriburu, even from retirement, continued criticizing, and scheming against Radicals and his uniformed nemesis, General Agustín Justo, the Anti-Personalist favorite.[2] By the end of the 1920s, the absence of Germans in official capacities had not dimmed the luster of Argentine *germanófilos*, and Uriburu was recognized as the leader of an authoritarian-nationalist wing of the army officer corps with ties to civilian nationalists and proto-fascists.

To the north, Brazilian *germanófilos* were forced to "bite their own bullets" when a French mission led by the prestigious General Maurice Gamelin came to Brazil in 1919. French officers stayed in Brazil until 1940, but not without difficulties. There was opposition to their presence from both the officer corps and political circles. Junior officers, most of whom had been denied advanced training owing to the failure of Brazil to obtain a formal German mission prior to the war, flocked to the French. The pre-war junior officers, now in middle and high ranks, reminisced and, having passed the stage where they could profit by specialized training, resisted the wholesale renovation of their army by Frenchmen. Meanwhile the Old Republic foundered through the "Dance of the Millions" and escaped serious danger when, in the mid-twenties, nationalist junior and senior officers, collectively known as *tenentes*, revolted, then attempted to arouse the interior against the government.[3] The revolt of the *tenentes* failed, but it spawned *tenentismo*, a broadly-defined program of economic nationalism, effective national government, and social reform, much of which was based on the blending of French military professionalism and colonial military theory with Brazilian reality.[4]

Like their Argentine and Brazilian neighbors to the east, Chileans no longer enjoyed the prestige of being associated with Europe's military titan. Nevertheless, the old ways did not cease to obtain; the lessons of the past were useful in confronting the present. Denied their German link and embarrassed by conspiracies in 1919 and a politically-motivated mobilization in 1920, proud Chileans watched as the political process sputtered to a stop during the administration of Arturo Alessandri Palma (1920–24, 1925).[5] Alessandri was the first non-aristocrat to wear the presidential sash; the first since Balmaceda to combine (however vaguely) strong executive leadership with a social and economic reform program. No extremist in all this, he committed the unpardonable sin in Chilean political circles of appealing to the lower classes and to the armed forces for support to gain a favorable parliamentary majority in 1924, and then tried to push programs through congress when his followers and the opposition proved recalcitrant. In 1924 Chilean officers pronounced in the first "problem-oriented" military movement of the century in Latin America.[6] The 1924 movement, a 1925 putsch, and the 1927–31 administration of General Ibáñez constitute the earliest example of professional militarism on the South American continent.

Peruvian officers of the 1920s were privileged in comparison to their Argentine and Chilean counterparts in that they were allowed to reestablish their European link.[7] No provision of the Versailles accords banned French military missions. As soon as the war was over, the French were back in Chorrillos; even Paul Clément returned, thus providing additional continuity. Maintenance of continuity in doctrine and training methods did not mean there were no problems in Franco-Peruvian military relations or in Peruvian military-civilian relationships. Augusto B. Leguía's *oncenio* proved an awakening experience for military professionals, for Leguía, despite his assurances that the army was inviolable, did everything he could to manipulate and control it. Peruvian military anti-politics can be traced to the 1920s, when even the staunchest professional officers were entrapped in politics by Leguía and his foes. The politico-military careers of Ernesto Montagne Markholtz, Luis María Sánchez Cerro, and Oscar Benavides compare somewhat with those of the Chileans Bartolomé Blanche, Marmaduke Grove Vallejo, and Carlos Ibáñez, the Argentines José F. Uriburu and Agustín Justo, and the Brazilians Bertholdo Klinger and Luis Carlos Prestes.

These men, *la flor y la nata*, intellectually and professionally, found politics very much a part of their career. Some preferred it that way, others did not. By the time Leguía was driven from power in 1930 he had meddled with the officer corps in every conceivable way, even appointing a former German staff officer inspector general for a brief time and recurrently threatening to break the French grip (i.e., the grip of the past) on Peru's army by bringing in a U.S. mission. Leguía's actions constitute the first serious thought of attracting North Americans to the parade grounds and military classrooms of South America, the first instance of a South American country considering the United States as a source of military (as opposed to naval) influence.

It was in the 1920s, then, that South America's incipient professional army officer corps confronted first-hand the world of politics and, in the case of Chile, the responsibility of overseeing governmental affairs. These confrontations did not cease, rather they continue to this day in altered form, still heavily influenced by decades-old professional military ideals and values.

The Radical Era in Argentina, the Old Republic in Brazil, the Chilean Parliamentary Republic, and the Peruvian *oncenio* bear some resemblance, as much as do the professionalization programs of the four armies. The political troubles of the post-war decade were all manifestations of the partial change wrought by the first stages of modernization, of politics based on recognition of socioeconomic inequality and regional conflict, of urbanization, economic vicissitudes, and challenges to the monopoly of government by socially—not necessarily temperamentally or culturally—non-aristocratic forces.

Along the Pacific Coast, Alessandri and Leguía mutually represented former political "outs" or elements nominally within the ruling class that yearned for power the way some of the original Radicals had in the past century. Alessandri's and Leguía's use of executive power, their demeanor and their arrogance, upset friend and foe alike in the same way Hipólito Yrigoyen baffled Argentines. Brusqueness, arbitrariness, at times bungling and corruption (if not personally in the cases of Yrigoyen and Alessandri), characterized politics.

It was all right for the *unicato* to function in Argentina as long as it did so in the name of the Córdoba clique, but, when Yrigoyen used and abused executive prerogatives, Argentine oligarchs objected strongly; his own party split asunder because of his high-handed methods.[8] Similarly, as long as Civilistas could benefit from the executive-oriented Peruvian system, they complained rarely, but Leguía served other constituents as well. His opening of Peru to the United States caused great concern, especially among middle-sector and business interests undercut by large foreign concerns. So did his manipulation of army, church, bureaucracy, and treasury. So did nepotism.[9] Chilean Conservatives and Liberals did not fear Alessandri's 1920 campaign platform; they did fear and resent his use and abuse of presidential powers heretofore circumscribed by gentlemen's agreements or constitutional interpretations made decades before. When Mineiros finally figured out the Paulistas sought to dominate Brazilian politics with or without their cooperation, they found fault with a political system they had helped to create and support since the 1890s.[10] The continued rise of São Paulo, far beyond the status of *primus inter pares* after World War I, and Paulista manipulation of power, especially during the presidency of Washington Luis Perieira de Souza, finally convinced enough state machines to support a movement against São Paulo, the Old Republic, and the idea of Brazil as a confederation.

The 1920s were dynamic years in South America. If some aspects of life changed little or superficially, the faces and economies of cities, and demographic distribution, diminished the ability of Argentina, Brazil, Chile, and Peru to withstand exogenous economic and ideological pressures. There is a correlation between the increasing involvement of South American economies in the world economy and their increasing susceptibility to fluctuations in commodity prices, foreign exchanges, and trade balances.[11] Progress, in short, was only relative; it victimized as much as it developed or modernized South America.

Some statistics—keyed to specific and appropriate national situations—indicate problems that figure in inter-war military-civilian relations.[12] In 1890, 37 percent of Argentines lived in urban areas, and 53 percent were urban dwellers by 1914. In the two European countries stressed in these pages there were comparable demographic shifts to urban centers, especially to large cities, certainly as dramatic and politically consequential as those in South America. France's slow-growing population was two-thirds rural in 1871, and was not 50 percent urbanized (i.e., living in towns over 2,000) until 1931, when France had 41 million citizens. The largest cities grew most rapidly. In Germany the larger cities also grew more rapidly than towns, and by 1914 50 percent of Germany's 45 million citizens lived in urban areas of over 5,000. Forty years earlier, only a quarter of Germany's population had qualified as urban.

During most of this period the urban literacy rate in Argentina was consistently 80 percent. Therefore Argentina showed a steady increase in the raw number of literate urban dwellers—most of whom were poorly paid, exploited, politicized, and only barely represented by the Radicals.These Argentines mainly fell under the influence of anti-political and anti-democratic schemes and their proponents. Despite the fact that immigration in the 1920s was nowhere near what it was in pre-war years (peaks of 200,000 per annum in 1890, 1905, 1910–12), post-war immigrants still clustered in Buenos Aires, adding to the European tone of urban society. As urbanized as Argentina's society was, it was not a true industrialized society. Between 1920 and 1940, agricultural and livestock profits consistently totaled between 94 and 95 percent of Argentina's exports. This meant that society and economy, if examined apart, represented two Argentinas. Nationalist army officers found this unacceptable.

The growth disparity between São Paulo and the other Brazilian states became more exaggerated between 1920 and 1940. Just after World War I, 31.5 percent of national industrial economic output came from São Paulo; in 1940, Paulista manufacturers turned out 43.5 percent of the industrial product. Rio Grande do Sul's share declined during this period from 11 to 9.8 percent; Minas Gerais's share increased slightly from 5.5 to 6.7 percent. São Paulo's political decline, as seen in the demise of the Old Republic, simply did not indicate an economic shift like that which accompanied the fall of the Empire in 1889. Indeed, Paulista industry (along with Brazilian industry in general) fared much better from 1930 onward. The population of Brazil grew by one-half between 1920 and 1940, from roughly 30 million to 45 million. About a third were literate. During the inter-war years a third of the population clustered in São Paulo, Rio de Janeiro, and Espíritu Santo.

The city of São Paulo was still not as big as Rio after World War I, but it soon would be. In 1920 São Paulo was the country's second-largest city; its 580,000 citizens amounted to twice the total of the next two largest cities, Salvador and Recife. The disparity grew greater by 1940. Giant Brazil was, to put it lightly, a victim of uneven population distribution. Until 1930, and despite the dynamic growth of São Paulo city, a rural-based political machine continued to control both state and city politics. Brazil was an anachronistic country, an unsynchronized polity, economy, and society within her national boundaries. This did not go unnoticed by army officers eager to reduce everything to statistics in the name of national defense and security.

Urbanization was significant in Chile as well. Between 1920 and 1940 the urban population (towns over 2,000) increased from 28 percent to 35 percent, and half of all Chileans lived in towns over 10,000 in size. As late as 1930, 50 percent of these were illiterate. Population growth was not as pronounced as it was in urbanized Argentina. Chile's population increased from 3,785,000 in 1920 to 5,063,000 in 1940. Copper production rose annually between the wars, with a hiatus between 1930 and 1934. Government services, begun for the most part in the 1920s, steadily expanded. Many indicators made Chile look healthy economically, but on closer examination they show that the Santiago-Valparaíso complex grew disproportionately to the rest of the country. Fully 25 percent of Chileans lived there from 1930 onward. Thus Chile experienced uneven demographic change. Of the four countries under consideration, however, Chile does represent the closest thing to a case of coordinated socio-economic development and political adjustment between 1920 and 1940. Nevertheless, it was in both the cities and the towns where the Marxist left made its strongest showing in elections and where army officers awakened to Marxist designs on the political system.

The population of Lima doubled, and then some, between 1920 and 1940; from 233,807 to 562,000. Of Peru's total 1940 population of 6,207,967, less than 10 percent lived in the major urban center, just over 10 percent if Lima and Callao are lumped together. Peru can be compared more profitably with Brazil than with either Argentina or Chile in this respect. In only four departments (provinces) did urban dwellers constitute over 50 percent of the population: 99 percent in Callao (little more than an urban zone, after all); 76 percent in Lima, the capital; 59 percent in Arequipa, to the south; and 15 percent in Lambayeque, to the north. Demographically (and culturally) Peru more closely retained the heritage of the past than either Argentina, Brazil, or Chile. The disparity in economic output, literacy, and political awareness between the coast and the sierra showed no decrease between the wars. A post-1920 decrease in defense expenditures as a percentage of the annual budget (cited by one expert as a significant factor in the alienation of the army) was reversed in the 1930s under Sánchez Cerro and Benavides, but actual expenditures in *soles* showed a steady increase.[13] Officers linked their fortunes, both figuratively and literally, to strong government, internal order, and economic growth like that achieved under the good marshal between 1933 and 1939.

Economic expansion, urbanization, and political awakening meant little when the Great Depression struck Latin America. The initial stages of economic collapse caused governments to fall in Argentina, Brazil, Chile, and Peru. In each case the armed forces, led by the army, played a critical role in the unmaking of an administration and the making of a new one. Not since the nineteenth century had the military presence been as great as it was in the depression *golpes de estado.*

Chileans, of course, had been at it actively since the movements of 1924 and 1925. Carlos Ibáñez played a role comparable but not identical to that played earlier by Caxias in Brazil, and contemporaneously by Benavides and Justo, in that by keeping himself involved in politics he was able to prevent full-scale participation by men in uniform. His 1927–31 administration was neither military rule nor dictatorship, but it surely reflected military priorities vis-à-vis the role of government.[14] Similarly, it represented the priorities of a growing segment of the civilian sector: urban, middle-income, desirous of internal order, wary of both rightist and leftist extremes. Military-civilian concurrence obtained only as long as the economy continued to expand. When outside sources of capital dried up, and Finance Minister Pablo Ramírez's *política prestamista* failed to maintain economic growth, previously-allied civilians joined the opposition. Members of the officer corps who chafed at civilian criticism, who did not like Ibáñez and his clique, or who feared leftist agitation would lead to violent conflict let Ibáñez know of their displeasure. He got the message. Confronted with defections from the ranks (but no large-scale mutiny), a middle-sector and labor general strike, and an empty treasury, the general left Chile in the hands of a caretaker administration on July 26, 1931. For the next fifteen months Chile underwent a politically masochistic experience.[15] Military meddling in civilian affairs and civilian interference in military matters were the rules, not the exceptions. After two mid-1932 essays in socialism (providing examples and legislation that would be useful to Salvador Allende Gossens forty years later), enough officers became convinced that no politics was the best policy. Civilians restored the pre-1924 military-civilian balance by electing the man ousted by army officers in 1924 and 1925, Arturo Alessandri.

Between 1932 and 1938 Alessandri held the line against a chastened but resentful military. He supported a civilian militia that to many was little more than a Fascist goon squad. He limited defense expenditures and he sacked officers who showed signs of political interest. He reluctantly passed his responsibilities on to Popular Front candidate Pedro Aguirre Cerda in 1938. Soon after long-time Radical leader Aguirre Cerda took office, an anti-Communist general attempted a putsch, and by the end of the decade the army conviction in regard to Marxism in any form was quite clear. Cold War confrontations merely personalized and renewed the strength of the institutional stance.

Throughout the inter-war period, Chilean officers showed a preference for energetic, coordinated administration of the country; the addressing of social problems from non-partisan approaches designed to maintain social order yet provide for satisfaction of material aspirations; and the development of a modern, self-sustaining economy. Their apparently moderate views, compared, say, to those of Argentines and Peruvians, were the result of governmental action in the 1920s, state responsibilities assigned by the 1925 constitution, and the attending to those responsibilities by Alessandri between 1932 and 1938.[16] Wary of democracy, Chilean officers tolerated it as long as it was not synonymous with egalitarianism and extreme socioeconomic policies. Their literature indicates this vividly.

The fall of Hipólito Yrigoyen in Argentina barely a year before the departure of General Ibáñez was but one of the 1930 movements that brought the officer corps directly into politics. Long-time concern over democracy, extremism, and the failure of government to attack certain problems or "to treat the army properly" finally resulted in political action based at the inception on professional military ideals and values. But 1930 was too early for the inspiration of a long-term political action by professional militarism.[17] In neither Argentina, Brazil, Chile, nor Peru was the officer corps cohesive enough to pose a united threat to disunited parties and factions. It was too early for civilian political systems to be seen as definitely self-destructive or as menacing to the very existence of the military profession.

Uriburu's *golpe* of September 6, 1930, had the support of labor, ranchers, merchants, businessmen, and Argentines involved in foreign trade. This led the general and others to believe they had a mandate to make changes in the political system beyond the one they had made at the top. The usual reasons cited for Yrigoyen's ouster—the onset of economic depression, inflation, unemployment—perhaps overshadowed army anger at the senile Yrigoyen's incompetence, his failure to delegate responsibility, and the malfeasance of Personalist Radicals. Perceptions that the country had reached an economic nadir were, no doubt, widespread, but Argentina had a ways to go (until mid-1933) before the depression bottomed out. By that time Uriburu, terminally ill with cancer, had been forced out of office, and his plans to create an Italian-style corporate state had been quickly forgotten by all but a few civilians and officers. The Anti-Personalist Radical favorite, General Justo, became president.[18] Supported by a coalition of influential army, civilian, and church leaders known as the Concordancia, Justo did his best to reduce labor's influence to a minimum and restore pre-1920 business and foreign trade patterns.

In so doing, Justo was accused of turning back the clock—the same accusation leveled against Alessandri across the cordillera. The two were as comparable as were the polities in which they operated. Those now in control reacted to what they considered political excesses of the previous decade. Again it is the perception that counts. Those in control of Argentina perceived the Yrigoyen administration's labor policy as excessively libertarian (it was not) and detrimental to economic expansion (it was not). They believed modest moves in the direction of economic nationalism had driven foreign capital away (a belief based on lack of understanding of the world economy). So they sought to restore the *unicato* with "the right kind" of man at the top: Justo, then the aristocrat and Anti-Personalist Roberto Ortiz, 1938–42. The Concordancia's neo-*unicato* failed to take one major, recent development into consideration. A number of officers believed firmly that Argentina needed an active policy of economic nationalism in order to survive economic crashes like that which had befallen the country following 1929. Industry, a contented and docile labor force, a better price for agricultural and pastoral exports, an aggressive foreign policy— all these figured in the thinking of what observers call the "integral-nationalist" faction of officers. Some of these men would form the Grupo de Oficiales Unidos (Group of United Officers, GOU) to plot the creation of a military-led corporate state to do for Argentina what military-civilian corporatism had, they thought, done for Germany and Italy.[19] By the end of 1930 the literature of the Argentine officer corps showed an overwhelming interest in industrialization and economic mobilization potential akin to that being touted in Germany and Italy as the direct result of the corporate state.

Brazilian officers, too, showed great interest in the economic development of their country. Brazilian military-civilian relations were not unlike those of the Spanish American republics, indicating that throughout the continent economic nationalism was an important force. It came to fruition among the various officer corps as early as it did in the civilian sector. During the 1920s South American military literature as well as political action emphasized the role of the state in economic development, and continued to emphasize it in the decade to follow.

The *golpe de estado* of 1930 and the subsequent rise of Getúlio Vargas through the provisional presidency, 1930–34, and constitutional presidency, 1934–37, to become supreme head of the Estado Novo, 1938–45, coincided neatly with military aspirations regarding economic capabilities. From the standpoint of military-civilian relations, what happened in Brazil between 1930 and the fall of France ten years later had the overtones of a partial return to the imperium with adjustments made for the passage of time. Vargas and the New

State represented centralized authority (far more than did the imperium,), national sovereignty, and a zealous nationalistic faith in Brazil's present and future.[20] This is not to say that all officers concurred with steps taken by Vargas and his military allies, including generals Gaspar Eurico Dutra, Eduardo Gomes, and Pedro Aurélio de Góis Monteiro.

Nor is it to assert that the officer corps was entirely pleased with governmental (i.e. civilian) dictates as to the source of technical and strategic training. Despite the strong attraction Brazilians felt for their French mentors, there was, dating the early 1930s, a yen for a U.S. mission or individual training personnel. In Brazil, and in Peru as well, a shift of preference from France developed for two distinct reasons: increasing penetration of the domestic economy by U.S. interests, and French insistence on control of armaments purchases. The latter usually meant purchases of surplus, obsolete French material of pre-1914 vintage. There was also a leaning toward the United States as a counterpoise to the French, owing to rising U.S. naval influence in hemispheric waters.

If only outwardly, the Brazilian army enjoyed harmonious relations with its government and approved its government's economic programs during the 1930s. In marked contrast to its actions in the previous decade, the central government took action—at the expense of the state administrations, party organizations, and extremist groups, particularly those of the left. More than a few officers were hostile to the continued influence of the French because of Brazilian pro-German and pro-Fascist sentiments. This provided for some exciting diplomatic episodes, some of which solidly confirm recent assertions about Brazil's manipulative powers over the United States at a time when the United States was presumed capable of exerting hegemony.[21]

By the end of 1939 the shift toward the United States was definitive, and when German armies marched into Paris on June 13, 1940, a U.S.-Brazilian military tie was a strategic and tactical foregone conclusion. Though by no means devoid of sociopolitical content, Brazilian military literature emphasized economic development, preparedness, and the like. As in Argentina under Justo, there was enough military-civilian concurrence to preclude much literature dangerously critical of polity and economic policy or works proposing alternative solutions for social problems. In certain respects, Vargas–New State accomplishments mollified Brazilian officers, as the GOU-Perón accomplishments of 1943–1951 would impress Argentines.

Despite the presence of the Justo-like Benavides, Peruvians continued to harp on the need for social development schemes and a coordinated national mobilization policy. Like their South American counterparts, Peruvians went through the brief period of tension and uncertainty during which civilian parties of military-civilian coalitions struggled for national leadership with army cabals.

Oscar Benavides succeeded the mercurial Sánchez Cerro and restored to power the Civilista and Anti-Leguía forces of the past.[22] Between his second assumption of power of 1933 and the carefully arranged election of Manuel Prado y Ugarteche in 1939, Benavides governed with extraordinary powers and consummate skill. His historical image, when subjected to objective scrutiny, will doubtless indicate he was far more sagacious and genuinely concerned with national development than thought heretofore.

Yet it was during the Benavides administration that a clearly defined, almost "patented" military ideology crystallized in Peru. In formation since the arrival of the French, this ideology was more attributable to foreign influences than were the ideologies of Brazilians, Argentines, or Chileans attributable to their European mentors. Brazil-like squabbling over armaments contracts notwithstanding, the French emphasis on hostility to political factionalism, politicians, "unbridled capitalism" (whatever that was), and ideological extremes held fast in Peru. This was because of an early rise (1924 forward) of an indigenous extremist movement in Peru, the Alianza Popular Revolucionaria Americana (APRA), by contemporary standards considered a danger to all that was sacred to the army and propertied classes alike.[23]

If confronted with a list of general solutions for Peru's most pressing problems submitted by APRA and with another submitted by the Peruvian general staff, one would find much in common at any given time after 1930. But there have been great differences of opinion regarding the means of achieving comparable ends.[24] In the 1930s, APRA appeared to a majority of the officer corps to be an extreme-left organization, and an enemy to army military discipline to boot. The Aprista uprising and the execution of officers in Trujillo in 1932,[25] resulting in brutal army reprisals, and the assassination of Sánchez Cerro by an Aprista in 1933, followed by repeated attempts to subvert discipline in the barracks, set the two forces against each other so firmly that to this day one can easily evoke a visceral reaction from militants of each side. Much of recent Peruvian political history can be written in terms of a contest for power and brief tenuous alliances between professional militarists and APRA.

Reacting to the menace of Aprismo (illegal and persecuted under Benavides), Peruvian military literature of the 1930s evinced a solid conviction that the army had a peacetime social role—*la misión civilizadora*—to carry out. Benavides continually affirmed this and devoted energies of the state to material modernization projects, most visible in the Lima-Callao metropolitan area, Arequipa, Trujillo, Chiclayo, and Cuzco. Moreover he kept the Apristas at bay quite forcefully. This did little to convince officers they would never have anything to fear, but it kept them in Benavides's camp. Material modernization, authoritarian rule, and a placatory military policy kept the army at bay while serving to confirm the belief of military authors in military political action in the service of the fatherland.

Throughout these years the French, in gradually reduced numbers, held on to their mission in Peru. Not until the fall of France and the erection of the Vichy regime would they depart. Some joined the Free French organization of Charles de Gaulle in London, others went home to France. By the time they did so, Peru had a civilian government once again.

Similarities among France's and Germany's client states abound in the twenties and thirties. These were reflected in military-civilian relations, relations that, along with tradition and European orientation, shaped military professionalism and turned it into professional militarism. At each and every stage the values and ideals, thought and self-perception of the officer corps of France and Germany and of Argentina, Brazil, Chile, and Peru are convincingly similar. In some instances the comparisons are sharply defined.

In both the Old World and the New, political contests were characterized by a struggle between the forces of authority or "limited democracy" (usually defended in terms of "the good old days, and how to return to them") and those of either libertarian democracy and egalitarianism or of the far left (normally defended by promises of "a bright future through reform and revolution"). Marxism terrified officers; fascism, while not altogether attractive, was far more preferable. Officers, Fascists, and authoritarians who yearned for the good old days, then, had much in common.

To be sure, there were differences galore between the Marxists of Europe and America, between Spartacists and the *Partie Communiste*, Socialists and Communists; between the indigenous movements like APRA, Radicalism, *tenentismo*, and *Ibañismo*; and between corporatist movements like the Nazis and Action Française, Argentine integral nationalists," Brazilian Integralistas, Chilean Nazis, and the Peruvian Unión Patriótica. But they all polarized politics in a similar fashion. To officers of these years it appeared that "the factions" were responsible for the disruption of order and always had been. Similarly, South American officers viewed extremists as anti-nationalistic, as had their European mentors of pre-war decades. Some South American officers were concerned that foreign economic interests, if left uncontrolled or unsupervised by the government, would work against the best interests of the state in peacetime as well as in the event of war. Even the most superficial aspects of change worried officers, attuned as they were to routine and tradition. Long-standing hostility to civilian democracy made of them authoritarians by default. Their professional attributes bound them to defend order and stability. Their endlessly-professed devotion (at times in the form of lip service) to abstractions of discipline, honor, patriotism, abnegation, hierarchy, and non-material pursuits, already had made them anachronistic in an age of flux.

Between the world wars the United States became increasingly involved in Latin American affairs. Seen by some South Americans as a threat to their cultural integrity, by others as an expansionist economic power, the United States had been quite active in the circum-Caribbean area prior to 1914.[26] The Washington government maintained diplomatic ties with all South American republics, of course, and especially with Brazil. Despite the warnings of attachés like Constant Cordier, there was little interest in anything but commercial relations with South America. Isolationism, failure of ratification of the Versailles accords, refusal to join the League of Nations, and arms limitations policies held the administrations of the 1920s from any move to relace Germany and France as military models. There is evidence of minimal interest in sending military missions to Brazil to complement the naval mission there, to Peru (where the United States would also send a small naval mission) and to far-off Chile. A few individuals did serve in South America as advisors and aviation instructors. On occasion, South American politicians made overtures to the United States, as Leguía would do, but only for political reasons. (Leguía, of course, did it thrice, hoping to gain more influence in the officer corps by getting rid of the influential, if controversial, French, whom he considered agents of the Civilistas.) Not until late in the 1930s, however, was there anything resembling a consensus that missions from the United States would be of long-term benefit to Argentines and Brazilians, Chileans and Peruvians. A U.S. naval mission had little political impact in Brazil.

Owing to this, there was no cordial relationship between U.S. and South American military establishments during most of the pre–World War II era. The occasional advisor and instructor simply could not exert the influence that a mission did. The visit of Chief of Staff George C. Marshall in 1938 made quite a splash in Rio de Janeiro because Vargas and his canny foreign minister, Oswaldo Aranha, wanted it to. Eight years earlier the unofficial visit of Chilean General Francisco Javier Díaz to the United States was a disaster that nearly ruined relations between the countries.[27] The first timid steps taken by the United States on South American terrain caused as much furor as they helped to open new areas of activity, for the Americans were not sufficiently aware of power rivalries to enable them to take advantage of the situation to expand U.S. military influence.

Late in the 1930s, Brazil and Peru showed some serious, professional interest in contracting U.S. air missions (and in the case of Peru, some navy instructors). When the War and State Departments began to treat these inquiries seriously, there were protests from the Argentine and Chilean embassies and the foreign ministries in Santiago and Buenos Aires. Pan Americanism and hemispheric defense made little headway in the *cono sur* until late in World War II. U.S. arguments that one military mentor serving all interested parties would assure parity and foster the decline of conflict potential made little sense to either fervently nationalistic Argentines or tenaciously Germanophile Chileans.

There is reason to believe that struggles went on within the officer corps in Peru and Brazil during the 1930s—struggles between die-hard *afrancesados* and those who wanted U.S. missions. These struggles were reminiscent of those waged between senior officers and the *jóvenes turcos* or *jovens turcos* prior to World War I and between the Brazilian *germanófilos* and *afrancesados* following the war. Generations of officers identified with the army whose officers had trained them when it came to international affairs and loyalties. Through World War II and later, there were still die-hard *germanófilos* in Buenos Aires and Santiago. In Brazil the situation was even more complicated by the fact that the New State smacked so of Italian fascism, and the German embassy did such a good propaganda job that a group of influential senior officers was openly pro-Axis until 1940. This meant that there was a three-way struggle for influence going on within the corps, involving cliques favoring France, Germany, and the United States. The situation was neither so complex nor so pronounced in Peru. There the French went unchallenged (as opposed to going uncriticized) until the fall of Paris.

Thus the arrival of the Yankees on the South American military scene hardly provoked hearty, enthusiastic welcomes.

The United States's lack of a European-style military tradition convinced many South Americans that the Yankees did not make good soldiers. After all, the United States had entered the war only in 1917; South American writers gave little credit to the United States for the defeat of the Central Powers. The end of France's and Germany's grip on training, education, and armaments supply would not be achieved fully until well into World War II, and then only in relative terms. As of 1940 the U.S. army had not yet proved itself worthy in the eyes of South American officers of association with the armies of Argentina, Brazil, Chile, and Peru.

U.S. willingness and ability to work with South American military establishments came about for two principal reasons. First, the United States had emerged from World War I a creditor nation with an expanding economy, expanding markets, and convenient sources of finished goods. There was also a surplus of armaments and equipment to sell. The Great Depression set the U.S. economy back, but recovery in the form of markets and sources restored developing trade patterns with Brazil, Chile, and Peru, and motivated interest in improved relations with Argentina. The sword followed the ledger to South America following World War I, whereas the reverse had been the case before 1914. Second, neither France nor Germany was able to maintain close ties from 1939 onward. Germany's ties were by this time tenuous, ideological, and based on propaganda anyway. French ties had loosened greatly during the 1930s. In a sense, the United States usurped the Europeans' role, but could not hope to end the European military tradition.[28] South American motives for collaboration with the United States were not identical to those of the United States. North and South American motives were at best those of expediency.

Through all this, European military professionalism did not diminish, it actually gained strength. The apparent changes occurring in the sociopolitical matrix of which the army was a part convinced officers that there was little chance of closing the distance between civilian liberal democratic theory and practice. European and South American military concepts of democracy, developed during or before the first phase of professionalization, contradicted civilian democratic norms of the inter-war years. Equality, objectivity, opportunity, discipline, obedience, freedom, authority, order—all these had specific meanings to officers, but civilians defined them as they wished, for the moment. Continuity, consistency, efficiency—these were lacking in politics, thought many European and South American officers.

Society was in trouble too. An old order, idealized to the point of absurdity in military circles, had vanished, swept away by the Great War. The materialistic, individualistic bourgeoisie had triumphed. Before the war the world had been a better place, they thought, ignoring what they themselves had written from the 1890s forward. The young were still undisciplined, unpatriotic, superficial, and insufficiently imbued with respect for authority; the bourgeoisie was still to blame for economic troubles, the high cost of living, and the decline of cultural levels. Army officers in Europe and South America continued to complain about low pay and lack of appreciation for their devotion to duty.

Nationalism, the veneration of the state (in its objective, impartial, yet activist sense), strengthened between the wars. No League of Nations, no arms limitations treaties (especially when championed by non-member United States), convinced South Americans that war had ceased to be a danger. Between 1932 and 1936 Ecuador, Colombia, Bolivia, Paraguay, and Peru were involved in war. Chileans shot at each other during the "100 days of socialism" in 1932. Argentines and Brazilians watched each other in all sectors of the Paraná–La Plata basin. To many Brazilians and Peruvians the French had won the war and U.S. participation had been incidental; the war had been fought on French and German soil, not in the British Isles or in the United States. To Argentines and Chileans it went without saying that leftist extremism had undermined the greatest army the world had ever known, and only with the aid of the "British shopkeepers and their North American cousins" had France been able to defeat the Kaiser's finest.

Experiments with democracy in South America—the Radical administrations in Argentina, the Alessandri administration of the early 1920s, the Old Republic in Brazil—did not satisfy army officers. The authoritarianism of the civilian Leguía did not satisfy the Peruvians. In each case there was constant meddling with the internal workings of the army. Post-World War I administrations reflected the pacifism and anti-militarism of the age. Extremist groups were allowed to grow and feed on the discontent of the ignorant, the untrained, and the unincorporated members of society. Army officers definitely favored authoritarianism, but only if civilian leaders behaved according to military norms, provided the army with what it needed to defend the fatherland from all its enemies and refrained from meddling with intra-service matters.

Officer-corps thought, self-perception, ideals, and values of the inter-war years were interchangeable with those of the 1890–1914 era. Specific issues changed according to the times, and there was a new exogenous influence to contend with, but military professionalism remained much the same as it had been before the war. The lore of the profession set it apart from society, but peacetime duties of officers made them ever conscious of their role in that society. This uncomfortable dilemma affected the second-stage metamorphosis of military professionalism into professional militarism in South America. By 1940 the ideological contours of the post-war years, of the Cold War and beyond, had taken shape in Argentina, Brazil, Chile, and Peru.

"Before the establishment of the French mission the army was ignorant of its duty and national role, and even among its leaders patriotism did nothing more than conceal a profound ignorance of military science. Now everything has changed, and health and order reign in the barracks."

Francisco García Calderón, *Le Perou contemporain: Étude social* (1907)

"The army officers are strongly nationalistic. They have a tendency to think…in terms of [what is] best for the army; they look upon foreign powers as potential dangers…and fear domination by Anglo-American interests as much as, if not more than, domination by the Axis powers."

OSS Research and Analysis Report #154, "The Attitude of Brazil toward the Establishment of Naval and Air Bases by the United States" (1941)

CHAPTER SIX

Missions & Missionaries: Professionalism in a New Setting

■

As soon as possible after the conclusion of the war and the peace negotiations that ensued, the French returned to Peru. The French government also agreed to send a mission to Brazil. By the end of 1920 there were more French officers in Brazil and Peru than had served in Peru during the entire 1896–1914 period. Ten years later the number of French officers in South America had decreased markedly, and by the time Germany invaded Poland in 1939 there were but a handful. While the number of French officers decreased during the 1930s, there was a perceptible increase in the small number of German officers serving in Argentina, Bolivia, Chile, and Colombia. A few Germans served in Peru and Brazil as well during the inter-war years. Despite the fact that the Versailles Treaty barred Germany from maintaining a large army and a general staff, or from sending missions abroad, Germans did continue to serve in South America. They did so under the guise of host-country citizenship or as citizens of Danzig. After 1933, Germans flaunted their own citizenship and cast off their oath of loyalty to the Free City.

European training thus continued in schools and academies of the major military powers of South America. At one time or another, in fact, there were Frenchmen, Germans, Italians, Spaniards, Swiss, and assorted Central Europeans serving in each of the South American republics. Not until war again appeared inevitable did the U.S. government formulate a military cooperation policy; that policy eventually substituted the United States, at least superficially, for France and Germany as military model in the four countries. It is with the post-1918 emergence of the United States as a hemispheric and world power that Washington's considerations of European military influence appear to concern anything more than the commercial significance. Because of the slow development of U.S. interest, it becomes useful here to take heed of political and diplomatic developments from chronological, continental, and hemispheric perspectives in order to ascertain just what military professionalism was becoming in Argentina, Brazil, Chile, and Peru. Frequent policy shifts and the fact that each of the South American powers underwent changes in regimes during 1930 and 1931 comparable to those of 1889–91 render this approach particularly revealing.

The United States did not maintain appropriate military contacts with Argentina during the 1920s, and therefore neither specialists in the Department of State nor those in the War Department (with few exceptions) grasped what was going on between military professionals and politicians or between factions led by Generals Justo and Uriburu. Not until the 1930s would anyone in Washington seriously consider the army as a political interest group, possessed of its own identity and ideology. Policy-makers in this country were barely aware that the army resented being placed in charge of internal order during the difficult economic times just after the war. This was nothing more than a natural reaction akin to that of Brazilian officers who bridled at being sent out in search of escaped slaves or resented having to slog their way to Canudos in the early days of the Republic. It was clear to U.S. observers that most army officers favored Marcelo Alvear's pro-military policies to Hipólito Yrigoyan's incessant meddling in army internal affairs, for if Alvear interfered, he also placated.

More vivid was the Argentine-Brazilian power rivalry and its implications for military and foreign policy and for military-civilian relations. The presence of a U.S. naval mission in Brazil from 1919 forward did nothing to endear the diffident Argentines to the United States. Argentine officers remained Germanophiles, and gradually a few veterans of the Kaiser's army filtered into Buenos Aires during the 1920s.

From 1917 on there was controversy within the Brazilian army officer corps over the negotiations for a training cadre from France. When the contract was signed and approved in 1919, and Brazil welcomed its first full-fledged military mission, there was a division of opinion. The results of the war had changed most minds, but not all. The Brazilian Germanophiles—now majors, lieutenant colonels, and colonels—were disappointed that Germany had lost. Like their own superiors a decade and a half before, they saw little need for foreign penetration of the corps. For essentially the same reasons a decade after the war, Francophiles themselves would agitate for an end to active French influence, insisting they were prepared now to supervise all aspects of military training and education.

One of the galling aspects of the French mission contracts in both Brazil and Peru—an aspect of which both South American governments were aware when missions contracts were initially approved—was that of French control over armaments and material supply procedures. In both Brazil and Peru there was continual sniping at the French and their heavy-handed methods. It was this antipathy, not a rejection of French military professionalism, that caused some officers to turn to the United States as alternative supplier, trainer, and role model for their army.

In Peru there was also the problem of Leguía. He threatened repeatedly to cancel the mission or exercise Peru's option not to renew the contract. Because the French mission arrangement predated him, Leguía saw the French as allied with the Civilistas, and a threat to him. For this reason he would go so far as to import General Wilhelm Faupel from Argentina (to where he had emigrated after the war) and make him inspector general. This, he thought, would assure him of officer-corps loyalty by blocking the access of Francophiles to overall command. Faupel made little impress on the Peruvian officer corps during his short tenure, and French influence remained dominant throughout the period. By 1925, when General Gabriel Velarde Álvarez, the lieutenant colonel who coined the phrase "misión civilizadora" in 1904, became chief of staff, there were more than a few officers who thought the French had served their purpose.[1] The Catholic press urged the government to turn over supervision of Peruvian military affairs to good Peruvians. As in Brazil, then, the French ran into controversy as soon as enough of their pupils considered themselves fit to take over. What more natural result of the French insistence on Lyautey's "the right man in the right place." Brazilian and Peruvian officer-class tyros were in this sense a credit to their mentors. But throughout it all the French hung on.

Further south, the Chileans continued as disciples of Germany, well and good, but of pre-World War I Germany. Despite inroads made by French military doctrine emanating from the successful prosecution of World War I, Chileans were embarassingly steadfast in clinging to the past. Like the Argentines before them, Chileans took military matters into their own hands—they did not have much of a choice. Like the Brazilians and Argentines, they opened their military school to foreigners.[2] Carlos Ibáñez's foreign minister went so far as to offer scholarships to cadets of all Latin American countries in a short-lived attempt to make Chile a new Prussia in military circles, and General Hans von Kiesling, one of Goltz's most fervent disciples, briefly served with the Chilean army during the 1920s, but there were plenty of Chilean Germanophiles to keep the faith throughout the 1920s.[3]

Until the time of the Great Depression the South Americans still looked toward Europe for inspiration. At the time the United States became involved in "policing" the circum-Caribbean there existed both a staunch U.S. resistance to any idea of sending missions to South America and a convincing lack of interest on the part of most South American military leaders. The following examples suffice to verify U.S. resistance to military missionary activities south of the Caribbean.

In the case of Brazil the United States might have gained military influence at the end of World War I. Diplomatic correspondence of 1918 made it clear that Brazil's plans to attract students from other Latin American countries to her military and naval schools fell on deaf ears in Washington.[4] No attempt was made to involve the United States in the Brazilian venture or to assist in the training projects Brazilians had in mind.

A decade later there existed a consensus among Brazilians that the United States wanted nothing to do with the military training of South Americans. Senator William Henry King (D-Utah) introduced a bill to prohibit the United States from sending missions to Latin America. The isolationist, non-interventionist bill caused *O Jornal do Brasil* to praise both the French and the Americans and to hope the bill would fail.[5] It did not get to the floor of the Senate.

King was not the only isolationist to blast U.S. policy in Latin America. Earlier in the decade Samuel Guy Inman, referred to as a "professional trouble maker," was the subject of a 1923 letter from Henrietta Livermore to Joshua Baxter Wright. Mrs. Livermore, of the State Department's Commission to the Brazilian Centennial Exposition (1922–23), brought it to the department's attention that Inman had done damage to U.S.-Brazilian relations by taking sides in the Atlantic-Platine rivalry. Inman publicly followed the line that Brazil was the belligerent party in Argentine-Brazilian relations. With the aid of the United States she had built up her navy to a point where she could threaten Argentina. This had forced Argentina to build up both her army and her navy to a point where both countries posed a threat to peace in the Southern Hemisphere—to a point where they were spending entirely too much on armaments.[6] The U.S. naval mission and French military missions in Brazil and Peru had ruined chances for success of the Santiago disarmament conference of 1922. Inman, Mrs. Livermore protested, had linked U.S. businessmen, diplomats, naval personnel, and munitions dealers with European counterparts in an unholy alliance to militarize South American and profit by it. Just a year after Mrs. Livermore's letter, the intemperate words and actions of a U.S. admiral serving in Peru caused the State Department to request his censure by the War Department for fear the small mission in Peru would alienate the Chileans.[7] The U.S. naval presence in Brazil and Peru could hardly be termed either auspicious or non-controversial.

Indeed, it appeared that such tentative steps toward armed forces cooperation might be more detrimental than helpful to the United States. Both Argentina and Chile considered the United States to be closer to Brazil and Peru in South American military and diplomatic circles and to be acting against the interests of peace and disarmament. However specious the reasoning on the second point may be, the record of U.S. diplomatic policy in the early twentieth century corroborates the first. Then, when the United States championed the Kellog-Briand accords, Argentines and Chileans used that stand, too, as evidence of a hypocritical attitude toward the continental power balance. Naval missions and peace accords did not mix in Argentine and Chilean minds (nor in the minds of many Brazilians and Peruvians either, if it meant halting naval cooperation).

By the end of the decade the United States fared no better; indeed, it already appeared to be a target of criticism. With regard to officers, the United States could not possibly please all members of any officer corps. Diplomatic entanglements were so complex and military rivalries so intense that even Washington's light touch in naval affairs had been too heavy for "injured parties." But there were, nevertheless, isolated official signals late in the 1920s that some form of U.S.-South American military relations might prove advantageous to the United States. As yet these signs had no more effect than the pre-war admonitions of Constant Cordier and Winfield Jones.[8]

An interesting letter from Captain H. B. Grow in Lima to George Akeson, an adviser to President Herbert Hoover, pointed out the difficulties faced by a small U.S. air force mission in Peru. Grow did not press a case for military involvement, but he did lament the fact that "New York bankers" were reluctant to help Peru build up an air force. He likewise regretted that American industry did not stand ready to assist. This, he said, forced Peruvians "to go to English firms for materials and money." He continued: "If the South American countries whom we so generously protect with the poor old Monroe Doctrine, base their entire economical existence on foreign sources of capital, there is sure to be conflict some day and we may be placed in a disagreeable situation through a sincere effort to support our promises in this same doctrine."[9] Despite the fact that Grow was hopelessly and typically unaware of what the Doctrine said or meant (though probably sure about the "Roosevelt Corollary"), his message was quite in keeping with European military thought: business, industry, and military strength went together in the protection of national interests.

Peruvian President Leguía's reported toying with the idea of a U.S. military mission resulted in serious consideration in Washington, and on one occasion, in 1924, Miles Poindexter wrote Secretary of State Hughes that State and War ought to think before responding definitively to an offer—an offer that never came. For the reaction in the Chilean and Argentine foreign and war ministries would offset any advantage gained by a U.S. monopoly on army and navy missions in Peru.[10] Later correspondence indicates that State was very wary of such a move, even if there was a chance Congress would pass enabling legislation. It was this ambivalent attitude, this difference of interests in the branches of the U.S. government (from late 1924 to early 1927), that prompted Leguía to appoint General Faupel to be his army watchdog in 1926. Leguía, of course, wanted only to displace the French—with whom mattered little. In 1930 there was again some evidence that State and War were taking more serious notice of South American military affairs. The venerable Francisco Javier Díaz visited the United States en route to Germany. His purpose in crossing the Atlantic was to return a recent visit to Chile by General Wilhelm Freye and to witness German maneuvers. Captain Ralph Wooten, the attaché in Santiago, was alarmed that little attention was paid to Díaz's visit by authorities in Washington, for he represented not only an army but an army that had created the government of Carlos Ibáñez. "It is needless to say that in general the military groups in practically all South American countries, and especially in Chile, place what may appear to us to be undue emphasis on the so-called military courtesies, both from and to foreign military men."[11] Díaz's visit was, of course, unofficial. He met the president, however, and toured West Point and the Army War College. Wooten was tersely informed of this.

Aside from these isolated manifestations of interest and awareness, the U.S. government showed no inclination either to offer military missions to South American countries or to expand operations in Peru and Brazil. In the case of these two countries, enough evidence exists to indicate that the United States was reluctant either to assume a military role or to alienate Argentina and Chile. Owing to the fact that no serious, formal requests ever arrived in Washington, however, such conclusions remain only conjecturally firm.

Following World War I, rumors circulated in Santiago and Washington that Germans had offered their services to Chile, presumably with the idea of using Danzig as a port of embarcation. But the Alessandri administration demurred, and when it was brought up in the Versailles dealings, the issue died.[12] Germans thus did not return in a post-war mission to Chile and never in a large enough number to enable them to revitalize their brand of military professionalism. Chileans did that themselves, and blended it with what they learned by sending officers to study in France. The Ibáñez administration merely confirmed the continued existence of German-style military professionalism in Chile.

At the beginning of the decade, Chile's army strength stood at 23,782 men: a population ratio of 6:1,000. Chile had a trained reserve of 178,000, or 51:1,000, and an untrained reserve of 431,734. In 1921—a full four years before military men began to exercise extraordinary influence over budgetary matters—War and Marine expenditures amounted to 32 percent of government expenditures.[13] During the Ibáñez presidency the military and naval budget dropped in percentage of overall expenses, but the actual peso amount increased, owing to enlargement of the national budget and to inflation. By that time the Germanophiles and military Germanophilia had staged a comeback, and French influence stood no chance of replacing it. Even before Ibáñez assumed the presidency, his cabinet colleague, Conrado Ríos Gallardo, proposed the scheme that would have established Chile as South America's Prussia by expanding military training programs to allow full scholarships for study at the Escuela: three each to Mexico, Colombia, Ecuador, Venezuela, Uruguay, and Paraguay. Like Germany and France, Chile sought to use her purported military prowess as a tool of diplomacy. Hans von Kiesling was an ornament; Chileans were in charge of all training programs.

Across the Andes the same did not obtain. Faupel's arrival in 1923, his hiring of six German "retirees," and his departure three years later caused more than just a ripple. The same can be said of General Johannes Kretzschmar and his colleagues. Just as the Chileans were doing (and as Brazilians would do), Argentina sought to use military influence in diplomacy. At the beginning of the 1920s the Argentine army stood at 24,400 men, a ratio of 2.9:1,000. There was a 309,000 reserve (37:1,000), and the army and navy enjoyed approximately 26 percent of the budget.[14]

Despite the "distinctly pro-German" Uriburu's resignation and Faupel's "defection" to Peru in 1926, the army maintained its Germanic image, and Uriburu's *golpe* in 1933 briefly strengthened that image. The Justo clique, which controlled most of the high-level posts, was less blatantly Germanophile than were Uriburu and his followers, like Colonel Basilio Pertiné. Argentina continued to welcome Latin Americans to the Colegio Militar. Paraguayans and Bolivians studied there, and there were a few Peruvian exchange students.

U.S. embassy personnel became alarmed midway through the decade when it was rumored that a Mexican mission had arrived in Buenos Aires. U.S. citizens staying at a downtown hotel had seen the Mexicans, though how they knew they were actually Mexicans is not known. The Argentine War Ministry denied their presence. What were General Andrés Figueroa, Colonel Paulino D. Madrazo, and two physicians doing in Buenos Aires? No one ever found out; Argentina sent no mission to Mexico to depoliticize the Mexican army and Mexico sent no mission of cadets to Buenos Aires.[15]

In the Southern Cone, then, German presence was, for the most part, second generation in nature. Although Faupel and

Kretzschmar did restore content in Argentina, it was not without officially-expressed hesitation similar to that expressed over a decade earlier by Maligne.[16] For various reasons, all linked to domestic or foreign policy, neither Argentina nor Chile saw fit to "bootleg" formal German missions via Danzig. Nor did they think it necessary to hire Swiss or Italian missions. Both the Argentines and Chileans let the United States know in set terms that they would take umbrage at persistently-rumored expansion of U.S. naval activities in Brazil and Peru, but nationalistic civilian and military leaders like Yrigoyen and Alvear, Alessandri and Ibáñez, saw little to gain and probably much to lose from German army missions. Frustrated military Germanophiles cited the Treaty of Versailles and blamed the British, French, and Americans-selectively and opportunistically—for their plight.

Early in the post-war decade Brazil had an army of 42,808 men. The ability of this mass of soldiers to do much beyond drill and exercises was, to put it mildly, limited, despite earlier efforts of the *jovens turcos*. The French learned this when they arrived in 1919 to provide strategic and tactical knowledge gained in World War I to their new charges. After the French had been six years on the job the U.S. military attaché Captain Hugh Barclay reported: "I think little of this knowledge has penetrated to the individual soldier. The officers of the general staff, however, have benefitted greatly from it." There was an apparent class line between officers and men, just as there were clear social divisions in civilian life. Brazil was such a backward nation—something army officers had been writing about for years—the attaché concluded, that out of one year's active duty most of the conscripts spent fully six months in basic physical education (i.e. just getting into good physical condition) and learning drill formations. This left barely six months for true military training, which thus "might be said to be non-existent." The individual soldier, he went on, "as a rule is ignorant, illiterate, can be easily led and will follow his immediate superior without knowing why".[17] It was not a very impressive picture of Brazil's new army. The French had begun nearly from scratch, but they were used to doing so, and they were making improvements from the top down. "Bemvinda seja" headlined *A Defeza*'s lead editorial in April 1919.[18] From this point forward there was an official public policy of cooperation between the Brazilians and the French. Despite the wrangling of the 1920s, most of which was kept within the officer corps, the outward appearance was one of amicable relations.

Marshall Foch personally selected the mission's leader, General Maurice Gamelin, after being contacted by the Brazilian government. Negotiations went on between War Minister João Pandiá Calógeras and the French attaché in Rio, negotiations in which the Brazilians, according to one general, stressed "the difficulties that the mission would have to confront with much skill."[19] Gamelin was accompanied by General Eugene Durandin, his aide; Colonels Albert Barat and Louis Buchalet; Lieutenant Colonels Louis Derougemont, who taught tactics, Lucien Lelong, who taught strategy, August Vallaume, Gabriel Barrand, who took over infantry instruction at the Escola de Estado Maior, and Ferdinand Pascal, an artillery instructor; Majors Chavanne de Dalmassy, an artillery specialist, Louis Thiebert, Jean Gueriot of the engineers, Raymond Dumas, who taught tactics, Jean Petibon, Paul Richon, Pierre Bresard, Sebastian Saly, and Henri Marleanger, a veterinarian; and Captains Robert Duran de Mareuil, Paul Dieloulard, another veterinarian, and François Le Meliante, an armaments specialist. There were a number of civilians as well. These men and those who followed them taught at the Escola de Estado Maior at Praia Vermelha, at the Escola Militar, and at the Escola de Aperfeiçoamento, but they were not given authority over military institutions as Europeans had been in Chile and Peru. French officers were not active at the Realengo school, which remained the preserve of the *jovens turcos* and their *missão indígena*.

The French found difficulties from the beginning at the staff school. It offered a three-year course for alumni of the speciality schools to prepare them for staff and planning assignments and the elaboration of doctrine. Brazilians still used translations of outdated, pre-war German manuals and old Brazilian publications. From its inception, the French mission to Brazil had to write new guides and textbooks or have existing French works adapted for use in Brazil. They did this for artillery, cavalry, infantry, engineers, tactics, strategy, geography, staff service, administration, and sanitation courses. Even though they were denied command or administrative authority, the French were able to affect Brazilian military thought through instruction and advising. Limitations, stressed by more than one officer-author, made the mission no less significant as a source of intellectual stimulation.[20]

Inevitably, those who gained most from the mission were the officers who attended classes at the Escola de Estado Maior. For this reason there were, early on, divisions of sentiment. The pre-war Germanophiles became the middle-ranking senior officers of the 1920s. The Francophiles were the most up-to-date in technical matters.[21] Thus the generational clash, significant in Chile and Peru, was a feature of military professionalism in Brazil as well.

The French also went to work on rewriting the codes and ordinances by which the Brazilian officer corps was governed. After some fifteen years, promotion, salary, and retirement regulations were thoroughly French in inspiration. The legislation on the "military situation," or the legal status of the officer corps, the organization of the army, recruitment regulations, and the army's finance and administrative structure, was similarly French in design. "Nothing more noble or more worthy of Latins from both shores of the Atlantic than this admirable example of solidarity and fraternity of race" was the way War Minister Calógeras viewed the Franco-Brazilian mix that molded a modern officer corps in the inter-war years.[22]

Three years after the French began to participate in this aspect of "Latin solidarity" they supervised the organization of large-scale maneuvers. It was the aftermath of these maneuvers that caused Captain Barclay to cable his comments on the capabilities of Brazilian officers and men. The 1922 maneuvers were disastrous, with the older *chefes* showing themselves to be outmoded, as outmoded as their own superiors had been in Marshal Hermes's day.[23] This convinced the French they had much more to do; it convinced many young Brazilians they had much more to learn. It served as well to convince the French, in the words of one participant, that they had to "appreciate the necessities of adapting to the Brazilian milieu, temperament, and field of operations." Only by so doing would they be able to inculcate professional ideals and values, to blend post-war professionalism with Brazilian socio-political reality, then to engender professional militarism.

The same commentator emphasized that the French stressed originality and creativity, that they discouraged learning by rote; that they prodded their pupils with new problems, sought new and original solutions, and encouraged discussion, debate, and freedom of expression.[24] In doing this the French apparently were encouraging Brazilians to think for themselves about acting politically. Gamelin's interest in the development of telecommunications in the Brazilian far west under the aegis of General Cândido Mariano da Silva Rondón doubtless awakened many Brazilian officers to the backward conditions in their fatherland.[25] One Brazilian went so far as to link French training, with its emphasis on originality, creative thought, and independence of action, to the revolts of 1924, collectively known as the *tenentista* movement. The rebels used the term *missão indígena* to describe their goals. They were "a select group of subaltern officers...imbued with renovation of military instructional methods [and] with the teachings of the French military mission, which began and encouraged the modern, professional education of the army."[26] Tactics employed in the São Paulo revolt smacked of World War I, but the intellectual and ideological origins of the movement, in addition to being a response to the political oligarchy of the Old Republic, did stem from the teachings of Brazil's new military mentors.

Within three years of his arrival, Colonel Derougemont would tell his listeners and readers that "the officer's profession must be a priesthood, and not a trade that one takes up like any other, simply to earn a livelihood." He wrote of a vocation, of a willingness to take orders and give them, of service, of the officer's disdain for material rewards, of his disinterest in money. He also stressed that the officer should in no way involve himself in partisan politics. Derougemont, in short, pleaded the case of officers in the same ways pre-war French military officers had done. The only real difference was that he was pleading the case in a Brazilian, not a French, military journal and that his readers and followers were Brazilians caught up in the maelstrom of the post-1922 military-civilian stalemate. The army was "of the nation and the fatherland," not of any particular party or regime. It was not a caste apart, as in some Central or Eastern European countries. Officers lived to defend their countries against aggression and to perpetuate a social order, and they should mix with *o povo*, not shun contacts with those in civilian life.[27] This clear expression of the French military mentality appeared in the same year that army officers attempted to lead the Copacabana barracks against the government in downtown Rio, initiating, thus, Brazilian *tenentismo*.

Throughout the tenure of the first French mission (1919–24), Gamelin, Derougemont, and the others stressed results and action over specific means and theories. Gamelin took special note of the fact that nearly two-thirds of the troops were illiterate. He hoped a year's military service would turn them into literate, physically fit citizens, capable of fighting for Brazil.[28] Owing to the contemporary Brazilian situation, the French were unable to pursue their work without encouraging military men to think politically. Stress on being a part of the nation, not apart from it, pushed staff officers toward the application of military solutions to national problems.

In 1924 General Frédéric Mathieu Marie Coffec succeeded Gamelin; Gamelin stayed beyond his term, but the rest of the French mission had served its four-year tour and departed. Coffec served as chief of mission until 1927, when he was replaced by General Joseph Spire. During 1926–27 there were forty-one French officers and civilians serving in Brazil; by

1929 there were forty-three; in 1933 the number had decreased to twenty-one. During the 1929–31 years the mission grew in size, so that by 1931 Spire had ten colonels and lieutenant colonels alone under his command. By this time the United States was reporting on the new "generation gap" in the officer corps, for many Brazilian majors and colonels believed themselves ready to "go it alone."[29]

Any evaluation of the role of the French mission in pre-Depression Brazil must take into account the fact that Brazilians were experiencing a political situation with attendant socioeconomic and cultural problems comparable to those experienced between 1889 and the Great War, somewhat less comparable to those experienced by Peruvians between 1900 and 1914, but from the very same standpoint: that of an officer corps enjoying for the first time a heavy dose of professional orientation administered by members of one of the world's leading military organizations.

There were repeated admonitions to Brazilians, aside from those of Derougemont, that they had no business in politics, that they were not "janizaries," but enjoyed a privileged position.[30] Captain Luis Correia Lima wrote that officers were indeed inseparable from the rest of the population: "Let us march side by side, not face to face; let us march shoulder to shoulder, not chest to chest," he echoed. There were repeated outpourings of admiration for the French, from their being *Bemvinda!* forward. The French provided unity, standardization, and an appropriate doctrine. French tactics and strategy, though demonstrated poorly by Brazilians in war games and maneuvers, would soon make the army an up-to-date organization, wrote a uniformed enthusiast.[31] When Gamelin returned to France in December 1924, he was given a formal military send-off with banquets, speeches, testimonials. The death of the famous general Charles Mangin, a popular figure in both Brazil and Peru, was noted by Brazilians with appropriate commemorative ceremonies and messages of sympathy. Brazilian journals published increasingly more extensive coverage of military events and general news from Europe during the 1920s and concurrently decreased their coverage of

Latin American affairs. To Brazilian officers the world was shrinking as their self-perception took on increasingly complex characteristics; they thought increasingly like Europeans. They believed from the first years of the decade on that their profession could achieve the necessary heights of perfection only if Brazil were industrialized and had a modern transportation and communications network: that a country was only as good as its army.[32] These things the French told them as well. And far off to the west, less affected by the complexities of the 1930s, other French officers continued to do much the same to their long-time clients and colleagues, the Peruvians.

The sixth Franco-Peruvian mission arrived May 1, 1919. Serving were the commander, General Bonaventure Vassal ("don Buenaventura"), and Colonels René Mascarel, Charles Menú, and Georges Marcel, who specialized in infantry, artillery, and cavalry respectively; Colonel Jules Baudiez, Major Louis Conduret, and Lieutenants Abel Brenaud and Pierre Cousin, all aviators; and Major Camile Houdelot, a veterinarian. Also included were Lieutenant Colonels Omar Paucheu, a gymnastics instructor, and Émile Bruyère and Lieutenants Émile Danudoux and Albert Chabrier, both pilots.

A seventh mission took up its duties three years later. This group was commanded by General François Pellegrin (Lyautey's aide-de-camp during the war) and Colonels Louis Bourgignon, René Prioux, Joseph Chevalier, Gaston Hébert, Paul Goubeaux, Andre Ducep, and Georges Thomas. Bourgignon, Prioux, and Goubeaux were infantry officers; Chevalier, as might be expected, was from the cavalry; Hébert was an engineer; Ducep and Thomas served in various capacities. Also among the officers making up the seventh mission were Colonel Bernard Verdy, a horseman and pilot, Lieutenant Colonel René des Borderies, a cavalry instructor, and Major Houdelot, veterinarian.

From 1922 until the beginning of World War II, officers served on an individual basis, although groups of Frenchmen are still referred to by Peruvian authors as *misiones*. Clément returned briefly to serve as chief of staff—not as a mission member—which caused some ill feeling among those less privileged than he. Other notables to sign on for three- or four-year tours of duty were Lieutenant Colonel Verdy, (1924–27), Colonel Georges Paris (1932–35), Major Pierre Demoreulle (1936–39), Colonel Raymond Laurent (1936–39), Colonel August Pillegrand (1936–39), Colonel Joseph Weller (1939–40), Lieutenant Colonels Hector Dassonville and Marcel Pilot (1938–40), and Major Etienne Caminade (1938–40). Individual French officers served in a range of capacities: Clément as chief of staff, Verdy as instructor of tactics, Paris as a technical adviser to the War Ministry and as director of the Escuela Superior de Guerra, Demoreulle in communications, Laurent as an advisor to and instructor of staff service at the Escuela Superior, Pillegrand as director of infantry application courses and adviser to Laurent. Weller directed the artillery application school, Dassonville and Pilot were advisers to the general staff, and Caminade was an engineer's adviser. Although reduced in numbers, the French retained influence throughout the officer corps, advising, directing, and teaching at all levels. "Of common concern since the first mission had been the offering in our schools and in the barracks of military instruction to prepare the country for war."[33] There was as yet no doubt as to the mission's prime responsibility.

From 1919 to 1925 a total of twenty-four French officers served in Peru; from 1925 to 1940, a total of ten more. Throughout this period French officers sought to mold the Peruvian army in their image. In 1924 Lieutenant Colonel Georges Thomas (as director of the army's geographic office) again told officers that Peru needed a top-quality map. Clément's promise of 1898 still had not been carried out. Peru's topography and regional characteristics made the map just as much a necessity in 1924 as it had been in 1898.[34] National defense depended on it. A year later, General Pellegrin informed officers of the French institute for higher military studies—forerunner of the Peruvian Centro de Altos Estudios Militares. His lecture to officers of the Lima garrison appeared in translation thanks to Lieutenant Colonel José C. Pérez Manzanares, one of Peru's leading Francophiles. Pellegrin impressed his listeners and readers with France's dedication to preparation for total war through this unique civil-military institute. He called his work "the total preparation of the country" for national defense, a task that appealed to Peruvians who wanted to "prepare their country for support of the army." Pellegrin also allowed as how the high-level training in social sciences as well as advanced military subjects helped mission, mandate, and colonial officers alike. In so doing he compared French missionary work in places like Peru, Brazil, Poland, Czechoslovakia, Rumania, and Greece with mandate enforcement in Syria and the colonial operations in Africa and Asia.[35] French theories of non-European military operations thus spread directly in both Peru and Brazil.

Bernard Serrigny's essay, translated by Pérez Manzanares as "La organización de la nación para el tiempo de guerra," appeared midway through the first decade of post-war French missionary labors.[36] Serrigny, of course, had always emphasized the preparation of civilians as well as officers for "total national preparedness." His emphasis on a national scheme for economic and social organization to facilitate mobilization under military leadership differs from his pre-war stand in its emphasis on military supervision of mobilization. There can be no question of the direct transmittal of military and sociopolitical theory by the French to Peru. Their emphasis on combined civilian and military national defense courses, plans for mobilization and coordination of efforts, and the interest in "colonial" tactics and theories drove home to Peruvians the point that in a non-conventional environment the army ought to expect to play a greater role. This role was already in the mind of Peruvian officers. It had been since 1904—*la misión civilizadora*. To discuss the mechanics of French military missionary efforts in Peru is to discuss *la misión*.

To raise these subjects without noting the difficulties faced by the French, however, is to cloud the issue of their presence. In both Brazil and Peru the French had to deal with politicians who sought to manipulate the army; nationalists who, for various reasons, saw no need of a foreign training mission; and generational gaps in training and experience that made total penetration of the corps impossible. There is no case in South America—Argentine, Brazil, Chile, and Peru being the most representative, with Bolivia another, though peculiar, example—where Europeans had an easy time inculcating the military virtues of the Old World. The public praise and the ceremonies were real enough, and so were the objections. Through it all, however, the transmittal of professional thought and self-perception went on. Few officers questioned French professionalism or the French concept of the role of the officer corps as leadership group of a national army.

Early on in the *oncenio*, Leguía's followers considered the French as representatives of the past, as maintaining an officer corps sympathetic for the most part to Civilista leaders. The Leguía *golpe* of 1919 had ousted Pardo, a Civilista, and since it had been Pardo's administration that had renewed the Franco-Peruvian tie, Leguía did not trust his French guests.[37] In 1923 the head of the mission was the subject of numerous stories alleging his complicity in graft schemes. General Vassal swore innocence, but the Leguiístas did not let up; they began at this point to discuss seriously the United States as an alternative, just as they began to expand commercial contacts with American companies and financial institutions.

Soon thereafter the French ran into trouble again, this time with the church hierarchy. Out of the blue, according to Peruvian and U.S. observers, *La Tradición*, the episcopal organ, unleashed an attack on the French—and the Americans as well. On January 30, 1924, the editors warned the government against contracting a "Yankee general" (unnamed) to direct Peruvian military education. *La Tradición* said it was common knowledge that the French officers were grafters, that they served as agents for French munitions concerns, and that they had little new to offer Peru. French successes in World War I notwithstanding, Peruvians could handle the job of educating officers and training conscripts. It was "indeed high time that the Peruvian army stood on its own feet and…used the nucleus of young Peruvian officers who had received sufficient schooling and training abroad to effectuate the methods of organization that the army needs." The essay went so far as to state a case for a U.S. mission based on the presence of the naval mission, but only on this basis; the editors maintained throughout that Peruvians could do the best job. *La Tradición*'s unequaled anti-French reportage (thought by some to be a Leguía-instigated ploy despite the president's difficulties with the church) evoked no response from the officer corps. According to the U.S. attaché, Peruvians were, for the time being, happy with the French.[38] This was true only so far as instruction and technical advice went.

Some of *La Tradición*'s allegations and insinuations did cause Peruvian officers to wonder why civilians and church leaders might not favor continued French presence in Peru and to consider the sources of their own displeasure with the French, if not with their teachings. Vassal did make a number of doctrinal changes based on World War I experiences, but they had little application to Peru. Clément and Pellegrin did have salaries quite a bit higher than other French or Peruvian officers who were their equals in rank. The activities of the French in administration gave them more authority than even the war minister; they taught concomitantly that foreigners had no business to be in control of another nation's army. It all came down to the fact that many now thought that neither the French nor the United States, a country with no "military lineage," could do better than French-trained Peruvians.

Velarde Alvarez succeeded Clément in 1925 as chief of staff—a step in the right direction for readers of *La Tradición*. Soon, Leguía revived his interest in a U.S. mission, was rebuffed, and turned to Faupel. This move—no pleasant thing to the French advisers—pleased German merchants in Lima and caused but mild concern in the United States. Faupel stayed in Peru until 1930 (beyond the time he exercised any real authority), when his contract was bought up and he was relieved of duties as adviser. He did not succeed in substituting German armaments for French, despite rumors that he strove to do so.

An assessment of the Peruvian officer corps in the mid-1920s revealed that the Peruvians found themselves in much the same position occupied by Chileans following the reforms of 1906: numerous junior and middle-grade officers filling staff positions because of a lack of qualified, fully-trained seniors. Elmore Steward, the U.S. attaché, wrote that, despite French efforts, politics still dictated promotion to the ranks of colonel and above. The old Leguía-Pardo rivalry still dominated entry into the upper echelons. Steward considered the lieutenant colonels of this era the backbone of the army. Among the high- and middle-ranking officers he considered the very best in Peru were General Oscar Benavides (in exile in Ecuador at that moment), Colonels Manuel María Ponce and Pedro Pablo Martínez, and Lieutenant Colonels Germán Yáñez, José Ricardo Luna, Ernesto Montagne, and Aurelio García Godos.[39] All of these highly-qualified professionals participated actively in the political life of their country when the dictator fell in 1930.

The overthrow of Leguía in Peru and the demise of the Old Republic in Brazil produced major changes in politics and government in both countries. Army officers played a significant role in the dramatic events of 1930. Lieutenant Colonel Sánchez Cerro delivered the *golpe de estado* in Peru, and Francophile Brazilian officers turned their backs on the administration of Washington Luiz Pereira de Sousa to form the *Junta Pacificadora*, avoid an intra-army armed confrontation, and tip the balance toward the opposition led by the defeated candidate, Getúlio Dornelles Vargas. Sánchez Cerro held power briefly in Peru; Vargas began his climb toward control of the national government in Brazil. The tumult of *golpes de estado*, provisional governments, and military-civilian political cooperation did not end—or even seriously interrupt—French mission activities in Peru or Brazil, but the incertitude of the early 1930s did force professional officers to see politics and government with different eyes. Old problems were exacerbated and new ones made dramatically obvious. From 1930 forward, European missions and military presence were intricately involved in the elaboration of a U.S. military policy for South America.

Early in 1930 the Sousa administration showed dissatisfaction with the French over the sale of munitions. Walter Edge of the U.S. Embassy in Paris wrote Secretary of State Stimson that Brazilian officers serving on an armaments commission in France were greatly annoyed because the French, they believed, were attempting "to unload...a large quantity of French worn or obsolete war materials. The insistence of the military mission...has been annoying to the Brazilian government."[40] Edge opined that Brazil might not renew the mission's contract. Soon thereafter, Edwin V. Morgan in Rio informed Stimson that the constructive work of the mission "overrides the defects which have been found in this conduct," that is, the hard-sell tactics associated with armaments. Morgan said that the rumors of an imminent rupture of Franco-Brazilian military ties were largely attributable to navy officers who wanted the army to end its dependence on a "continental power." He added that a response to such naval overtures would cause problems in Franco-American relations. Morgan assured State that "the French military mission has handled a difficult situation with considerable judgment and had effected improvement in the morale and technical skills of the Brazilian army."[41] As the new decade began, there were significant differences between State's and War's appraisals of the technical and professional skills of the Brazilians. As U.S. diplomacy developed during the decade this State-War difference of opinion significantly promoted the further involvement by default of the United States in Brazilian military affairs.

The French were not to be outdone, however, until the end of the decade, when war again consumed the European powers. With the Old Republic not yet a year deceased, Major Lester Barker filed a G-2 report early in 1931 that indicated a blending of the Franco-Brazilian military relationship with interest of the Vargas-led provisional government in a closer relationship with Brazil's traditional diplomatic ally in Washington. Barker referred to the continuing question of French permanence, and noted that austerity measures might make it impossible to continue the mission. The United States was very popular with the Vargas government, he said; on the other hand, the French mission was popular with the army but not with the government.[42] The French contract was renewed, of course, but Barker's text should have made it apparent that the officer corps still showed no affinity for the U.S. army. The fact that the government leaned toward Washington ought to have indicated that, appearances notwithstanding, Vargas and his army commanders did not see things eye to eye. This is evidence in retrospect of the emergence of a military mentality quite distinct in at least one respect from that of the authoritarian regime supported by the officer corps.

After Charles Huntziger arrived in February 1931 to direct what was left of the mission in Brazil, he stated that "the hands of friendship which united the Brazilian and French armies are very intimate, and it devolves upon us to draw them even closer. For my part I will devote my best efforts to that end."[43] To the charges that the French were teaching obsolete methods and doctrine, Huntziger replied to the effect that he would attempt to outdo Gamelin in adapting the teachings of the recent war to Brazilian realities.

A year later, as loyal elements of the army swung into action to block the rebellion in São Paulo, Brazil had 43,700 men in uniform.[44] This, reported the U.S. military attaché's clerk, was an increase from 35,200 in 1930. Early in the last decade of the Old Republic the army had stood at 42,808, then in 1922 the Arthur Bernardes administration (allegedly an anti-army government) had reduced it to 31,765. Sousa reestablished the 42,000 level, reduced anew in 1930 because of overall budget cuts. Sharp fluctuations in the size of annual conscription levels and manpower were prevalent in post-war Brazil, just as prevalent as they had been prior to 1914. Consequently, professional officers continued to resent a lack of continuity they deemed necessary for the maintenance of defense preparedness.

Also in 1932, Brazilians began to replace French in certain posts; most of the subdirection of instruction was in the hands of Brazilians. New rumors began to circulate (if indeed rumors ever ceased) that the French would not be invited to return. Reports on this continuing rumor are remarkably similar to those coming out of Peru concerning Leguía's interest in replacing the French there. Vargas may have considered it to his advantage to bring a new influence to bear on the officer corps. Other rumors had it that the new four-year contract would be cancelled immediately and that Vargas was displeased with the U.S. naval mission.[45] Brazil's new nationalism and Vargas's desire to exert as much control as possible over the armed forces was responsible for both his ambivalence and the rumors. His tactics were indeed similar to those of Leguía. Vargas cut the size of the French mission from twenty to five officers; he ordered armaments commissions to be more selective in purchase of items not specified by the French, such as aircraft. Major William Sackville, attached to the U.S. embassy in Rio, saw changes in the offing: "Prior to the World War our military organization attracted no attention from Latin American nations. Also there was a general conviction that cost of living and expenses in general were notably higher in the United States than in Europe. And, perhaps most of all, Paris is in Europe."[46] Vargas no doubt reasoned that Washington was in the United States, Brazil's close ally, after all, and that the cost of living was no longer a deterrent to relations.

By 1934 there were two U.S. coast-artillery officers serving as advisers in Brazil. Two more officers joined the mission that year, and the contract was extended in 1936 for two additional years. Four American officers serving in Brazil by 1935 were an indication that the United States now had only one less officer serving there than did France. Carrying on the work of France in Brazil were Colonels Baudoin and Corbé and Majors Carpentier, Vignon, and Fay. Huntziger had left by the end of the year. The French mission, which had peaked at forty-three officers in 1929, stayed at five officers during most of the 1930s.[47] The United States still had not replaced France as a model, however, nor had the Brazilian army shifted to a definitive pro-U.S. stance.

In the second half of the 1930s, splits in officer corps sentiments became public. One group of high ranking officers openly expressed support for the regimes in Italy and Germany and for the military-civilian relationships that appeared to obtain there. Vargas's declaration of the Estado Novo by fiat and by natural favoritism for corporatist and authoritarian rule caused this shift of officers toward the Axis powers. Some officers held back from open applause for Germans and Italians. The staunch Francophiles favored Vargas's centralized government and his promises of economic nationalism and development, but a pro-German attitude was going too far. A third group began to look toward the United States as the best available source of military advice unfettered by ideological or political overtones.

The government moved slowly and deliberately.[48] Vargas's feeling of kinship with regimes in Portugal, Spain, Italy, and Germany caused concern in Washington, to the point where Cordell Hull was called upon in 1937 to respond to a letter of Mrs. Pauline Nimkoff writing on behalf of the Brooklyn Women's Anti-Fascist League. Mrs. Nimkoff protested the blooming relationship between Washington and Rio and the bare beginnings of military cordiality: "The continuance of our aid and advice in Brazil will mean the support of fascist dictatorship which is against the principles of every real American."[49] Hull's reply was one of cool reassurance of the compatibility of American ideals with Brazilian friendship.

Near the end of the decade the French mission expanded slightly to seven men: Major General Chadebec de Lavalade, chief of mission, had replaced the popular General Paul Noel. Also serving were Colonels Samuel Nalot and Jean Schwartz, Lieutenant Colonels Pierre Grausot and Armand d'Arnoux, and two majors, Pettier and Leroy. At this time there were five U.S. artillery and eight navy officers in Brazil. There were also ten German aviation technicians.[50] Germans began to show up in Brazil (as they began anew to be visible in Argentina and Chile) after Hitler's rise to the chancellery. Their presence, the continuation of the French mission, and the new group of Americans helped turn the military into an armed ideological arena. Officers from Brazil were studying in Belgium, France, England, and the United States. The French still insisted on monopolizing armaments acquisitions, and this still caused problems. Brazilian officers, especially at the senior level, complained that they were competent to direct the army. There was some defection from the ranks of the Francophiles. Still and all, the official U.S.

view was that the French had accomplished "excellent results" and that Franco-Brazilian relations were as good as ever.[51]

Oswaldo Aranha, Vargas's canny foreign minister, was by this time at the height of his manipulative powers. He had persuaded Vargas to hold down the size of the French missions in order to justify allowing in only a few Americans. His balancing act and gradual easing out of the French was an artistic display of diplomatic expertise even if it was aided measurably by the onset of war in Europe. He successfully brought the army officer corps into line with Brazilian foreign policy: disestablishment of ties with European countries (as that became expedient). This enabled Brazil to supersede Argentina as the dominant power on the Atlantic coast of South America and, authoritarian regime notwithstanding, to align herself early with the forces of democracy against those of fascism. The Vargas-Aranha foreign policy and World War II disentangled the officer corps from the French, but did little to change the thought and self-perception of that corps.

Between Leguía's fall on August 25, 1930, and the end of 1933, the loyalty of the Peruvians to any of their national administrations was ever in doubt. This was the case during Sánchez Cerro's 1931–33 presidency. The thrust into political life under Sánchez Cerro and the confrontations with APRA made it extremely difficult for the army to extricate itself from the arena of government and politics. It is probable that even the most staunchly professional officers understood, if reluctantly, at this time, that political participation was a necessary evil.

Sánchez Cerro himself was living, then dead, evidence of the dangers inherent in military involvement in affairs normally reserved to civilians since the 1890s.[52] Sánchez Cerro reinstated some officers who had been retired or relieved of duties by Leguía after the beginning of the *oncenio*.[53] These officers—none of whom was a significant figure—were still known as Pardo-Civilista officers, that is, they were linked to the politicians of the pre-1919 years. They were the Peruvian counterparts of the Bolivian Ismael Montes–Partido Liberal faction. The doughty little *cholo*'s move won him no kudos from army professionals or those civilians hostile either to Civilismo or to Leguiísmo.

The French did their best under the circumstances. The mission limped along, in effect, and somehow the army survived the tumult of a *golpe de estado*, political struggles, the rise of APRA, and the Sánchez Cerro assassination. Wilhelm Faupel's 1926–30 tour of duty provided only a slight interruption of continuity, and by 1932—Guillermo Thorndyke's "año de la barbarie"—the French were back in control once again. Peru figured very little in U.S. policy interests of this time, but Fred Morris Dearing did write Henry Stimson in late 1932 that a new group of French instructors was on its way to renew the Franco-Peruvian arrangement which had weakened under the late president (Leguía), under whom "everything [anent military affairs] was done in secret and for improper motives." "Since the course of the [Sánchez Cerro] government at the present time," he went on, "is unreservedly honorable and patriotic...Peru finds it timely and convenient to renew the French military mission."[54] Dearing thought the Peruvian officer corps was of "high quality" but needed updating in technical matters. And so officers from the "heart and brain of the western world," as Sánchez Cerro had called them, regained their hegemony. Either his brief service in France during the *oncenio* had endeared him to France, as it had done to other Peruvians, or he knew a good opportunity to make friends inexpensively. State Department papers consistently referred to him as pro-French in contrast to the pro-U.S. Leguía.

In 1932 the Peruvian army had 6,000 men and 1,340 officers. The police force had a contingent of 7,000 commanded by 348 officers. Both were armed with French or Spanish weaponry, mostly pre-war rifles and pistols, although there were some post-war French pieces in use.[55] The staff school was commanded by the popular Colonel Georges Paris, but the army's planning and warmaking potential was found wanting that year in the Leticia confrontation with Colombia. The army's ability to defend the country against foreign threats to national security was still virtually nil.

In 1936, when Colonel Laurent, Lieutenant Colonels Pillegrand and Weller, and Major Demoureille took up their duties, French strength, as noted, was a far cry from what it had been. But it still constituted a link to the past. Rumors now circulated widely along the west coast of Orientals (i.e., Japanese) serving as military instructors in both Peru and Chile. No evidence exists, however, that the Japanese did anything more than send representatives to demonstrate the available products of their flourishing armaments industry.[56] They advertised widely in South American military journals of the time. President Benavides was considered pro-French, but less obviously so than his dead predecessor. He was extremely affable with members of the U.S. diplomatic corps. The fact that appraisals of the Vargas clique and the Benavides government led observers in Washington to consider them pro-European is no coincidence. It may indicate there was a built-in intellectual and cultural resistance to the "replacement" of Europe by the United States as leading extra–South American power. No Peruvians advocated the replacement of French military instructors with Americans, in contrast to Brazil, where the urge to switch was building. The renewal of Colonel Paris's one-year contract in 1935 served as evidence of Peruvian steadfastness.

The French were still esteemed for their work, although the high pressure caught up with them again in the mid-1930s. They and the handful of British and Italian aviation specialists were less than subtle in trying to peddle surplus munitions and equipment. Dearing notified Hull in August 1935 that Benavides had hinted at an interest in closer relations with the United States.[57] Though hardly a dynamic or strategic shift, the realities of dealing with Europeans in the mid-1930s forced Benavides (like Vargas) to consider alternative sources of military support. Though their hearts might be with the Europeans, the world situation dictated that Brazilian and Peruvian military and civilian leaders consider seriously a break with tradition. Comparatively easy to accomplish diplomatically and fiscally—and so obviously owing to the mounting tension in Europe—this was no smooth break with the past. Peruvian officers, like their brothers to the east, remained Europeans at heart.

As late as 1939—weeks after Europe had gone to war— Peru clung to the military past. The high command and the government lamented the fact that French officers might have to return home. Having again reassured the United States that there were no "Asiatics" training the Peruvian army, Benavides praised the French mentors of his army.[58] There now remained seven French officers in Peru, and a nine-man police mission served with the Guardia Civil. Colonels Laurent and Pillegrand, Lieutenant Colonels Weller, Dassonville, and Louis Emmanuel Pilot, and Majors Demoreulle and Caminade were awaiting orders from home. Of them Benavides said on December 19, 1939: "The French military mission, one of the most complete of any which have come to the country is aiding effectively in the technical perfection of our command in the Escuela Superior de Guerra and in the general staff of the army, as well as in the service schools of infantry, artillery, engineers and communications."[59] Within a year, Frenchmen in Peru and Brazil made their decision between the Vichy regime and France. Benavides soon would be an ex-president and the United States would become the new military power of the hemisphere.

Down the coast in Chile, and to the southeast in Argentina, there was no dramatic return to the European past in the 1930s comparable to that in Brazil and Peru. But the German influence did hang on. In both Argentina and Chile the army was heavily involved in politics and government: in Chile until late 1932, when Alessandri returned to La Moneda, and in Argentina throughout the Uriburu provisional presidency until 1936 under General Justo. Justo was to the Argentine army, obviously, what Benavides was to the Peruvian army.

Despite the fact that Germany could send no mission, Germans were ending up in Chile and Argentina. Less is known about their whereabouts and dates of service. With some exceptions like Faupel, Kiesling, and Kretzschmar, these were anonymous figures, citizens now of Germany, then of Danzig, then of the South American country in which they found themselves. By 1930 there were more than a few Germans serving in Chile. These training officers and teachers of drill and tactics merely perpetuated what already existed in Chile. The U.S. consul general in Berlin, George Messersmith, a perceptive observer of things Germanic, sent a memorandum to State in mid-1930 that made the rounds there, then was passed on to the War Department. His "German Officer Attachment to the Chilean Army" made it quite clear that the German military tradition was to be reckoned with and that there were at least ten "former retirees" or "resigned" officers working in military schools and special institutes. The sole reason for the memorandum—indeed the prime reason for U.S. diplomatic attention to any German activity in Chile, Argentina, and Brazil—was the concern over possible violations of the Versailles pact. "From well-informed sources," Messersmith wrote to Stimson, "it is understood that the officers have been carrying out their duties in Chile with much dedication and have confined themselves entirely to the technical advice for which they have been employed." Socially and professionally they remained in the background, he went on, and they were not involved overtly in the armaments trade.

Messersmith believed the Ibáñez government would retain the army's Prussian qualities one way or another and that Chileans as a whole were favorably disposed toward Germany, her people, and her army. This did not bode well for U.S. interests, but it did not alarm anyone at State or War, for those interests were strictly limited at this time to U.S. security in the Western Hemisphere, and Germany was considered no threat. Messersmith called the Chilean army "one of the best-trained and equipped in South America." He noted that the navy inclined toward the British and that the recently-founded air force (one of Ibáñez's brain children) favored the United States. But the army was definitely European-oriented. If Germans were unavailable, he concluded, Chile would probably look to France rather than to the U.S. for military training personnel.[60] Most reports from Chile left no doubt as to lukewarm army sentiments about the United States.

Midway through the 1930s there were at least three known ex-Reichswehr officers serving in Chile. General Hans von Kiesling, once Goltz's aide-de-camp in the Middle East, was an advisor to the general staff and taught at the Academia de Guerra. A General von Kramer taught at the Geographic Institute, the center of Chilean geopolitical thought, and a Colonel Halbfuss also taught at the Academia. Kiesling and Kramer wore Chilean uniforms regularly.

Kiesling was no longer in Chile lecturing to Academia students in his Chilean uniform at the end of the decade. In 1938 there were eight Chilean officers studying in France and four in Germany. The War Ministry still encouraged foreign study, but there was no longer a German presence in Santiago. As the second European war of this century opened, the Chilean army had nearly 20,000 men and officers—a standing army of 7,250 and a 10,000-man annual conscription; over 1,400 officers were in uniform.[61]

Across the Andes, the Argentine army had endured a similar experience, withdrawing from its addiction to German influence. The German tradition was still strong on the eve of World War II, maintained by latter-day Germanophiles. As the 1930s wore on, Argentine military-civilian relations became deeply involved with Argentine-Brazilian relations and with the impending rise of the United States as a hemispheric and world power. The United States showed more interest in the military-civilian relations of the Atlantic powers than in those of the Pacific states, owing to developments on the European continent, their ramifications for South American military orientation, and the strategic location of Argentina and Brazil and their traditional power rivalry. European military influence in Argentina and Brazil—and the resultant maintenance of European military professionalism—were of strategic concern to this country, and affected U.S. policy toward the Atlantic neighbors.

"German ideas and methods appear to be fairly entrenched, and these are nourished by the half-dozen or more German officers now engaged as teachers in the Army War College [Escuela Superior de Guerra] and by the respectable number of Argentine officers who have pursued or are pursuing courses of study in Germany."[62] As in Brazil, numerous influential members of the high command were Germanophiles. Moreover, the Argentines had the direct link with Germany. In 1936, when Alexander W. Weddel made the above-noted evaluation, the Argentine army, war minister, General Basilio Pertiné, prided himself on having been Argentine attaché in Berlin and on having served as an official, neutral observer with the German general staff during World War I.[63] Pertiné was an outspoken admirer not only of the German army but of the government he thought had made the army great again: the Third Reich.

General Justo, the president, played a role vis-à-vis the United States remarkably similar to that being perfected by Getúlio Vargas and Oswaldo Aranha in Brazil. Justo, of course, represented more solidly anti-U.S. views, given Argentina's traditional wariness of the "Colossus of the North" and its Brazilian ally. Double-dealing with Washington was the main characteristic of relations between the Atlantic powers and the United States.

In 1936 Justo told Weddel, for example, that there was no need to worry about German influence in the army. German emphasis (soon to be a thing of the past) on a small army capable of rapid mobilization was particularly well suited to Argentina. "Argentina had its own ways and methods," Weddel quoted Justo as saying. Justo was saying that Argentina emulated Germans as far as it suited their purposes, i.e., in matters of military-civilian relations, and they devised their own systems when that suited them better. This conclusion confirms the retention of military-civilian relationships of pre-World War I configuration, made possible in the 1930s owing to the Uriburu and Justo military-sponsored administrations.

Weddel's report carried yet another of those suggestions that the United States devise a hemispheric military policy to expunge the European military influence. Like those before him, Weddel was apprehensive about European (German in this case) influence. By the time he wrote, that influence was no longer simply an adjunct of trade and commerce, of investment and emigration; it was a matter of ideology and security, of political influence and foreign policy orientation on the South American Atlantic littoral. The fact that the U.S. awakening of interest was associated with such factors significantly affected the ways in which South American Germanophiles viewed the Americans who replaced the Europeans during World War II. Weddel wrote: "The advantage of a unification of standards, both naval and military, between our own armed forces and those of other countries on this continent is one which I believe our government desires to promote, and a means to this end is through familiarizing officers of other armies with our methods."[64] He suggested that State attempt to influence the White House and the War Department to pursue such a policy. To Weddel, a military tie meant a better military relationship. On the basis of the evidence with which he had to work in Buenos Aires, this appears a logical conclusion.

In 1937 there were twenty Argentines serving in the German army (Bolivia, it was reported, had a hundred officers training in Germany).[65] This evidence had the same effect that Weddel's arguments did; the United States would enter into no formal relationship. Aside from token coast artillery missions in Brazil, the Washington government would have nothing to do with training South Americans armies.

Two years later the Argentine-Brazilian imbroglio, the war in Europe, and the convolutions of Argentine and Brazilian foreign policies dominated professional affairs. Jefferson Caffery cabled Hull that General Pedro Aurélio de Góis Monteiro had informed him that there were approximately twenty German officers helping to train the Argentine army. These were advisers, *informantes*, Monteiro claimed; they did not constitute a mission, but their work did constitute a potential threat to Brazil and to hemispheric peace. The inference was obvious: German military influence in Argentina meant a possible Berlin–Buenos Aires axis. In case the United States or Brazil (in which country the situation still lacked definition) became involved in the European conflict, this alliance might compel the Argentines to respond to a German call for assistance by attacking Brazil.

Caffery went on to note that a majority of the Argentine officers, led by General Guillermo Mohr, who attended the Brazilian Independence Day celebration (September 7, the

117th anniversary of Pedro I's declaration) were "Germanophilic in interest."[66] Caffery also commented on the rigorous discipline of the German cadet contingent marching in the parades as well as the visual impression created by the use of the goose step.

At this time the United States was negotiating with Argentina to take charge of aviation training. Preparation for and then engagement in war had forced Germany to cancel her training activities to a degree, and especially in the field of aviation. In mid-1938, cable traffic between the U.S. embassies in Rio de Janeiro and Buenos Aires and the State Department in Washington still dealt with little else. Caffery claimed the Brazilians were angry with the United States because Washington appeared to be helping their arch enemy without any explanation to the long-time ally.[67] He said he did not know what to tell the Brazilians. Hull replied to his cable of May 11 by saying that the United States was going ahead with plans (plans that had been kept secret, it should be noted) to assist the Argentines. He asked Caffery to be firm and circumspect in his dealing with Aranha. To the foreign minister's argument that U.S. aid to Argentina might help the latter in case of war, Hull advised Caffery to convey Hull's opinion thus: "You may add that I am sure he will agree that it would seem to me to be in line with the inter-American policy of this government [essentially the hemispheric application of the Good Neighbor Policy] and of the Brazilian and Argentine governments that services of this technical nature be furnished wherever possible by nationals of one of the American republics in preference to nationals of non-American powers."[68] This milestone in U.S.–Latin American military cooperation asserted in Monrovian terms (as interpreted by Theodore Roosevelt some years before) the role of the United States as military mentor, and it set the stage for an expanded role during World War II and after. It also asserted by implication that the United States would take a stand on military relationships between Latin American states. This was a far different policy from anything ever expressed by the French or the Germans. Hull's assent to involve the United States in the training of Argentine pilots, understandable and timely though it was, did not signify that the United States had replaced Germany "in the minds and hearts" of Argentine Germanophiles nor European military professionalism in the mind and heart of anyone else.

Soon thereafter, Hull had to contact Caffery to reassure Brazilians that news that the United States was about to train Argentine naval officers was nothing but rumor. His reasoning was essentially the same, providing a further opening for ties to the South American military organizations. No, he replied to Caffery, there would be no Argentines training with U.S. naval personnel, no joint maneuvers in the South Atlantic, but he registered amazement that the Brazilians would be upset by that eventuality, for, if the U.S. assisted Brazil, why should she not assist other countries as well?[69] The Brazilian ambassador also informed Aranha of State's opinion, and he concurred with Hull that "it is far more to the interests of Brazil to have American technical experts in the Argentine army than Germans or Italians."[70] Slowly the new policy took shape and new relationships began to grow, but it would take decades for intellectual and ideological similitude to be discernible. As Aranha fumed and tried to convince the Chileans of perfidy on the part of the United States, the Pax Americana developed from a strategic base point of Argentine-Brazilian relations. With officers trained by South American Germanophiles and Francophiles the United States would begin to fashion its military relationship with South America. In its earliest form this policy was destined to exclude the Europeans, especially Germans, from hemispheric military affairs; to insert the United States where expedient and possible, and where controversy could be kept to a minimum; and to ensure the power balance between military and diplomatic rivals through a training, equipment, and advising monopoly. World War II made it impossible for the French or the Germans to maintain their influence over South American armies, and U.S. policy anticipated this by nearly a year and a half. Despite even this, there still was no discernible change in the thought or self-perception of members of the Argentina, Brazilian, Chilean, or Peruvian army officers corps by the time France and Germany went to war.

Indeed, when the few Germans individually contracted in South America went home and the French officers still serving in Peru and Brazil made their choice between Pétain or De Gaulle, South Americans still idolized their European mentors. They were still influenced by European strategic concerns, for these were more applicable to their continent. A year after the war began, five months after the fall of France, the loyalties of the Brazilian officer corps were still in question. Dutra and Góis Monteiro, two of the most influential members of the clique supporting Vargas and of the New State, were quite close to the German attaché, General Günther Niederfuhr. Niederfuhr shuttled between Rio and Buenos Aires, where he also served as military attaché, and he made numerous visits to southern Brazil, home of a large German emigré community. Thirty years before, the existence of that community had frightened Brazilian legislators so much that they voted against Marshal Hermes's plans for a German mission.[71] The German community still alarmed Brazilians and many Francophile officers. Near the end of 1940 the U.S. military attaché reported that the Brazilian high command was for the most part pro-German, rather than pro-Vargas, and that it was "well lined up" in favor of the German war effort, whereas field and command company officers were favorably inclined toward France and the United States.[72] The fact that by this time the United States still had made little effort to counteract either French influence or pro-German attitudes—above and beyond aviation assistance and an official visit by Chief of Staff General George C. Marshall—simply prolonged European military professionalism's appeal in Brazil. So did the corporatist New State. German victories justified the corporatists' belief that authoritarian nationalism was best for the development of Brazil. France's collapse convinced them that democracy was weak and unstable. What pushed Brazilian officers toward the United States were practicality, Argentina's neutral policies, the question of loyalty of the southern Germano-Brazilians, and residual pro-French sympathies.

What remained of the French missions to Brazil and Peru reluctantly faced the Vichy-Free France dilemma. General

Chadebec de Lavalade was hostile to the Vichy regime. He had the poor luck of replacing the extremely popular General Paul Noel, a colonial officer par excellence, and he never achieved his predecessor's popularity with Brazilians. Nevertheless, he and his fellow officers maintained a high profile in Rio. The U.S. military attaché reported in October 1940 that he would go to London, not to the continent.[73] Across the Andes, the remaining French in Peru found themselves in the same situation. At least there was no comparable German involvement to complicate matters. German contacts with Chile were not as intense as with Argentina, for Chile—the entire Pacific Coast—did not figure prominently in German strategy. The German colony in southern Chile was far more Chileanized than that in southern Brazil, and not as large.

Late in 1940, Colonel Jorge Dellepiane, the military historian and Peru's attaché in Buenos Aires, informed the U.S. military attaché, Colonel M. A. Devine, Jr., that the French were on their way home from Lima. Peru, he told Devine, would be pleased to host a U.S. mission. Dellepiane was frank; in Peru, he informed Devine, the long-term squabbling among the French had tarnished their image. Insistence on armaments purchases from French suppliers (the complaints of the past decade had had little effect) still annoyed the government. France's army had fought poorly in 1940 against the Germans, and in the event of world war the United States was the only alternative source of supply and training.[74] He also alluded to the U.S. policy of hemispheric cooperation. For very practical reasons, then, Peru fell in line with the United States.

The recently-promoted chief of mission, Colonel Pillegrand, went home—to the continent.[75] Two of his chief aides (and rivals), Lieutenant Colonel Dassonville and Major Demoureille, left for London. The French era ended on a sour note in Peru, more ignominiously than the German era ended in Brazil and Chile in 1914. Despite such endings as the French came to in Brazil and Peru, intellectual influence outlived the missions, just as German influence outlived the German presence.

As the world went again to war, the South Americans were still dazzled by the Europeans. This was especially true in

Brazil and Peru, where the French missions had continued to operate. During the entire inter-war period the same Brazilian officers, while complaining about armaments purchases, routinely sang the praises of their French mentors. A 1921 editorial in *A Defeza Nacional* began this trend. Captain Bentes Monteiro continued it in 1923.[76] Ten years later, after more tension and questioning of the value of French training, a new contingent received an effusive welcome from the same journal. "We have now a certain number of elite officers with a high level of culture and professional mentality, but it is indisputable that the total formation of such elements is not yet perfectly completed; for the number of these [French-trained officers] is still not sufficient to command the army."[77] Clearly the editors believed that French orientation was still necessary. Seven years later a special volume appeared, published by the Biblioteca Militar. Entitled *Escola de Estado Maior, 1940*, it praised throughout the work of the French, especially their rewriting of training manuals.[78] The editors extended a special salute to Lavalade, leader of the last French mission, such as it was, to South America's largest country.

Benício da Silva, writing in 1941, lamented the departure of the French but offered the opinion that Brazilians had adjusted to a new direction before and could do it again. He praised the French, as did all other official sources, for having raised the military profession in Brazil to a high point. João Baptista Magalhães, writing almost two decades later, echoed these sentiments and reiterated the persistent dilemma of young officers trained by the French who found themselves at odds with their seniors.[79]

On the surface, it would appear, adulation for the French persisted beyond their tenure; beneath the surface there had been obvious problems throughout it. Civilian objections to the French and a slow redirection of policy toward the United States in the 1930s may have made military Francophiles just that much firmer in their sentiments, thus prolonging French military professionalism.

The same was true in Peru. From the outset of the inter-war years the French were officially welcome and apparently popular. French ability and willingness to adapt theory to Peruvian reality consistently merited them praise. French models served Peruvians very well, especially with reference to matters of discipline and nation-building. Proof of this was the reprinting of a French essay, "El oficial," in 1935. So was the reprinting of a piece by Gamelin the same year.[80] Two decades later, the Peruvians were still nostalgically looking back to the golden years, thanking the French for what they had done for the army, and praising French officers for having left a modern, professional organization.[81] Among the four armies discussed herein, the Peruvian has proved to be the least modest, both in officer-corps self-praise and in praise of former models. The Peruvian debt to France and to France's army is the easiest to discern in all respects; perduration of French military professionalism in South America is purest in Peruvian ranks.[82] The evolution of Peruvian military ideology since 1940 attests to this.

Had the Brazilians not entered World War II alongside their new military comrades from the north, had the Treaty of Versailles not prohibited Germany's sending of missions abroad, and had Argentina and Chile continued active contact with their Prussian idols, the same conclusion would be as obvious for these countries. This is to say that the same conclusion obtains: South American military professionalism in the inter-war period was no less European in inspiration (indeed, it was more so) than before 1914. Further, the evolution of military thought and self-perception in Argentina, Brazil, Chile, and Peru, so overtly dependent on European inspiration, continues to attest to the European impact. South American professional militarism of the post-World War II decades, especially that of the 1960s and 1970s, is a direct consequence of the durability of European military professionalism, in both pure and adapted forms before 1940, and blended with theories and doctrines derived from U.S. training and orientation since World War II. The concluding chapters of this work treat the metamorphosis of military professionalism into professional militarism: the search for an idealized past by men of a turbulent present whose thought and self-perception defied change.

"In its army the State does honor
to itself, hence nothing could be
more dangerous to the army than
to lose the status it deserves in a
State weakened by futile
pacifism."

Hans von Seeckt, *The Future of the
German Empire: Criticisms and
Postulates* (1930)

"Our young officers, eager and
motivated, imbued with the social
significance of their role...testify to
the continuity of French values."

Maxime Weygand, "L'Armée
d'aujourd'hui" (1938)

CHAPTER SEVEN

European Military Professionalism between the Wars: Tradition in a New Setting

The officers and non-coms who came to South American countries in the inter-war years were intellectually representative of pre-1914 Europe and professionally representative of either African colonial service or World War I action or both. Their intellectual formation made them representatives of an era forever gone, brought to an end by the last great dynastic war in Europe's history, and the first international conflict fought with strategy and tactics dependent on mechanization and mass mobilization for long-term campaigns. World War I gave them up-to-date military experiences. The conjunction of past and present, of tradition and innovation, of years spent in war as well as peacetime service gave them career experiences more intensive than those of most officers who had preceded them in Argentina, Brazil, Chile, and Peru, and had blended professionalism with tradition.

Officers like Gamelin in Brazil and Clément, back in Peru, represented the victorious French army. Out of the Great War came a new supply of lore that merely reinforced French military tradition and linked officers to an earlier age of military grandeur. The stigma of the 1871 defeat vanished. Lyautey-esque images of the officer as social worker, creator of citizen-patriots, and molder of the French youth did not diminish.

Germans like Faupel, who found a home in Buenos Aires and Lima, and Kiesling, who spent years in Chile, retained as much as they could of their own past. Despite the overwhelming evidence of military inferiority in the face of French, British, and American opposition, the likes of Faupel, Kiesling, and even Kundt in Bolivia showed little inclination to change. The German army had not lost the war because it was beaten, German officers convinced themselves; Germany had lost the war because "enemies within" had undermined the armed forces. Even without the presence of missions, Prussian-style professionalism still dominated military thought in Argentina and Chile. Out of date though they may have been, the thought and self-perception of the German imperial past prevailed among German army officers of the Weimar era and in South American officer corps formed by pre-World War I German cadres.

The Goltzes and the Lyauteys lived on, literally as well as figuratively, and this helped transform South American professionalism into militarism. The Goltzian concept of the nation in arms, after all, had reached fruition in World War I. Obligatory military service, economic organization for wartime purposes, the fusion of military and political goals, and the devotion of the *Volk* and the *Staat* to the military imperative that dominated German thought and self-perception prior to 1914—these all endured in the post-1918 decades. Political and economic developments in the 1920s and 1930s reinforced, up-dated, and popularized them. Peasants having become Frenchmen, the dream of Hubert Lyautey became as much a reality as Goltz's "nation in arms," and themes in French military literature remained essentially the same. Obligatory service was still a necessity if France were to defend herself against German revenge. If the army no longer made provincial farmers into nationally-minded citizens, it still could do much for the sons of the alarmingly materialistic and individualistic bourgeoisie. As a mood of ennui and alienation swept over a generation of Frenchmen, as intellectual disregard for the historical past became commonplace, as people wanted simply to forget the horrors of war, French officers decried what had happened to their victorious guild. They believed themselves forgotten, ignored, and betrayed.

In Germany the once-aristocratic officer corps now had to deal with a bourgeois republic, and it was not easy. From 1918 to 1933 the German officer corps suffered attacks from without and survived internal schism. Writings from 1920 through 1939 indicate that at no time did officers cease to believe Germany would one day send her armies into the field against France. The rise of the National Socialist German Worker's Party—by no means a pleasing development to old-style German officers—served to confirm to a goodly number the inevitability of strong, centralized government in the Germanic world. Throughout the pre-Hitler years, German military thought displayed a nostalgic reverence for authority in the civilian sphere; the National Socialists effectively manipulated this reverence.

The Third Republic continued to be the subject of much discussion by French officers throughout these years. Many clung to Maurras's Action Française, some joined lodges like the *Cagoulle* and the *Croix de Feu*. Monarchist, Roman Catholic loyalties did not fade. Strong government remained a constant wish, hence the interest in Action Française and the numerous flirtations with nationalistic political groups. In both France and Germany, corporatist, fascist movements responded to historical and cultural as well as immediate socioeconomic and political realities.

The thought and self-perception discussed in this chapter contain enough of the essence of the past to make it obvious that change is a relative term. When juxtaposed with earlier books, monographs, and articles, the works of French and German officers and civilians published in the 1920s and 1930s appear repetitious and derivative. This means, however, that most of what pre-World War I officers thought and wrote about themselves and their profession, and the state, nation, and society of which the profession was a part, was still valid in 1940. A half-century simply did not erase the past, and the European officer of the day indeed was, in the figurative sense, "yesterday's soldier." These conclusions hold for all forms of comparison.

No better examples exist than Charles de Gaulle and Hans von Seeckt. Representatives of distinct yet blended generations: the future leader of Free France and the Fifth Republic and the monocled epitome of *Rittertum* who rebuilt the German army in the 1920s were every bit as symbolic of their era as were Goltz and Lyautey of theirs.

These first-hand observers of military-civilian relations and defenders of the military profession portrayed an age of doubt and frustration, of dismay and disgust. They ably defended the military profession against any and all enemies and detractors. They adapted tradition to change, the past to the present. Better than any, their works indicate the peculiar situation of the French and German officers. Better than any, their works highlight issues discussed consistently in both widely-circulated and professional publications.

Hans von Seeckt died in 1936 at the age of 70. During the Great War he was August von Mackensen's chief of staff on the Eastern Front, and chief of staff of the Turkish field command during 1917 and 1918. From 1918 to his retirement in 1926 he was commander in chief of the army, the *Reichswehr*. Between 1932 and 1935 he reorganized Chiang Kai-shek's Chinese Nationalist army. His organizational skills and field achievements aside, Seeckt's greatest accomplishment was the maintenance and development of the post-World War I army. Author of several significant treatises, his most famous work is *Gedanken eines Soldaten—Thoughts of a Soldier.*[1]

Seeckt's most fervent wish was to keep the army out of politics and, in turn, to keep partisan politics out of the officer corps and the barracks. "The army should be political," he wrote, "in that it should grasp the conception of the state, but it certainly must not be political in the party sense. 'Hands off the army,' is my cry to all parties. The army serves the state and the state alone, for it is the state."[2] Seeckt also revived the concept of the army as "the purest image of the state," so often expressed in the past.

His ideal, the apolitical army as expression of the state, was "a combination of many men with the same aim. This gives the soldier's profession a quite peculiar bond of unity, a corporate sense."[3] Seeckt believed discipline was as important to civilian society as it was to the army, and the officer's role was that of educator as well as leader. His perception of the army as bound to the state, hence of the state as bound to the army, was absolutely unoriginal. Post-1918 circumstances in Germany solidified rather than altered the German concept of

Staat, *Volk*, *Reich*, and *Heer* as permanently and necessarily monolithic.

Some of Seeckt's most cogent statements are found in his less well known works, for example, *Die Zukunft des Reiches: Urteile und Forderungen* (translated as *The Future of the German Empire; Criticisms and Postulates*) and *Die Reichswehr*. In the former he stressed the transcendental qualities of Germanic culture in the historical struggle for a unified state representing all Germans. This was a living, organic state, but not an oppressive one. Divisive issues, i.e., partisan politics and parliamentarism, worked only to the detriment of the state, hence of all Germans, for these divisive phenomena precluded representation of a common will by the state.

Seeckt stressed the present as a transitory link between the past and the future. The latter were thus more important than the unpleasant here and now. In terms at times utterly fatuous he linked the army to the past, present, and future, to tradition, preparation, and innovation. "The man of action," he stated, "is confronted with the task of grasping the threads of the past, and within the working time allotted to him of fashioning them into a new fabric for the future. When I speak of the future, I mean thereby the continuity of the past to which the future is fatefully linked."[4]

Politics drew harsh words from Seeckt. Proportional representation, parties, plebescites, and parliamentary debate all tended to make factions more significant than the whole. The bureaucracy responded too much to partisan pressures. Parliaments were under the control of cliques that divided the populace. This meant that "the real interests of the people are subordinated to party interests which, in the long run, always aim at the maintenance, gain or growth of power."

Where were the general will and national spirit best represented? Where else? The German people's sense of history, indeed its sense of being, "obliges and entitles the army to cherish tradition, soldierly and national tradition. From these traditions it derives its sense of obligation towards the past and towards the state."[5] Thus the army was *the* national institution, transcending the chronological confines of history, from the monarchy and empire of the past to the parliamentary republic of Seeckt's present to the future he both hoped for and feared.

The state, represented by the army, was but a means to the common good. It was the state's (hence the army's) obligation to check freedom where necessary to assure that the common good be achieved and maintained. Too much discussion and difference of opinion detracted from the proper blend of past, present, and future. Hence there must be a time when "the man of action...is entitled to precedence over the debater; debate must lead to action on which discussion thence forward ceases and must not be allowed to exercise any influence."[6] Barely tolerant of civilian politics and democracy, officers eagerly subscribed to Seeckt's dicta.

Turned outward, toward what Seeckt called the "pygmies of Versailles," Seeckt's ideas had the effect of rekindling German cultural nationalism and xenophobia.[7] Democracy, bureaucracy, materialism, bourgeois values, anti-French and -British feelings, geopolitically-based complaints about Germany's lot—these all found expression in the works of Germans.

At the age of thirty-seven Captain Charles De Gaulle delivered a series of three lectures at the École Supérieure de Guerre. Later published as *Le Fil de l'epée* (translated as *The Edge of the Sword*), they formed the neat political testament of a young, ambitious officer. The young De Gaulle was as representative of traditional military thought and self-perception as was his aging German contemporary.

Of particular interest to the captain's listeners in 1927, to his future followers, and to South Americans who read his essays or heard second hand what he had to say were remarks in the chapter "Of Character."[8] Like Vigny, Lyautey, and Psichari, De Gaulle had a mystical conception of character. Like Seeckt's (and Goltz's and Clausewitz's) man of action, the man of character was one who seized the initiative, who took responsibility, a man who did not "hide behind textbooks or regulations." The man of character was prepared for action, could deal with both success and failure. He was self-reliant, reserved, aloof, confident. Political attributes to Seeckt were signs of character to De Gaulle; and their own personalities were no doubt influential in their works.

Men of character, i.e., potential event-makers, were not popular men, hardly hail fellows well met. "The authorities dread any officer who has the gift of making decisions and cares nothing for routine and soothing words."[9] Politicians only listened to men of character, thought De Gaulle, when the country was in real trouble. Routine and soothing words were to De Gaulle what the "bouton de mandarin" and garrison duty were to Lyautey. De Gaulle specifically referred to lack of discipline and initiative as signs of character. Lyautey's conduct in Morocco in defiance of orders from home was an example.

De Gaulle railed against the parliamentary system, claiming that it would ultimately destroy the "military order whose strength is drawn primarily from soldierly virtues."[10] He chided civilians for their ignorance of the military, using the terms of pre-war French officers to do so. He attacked what he considered to be the neglect of the army by the Third Republic, just as Seeckt decried the condition of the army under the Weimar regime. Like Seeckt and many Germans—and like Argentines, Brazilians, Chileans, and Peruvians—De Gaulle and many of his fellow officers were convinced that civilian society was self-destructive, fractious, without direction. The army was corporate, organic; military training developed leaders (men of character); obligatory service made men into full citizens. Only in the army did men of all classes "rub shoulders."

In "Of Prestige" the captain lamented the decline of discipline and authority in everyday life. "This decay of public authority has followed hard on the heels of a decline in moral standards, both in society and politics, from what they were in an older Europe. Men in their hearts can no more do without being controlled than they can live without food, drink and sleep." Again a man in uniform ticked off the culprits: individuality, audacity, mass participation in politics, lack of respect for leadership. "Men of action" and "men of character," therefore, could not be civilians; only army officers were expected to display indiscipline and have it pass for a positive character trait. The major remedy for the decline of European culture and civilization was "prestige." Prestige counteracted the disturbing of traditions and institutions by contemporary reality; but how to exude prestige, how to captivate other men and persuade them to obey and follow? Like character, prestige had intangible qualities: mystery, creativity, secretiveness, taciturnity, silence, sobriety.[11] These qualities, necessary for maintenance of social solidarity and retention of historical consciousness, were inherent in the officer corps.

De Gaulle also discussed soldiers and statesmen, clearly viewing the soldier more capable of being a statesman than vice versa. Collaboration was necessary, especially in time of war, when the soldier became involved in national policy making, but even in peacetime his counsel was valuable. "One would think that an enlightened state would see the wisdom of training a political, administrative, and military elite by means of studies undertaken in common, so that there might be a body of competent men in all these departments ready to direct the nation in time of war."[12] De Gaulle's argument in favor of the École des Hautes Études Militaires was very much in keeping with traditional elitist French education policies.

The general and the captain represented different generations—Seeckt was a captain when De Gaulle was an infant—but they were professionals whose careers spanned most of the half-century dealt with herein. Their ideas on the politics of modern democratic systems and republicanism, on leadership, on the differences between military and civilian ways of life, and on the nature of the military profession and its "soldierly virtues" were so similar as to constitute hard evidence of continuity in officer-class self-perception regardless of nationality.

The fact that the general's army, that modern version of *Rittertum* and *Junkertum*, had lost the most costly war in the history of mankind, or that the young captain's army had won (albeit with the "assistance" of allies), made only slight difference when it came to appraising the corps, the profession, and the army's social responsibilities and its relations with civilian institutions as part of a grand historical continuum. Whether by Vigny or Clausewitz, Goltz or Lyautey, Seeckt or De Gaulle, publicly expressed thought and self-perception were much the same as they had been for decades. There was still a gulf between military values of authority, hierarchy, and corporatism, and values that officers and some civilians, too, perceived as dangerously and excessively dominant in the world of civilians: liberty, equality, and individualism. Seeckt and De Gaulle were not the only ones to realize this.

What appears as resignation ought not to be mistaken for acceptance in toto of democracy and the third Republic by the French officer corps. Publicly, French officers were relatively quiescent in the 1920s, but quiescence need not indicate lack of concern.

Four great French generals died between 1916 and 1931: Gallieni in 1916, Mangin in 1925, Foch in 1929, and Joffre in 1931. Lyautey himself died three years later. Inter-war attrition left the high command to the likes of Pétain, Gamelin, and Huntziger, and the role of critic to De Gaulle. By the end of the 1920s, Gallieni, Mangin, Foch, and Joffre had become symbols of grandeur, devotion, and abnegation. Charles Maurras, praised them in a volume of essays published in 1931 entitled *Le Quadrilatère*.[13] He portrayed France's dead heroes as representatives of the true France, as worthy opponents to the politics of civilians like Aristide Briand, Raymond Poincaré, and, of course, Georges Clemenceau.

Maurras's words flattered officers, for he alleged that they had been antidotal to the excesses of parliamentary democracy and the easy terms of the Versailles treaties, and that they were the defenders of the French nation not only against the Germans but, in the years after the war, against the British, the United States, and international-minded Woodrow Wilson.[14] Maurras was not the only civilian to curry favor with the army, and more than a few officers displayed in print a susceptibility to his blandishments.

The French were ever aware of the need to stay abreast of military developments east of the Rhine. French behavior in the decade after Versailles makes it crystal clear that, win or lose, military professionals can make a case for greater military expenditures, better equipment, expanded obligatory service, and a more significant peacetime role. Under any and all conditions French officers complained, felt unappreciated, aspired to a wider scope of domestic activity, and worried about their future.

Looking at the German army in 1929, Paul Gentizon correctly perceived it to be in a state of flux, its officer corps divided and weakened. The new constitution, he noted, submitted the army to civilian controls as never before, causing the older generation of officers to oppose the system they had sworn to defend. It was an *officiersdämmerung*, their "twilight."[15] Gentizon's point was that Germany was in a situation somewhat analagous to that of France after 1871. It was "as if the majority of the officer class in the Imperial Army had been Social Democrats."[16] As much as French officers lamented "easy terms" forced on the Germans, he claimed, Germans considered them an undue hardship.

Evidence for allegations of easy peace terms came from Foch. His *Precepts and Judgments* contains a distinctly hostile appraisal of all politicians, the parliamentary system, diplomats, and most foreigners.[17] Despite his admonition to fellow officers that "one must take a wide view; you all know how much I hate blinkers; one must not have an exclusively military outlook," Foch had no doubt that Clemenceau and others had been soft on the Germans and accommodating toward the British and Americans.[18] "Frock coats" had allowed Germany to hold on to the Rhineland (temporarily). By inference, civilians were unrealistic; soldiers had a clearer view of reality. No matter Clemenceau's disclaimers, he was no favorite among members of the officer corps.[19] Foch, as well as Lyautey and Goltz, De Gaulle and Seeckt, decried the inability of orators, candidates, statesmen, and prime ministers to solve problems.

Politicians wanted to "satisfy the electorate"; they were not competent administrators as a rule and cared not a whit for the state. "France's land is rich; as a state she is in ruins, and it is the government that has ruined her."[20] Foch also believed in military-civilian cooperation. His 1909–10 Centre des Hautes Études Militaires had been an attempt to remedy the lack of administrative expertise among army officers, but had been abandoned. Reopened in the 1920s, it became a joint civil-military institute (although never what Foch wanted it to be) for high-level administration and cooperation in security and national defense matters. It provided a model for a more successful institute, the Peruvian Centro de Altos Estudios Militares.

Gallieni, the colonial genius and savior of Paris; Foch, commander in chief and defender of the army against civilian "meddling"; Joffre, "Hero of the Marne"; Mangin, the African veteran who helped create France's Black African Legion,[21] which simultaneously terrified and disgusted Germans: the roll of French heroes was diminished noticeably. Through Mangin, South Americans learned details of France's victory and of her army's plight. During 1921 he toured and lectured extensively in Peru, Chile, and Argentina and later wrote a book about his tour.

As Mangin toured, Maurice Gamelin was head of the first French mission to Brazil. Although he served abroad between 1919 and 1929, Gamelin rose to the post of chief of staff in 1931. By this time he was already convinced of the sad state of affairs in the army, for he thought the best and brightest of French youth would have nothing to do with an army career. Who wanted to enter St. Cyr if there were no wars in which to achieve glory and promotion, like Gamelin himself and others of his generation? Who wanted to spend years languishing as a captain or major for low pay? Who wanted the dull routine of provincial garrisons?[22] The empire no longer had the appeal it once had, and opportunity for economic gain lay elsewhere.

French officers, though not confronted by a new political system, perceived themselves in no better a situation than did Germans. The values of both were, in the words of one contemporary, "old goods in new wrappings." The essentials of leadership had not changed; leadership was the "conductor" or wire for the "current of morale generated by the dynamo of nationalism."[23] The Great War had changed only the metaphors for the French, the Germans, and others. The past was with them; so was the future. This is vividly evident in the literature on education, a long-standing interest of French officers.

"If you compare the scholar that I was yesterday to the soldier that I must be tomorrow, you will appreciate the necessity of a rigorous regimen and well understand that St. Cyr is a factory, a special military factory, that manufactures soldiers who will one day be our leaders."[24] Lieutenant Federphil's nostalgic glimpse of France's military school convinced him that the "special military factory" was the only place (aside from the Polytechnique) where young Frenchmen learned discipline, obedience, loyalty, service, and the fulfilling of an assignment. Preparatory schools taught useless things like poetry, art, debate, and pure science. Such a shallow education served no useful purpose. Military education created potential leaders.[25] It mattered little that civilian receptivity to such arguments had dwindled greatly; officers continued to pose them.

The most widely circulated military tract on education was that of General Maxime Weygand. In his 1937 *Comment élever nos fils?* Weygand was more than just mindful of the youth programs by now well under way in Germany. In contrast to Germans, he thought, French youths were undisciplined, individualistic; they had too many choices. French education needed a military-patriotic component in which national heroes, great events, morality, and discipline could be inculcated quickly. French youth had forgotten fifteen centuries of history, and lived only for the moment.[26] Further, the public and private schools were simply not doing their job. Official government statistics indicated that 4 percent of the army-age men were illiterate; army-administered *dictées* given to conscripts showed an annually varying rate of between 22 percent and 31 percent. Weygand agreed (inadvertently), with Jaurès, who had pegged the illiteracy rate at 36 percent a quarter-century earlier. Some conscripts, he lamented, thought that Henry IV (king, 1594–1610) had assisted Pétain in leading France to victory in World War I, others believed Russia to be a French colony.[27] How could such ignorance contribute to national defense?

"Directors of business, industry, stores, and banks deplore the young graduate's lack of aptitude for writing a letter, a report, or an account rendered with order and clarity, in correct language with impeccable orthography."[28] A "practical" military education, of course, eliminated such shortcomings, but in lieu of a large-scale militarization of the educational system, only intensive reform would provide France and her army with functionally literate and capable young men. Weygand's points found a ready-made audience in South America if not in his own country.

Education was not the sole issue French officers continued to discuss publicly. Deputy Paul Reynaud championed a stronger army in 1937, citing the new, blatant rearmament of Germany and Germany's bellicose behavior as his chief justification. Was France destined to be "the sheep in a world of wolves?" he asked. The Centre des Hautes Études de la Défense Nacional (Foch's legacy), under a new name, needed expanding in order to provide France with a military and civilian administrative elite to plan and execute economic and military policy. Defense must take into account joint command of all operations.[29] The pseudonymous "Video" responded affirmatively to Reynaud's suggestions. France's army, her entire defense capability, depended on the political, social, and economic "wealth" of the nation. In short, France was in a desperate condition. Owing to divisions within the political system, France was "sitting and waiting" while Germany rearmed.[30] Foreign affairs, political affairs, social problems, and military potential were thus inseparable.

Germany's increasingly aggressive actions drove Frenchmen to look within the army as well. Discipline was difficult to ensure in a modern military context. Whereas career-oriented professional officers were constantly steeped in it, the citizen-soldier did not respond well. Lack of response, General Tanant wrote, had increased since World War I. This meant the army must present discipline as a positive, valuable, beneficial aspect of modern life. Frenchmen were sociable, gregarious, unused to discipline for its own sake. "One cannot, for example, treat the French soldier as a German soldier is treated."[31] Prussian-style militarism was unsuitable, but this did not mean France could not have a disciplined army.

Initiative, questioning, and interpretation ought to be permissible, Tanant wrote, but not to the extent that they cancelled out commands—not to the extent that they dominated civilian life, he might have added. The native intelligence of Frenchmen could be manipulated psychologically to assure a disciplined fighting force. A disciplined army, above and beyond being capable of defending *la Patrie*, also played an important social role.

Late in the 1930s another captain promoted the *rôle social*.[32] No army could function unless moral education was a part of basic training; France's army was truly democratic because the officer corps—the elite of leadership—was open to men from all social classes. Could civilian elite groups claim the same? In the army, at all levels Frenchmen submitted to discipline, shared responsibility, responded to their country's most urgent and serious needs. The army was uniquely homogeneous in function, yet heterogeneous in its make-up. Could civilian institutions be described in the same way? The army was a microcosm of France; it was like a family, with the officer assigned the role of *pater familias*.[33] This essay could easily have been written in 1891, when Lyautey wrote *Du Rôle social*.

On the eve of Germany's invasion of Poland, Henri Phillipe Pétain published an appeal for greater coordination of defense matters.[34] In doing so, he echoed Foch, Reynaud, and "Video." Pétain recalled that a quarter-century earlier civilian and military leaders were so far apart socially, politically, and philosophically that coordination of policy and action proved extremely difficult throughout the war. Foch's post-war complaints proved his point, Pétain claimed. Now, faced with inevitable war, France needed a fusion of military and civilian talents to survive. Officers in the École Supérieure studied international relations, law, and economics as well as technical subjects. It should not be permissible, therefore, that "the young men who one day will be statesmen or high functionaries remain indifferent to the questions of national defense."[35]

At this point in the history of military professionalism, the French opinions expressed openly in publications for wide dissemination had not changed much in a half-century. Alarm at the perpetually sad state of affairs in "civic culture" was increasing. Democracy still looked chaotic, education a mess, individualism exaggerated, youth undisciplined, politicians (most of them, anyway) corrupt and irresponsible. The army remained a flickering light in a darkening world. The army remained France's salvation, her preserver and nourisher. The army was *la nation en armes*.[36] If anything had increased visibly, it was the call for military-civilian coordination of defense procedures during peacetime as well as in war; on that issue the essence of officer-corps thought and self-perception was precise. It became precise in Germany, too, owing to the rise of National Socialism.

From the euphoria of the fall of 1914 to the defeat of 1918 and the near social revolution following that defeat was quite a distance for German officers. They traversed it bitterly. What had been called a "People's War" and a "Holy War," in keeping with German myths and propaganda, had ended ignominiously. The belief that *"Sie haben alle nur einen Feind: England!"* (You have only one enemy: England!) appeared painfully true to German officers and reinforced their chauvinism.

Lieutenant General Graf von Freytagh Loringhoven's works *Deductions from the World War* and *A Nation Trained in Arms or a Militia?* both confirm this.[37] He posed two principal deductions from the 1914–18 experiences. First, no matter the changes in technology or the innovations in strategy or tactics, what counted most in war was leadership. If leadership talent was lacking, the most modern materiel meant absolutely nothing. Second, uniformity of training through coordinated obligatory service was the only way to make components of the army function like "machines with interchangeable parts."[38] The earl was not alone.

The infamous Bernhardi also remarked on lessons of the war. Germany, he believed, had trusted her allies too much. France and England had hoodwinked the United States, Italy, and Russia into opposing Germany.[39] The *Reichswehr* had been brought down from within by cowardly civilians who were unable to bear the awesome burdens of war. Bismarck would have "turned in his grave" had he been unaware of the "unprecedented poverty of ideas" in civilian political life.

Bernhardi's principal conclusion was that in times of emergency "military and political direction should be in one hand."[40] There was need for trained professionals to direct the affairs of state during wartime, in order that military and civilian administration be coordinated for the common good.

Erich Ludendorf agreed with Bernhardi. Ludendorf absorbed much of the blame for Germany's late-war difficulties, and in his retirement years he lashed out at his critics. The lack of combined military-civilian administration during the war made it possible for Germany's enemies—the Jews and the Communist International—to defeat her from within. The Russian Revolution (aided and abetted by the Jews, French, and British) also helped defeat Germany.[41] The army had not lost the war, in short; Jews, Communists, foreigners, and civilians had lost it.

General Bernhard Kiesling tried hard to reconcile the military with the new state, nevertheless. The impositions of Versailles forced Germans to make the necessary adjustments (for a while, at least). Kiesling rationalized that Germany had not collapsed at all; Prussian-led Germany had. Germany had survived, and so had her military zeal and expertise. A new form of government would, if nothing else, make it possible for Germany to have a truly representative army, one in which aristocrat and commoner would not be at odds.[42] Kiesling's attempt at rationalization did not prove acceptable to very many officers of the old school, but it did indicate a professional's willingness to make adjustments in order to survive under difficult circumstances.

The civilian Arno Voigt proved no more successful in convincing anyone of the need for a dispute. A self-declared "*Unmilitärischen*," ("unmilitarylike"), Voigt castigated the officer corps. Officers were arrogant, elitist, cold toward their subalterns, narrow-minded, and out of touch with the times. They had to adjust to the Republic and to democracy, and their military effectiveness need not suffer for it when they did so. The officer of the future, Voigt averred, "must be socially oriented, the citizen is not beneath him, for he himself is a citizen."[43] Out of the crucible of war, defeat, and dynastic collapse, he believed, had come an *Offiziersdämmerung* and the dawn of a new age.

Liberty, democracy, and equality would prevail, and so would permissiveness. This signified an end to order, discipline, and defense capabilities unless the army maintained a high level of training. This was Seeckt's responsibility by the time Major Fritz von Rakenau wrote about it in 1925. The army could be an institution of "socialization" for Germany's youth only if officers preserved traditional methods of discipline. But officers need not ape chauvinists like Moltke and Schlieffen, the Prussian militarists associated with war and conquest. They had plenty of other examples to follow in terms of drill, education, nationalism, and discipline.[44] The point was that one did not have to be an autocrat, exhibit a dueling scar, and be able to quote Bernhardi to be a good officer. In a democratic-republican milieu the Lyauteyesque *rôle social* took on a new meaning for Germans. It was a way to preserve the past and adapt both present and future to it.

Totalitarianism was another. It made the army and the state synonymous, at least for propaganda purposes. From 1933 forward, the officer corps lost its aristocratic mien; it ceased to be a class.[45] The war and the Weimar era had begun this process. The "Nazification" of the corps and the expansion of the size of the *Reichswehr* in the 1930s completed it. Despite the dramatic changes in Germany from 1933 forward, however, officer-corps thought and self-perception remained steadfast. Nazi sympathizers and old-line Prussians could agree on certain principles—on history, myths, and the lore of the profession.

General Franz Ritter von Epp, a neo-Bernhardian Nazi loyalist, spoke for both totalitarians and the officers when asked what qualities he had to stand for the Reichstag in 1928: "I have no such qualities. I will never have those qualities."[46] Epp thought the Reichstag was a "hospital full of sick men." Politics was anathema. Education and social class also came under scrutiny in the new Germany. Professor Ewald Banse, exhorting Germans to war in 1934, opined that "the selection of officers should depend less on school reports and family than on 'bearing.' " Banze's geopolitical tract on expansion and war, *Raum und Volk im Weltkriege*, was blatantly racist in tone, and just as outré as Bernhardi's *Kriegsbuch*.[47] Still, he could calmly specify discipline as the officer's principal concern.

To Nazis—and to a number of army officers—the successes of the 1933–39 years indicated that Germany and her army had risen from the ashes. Military professionalism and National Socialism provided a new ambience for discipline, honor, patriotism, and service that assumed grotesque proportions.

Old explanations revived and thrived. Herman Gauer's *Bauerntum Bürgertum und Arbeitertum in der Armee* stands as an example. Writing in 1936 he argued that the army united all Germans. Peasants, bourgeoisie, and workers wore the uniform together for the sake of the *Volk*. Gauer insisted that arms had spread culture and civilization. Nations had prospered, Greece and Rome had fused armed might with political stability and national prosperity—a convenient view of antiquity. Now National Socialism similarly brought citizens and soldiers of all classes together more effectively than they had ever been before.[48]

Kurt Hesse concurred with Gauer. Young Germans ought to be honored to serve the Reich, he wrote. Obligatory service was a patriotic duty. The army was the "school of life."[49] Young men learned anew the meaning of discipline, respect for one's superiors, good conduct, patriotism, self-awareness, and comradeship: the basic elements of a good life. To an imaginary father he wrote, "Your son is now a soldier for a year. He serves the Fatherland, the state, the Führer. These are his new parents."[50] Germany, he claimed throughout, found herself on a historical continuum begun by Scharnhorst and Clausewitz, broken in 1919, and restored in 1933. Germany, grandeur, National Socialism, and the army were inseparable. Stripped of obvious objectional references to the mystical wonders of National Socialism, these pro-Nazi works appear no more authoritarian in theory than the thought of pre-1914 military professionals.

Axel Freiherr von Maltzahn's *Der deutsche Soldat: Ein Aus-blick und Rückblick* was no different. To Maltzahn, Germany was merely the contemporary expression of the warrior-nation tradition *vom Volksheer zum Heervolk*, "from citizen's army to armed citizenry." The mission of *Volk*, *Heer*, and *Staat* was still a spiritual one, sacred and decidedly humanistic. The *Heervolk* waged war against a present of excessive liberalism, materialism, capitalism, individualism, *and* Marxism to restore mankind's spiritual qualities.[51] The army was Germany's soul. From the pen of a Nazi hack these claims appear absurd, but they differ little, really, from past mutterings of German officers. "The army is the defender of the German nation," wrote another. "It protects the German Reich and Fatherland, which through National Socialism are united as nation and living space, *Lebensraum*. The roots of its power lie in a glorious past of nationhood, land, and toil. Service in the army is a debt of honor to the nation."[52] This propaganda piece summed up the new version of the army as provider of historical continuity and national identity. Continuity and identity were now, more than ever before, linked to racial superiority. All post-1933 works stressed this, and not just out of expediency. Did not everyone know that Germans had the finest army in the world, the defeat of 1918 notwithstanding? Now, National Socialism, wrote Egon Hundeiker, could even provide a substitute for racial purity in Mediterranean Europe and elsewhere, for it assured discipline and hierarchy.[53] Hundeiker's equine racial analogies—Nordics as thoroughbreds, non-Nordic Europeans as plowhorses, and Non-Europeans as asses—did not appeal, one ventures, to all South Americans.

General Georg Wetzel's war-mongering *Die deutsche Wehrmacht, 1914–1939: Rückblick und Ausblick* echoed Maltzahn's similarly titled work and completed the process of fusing past, present, and future through retrospect—*Rückblick*—and prospect—*Ausblick*. He emphasized German achievements since the eighteenth century as the results of close ties between state, nation, and army. Scharnhorst and Moltke had been close to their civilian counterparts; now Hitler provided an even stronger bond. "Whatever the war brings," he noted, "perfect coordination of military and civilian energies will produce victory."[54] By the time Wetzel's book appeared, the lines between civilian and military, between party and officer corps, between paramilitary and professional organization had blurred to the point where some officers began to think seriously about rectifying the situation. The war postponed their plans.

Perusal of official French and German journals of the interwar years indicates further consistency and continuity. Essays in professional reviews were identical in theme to works written for a greater audience. Thought and self-perception still were comparable, whether internally or externally generated. Economy measures in the post-war years resulted in the publication of only one official review in France, the *Revue Militaire Française*, a combination of the *Journal des Sciences Militaires*, *Revue Militaire des Armées Étrangères*, and *Revue Militaire Française*. The bulk of the literature appearing in the 1920s was of a technical nature, but non-technical material was equal in quality to that of the past.

Obligatory service received much attention, because it was a "nationalizing force." Lieutenant Colonel Émile Mayer, a frequent contributor to the *Revue*, argued in 1921 that if basic education was obligatory for all citizens, military service should be too. Responding to all "anti-militarists," he cautioned that peace would not endure if France became weak; defense demanded the rendering of military service by all in peacetime. "If the intellectual elite is useful in the liberal professions and in civilian life, it is no less [useful] in the army."[55] Mayer made a new case as well for national service as a real benefit to the uneducated man.

Colonel Viotte took exception to Mayer's arguments in 1922, continuing the continental tradition of using the military journal as tribune. Mayer had suggested the retention of a "small, mobile army." Viotte responded that to keep the Germans at bay, to maintain order in the colonies where "dangerous revolutionaries" were at work, and to insure against "undependable allies," France needed a much larger army, even larger than she had maintained in the past. The colonial army should be autonomous, for backward peoples accepted force and authority because they respected them. "If [force and authority] were to diminish, they would foment disorder, for the threat of punishment would be there no longer."[56] This argument appealed to South Americans.

Whatever the size of France's army, her officers were "spiritually oriented." Henri Michel's 1922 comments on grandeur, devotion to duty, morale, and tradition were reminiscent of Vigny's. So were those of Colonel Dessofy de Czernek, who also responded to Mayer's plea for military-civilian fusion. The colonel stressed that war demanded a psychological orientation different from that of businessmen or civil administrators, and there were obviously few who could make the transition.[57] French military wariness of civilians was fully comparable to that of Germans.

Frenchmen knew full well that Germany remained their enemy. Freytag Loringhoven's monograph of 1917 provoked a response by Major Grenier in 1924. He called the new German officer corps as much a caste as a military organization. *Junkertum* and *Rittertum* had given way to professional *Kameradschaft* and *Offizierbund*, "comradeship" and "officers' covenant."[58] Grenier believed these were just as binding.

Obviously the French officer corps had changed too. There were fewer with noble surnames now and more bourgeois officers.[59] But the officer, no matter his social origins, retained the moral and intellectual attributes of the past. The French *cavalier consommé* combined qualities of the past with the sophisticated technology of the present. "Let us not forget that Minerva is sister to Mars," wrote Captain Damidaux, proclaiming the intellectuality of the modern fighting man. Consummate cavaliers, intellectuals, and more; at the École Supérieure, instructors repeatedly urged staff aspirants to think of themselves as *mosquetaires et Benedictins*, i.e., as valorous armed servants of the state and as ascetics.[60] Despite the new metaphors, some of the old ones still appealed to officers.

Hierarchy still appeared to authors as a natural (therefore eternal and correct) selective process; those who possessed the talent for field command or staff service found their way to posts they were capable of filling in an objective way. All officers shared most of the same qualities, but some had greater intellectual, theoretical, or administrative talent. The latter became the elite of the army.[61] Such idealized views of the officer class were now common in South America.

The outspoken De Gaulle wrote on coordination of the national defense effort in a 1934 *Revue Militaire Française* essay. "All falls within the domain of national defense," he claimed in 1934. A country without a defense plan and military-civilian coordination of the plan's implementation was a lost country. One of his colleagues urged the government to provide statistical data on the economy, resources, and manpower to the general staff—old arguments in France, and by this time in South American countries as well.[62]

So convinced of the necessity for military-civilian coordination and unity of command were men like Pétain, Debeney, Castex, Gamelin, and General Paul Azan that they succeeded in changing the entire editorial policy of the *Revue Militaire Française* in 1937. The *Revue Militaire Generale* replaced it as chief organ, not just of army but of air and sea defense experts as well.[63] Its contents reflected the wishes of graduates of the Collège des Hautes Études de Défense Nationale, masterminded by Castex himself. There colonels and generals studied politics, colonial policy, sociology, mobilization procedures, public relations, and economics.[64] They strove for a unity of nation, state, and army as strong as that of Germany but free from the ideological trappings of the new Reich.

In downright touching essays of 1937 and 1938 some French officers tried to reassure themselves that all was well. In "Esprit guerrier allemande et française," one officer contrasted German aggressive tendencies and revenge motives with French passivity and doctrinal conservatism. He believed that the German army indeed was fused to nation and state, hence to society, but that the French army never would be. France's officer corps was refined, cultured, and sophisticated; Germany's was crude and intellectually limited. Such a contrast, he hoped, somehow would aid France in the long run.[65] In the face of imminent war other officers dwelt upon

the past, on Lyautey, on the *rôle social*, on themes so traditional as to be hackneyed.[66] This made their professional confrontation all that more difficult.

Early on after World War I, *Militär Wochenblatt* editors put
the question of political participation to their readers in "Soll
der deutsche Offizier Politik treiben?" They answered their
own question: "No, the German officer shall not practice politics." Political participation would destroy the entire army
(or what was left of it). The *Offizierbund* must stand above
the politics of opportunism, *Opportunitätspolitik*, in the interest of self-preservation. Other writers also warned in set
terms against "political practice." Social Democrats were now
Communists, and their Bolshevik allies controlled Russia. German officers saw the red flag everywhere, literally and figuratively. The army had to resist communism.[67] The
relationship of state and army must have a new "foundation
of trust and mutual respect." Army, state, and nation remained one in the mind of the German officers.[68] If one were
perforce pried away from the other two, Germany would dis-
integrate, for Germany was beset within and on all sides by
enemies.

Obligatory service, forbidden to Germany at Versailles, still
impressed Germans as a binding agent and the builder of
trust between government and populace, of critical importance under the Weimar regime. In the mind of most officers
the state remained an omniscient thing. The corps might not
prefer Weimar Germany to the Second Reich but the French,
thought one writer, did appear to have survived republicanism and democracy. Germans were brothers, first of all, and
politically-minded people second, so Germany might still
have "the best army the world has ever seen."[69] Division
spelled doom; unity against the political storms of the present
assured salvation; but how to achieve unity?

Germans began writing in official sources about military-
civilian fusion on a more practical plane in the mid-1920s.
Colonel von Notz discussed the salutary effects of a national
labor service in a brief note of 1925. If Germany could not
maintain a large standing army based on obligatory military

service, *allgemeine Wehrpflicht*, then why not a labor obligation, *allgemeine Arbeitsdienstpflicht*?[70] If not truly military experience, it might provide a vehicle for the inculcation of
discipline among German youth. As the army underwent restructuring, German officers thought hard and long of ways
to rebuild without evoking either rebuke or reprisal.

Politics affected German officer-authors in the early 1930s
just as it always had. The army feared the Communist party
despite General Kurt von Schleicher's attempts at political
bargaining. Communism was a menace to the fatherland, the
army, and society. Officers were warned to be perpetually "on
guard" against seditious propaganda, just as they had been
since the opening years of the century.[71] The army was never
politically neutral when Marxism was the issue.

Officers told each other that they still must represent
"knightliness," *Ritterlichkeit*, they still must set a proper example as teacher, drill master, and social role model. Being in
mufti did not release the officer from his commitment, wrote
one officer, rather it increased the necessity for him to behave
always as an officer.[72] "Nationalism and socialism," wrote another in 1930, "contend for the mind of the German youth,"
and it was up to the officer corps to see to it that "nationalism" won out.[73] Unity, political neutrality, and staunch defense of national values would strengthen all German
institutions.

Discussions of National Socialism per se began to appear
regularly in the *Militär Wochenblatt* in 1931. An August editorial deemed it "preferable to socialism," for it raised "nation"
above "class" and "fatherland" above "internationalism."[74] But
the editors made no formal commitment yet. They cautiously
adapted tenets of National Socialism to certain professional
tenets such as leadership, authority, action, hierarchy, solidarity
in the face of partisan politics, and the officer as teacher-
leader.[75] By 1933, authors were perforce writing about the army
as a binding agent but beholden to the NSDAP. "The army lives
off the energy of the nation." "Military service is a service to the
German nation." "One for all, all for one." The army and
National Socialism were identical in spiritual values, for they
sprang from the same spiritual source, and united the German

people. National Socialism was, after all, "not a real political party," it was a *Weltanschauung*.[76] Hitler coopted the officer corps enough that opposition movements to him and to the NDSAP sputtered.

By the end of 1934 *Militär Wochenblatt* had returned to technical themes. Political discussion was once again off limits to officers who aspired to anything beyond platitudinous praise of the Third Reich and its *Führer*. Officers still perceived themselves as teachers, leaders, and servants of the state; the army was still the "bearer of arms" of the nation, and now the nation was organized properly—along functional lines.[77] All males were "eligible" (not "obliged") to serve the fatherland. This made the army's job much easier, thought *Wochenblatt* editors. Officers rationalized their accommodation with Nazism using the same words and values with which they had always discussed political problems.[78]

A prominent German historian compared Hitler to Frederick the Great; the chancellor symbolized greatness in the present as the crown had done in the past. And officers could still write of war as a "creative force."[79] The chancellor himself gave the Happy New Year message to all officers on the cover of the first *Wochenblatt* issue of 1937. He thanked "his" officers for another year's devotion and service to the Reich, for the successful implementation of the new two-year military service system—and for the militarization of the Rhineland.[80] In the last full year before the war, *Militär Wochenblatt* proclaimed anew that the officer was a teacher, leader, inculcator of virtues, role model, and paragon of citizenship; that the army molded good citizens, patriots, and men of good faith.[81] A macabre mask of National Socialism was superimposed on the stern face of the German officer. Years had passed, composition of the officer corps had changed, but values remained the same. German military professionalism had retained its essence between 1890 and 1940 despite political, social, and economic vicissitudes.

And so, to the brink of another war in 1939 both French and German officers continued to treat the same themes their predecessors had treated between 1890 and 1914. The army was a school; the officer and the noncom composed a faculty of teachers and surrogate fathers. Obligatory service was a duty and an honor. Politics was evil; the army should be free from partisan pressures. National defense was impossible without joint coordination of all activities; military-civilian fusion would only be successful, however, if the officer could dictate to the bureaucrat.

Officers still proclaimed themselves to the public as virtuous, incorruptible, and devoted to duty. They still believed—they said they believed—that abnegation was a virtue, as was unswerving loyalty to the state. They claimed to represent the past of Napoleon, Clausewitz, Lyautey, and Goltz, as well as the present of armor, mechanized warfare, and advanced study of economics and international relations.

Frenchmen and Germans remained steadfast in their assertions that Socialists, Communists, capitalists, the internationally-minded, the English, the Jews, and those pushy Americans sought to destroy their world—a world defined in traditional, continental terms. Democracy was as chaotic to the defender of the Third Republic as it was to the servant of the Third Reich. Parliaments were useless. Students had no love of country unless their enthusiasm were channeled; they could have no sense of duty unless they received military training. Western culture and civilization, Christianity, social harmony, economic well-being, political stability, and human dignity were doomed to extinction. Europe's traditional military rivals, enemies to the end, imparted such a professionalism to South America. What had failed to wither and disappear in France and Germany was now in vogue as well in Argentina, Brazil, Chile, and Peru, where yesterday's soldiers also confronted the present.

"The government of a new nation shares in the constructive activities of orientation and of fomenting creative efforts, [activities] that are incompatible with the absorbing preoccupations of crude politics."

José F. B. Uriburu, Speech at the Colegio Militar (1930)

"In the Indo-Hispanic nations of our continent, which are not the repositories but the workshops of civilization, which do not represent the fruition of civilization but the continuous forging of a culture, a firm and active form of government is imperative."

Manuel Morla Concha, "Función social del ejército en la organización de la nacionalidad" (1933, 1952)

CHAPTER EIGHT

South American Military Professionalism between the Wars: The Origins of Professional Militarism

■

The meeting of minds that recessed in 1914 reconvened as soon as the war ended, and the devotion of South Americans to European models continued through the inter-war decades. Aspects of professionalism concerned with military-civilian relationships, officer-class thought and self-perception, and the social responsibility of the military remained as firm in South America as in Europe. The possibility of war in South America (at times "probability" became the operative word) became one of the prime justifications for interest in foreign policy, world affairs, and maintenance of a defense establishment.

National defense did not begin at the frontier, but during peacetime, at home. One of the great lessons brought home by South American observers of the European war was that a mobilization scheme was absolutely necessary. Mobilization, however, was impossible without a properly-developed political, social, economic, and, in some cases, cultural infrastructure capable of supporting the armed forces. The necessity of sustaining over a long period forces capable of attacking as well as defending was clear. The "war to end all wars" convinced few South Americans that its purpose had been achieved. The Kellogg-Briand Pact, signed a decade later, was no more convincing. Several mobilizations and brief conflicts involving Chile, Peru, Ecuador, and Colombia bore this out. So did the 1932–36 War of the Gran Chaco involving Bolivia and Paraguay. The mechanics of national defense vividly proved that an industrial base was prerequisite to successful prosecution of war aims, so officers showed concern for the slow pace of economic diversification and industrialization. In Argentina and Brazil, ideological ties with civilian groups were visible early on, ties that led to a military-civilian fusion like that favored by members of Action Française and the NSDAP.

Officers remained steadfast on "the enemy within." Socialism in its militant form remained the bugbear. The experiences of the 1920s in South America made it appear more so; the effects of the Great Depression reinforced the belief that Communists were out to destroy the army. It would be decades before sophisticated national security ideology dominated Argentine, Brazilian, Chilean, and Peruvian officer-class thought and self-perception, but evidence abounds that its intellectual origins stem from the 1890–1940 half-century. Making a better case for national defense, and basing it on "the lessons of the war," increased officer-corps self-esteem. This encouraged even more forceful formulations. South Americans began to sound even more like archetypal Prussians and French colonial officers. Military professionalism, obviously adaptable in the Old World, was just as adaptable to the plains, forests, deserts, and high country of the New. The involvement of the United States in South American international and domestic affairs, it is clear, did little to dilute European military professionalism, but contributed to its flowering by providing new elements of uncertainty to confront the military mind.

Europeans were still aware of what they had wrought across the Atlantic. Charles Mangin, one of Maurras's *Quadrileatère*, was fortunate that César Vallejo, the poet, translated his *Avec le Jules Michelet: Autour du continent latin*, for the book is more readable in Spanish than in the original French.[1] Mangin toured South America in 1921 at the behest of President Alexandre Millerand.

The general saw France everywhere as he went about his business in Callao and Lima. Frenchmen ran the port. There was a French chamber of commerce. At the Palacio Pizarro in Lima "a squadron of cavalry, armed and equipped like our dragoons of 1914," was in residence.[2] The country was ripe for the expansion of French influence. Nowhere was this more obvious, he wrote, than in the army, but even among Peru's finest there was altogether too much political influence in matters of promotion, salary increases, and duty assignments. French training officers were doing their best, but had not overcome the pressures of politics. Mangin did not name Leguía, but the reference to politics was clear enough.

Mangin viewed the army as the country's crucible, the symbol of its unity. This was so because the army was a microcosm of Peru: "Peru's two races are fused in her army." Creole and mestizo officers were aware already of the tenuous nature of racial fusion in Peru, and were writing about it, but Mangin's observations were nonetheless significant. Southern Peru captivated Mangin to the point where, suffering from *déjà vu*, not *soroche*, he compared the terrain, climate, and defense possibilities with Algeria, where he had once served. In Sicuani, Lieutenant Colonel Montagne, the Francophile, fussed over Mangin. Mangin agreed with Montagne that Peru desperately needed modern communications and transportation, education, obligatory military service, Indian social and political integration, and greater insulation of the army from politics and patronage.[3] His monograph is full of allusions, comparisons, and conclusions identical to those made by Peruvian contemporaries.

The durability and adaptability of European models also pervades much of General Charles Maitrot's *La France et les républiques sud-americaines*. He saw Franco-Latin ties in the South American countries as an effective countermeasure to growing Anglo-Saxon influence, "for France is their model; they are impregnated with our civilization."[4] He was convinced that the war had established France as the role model for South Americans, despite the presence of "Germanized" organizations in Argentina, Brazil, and Chile.[5] South America was a case of "French genius assimilated to live anew," and that genius thrived, particularly in the military, owing to the numerous international disputes still pending. General Wilhelm Faupel would say much the same ten years later.[6] Because war was a possibility, defense was a necessity.

But too many Argentines avoided conscription; mobilization was impossible in a country the size of Brazil unless greater centralized control was exercised; Peru was socially and economically backward (no matter Mangin's thoughts on racial fusion). There was hope for Peru, however, owing to the longstanding and highly successful French mission. "Of all the South American armies," though, "the Chilean is the most serious, most solid, that which is the most unified in its composition and cohesive in its organization." Chile had no "race problem" like Brazil and Peru and was better governed than Argentina. The Chileans, Maitrot wrote, were "les prussiens de l'Amérique,"[7] Four years after Maitrot wrote, those "prussiens" found themselves in a Weimar-like situation. Fellow South Americans were hardly better off.

In both Europe and South America, it should be obvious, it was the outspoken activists who, through their writings in journals, shaped a professional lore based on close ties to the state, involvement in national affairs, and a social educative role. Memoirs and most works intended for public consumption were so heavily weighted toward *golpes* and their aftermaths that they are not as valuable a collective reservoir of professionalism as are the essays in professional journals. That a minority should dictate policy to a majority is consistent with the fundamental canons of the military profession anywhere.

By 1930 South American officer corps thought and self-perception indicated the military profession had come of age. Attention to external and internal roles and political awareness had made South Americans *más alemanes que los alemanes y más franceses que los franceses.* Not all officers were "thoroughly professional." Not all agreed on each and every issue, any more than their idols did. Those who published with official sanction, however, did concur on points critical to the perpetuation of values and ideals.

With *képi* and *Pickelhaube* (still), monocle, swagger-stick, and pencil moustache, with military haircut and goose-step drill, the South American officer cut a dashing figure. But like his European comrade-in-arms he was convinced that civilians did not appreciate him, that war was ever-possible, that Marxists plotted everywhere, and that the crusader-educator-priest, the silent servant of state, nation, and society, had a responsibility to make things right.

On both continents, past, present, and future blurred with the passage of the post-war decade and the beginning of the 1930s. In 1930, France withdrew troop occupation from the Rhineland. Poincaré had resigned as prime minister the year before, and France was in the midst of seven years of shifting coalition governments that dismayed officers and civilians alike. Coalition politics achieved heretofore unheard-of extremes: victory for the Popular Front in 1936, then the breaking of a *Cagoulle*-monarchist-army plot in 1937.

On August 28, 1930 Lieutenant Colonel Sánchez Cerro overthrew Preisdent Leguía. In October 1931 he defeated Víctor Raúl Haya de la Torre, the Aprista candidate, in a disputed election. A year and a half later he fell to an Aprista assassin's bullet. Marshall Benavides became president, annulled the 1936 elections, and served until 1939.

A week after Sánchez Cerro deposed Leguía, General Uriburu deposed President Yrigoyen. The old Germanophile reluctantly gave up the presidency two years later, after failing in an attempt to establish an Italian-style corporate state. His arch-rival, General Justo, headed a 1932–38 administration supported by the Concordancia, a grouping of political leaders who wished for a return to the politics of the pre-Radical years.

By the end of the year, defeated presidential candidate Getúlio Vargas had deposed the incumbent Washington Luiz and barred his hand-picked candidate Júlio Prestes from assuming the presidency of the Republic. Within two years Vargas and his army allies had broken up the resistance of Brazil's industrial and commercial center, São Paulo. He and his *tenentista*, high-command, proto-fascist, and other civilian backers maneuvered Brazil into the Estado Novo in 1937.

Nine months after Vargas seized power, General Ibáñez fled Chile. His military companions stood aside rather than shed blood in the streets of Santiago to keep him in power. In

1931 and 1932 Chile endured ten distinct governments, including the "hundred days of Socialism" of June-August 1932. Ibáñez's nemesis Alessandri returned to La Moneda in December 1932 and held power until 1938, when he delivered the presidential sash to the Popular Front candidate, Pedro Aguirre Cerda.

In 1932 the Nazi leader Adolf Hitler lost the presidential election to Paul von Hindenburg by seven million votes, yet by the end of January 1933 Hitler was chancellor. In August 1934, with his party in control of Germany and Hindenburg dead, Hitler combined presidency and chancellorship. The Führer's Germany rearmed, occupied the Rhineland, and moved toward war. Frenchmen and Germans, Argentines, Brazilians, Chileans, Peruvians, all were caught up in the agonies of post-1918 readjustment, of economic depression, political extremism, and social upheaval.

One of the most persistent themes in military literature prior to 1914 had been that of obligatory service. Argentina's and Brazil's relative intimacy with the recent conflict and their national rivalry combined to make comparable their approach to obligatory service and their expansion of the topic to include all military-civilian matters. Since so few believed that Mars really lay dead (as Seeckt put it) after 1918, it is not surprising that officers continued to regard universal military training as vital to defense. Already a nation-building device, it soon became the basis for the military's advocacy of permanent expansive peacetime roles.

The Argentine *Memoria* of 1926 equated obligatory military service with primary and secondary education—under discipline and free from partisan influences.[8] This merely gave official cachet to what Major Miguel Gallardo had written the previous year: if men could be formed into healthy, good-humored, and disciplined individuals they would be useful not only to the army but eventually to society at large.[9] Foundation of the Argentine government petroleum monopoly, *Yacimientos Petrolíferos Fiscales* (YPF), and its direction by General Enrique Mosconi may have encouraged Argentines to expand their horizons. The educative-integrative role of obligatory service meshed neatly with Lieutenant Julio López's nationalist scheme, for example. He believed that the army molded immigrants into Argentines—a significant contribution "in an age of reaction against anti-nationalist and disruptive ideas."[10] Argentine insistence on obligatory service as a perpetrator of xenophobic zeal was nothing unexpected given the dependence on German ideas; nor was it all that unusual by South American standards.

To the north, readers of *A Defeza Nacional* saw the same opinions in print and continued to lament the poor application of Brazil's military service law. The principal editorial of the July–August 1925 issue noted that there were no penalties for draft dodgers, that recruitment programs lacked organization and coordination, and that training was spotty.[11] If Brazil wanted adequate defense, the government had to take steps, for obligatory service as a systematic program functioned only when men were actually in the barracks, the "school of abnegation" where brotherhood and patriotism—and a number of other virtues—were formed.[12] Patriotism and obligatory service were considered inseparable, and military literature from the end of the Great War to the advent of the Great Depression would not let Brazilian officers forget it. The army's most important role was that of civilizer and integrator. The army was called *o grande mudo* (*le grande muette*); it was that "filter" through which passed the sons of the fatherland—obvious French touches. The army, the flag, the people, and the nation were inseparable.[13] Discipline was a "moral force" brought to bear on individualistic, undisciplined society by skilled officers. "Discipline, the will to obey or be obeyed, is a principle of the national spirit."[14] If Brazil was backward and disorderly, officers had a remedy.

Argentines and Brazilians frequently emphasized industrialization in the 1920s. Uniformed authors, wary of politics, expressed their ideas in cautious tones until the early 1930s, when economic collapse freed them somewhat from constraints. Industrialization and national defense were inseparable from the beginning, therefore, but became more openly debated when associated with mobilization and development in the 1930s. The Argentine economic nationalist Luis

Vicat wrote in 1925 that "true national defense is a vast, complex subject and may be defined by saying it encompasses all those activities and all those measures necessary to assure the tranquillity, prosperity, and independence of a country—such as a rapid victory in case of conflict."[15] Needless to say, Vicat based his definition on an assumption that Argentina's neighbors menaced her on all sides; his thinking was clearly based on European thinking.

General Ramón Molina's 1926 essays on defense, first published in *La Nación*, found their way into monograph form that same year. He stressed preparedness, proper government action and legislation, and the necessity of thinking of a two-front effort. His assertion that the government did not adequately support Argentina's defense needs were comparable to those expressed concurrently in Brazil's *A Defeza Nacional*. A year later, Molina's innocuously-titled "La defensa profesional" tied national defense adequacy to the overall status of the officer corps. If officers were not properly trained and appreciated, he warned, could they be expected to defend their country effectively?[16] Molina's argument was opportunistic and self-serving. It was supposed to be.

Brazilians pondered their huge country's geography in connection with their defense of it far more than they considered the possibilities of a two-front war. Brazilians were concerned about adequate maps, a poorly-developed railway system, and the woeful condition of military education outside the barracks. Brazil was just not ready to fight—whether or not there was a war in the offing.[17] By blending obligatory military service with industrialization and internal infrastructure problems, Argentines and Brazilians asserted themselves precisely as did their European models.

South American military journals now carried international news (gathered by attachés) more often than did those of Europe. Argentines, especially, were worried about the international scene, developments in limitrophe states, and possible anti-Argentine consortia. In 1923 the Escuela Superior in Buenos Aires published volume 1 of *Estudios y Comunicaciones de Información*, a short-lived publication consisting of carefully-written appraisals of Paraguay, Brazil, and Chile as potential foes. Economic, political, and military information of an up-to-date nature thus was made readily available to officers. The *Revista Militar*'s "Sección América" strove to provide fresh data on events in Brazil, Chile, Peru, Paraguay, and Bolivia and on French mission activity in Brazil and Peru.[18] At times the editor made it sound as if one or a combination of these countries were poised to attack. It was not difficult for Argentines to link international relations and geopolitics to internal affairs. Traditional rivalries, German training, the lessons of 1914–18, and the domestic and international events of the post-war years made it necessary, they believed.

General Molina's militaristic essays of 1926 appeared in Portuguese translation that same year.[19] Brazilians believed that, if Argentina were the enemy, then they would be fighting only a single-front war, but by this time they were devoting attention to western and southern frontiers and the possibility of war with Uruguay, Paraguay, and Bolivia.[20] Questions of armaments and post-war disarmament conferences caused Brazilians to ponder their situation. Estevão Leitão de Carvalho wondered if Argentines and Chileans truly meant to curtail military expenditures, as they claimed, or if they simply wanted to gain the advantage over Brazil. He believed that Argentina and Chile were still ahead of Brazil and that their advocacy of arms reduction from the Santiago Conference of 1922 forward would freeze Brazil in an inferior position—an appeal to the nationalism of Brazilian lawmakers to support the army in a more generous way. His equally prolific comrade, João Baptista Magalhães, was of like mind.[21] Geopolitical arguments buttressed the defense theories, based as they were on domestic and foreign, military and civilian variables.

The earliest outright criticisms of democratic politics and linkages of domestic political affairs with national defense on the Atlantic coast of South America occurred in two Argentine essays of 1917. In the first, a pseudonymous "Mayor Diana" wrote caustically of the congress's slowness and carelessness in treating military legislation. He claimed that legislators were blindly unsympathetic to the army's needs.

This was a dangerous attitude, for, if politicians did not understand what was needed for defense, who did? Captain Gaspar Soria made yet another call for national integration under military aegis and cunningly treated the immigration issue. Since Argentina had become a haven for immigrants (which it soon would cease to be in such a magnanimous fashion), many undesirable extremists had come to the country. These had avoided military service. Perhaps Argentina ought to mind her frontiers more carefully.[22] Congress should act to assure this. By the time the likes of Molina and López wrote, Argentines saw that the role of the army and all it stood for depended on political action.

Brazilians had to confront the Old Republic from its inception. To them *o exército e a política* was old hat by the time Argentines "Diana" and Soria wrote. Argentines might lament the lackadaisical nature and foolish behavior of legislators, but Brazilians knew they were responsible for the republic the legislators helped to govern. This gave them no comfort and caused them frustration. During the election tension of 1921–22 *A Defeza Nacional*'s editors had to state bluntly that "officers are not janizaries," that they would not play at politics.[23] Three years later the editors meekly called for government action to foment industrialization.[24] In 1926 an editorial lamented the lack of civilian respect for the army— while saying nothing about the ongoing adventures of the Prestes column tramping the far interior in its search for civilian support.[25] Many of the *jovens turcos* were in fact far more interested in learning from the French than in preaching to civilians. The fact that the army was divided against itself for a good part of the decade eroded much of the credibility Brazilian officers hoped to establish.

This changed near the end of the decade, for the Old Republic's own credibility was fading. A year before the overthrow of the Republic, Colonel Parga Rodrigues stated that Brazil's government was not "systematic and orderly." Politics made for lack of continuity in policymaking. Lack of consistency in policy precluded an adequate defense capability.[26] The conclusion was obvious to all but the most thickheaded readers: if politics, perforce associated with the Republic, meant inconsistency, and if inconsistency precluded a defense capability, then the political system needed reform. Within a year the Republic had fallen and *A Defeza Nacional* editors were urging a more aggressive policy on Brazil's provisional government. In the same year, the Argentine army ousted President Yrigoyen. Superficially democratic systems in two of South America's great powers were replaced by more authoritarian regimes supported or led by military leaders. In both countries, it is true, the new order underwent metamorphosis between 1930 and 1940, but the overall military presence did not decline and the military stepped up its campaign for greater cooperation with civilian institutions.

Argentine officers now urged industrialization on Justo and Ortiz with vigor: the Radicals, the Depression, the Roca-Runcinan Treaty all confirmed their hard-line position. Brazilian officers urged industrialization on their new-found civilian ally, Getúlio Vargas, and encouraged him to mold the huge country around them in a more acceptable image.

Argentine official literature of the 1930s shows the clearest pro-German sentiment to survive in South America. Once the political turmoil following the overthrow of Yrigoyen had subsided, officers began to look again to Germany as their inspiration. They praised the German conscription system; they lauded the German pension and retirement program. Advertisements for German industry and weapons manufacturers appeared anew in the *Revista Militar.* Following the Munich debacle, Argentine officers began to think seriously of their country's position vis-à-vis the Axis and its enemies. They maintained that Argentina was as European as it was American; its interests lay with Germany, Spain, and Italy more than with the United States, Great Britain, and their associates.[27] It occurred to more than one officer that the United States and Great Britain had been hoodwinked by the Soviet Union and that the real struggle of the future was between nationalism and communism. National Socialism seemed suitable for countries with grave social, economic, and political problems.

France, Argentine officers were convinced, had fallen prey to anti-militarism—which they equated with communism.

But the French army was not to blame for this, for French officers had warned civilian leaders and urged an elaborate higher military studies center on their leaders. They had begged all along for military-civilian fusion, coordination of mobilization and command. No, France's officers were not at fault; her civilian leadership was. Because civilians had not listened, communism, individualism, internationalism, and labor unrest prevailed by the end of the decade. Unions and parties had ruined France and her army.[28] Unity, discipline, and resolve had made Germany strong. National Socialism or a variant appealed to many Argentine officers.

Most writers viewed Argentina's situation from a proto-fascist viewpoint. The "revolution" of September 6, 1930, wrote Lieutenant Colonel Enrique Rottjer, was a popular movement carried out by the military to stop politicians from deceiving the people and to protect the army itself from civilian meddling. Rottjer called the military *golpe* a "sacrifice" on the part of the officer corps, and he hoped the army would never have to make such a move again. The army, representing the people, had veered from its normal mission because this "integral part of the nation, whose members, from commander in chief to common soldier, were flesh of the nation and whose origins and development were intrinsically linked to the nation itself, could not remain indifferent to the situation."[29] Words like these could have been written by any Frenchman or German of the time.

So could those of General Juan Vacarezza, who stated that the military's mission was a cultural one: "a mission of culture, of order, discipline, and civilization."[30] Political involvement was a lamentable necessity. Several fellow-officers went further and blamed all Argentina's economic and social problems on civilians. Political parties, unions, international organizations, and foreign investment (all of civilian inspiration) had polluted the country and nearly destroyed the true Argentina. Argentines now had to "take possession of their own country." Other writers in the *Revista Militar* brazenly supported ultra-nationalist movements and excoriated liberal democracy.[31] In an age of "collective unrest," as Juan Beltrán called it, the army represented organized force and strength.

"Only the officer corps remains uncontaminated in this vortex of uncertainty."[32] Beltran's was a forceful if clumsy analogy.

Confronted by the crisis of the early 1930s, many Argentine officers gave up on liberal democracy. The appeal of fascism was strong, for it blended well with the officers' social function. The officer corps projected its self-perceived hierarchical and disciplined image on Argentine society far more vigorously than ever before. The demonstrable weakness of the political system encouraged them as much as events in the army's professional *madre patria*. Rottjer, Lieutenant Colonel Atilio Cattaneso, Lieutenant Oscar Uriondo, Colonel Enrique López Rivarola, General Vacarezza, Colonel Carlos Gómez, and Lieutenant Colonel Ricardo Miró all championed the *misión civilizadora*—Argentine-style—and the unique leadership qualifications of officers in strident terms between 1930 and 1935.[33] In that year, Jacinto Hernández published a brief essay in which he cited both Alfred de Vigny and Colmar von der Goltz as "defenders of the faith."[34] His arguments were outré, even by contemporary standards, but his insistence that the officer be respected and obeyed appealed to many colleagues. That he cited Vigny and Goltz by name lends at least a touch of respectability to his tortured little essay, for most South Americans did not cite the words and ideas of others in a scholarly fashion.

Self-perception of the officer as historically both social worker and leader, servant and commander, became more integrated than ever.[35] The army's civilian champion, Alberto Baldrich, praised the officer corps for its "historical and spiritual grandeur" in a lecture to the Círculo Militar on July 26, 1940. In terms no less grandiloquent than those used by the army's first civilian spokesman, Leopoldo Lugones, he compared army officers to heroes of Greek and Roman tales and to the crusaders of the Iberian reconquest. "The Argentine army is a holy order," he concluded, "and should be called the 'Order of the Caballeros de San Martín.'"[36] This was as heady and romantic as anything conceived by Vigny or Psichari or the Chilean Barros Ortiz.

Officers of the 1930s were strident critics of the entire fabric of civilian-led democracy. The fact that Baldrich was a civilian made this even more significant. Once the floodgates of publication opened, the cumulative effects of years of frustration were overwhelming. Military thought of the 1930s teemed with accusations that civilians had made a mess of government, education, and defense policy; that foreigners were sapping Argentina of her resources and had made the country dependent on foreign sources of industrial goods. Officer-corps thought and self-perception became intimately associated with cultural, political, and economic nationalism. Although made at the beginning of the decade, General Uriburu's conclusions on the role of the army were still widely accepted in 1940: "The armed forces must be above political parties, whatever tendency these represent. [The armed forces] are a guarantee to all, but cease to be so whenever they respond to one [of the parties]. Of genuinely national character, composed of Argentines from all classes and regions, they must serve only the nation."[37] The gulf separating theory and practice does not escape the eye.

Argentines of the 1930s fervently wanted an industrialized economy capable of turning Argentina into an exporter of finished goods. Geopolitical and economic thought blended in their classrooms and discussion groups. On the assumption that there would be another war, *Revista Militar* editors published a number of essays dealing with mobilization and economic diversification. Although this might have been the primary focus, they usually treated military-civilian relations, obligatory service, and political instability as well.

Since modern wars were fought between nations, not dynasties, wrote one anonymous officer in 1930, entire nations needed to be mobilized.[38] This essay refined ideas promoted by South Americans and Europeans since the turn of the century. But these were sensitive times in Argentina. Industry meant grandeur, wealth, independence, pride, honor, and international respect—just as a powerful army did. A strong army meant a healthy Argentina as well.[39] Economic development, however, meant nothing if it did not go hand in glove with military necessities, or if it did not count regional needs; in short, if it were not uniformly planned throughout the interior. Because there were enemies on Argentina's western and northern frontiers, her industry, commnications and transportation must be coordinated to serve the army in a two-front war.[40] If it were to carry out mobilization and campaign alike, the army must have statistical information on all aspects of the economy in order to prepare plans and schedules, along with complete cooperation from all civilian authorities. Colonel Jorge Crespo's above-noted essays of 1936 provided an elaborate policy for the coordination of geopolitical considerations, mobilization plans, industrial development, military-civilian consultation, and obligatory military service.[41] The meaning was clear when viewed in the context of contemporary thought and self-perception: if the government did not respond to army demands, then the government simply did not serve Argentina's immediate interests.

The thesis proposed by Crespo dominated essays in the late 1930s. For example, Captain Ricardo Marambio's "Industrias argentinas y tecnocracia" was a strong plea for turning over all national planning to the army high command.[42] Lieutenant Alvaro Alsogaray's translation of a *Revue des Deux Mondes* essay published in 1937 presented the familiar French argument to Argentine officers. Colonel Gómez and others exposed Argentina's vulnerability to a combined Brazilian and Chilean attack à la Japan's seizure of Manchuria. The well-published Colonel Crespo put it tersely in his "Si vis pacem, para bellum" of June 1939. "Argentina must be prepared for any eventuality," he said, "or suffer the consequences."[43] Two months later he and his colleagues were doubtless smug.

Radicalism and the Great Depression and its aftermath confirmed the Argentine officer in his thought and self-perception about state, nation, and society; the new international conflict confirmed his convictions concerning industrialization and national defense. War in Europe made linking of national security and socioeconomic development indisputable. French and German officers had said it; Germany's victory of 1940 confirmed it. All this committed numerous Argentines to authoritarianism as the political style most akin to military professionalism. The GOU movement of 1943 was the immediate result.

Brazilian literature on the *missão indígena*, politics, international relations, and socioeconomic problems also indicates a response to both current German successes and traditional French points of view. Brazilian officers divided ranks in the 1930s with the corporatist mind clearly in the ascendance. The military-civilian example of the Third Reich, however, was hard to swallow for many Francophiles and those who could not swallow Nazi racial doctrines. Getúlio Vargas's own authoritarian tendencies, well known prior to the declaration of the New State, and the military's hostility toward the 1889–1930 regime prevailed. The tone of Brazilian writing was less strident than that of Argentine literature, for the Vargas administrations of the 1930s, after all, did champion social and economic programs favored by most officers.[44]

Early in the decade military editors cautioned officers against political activity—in terms that stimulated their interest. An editorial of 1933 in *A Defeza Nacional* entitled "Exércitos Modernos" pointed out that the army was Brazil's most truly "national institution," for it standardized education for many citizens and provided the entire country with an organizational infrastructure. In words no less dramatic than those of the civilian champion Olavo Bilac and legions of European militarists, the editors stated that "initial development of human society has only been possible owing to man's capability to defend himself in organized groups."[45] Defense was both a necessary adjunct of and a stimulus to civilization and culture. Another editorial urged the worthy citizens writing the new constitution (the document of 1934) to leave politics to the civilian sector and to protect the army from partisan debate: "Imagine what would happen in the garrison during election time where the field grade officers were conservatives, the captains liberals, and the lieutenants 'advanced reformists.'"[46] Its interesting breakdown of political sentiment and rank aside, this was a plea for an inviolate, united, professional, non-partisan army. Rarely were the *tenentes* mentioned in official sources, despite the adaptation of much of their thought. One mid-decade editorial stated: "The army should be a great mute, but an active and productive one."[47] Vigny would have been pleased to read this translation of his concept of *la grande muette*, hence to see it alive and well in Brazil. It stimulated rather than placated.

A Defeza Nacional, for two decades the conscience of the profession, fell silent with the return to constitutional government in 1934. Except for self-criticism, i.e., officers who played at politics or who agreed to serve in a government position were by definition ill-prepared to carry out professional assignments,[48] this journal ceased to give a clear picture of officer-class thought and self-perception. The *Revista Militar Brasileira* took its place as official periodical. Both the *Revista* and the annual *Relatório* turned the apolitical line once championed by *A Defeza Nacional* inside out. By the end of 1937 the official line was that the non-partisan quality of the officer corps made it an ideal partner of the Estado Novo. Chief spokesmen for this new position were Division Generals Pedro Aurélio de Góis Monteiro, army chief of staff, and Gaspar Eurico Dutra, the war minister. Their leadership meant, essentially, the same in Brazil that pro-Nazi army readership meant in Germany: fusion of state and army, providing (ostensibly) a concurrence of priorities in the fields of foreign policy, national economic development, and domestic affairs. Anticommunist pieces emphasized the need for militance in common civilian and military interests.[49] An uneasy relationship ensued, lasting until the closing months of World War II.

In discussions of France and Germany, the former received favorable treatment early in the decade and the latter received fawning coverage from the mid-1930s until 1942—even as the United States became Brazil's military partner. The French mission contract of 1933–35 was hailed as one that brought to Brazil a group of outstanding officers, "members of an elite." Just a half-year later, the same editors showed a distinct preference for the Italian political system[50] Like Argentines, they blamed France's collapse on internal as much as or more than on external influences.[51] Unlike Argentines, Brazilians accepted the United States as surrogate military mentor once the advantages were clear.

Brazilians, like Germans, experienced a theoretical fusion of army, state, nation, and society. They appreciated the relationship between military and civilian interests in matters of national defense. Brazil probably represents the best South American example of realization of military-civilian concurrence prior to World War II. This would not have been possible were it not for the flourishing of a political system that made military-civilian fusion theoretically acceptable to both. If Brazilian officers were less openly and stridently corporatist than Argentines were, it was because they had less reason to be. The Vargas machine was beholden to the army for suppression of regionalist and ideological oppposition. The army was beholden to Vargas for destroying the influence of the state militas, the hated *forças públicas*. This mutual dependency made for some strange bedfellows, but it promoted amicable relations.

Economic development under army control became a rallying-point early in the 1930s. Editorials and essays on the subject compared military participation in the economic development of Brazil to military frontier colonization schemes of the past century. All Brazilians must be prepared to work or fight in the event of war. The Old Republic had "betrayed" the heroes of Caxias, wrote Monteiro in 1935, to the point of endangering Brazil's leadership position in South American international relations. The very next year, General João Gomes Riberão Filho warned that unless state and nation united stood ready to support the army, Brazil would be defenseless.[52] Both blamed Communists and state leaders for Brazil's weakness as much as "aggressive Argentines."

Writing in 1936, Fernando Magalhães averred that the state in Brazil was the "tangible creation of society" and that "the nation was Brazil's collective 'conscience.'" The army was the condensation of that conscience, equal in importance to the state, indeed inseparable from it.[53] The following year's single most important issue of *Revista Militar Brasileira* proclaimed that the "new regime" meant authority for the state and liberty for the people. Authority meant true liberty; the former was impossible without the latter.

At the end of the decade the *Revista Militar Brasileira* as well as *A Defeza Nacional* published primarily technical materials. *Nação Armada* took over the role of spokesman on military-civilian opinion and relations. It contained much of

the philosophical basis for the creation following World War
II of the Escola Superior de Guerra.

With the coming of the war, Brazilian officer-class thought
on the defense mobilization and military-civilian relations finally came of age.[54] Geopolitical considerations, industrialization, and participation in the war freed officers from the
constraints imposed by the sometimes smothering military-
civilian fusion of the 1930s. This did not change dramatically
officer-corps self-perception, however, for economic development, cooperation with civilians, and close ties with the state
all predated the rise of the New State. The superiority of military to civilian institutions was implicit (when not explicit) in
material published from 1930 to 1934. Stabilization of the
Vargas regime by the mid-1930s indicated strength in the civilian sector, and officers responded accordingly, but at no
time did they cut off their ties to the past, to the *missão indígena*, and to French tradition.

Captain Aloysio Miranda Mendes emphasized the solidarity,
sense of fulfillment, abnegation, and spirituality of army officers in an essay of 1936.[55] The hard-line anti-Marxist M.
Paulo Filho wrote on the barracks as a center of learning the
same year in precisely the terms in which pre-1930 South
Americans and Europeans had discussed it.[56] So did Captain
S. Sombra in "O Exército y o Plano Nacional de Educação."
Sombra stressed the army's educative role as both supplemen-
tary and complementary to civilian education; in the army,
the "formally educated" civilian became physically, morally,
and technically educated, disciplined, patriotic, and coopera-
tive. Things had changed little, then, as Brazilians went off to
battle alongside their new allies. In a war fought against exponents of authoritarian systems with which Brazilians identified intellectually and professionally, they experienced a new
confrontation of past and present.

Chileans and Peruvians were less immediately affected by
World War I than were the Atlantic Coast powers. On the
Pacific, military literature provides a relatively sharper contrast in the inter-war years owing, probably, to the early adaptation of European professionalism to national tradition.

By the end of World War I, the thought and self-perception of junior- and middle-grade Chilean officers were very much "up to date." Soon Chileans had their own counterpart to Goltz and Lyautey. In 1920 there appeared the first edition of the incomparable *Vigilia de armas* by Captain Tobías Barros Ortiz.

In this book the young captain expressed Chilean military professionalism in a new way, establishing a model for officer-class self-perception that is used to this day. Its touches of romanticism notwithstanding, *Vigilia de armas* is more a positive exposition of military philosophy, views, and aspirations than any earlier South American work. In places its prose is distinctly reminiscent of Alfred de Vigny.[57] Barros dedicated the book to his father, General Tobías Barros Merino (who had written the preface to Medina's *El problema militar de Chile*), and addressed it to his brother, Mario Barros Ortiz, a cadet about to graduate in December 1919 from the Escuela Militar. In conception and production *Vigilia de armas* is the magnum opus of Chilean officer-class thought and self-perception. It is the most significant piece of South American military literature published prior to the 1930s, unlike any other in the profundity of its attachment to the idealized past. It is a classic example of the lore of the profession, as worthy of attention as the works of any European.

The purpose of the book was "to aid young officers of today [i.e., 1920] to understand that the military institution is the product of the ongoing perfection by thousands and thousands of comrades who, over the years, have maintained the eternal and unshakable principles of loyalty, valor, patriotism, spirit of sacrifice, noble ambition to distinguish themselves, and abnegation, symbolic of our profession." Barros compared the profession with knighthood, the struggle of "modern life" with a state of permanent war (the latter being "divine in its origins"), military life with chivalry.[58] Shades of *Rittertum*, of *servitude et grandeurs*.

Vigilia de armas solidified, early on, a "we vs. they" military mentality in Chile, for Barros pointed out sharp distinctions between things military and civilian. He also reiterated

South American and European arguments for a military-social role. "The army is society's arm" and is "the origin of abstract, unalterable discipline," to Barros a civil as well as military necessity.[59] The "nerve" of society's arm was obligatory military service, seen by all Chilean officers as a symbiotic military-civilian unifier and nation-builder. Its product, the "citizen-soldier," was "the very essence of patriotism and nationalism, the salvation of society...a new creation in the social order." "Neither family, nor education, nor birth exempt one from obligation [to serve] in common," he wrote, for "the family is the fatherland in miniature, the fatherland is the home on a grand scale; when these are threatened, everyone must aspire to the honor of defending them."[60] All Chilean military writers since Barros concur that obligatory military service for "sons of the national family" is a necessity as long as there is illiteracy and lack of civic education as well as a need for national defense.

In the Barrosian view, most sons of the Chilean national family "lack the most elemental notion of public spirit, morals, and even civilization"—this in a country that prided itself on its efforts in public education. He debunked two popular Chilean myths: that of the "docile, patriotic peasant," whom he considered as having "the stupid docility of a beast" and absolutely no substantive grasp of patriotism, and that of the patriotic *roto* (urban worker), "who is not patriotic at all, although he might be attracted to parades and the like." But Barros was convinced they could find a kind of salvation through military service. "Unlettered and ignorant to the point of resembling savages with no knowledge of hygiene or morals, thus they arrive [at the barracks], these unfortunate creatures; and have you seen how they leave at the end of their service? Each one of them leaves knowing how to read, write, and cipher; he knows the history of the fatherland and his civic duties; he knows and observes the rule of hygiene and the moral precepts of the civilized man." The army represented everything that was good; civilian society contained (fostered?) everything that was evil. Chilean officers, "knights," "educators," "spiritual leaders," soon had an opportunity to apply their reading to national reality, even though Barros instructed them to devote themselves to a two-fold mission, the fulfillment of military duties and the personification of "silent testimony to the moral superiority and dignity of those who wear the uniform."[61] These roles, apparently purely professional, also encouraged political deliberation.

In 1920 the demagogic Arturo Allesandri Palma won the presidency. By the time he was inaugurated, gone but not forgotten were the Liga Militar and Liga Naval, military political organizations dating from 1907, and the Army Society for Regeneration and *Junta Militar*, both 1919 political lodges. These had existed for the purpose of transforming into policy the ideals and values that army authors had been writing about since at least 1912 but that had attracted no wide professional following or civilian support.

Over, but likewise not forgotten, was the "Mobilization of 1920," a massive hoax perpetrated by the incumbent regime to use the army to divert attention from Alessandri's victory and serious national, social, and economic difficulties. Memories influenced officers when they moved against Alessandri in 1924 and 1925 and when they threw their support to Carlos Ibáñez in 1927.[62] Chileans were the first South Americans to demonstrate a commitment to professional militarism.

Although political involvement provided the opportunity (and necessity) for justification of the imposition of military ideals and values on the polity, it was not accompanied by a quantitative increase in literature of a controversial nature. Not all army officers were eager to blend *lo militar* with *lo civil*, for fear of harm to the profession. Illustrative of the concerns of Chilean officers were essays that dealt with military aspects of defense and international affairs. An editorial of 1924 in the *Memorial* lamented Peru's gains under the newest French mission and warned that the French soon would make the Peruvian officer corps a match for Chile's.[63] That same year, Major Javier Palacios praised the Argentine army and singled out General Justo for special praise. Justo, he wrote, had kept the army out of harm's way (and out of the limelight) by dealing forcefully with the national congress and convincing legislators of Argentina's need to defend herself against her enemies.[64] The Chilean view certainly contrasted with that of General Molina and of other Argentines of this period who believed that the congress did not behave in a responsible way at all. South Americans, like Europeans, tended to appraise and interpret each other in a way that would be convincing to the proper audience.

Two years later, a Colombian serving in Chile effusively thanked his Chilean hosts for all they had done through military missions to make Colombia's army "the faithful incarnation of the nationalistic spirit of the people."[65] His terminology was identical throughout to that used for decades by officers in Europe and South America. That same year, the Germanophile Francisco Javier Díaz published a monograph soon reprinted in the Argentine *Revista Militar.* Díaz argued that Chile needed increased military expenditures if she were to match (not exceed) the growth of Argentine and Peruvian land forces. Chile needed a 30,000-man standing army, an advanced studies center where civilians and soldiers might share their expertise, an overhauling of all mobilization plans and administrative structure, new training bases and frontier outposts, and an industrial base to make the country self-sufficient for defense purposes: no small order. Díaz plumped for maintenance of the German tradition. Three years later, in heated response, a Chilean subaltern would write on the aforementioned concern about officers who were more German than the Germans themselves, more French than Frenchmen themselves, and urge them to "think Chilean."[66] Absence may have made some Chilean hearts grow fonder, but to some, if the Germans were not entirely out of sight, they ought to be out of mind.

Army literature that did treat controversial sociopolitical themes was just as strident as ever. The 1927–31 presidency of General Ibáñez may have served as a safety valve for some frustrated and military "reformist" officers, but it did not temper the written words of those who did publish.

Precisely as Díaz was advocating a stronger defense posture, for example, Lieutenant René Montero Moreno, a fervent Ibañista, wrote that the wealthy families who ruled Chile since independence were still blind to the needs of a majority of the population. Political parties (specifically the Radical party) served merely as vehicles for ambitious members of the bourgeoisie who lost their zeal for reform as soon as they became part of the political establishment (e.g., congress, the bureaucracy, party council). If civilian political parties could not provide effective, responsible government, it was up to the disciplined, patriotic, apolitical armed forces to do so.[67] What Tobías Barros had praised and championed as *unique* qualities, Montero now cited as evidence of *leadership* qualities. Such an interpretation was due in no small part to changing political times.

Some of Montero's contemporaries, though quite proud of their profession and harshly critical of civilians, were worried that structural weaknesses (caused by civilian meddling or legislative inattention) might limit army potential for leadership. They presented evidence of some soul-searching within the officer class anent the ramifications of political participation for the military profession. Captain Ernesto Würth Rojas was convinced that by 1920 Prussianization had alienated younger (junior) officers from the high command, for members of the latter had enjoyed no modern military training.

Military discipline, therefore, could not be based on prestige and respect (all-important to a modern military organization) until the high command consisted of officers with a similar background.[68] Another prominent officer stated earlier that lack of continuity in government and politics had made it impossible for the state to properly support or modernize the army, thus justifying military action to correct the situation.[69] Still another of Chile's finest would single out the congress as the specific culprit because of its failure to act on military legislation; he also linked the sad condition of the armed forces with overreliance on political connections for promotions and assignments.[70]

No mincer of words, Carlos Ibáñez expressed anti-democratic feelings as well as any of his contemporaries and coevals. On assuming the presidency in 1927, he stated that Chileans "must bear in mind that we owe our tragic social indiscipline to the exaggerated cult of our rights and the sad neglect of our most fundamental traditions."[71] This argument prevailed anew in the following decade as soon as army officers returned to the barracks following the military-civilian confrontations of 1931–32. By the end of 1932, most of the political officers of the 1920s had been cashiered. Disdained, purged, and blamed for the Ibáñez government, the Socialist Republic, and Chile's depression woes, the majority of the officer corps drew back from political activity until 1938, when some began to consort with National Socialists, *Nacis*. Commanders devoted their efforts to restoring the army's strictly military capabilities—and assuring its continued existence. But some authors reasserted their views on the army's peacetime, non-partisan mission. Owing to the strength of the revived political system, there was no need yet for a firm ideological stance. Indeed, the only ideological stance the army took publicly was the one that might be expected: anti-Marxism. They continued appealing to authority, much as other South Americans did (as Europeans had taught them to do), and relying on traditional sources in stating the profession's case. This perpetuated ideals and values of years gone by.

Chileans were still skeptical of liberal democracy; they still viewed it as both cause and result of all national problems. *"The barracks is the school of democracy par excellence.* In the barracks there exist no differences of caste or background; there are found [both] true equality and 'the anvil' on which the character, personality, and moral discipline of the citizen are forged and fashioned," wrote Major Víctor Molina in 1935.[72] Molina's essay restated views dating from the inception of professionalism in Chile. No matter the state of military-civilian relations, the Chilean army stood ready to educate and civilize, for civilians were unable to do these things properly.

General Sáez Morales, retired veteran of the political wars of the 1920s and early 1930s, agreed that democracy was more prevalent in the army than in civilian life. "The common man in South American democracies is only cannon fodder," he wrote in 1938. "He is not a member of society but the instrument of oligarchy." Culture, economic independence, hygiene, civic consciousness, discipline—these "indispensable" necessities of functional citizenship were his for the taking in the army, thanks to obligatory military service.[73]

Linking military service, education, and defense, Captain Angel Varela stated that the army's peacetime duties were easily as important as any wartime defense function. "In peacetime," he wrote, "the army has a preponderant role to play in the intellectual and social development of a people, and its influence is felt in a notable way in numerous civic, commercial, industrial, and social activities....the barracks is the temple of the civic virtues."[74] Varela believed the army was truly a "humanistic institution." In a 1937 essay Barros Ortiz again referred to the army as an "armed citizenry" and to the officer class as composed of teachers and leaders and now "technicians."[75] Chileans justified their championship of the army's intellectual and physical educational role by reprinting "La cultura militar francesa y su difusión mundial," by the Mexican Tomás Sánchez Hernández, Maxime Weygand's "Como educar a nuestra juventud" ("Comment élever nos fils"), and Lyautey's "La función social del oficial."[76] Chileans adopted an up-to-date French-style role definition, but it differed only slightly from what they had professed for decades.

At the beginning of World War II, military advocacy of an educative and civilizing role and criticism of liberal democracy reached a high point.[77] Aggressive advocacy of traditional ideals and values peaked anew briefly with the high tide of Axis power, when the fusion of political authoritarianism and militarism seemed successful. In the 1940 essay "El ejército: Escuela de civilismo e institución de equilibrio social," Colonel Guillermo Aldona bluntly wrote that civilian society bred mediocrity and that liberal democracy made it possible for mediocre political leaders to rise to national leadership through electoral decisions made by intellectually mediocre voters. Civilians, mediocrity, and democracy were inseparable. Aldona concocted a view of the army as the state's chief ally in a campaign to impose on all citizens duties and obligations commensurate with liberties and rights.

To Aldona, real democracy was only found in the army, for there one found true equality, "equality of opportunity."[78] But to rise above the mass, he agreed with Barros Ortiz, one needed a true vocation and a commitment to perpetual self-improvement.

The venerable Indalicio Téllez concurred with Aldona in a 1942 appeal for better facilities for army advanced education. Téllez drew sharp distinctions between the army (and the other armed forces) and other professions.[79] Unlike lawyers, dentists, engineers, and pharmacists, for example, army officers (doctors and architects, too) somehow needed to continue studying throughout their career in order to maintain professional currency.[80] Continued study and perfection: this was yet another facet of the army's existence and uniqueness. Like the healer and the planner, the professional soldier ought to seek and have opportunity for perpetual improvement. Tobías Barros must have been pleased, for the meaning was obvious: the state had a responsibility to provide the army with the wherewithal for modernity.

At the end of the era of European professional dominance, Chilean officer-corps thought and self-perception had advanced but little beyond its 1920 contours. World War II found Chileans uncomfortable with the present but able to do little about it, their past efforts at directing national affairs only bitter memories.

Peruvian officers picked up after the war where they left off in 1914. Their journals indicate the continuation and modernization of extant themes and attitudes rather than the development of new subjects. Change in thought and self-perception was slight and outward. Peruvians were as traditional as Chileans, yet as concerned with the lessons of the recent war as Argentines and Brazilians.

In an essay published in 1919, for example, General José Maravá wrote that the army was both "useful and necessary," contributed to national progress by spreading modern technology, prepared conscripts for the trades, and improved the cultural level of Peruvians by educating them in the barracks.[81] The tone of this essay actually was rather mild when compared to the 1914 and pre-war arguments of Fernandini and Echazú, Velarde and Escalona. An editorial of 1919 quoted newly-installed President Augusto Leguía: "My government will spare no effort whatsoever to accomplish everything possible relevant to the flourishing of our armed forces, for they constitute the basis, not only of national defense, but of national growth."[82] Leguía, of course, meant to mollify, to coopt, for he believed he would need military support to prolong his tenure in the Palacio Pizarro. Officer-corps response to his support did not disappoint him—at first. Officers stressed the army's political neutrality (a "legalist" position that did not preclude deliberation in a time of crisis) and stressed strong support for any government that represented "the will of the people." They denied institutional subservience to "the oligarchy," "arbitrary government," or any specific administration. They claimed that the army represented "the nation" and "the people." During the *oncenio*, Leguía introduced officers to the realities of partisan politics and the difficulties of representing the will of the people, good training for the turbulent decade to come.

Midway through the *oncenio*, military writers carefully assumed the offensive, reacting to Leguía's continued meddling in internal military matters and failure to treat the army in the style to which it wanted to become accustomed. The Francophile Lieutenant Colonel José M. Pérez Manzanares published his translation of General Serrigny's "La organización de la nación para el tiempo de guerra."[83] Insistence on close military-civilian relations became an official high command policy in Peru long before they were codified in the Centro de Altos Estudios Militares.

Peru's budding military ideology found additional expression during the *oncenio*. Captain Andrés Escalona, concerned about the number of conscripts fleeing the barracks, suggested that inductees be gradually introduced to military life, "broken in," and then kept busy. "Let them work, play, sing, and laugh; in fine, let them enjoy themselves, but do not let them think."[84]

General Francois Pellegrin's "El c.a.e.m. de Francia" (another of Pérez Manzanares's translations) outlined the pre-1914 origins of higher military studies involving officers and related civilians in the expansion of national defense now being advanced anew by mission officers. Pellegrin, Lyautey's aide-de-camp during World War I, was instrumental in popularizing the potential of such an institute in Peru.

Peru's controversial *conscripción vial*—road-gang levies in isolated areas—was the subject of a 1926 essay by Lietuenant Colonel Vidal C. Panizo. He related highway construction to economic development, defense, and nation-building. To oppose the program, he obliquely warned legislators and politicians, was to deny one's heritage.[85] Soon, Panizo hoped, there would be highways linking Lima with Bolivia, and with Buenos Aires on the Atlantic Ocean. Contemporary arguments for regional military-commercial highways to serve military and economic imperatives pale in comparison, for Panizo also emphasized the role of the highway as transmitter of Western culture and civilization to the Peruvian heartland.

According to Lieutenant Paz García, the Indian of that heartland could do with some civilization. Reiterating a now familiar theme, he thought the Indian could become acculturated (with or without a dose of roadwork) through military service. "The Indian," wrote Paz García, "has been and continues to be vilely exploited by those who will not recognize...that he is a principal resource for the future of our nation."[86] Civilian educational schemes as yet had done nothing to free the Indian from the *gamonal*. Better facilities, patience, understanding, and "strong but paternal" discipline would make it easy for the Indian to adjust, serve, and ultimately leave the army "healthy, moderately literate, and morally pure." Paz García was as unflagging and ingenuous as any of his predecessors in his belief in the ability of the army to civilize the Indian.

The well-published Vidal Panizo concurred. As the anti-Leguía forces began to gather in the last years of the decade, he proclaimed that "discipline is the soul of the army";[87] intraservice harmony was the rule because of the moral purity of the officer class; the orders of officers were just, their fulfillment necessary; the officer's mission was critical and its completion a prerequisite to national progress. Beset by *politiquería* on all sides, officers realized the precarious nature of their situation. Sounding more like their mentors every year, they sought solace and self-justification in their civilizing mission, just as Chileans were doing to the south. By the twilight of the *oncenio*, Peruvian military professionals began to evince the qualities of professional militarism.

Major Genaro Muro saw frontier area colonization, for example, as the key to Peru's future progress. Bolivians and Brazilians living in the Peruvian *oriente* posed a threat to national sovereignty, but agricultural settlements administered by the army would both protect and produce. This was an argument for the future as old as briefs for nineteenth-century military colonization in North Africa. Muro called the *oriente* the "land of the future" and believed that "civilization would conquer the wilderness."[88] Captain Francisco Valdivia expanded on the arguments of highway advocates Ernesto Montagne and Vidal Panizo in his own brief for national highways: "veins of the [state] organism" that transmitted industry, trade, agriculture, defense capability, culture, and civilization to all corners of Peru.[89] If the Inca had fresh seafood daily in Cuzco, reasoned Valdivia pithily, so should Peruvians of the present and future.

Captain Federico Gómez, writing in mid-1930, stated that defense depended on the proper assembly and maintenance of statistics, but he was convinced that existing civilian institutions were incapable of fulfilling this task. Provincial garrison commanders needed accurate data on resources, communications, transport, harvests, storage facilities, and manpower if they were to defend the country.[90] His debt to the French was obvious. His argument was legitimate. It was something on which to build.

Peruvians aped their French mentors naively, almost slavishly, out of the conviction that their situation was analogous to that of France's African empire. It was up to the army to civilize the entire country. Politics, civilians, and the lack of adequate means stood in the way. Officers had no reason to believe there was any other national institution as prepared as or more worthy than they.

It was in the 1930s that APRA and the army first confronted each other, most dramatically in 1932 and 1933. In the same year, the army became more intimately involved with government than at any time since 1890. APRA, the "Indian question" (rarely asked properly, rarely answered adequately), education, integration, national pride, development in all its senses—these were all discussed in print, and nowhere better prior to World War II than in a 1933 essay by Lieutenant Colonel Manuel Morla Concha entitled "Función social del ejército en la organización de la nacionalidad."[91] In this publication, Peruvian officers of generations to come could find historic inspiration and justification for a political role based on professional militarism.

Morla's essay is the most important piece of pre-World War II Peruvian military literature. It is crisply reminiscent of Lyautey's "Du Rôle social de l'officier" for reasons all too obvious. Morla directly adapted Lyautey's ideas from "Du Rôle social de l'officier" and "Du Rôle colonial de l'armée" to Peruvian circumstances. He discussed questions in 1933 that had been raised first by early French observers, then by their Peruvian pupils. In so doing he provided an important link between past and future.

The army was an agent of culture (in the Lyauteyesque sense of civics, patriotic orientation, and literacy) and of democracy (in the sense of equality of opportunity in the ranks). Obligatory military service permitted the common man to be educated and trained, transformed from a "vegetating mass" into a productive citizen. Morla insisted that military service could "tie the country together" through the shared experience of a structured institution.

Addressing the Indian question, Morla wrote that the indigenous Peruvian who served his tour of duty became integrated into "national life," was given the rudiments of an education, was taught personal hygiene, but was allowed to retain the "positive attributes" of his heritage. Military service, in short, worked miracles—a far cry from reality, needless to say. The barracks was a school, he theorized, and the army's mission was, how could one doubt it now, *una misión civilizadora.*[92] Agricultural colonies and cooperatives under military supervision, he thought, were ideal for the settlement of frontier areas that were unincorporated into the national life. Roads, railroads, and airlines linking the colonies and the frontier to the populated areas would serve both military and commercial purposes. Colonization, railroads, highways and airplanes, and the army engineers would "forge nationhood" and make a modern country of Peru.

Morla's essay stands as the primary literary counterattack to APRA's early, extremist schemes for reform. His emphasis on discipline, authority, and hierarchy made the army's position on reform crystal clear. Others in the 1930s expanded on his counterattack, lending a superficially conservative tone to the Peruvian officer corps. Lieutenant Colonel Isaac Portugal lamented Peru's inadequate surface transportation and communications in another 1933 essay. He also blended military interests with commercial ones by averring that World War I had proved the utility of modern highway networks.[93] Captain Mauricio Barbis agreed, praising the army as "the sentinel of the fatherland: its calling is to take up the reins of national development."

Early in 1934 Colonel Jorge Vargas, in "Charla sobre el ejército," told the burghers of Cuzco, his fellow Rotarians, of the army's contributions to national greatness. This bit of service-club professional boosterism must have been repeated wherever Rotarians gathered in South America for food and fellowship, but, alas, only Vargas's contributions remain as an example. Vargas tied national defense to internal development, education, communications, and the redemption of the Indian.[94] Like those before him, he discussed tersely the army's social role as a peacetime obligation. How else, he asked, but through military service did Indians have an opportunity to become literate, disciplined, healthy citizens?

Essays of 1935 by Captain César Velarde and Lieutenant Colonel Alejandro Aliaga reconfirmed the intensity of French influence on Peru. The first of two essays by Velarde attacked excessive individualism in civilian society by calling on Peruvians to be mindful of obligations to their fellow citizens. The army, he thought, set a proper example of corporate responsibility. Civilians ought to emulate the discipline and sobriety of men in uniform. The army was the prime agent of national integration because of obligatory military service. His second essay of the year was another concise call for an expanded military role, in this case as educator of the lower classes.[95] He claimed that 60 percent of each year's draftees were illiterate and that some 80,000 men had learned to read and write, absorbed the elements of civics, and learned the rudiments of personal hygiene in the years since 1912. He solidly backed Vargas's concept of a military peacetime obligation.

In "Papel social del ejército en tiempo de paz," Aliaga wrote that the army was the school of "civic spirit" and the inculcator of discipline, loyalty, and honor; the army was the integrator of Indian, *cholo*, mulatto, negro, oriental, and white. It provided technical expertise to the entire country. Moreover, the army was Peru's only remaining counterpoise to "los tentáculos del monstruo comunista."[96] Thus APRA was no longer the only political bugbear feared by army officers, not the only justification for the continued existence of conscription.

In 1936 (the year Benavides voided the presidential election and announced he would serve the full six-year term of an elected president), Major Enrique Barreto wrote that the army must not be affected by political squabbling if it were to provide adequately for national defense, a standard military argument since 1890. By implication, partisan politics and parliamentary government were detrimental to both the public interest and to national defense—a standard position among South American European military figures of the 1930s. Too, he thought, the general staff in peacetime could serve as the perfect coordinating agency for economic development and social mobilization.[97] Thus Peruvians, like their continental neighbors, accepted the European argument of the day.

In their 1936 editorial "La política interna y el ejército," editors of the *Revista Militar del Perú* opined that "the army is the purest condensation and experience of the national soul" (with nary an acknowledgement to either Vigny or Seeckt et al.).[98] "To menace the fatherland is to threaten the army," they reasoned in inverse order, and admonished their readers to think of "the fatherland above all." They cautioned officers to eschew partisan discussions and civilians against meddling in army affairs, a clear response to APRA's efforts to subvert discipline. The army was thus stationed above divisive politics and placed on the same level as the fatherland, the state, the nation.

On March 24, 1938, War Minister General Federico Hurtado went on a national hook-up to present the army's viewpoint on political affairs and touched on the themes discussed by many of his 1930s predecessors. Not surprisingly, he called the army the "most noble symbol of the nation." International respect and national security were safeguarded only by preparedness for conflict; preparedness could be assured only through obligatory military service, which educated and civilized the common citizen. The army remained above politics and parties.[99] Hurtado's views constituted a summation of Peruvian adaptations of attitudes prevalent in Europe and South America since the late nineteenth century.

As the decade drew to a close, the Chorrillos graduating class of December 1938 heard a commencement address by Marshal Benavides himself. "It is not enough for the army officer to possess the highest of military virtues, to enrich constantly his knowledge, and to train and drill soldiers and citizens for the defense of the fatherland," he told the graduates. "Simultaneously he plays a social and civilizing role. He improves and brings nearer a future for a race that, thanks in great part to military service, we have incorporated into the functional life of the nation."[100] Wishful thinking and hyperbole, beyond doubt, heady stuff to be sure, Benavides's words certainly encouraged cadets and young officers to perceive themselves as leaders.

By contrast, President Manuel Prado's charge to the December 1939 graduating class contained no mention of a "civilizing mission," a "noble symbol of the nation," or a "perfect condensation and experience of the national soul," no exhortation to guard against "the tentacles of the Communist monster" or to transform the "vegetating mass" of Indians and *cholos*.[101] In short, to Prado and his kind the army existed to fight war, to keep the right kind of people in power and the wrong kind of people at bay. In less than a year, the French officers returned to Vichy or London. Soon Peruvian officers would meet with success in the field in a war with Ecuador, yet would chafe at its government's decision not to continue the conflict until Ecuador was totally defeated. Unfulfilled in war, denied their self-proclaimed peacetime role, Peruvian Francophiles reached the end of an era and faced an uncertain future under a civilian administration considered hostile to their interests.

The inter-war years were years of change and adjustment indeed, but the decade between the financial crisis of 1929 and the German invasion of Poland produced some of the most startling political events and social movements that ever confronted professional officers. This was also the decade in which two devastatingly candid anti-military films dealing with military life appeared: Lewis Milestone's "All Quiet on the Western Front" (1930) exposed the horrors of war to American and then continental audiences. Josef Goebbels banned it in Germany. Jean Renoir's equally classic "La Grande Illusion" (1937) cast a critical look back at the officer of yesteryear and an era that ended with the Great War. With rapidity and impact, in both South America and Europe, economic collapse, political extremism, shifts in international relationships, and the need to adjust to new political orders forced officers to take a stand. Political pressures had always affected military writers and their civilian champions with respect to the quantity and tone of their works. At no time between 1890 and 1940 were the pressures on officers as great as during this final decade. But the recent past no longer served as a model, full as it was of frustrations and bitter experiences, of democratic experiments and diplomatic entanglements. This encouraged South American officers to seek a more comfortable past on which to base their appraisals of and prescriptions for the present. Corporatism in its various creole disguises appeared to be a panacea.

By 1930, while governments were tumbling in Buenos Aires, Lima, and Rio de Janeiro and the Ibáñez administration began to totter, a new generation of officers had gained control of middle-level administration and command positions. The majors and lieutenant colonels of the 1930s were all trained professionals, products of European missions or European-trained cadres of nationals. By this time the tangible, cumulative effect of European-style professionalism was all too obvious. To confront political events, the absolute and relative effects of the Great Depression, and the cumulative effects of social and economic retardation, South American officers now relied as well on the accumulated lore of the profession.

Because those assigning study topics and written projects in staff and specialty schools now were Europeanized professionals, their pupils received an education more than ever based on traditional themes and methods. They wrote, as they had for years, on standard French topics and themes. Most of the South American literature of the 1920s and 1930s was reactive in that it still responded to extra-professional realities or problems beyond the jurisdiction of the officer, but the tone grew stronger in the 1930s, more refined and less tentative—more professional.

The outbreak of war in 1939 reemphasized the totality of military professionalism to Argentines, Brazilians, Chileans, and Peruvians. Officers had specific reasons for championing professional causes and for relying on their own experiences and lore to buttress that championship. The ideals and values and the priorities and solutions expressed in official sources reveal, however, that they had much in common, too much indeed to indicate mere coincidence in levels of professional development.

Juxtaposition of French and German officer-corps thought and self-perception with that of their South American charges demonstrates vividly, at every stage between 1890 and 1940, that South American military professionalism was emulative of European models. Creole concepts of *Rittertum* and *rôle social*, the necessity of obligatory military service, close military-civilian cooperation for purposes of national defense, the dangers of political extremism, attitudes toward foreigners, political leaders and civilians in general—these were identical in general configuration.

A half-century of literal and figurative military tutelage came to an end in 1940. France and Germany ceased to lead the way in an organizational, tactical, strategical, and technological sense. A new military titan arose, and since 1945 the officer corps of South America have gravitated toward the United States for training, equipment, and technological expertise. But in their hearts and minds, in word and deed, the generals of the 1960s and 1970s resemble their predecessors of the pre-World War II decades. If it is true, as the evidence indicates, that military professionalism changed very little in essence during the decades of European influence, can it not be that it has changed at least as slowly since that time? For the social, political, and economic dilemmas confronting officers in the post-World War II decades resemble ever so closely the concerns that shaped the thought and self-perception of yesterday's soldiers, thus completing the transformation of military professionalism into professional militarism.

"Life is a struggle. Society is conflict, War is progress. Force is everything."

José Muñiz y Terrones, *Concepto del mando y deber de la obediencia: Cartas a Alfonso XIII,* "Carta I" (1893)

"Above and beyond external changes in uniforms, customs, and aspirations the values of the military spirit remain unchangeable, constituting the heart and soul of the true soldier's permanent vigil of arms."

Tobías Barros Ortiz, *Vigilia de armas* (1973 ed.)

Postscript

Several significant conclusions come to mind, some of which are firm, others of which are tentative. I believe most of the latter can be made firm with further research. I also believe that future research will show perduration of what I have called European military professionalism and its end result, professional militarism, after 1940, despite the dominant position of the United States as military leader in the western hemisphere. So many of the political, social, economic, and cultural dilemmas of modern South America resemble those of the 1890–1940 half-century in Europe that I believe South America to be more representative of that era than that of the Atlantic World of the Atomic Age. Claude Lévi-Strauss was most perceptive when he observed tropical culture-lag.

I think it is clear that there was continuity in the content of the thought and self-perception of European officers and their South American pupils. Missions, cadres, study in Europe, and outright adulation led to their meeting of minds. This conclusion is, really, composed of others. It is the most significant of those reached in this work. Superficial changes that occurred during the time in question affected officer corps, obviously, but under all conditions they continued over the years on both continents to think and perceive themselves in terms of *Rittertum* and *rôle social*, of *missão* and *misión*; this work might just as well have been titled *Rittertum and Rôle Social*: European Military Professionalism in South America, 1890–1940.

The opinions of the officers on the state—its qualities and transcendental significance—remained essentially the same. So did officer-corps thought on the nation—its needs, its relationship to the army and the state. They maintained their pessimistic view of the society surrounding them. The bourgeoisie, individualism, libertarianism, materialism, capitalism—these all were viewed through skeptical eyes.

Officers, unless they were independently wealthy, realized early on that they were economically in the middle sector of society, yet they disdained and resented the bourgeoisie. Those who could claim noble or aristocratic family background by, say, the 1930s were in a distinct and not very prestigious minority. The *Junker* class was defunct as a noble-military caste. National Socialism would see to that, as if the Weimar Republic had not. The French Roman Catholic-monarchist aristocracy no longer figured prominently as a contributor to the officer corps. The process by which the social backgrounds of officers became more representative of the bourgeoisie was under way in 1890. World War I accelerated it, and it was accelerated again between the wars. In South America the professionalization process itself completed the decline of military-aristocratic linkage begun in the early nineteenth century. Elitist ideas and values still obtained, however, *Chevaliers* and *Ritter* lived on, figuratively speaking.

But middle-sector social standing for the majority did not make the majority any more secure. Educated and trained as leaders, taught to hold themselves aloof, and charged with maintaining traditions associated with a bygone era when (they thought) life was simpler, officers were uncomfortable in the present. Their views of society showed them to be all too clearly *part of*, yet *apart from*, the society surrounding them. Education and career experience counted more vis-à-vis their thought and self-perception than did social backgrounds at all times between 1890 and 1940. This is true for both Europe and South America.

These, more than any other characteristics, encouraged the development of the *rôle social* in its various translations. Obligatory service served a two-fold purpose: it provided the human wherewithal for national defense capability, and it availed peasants and workers, and in theory all young men of the more privileged classes, with a civilizing, nationalizing experience. It was the natural role of elitist, idealistic, tradition-bound officers to educate and train the male populace to be both soldiers and citizens.

It was the responsibility of a government—as temporal manifestation of the state—to see to it that the nation was both cultured and civilized, if not by outright involvement in the daily life of citizens, then by providing the appropriate ambience. The army was an agent of this responsibility. Governments that did not indicate their willingness (ability being dependent at all times only on willingness) to recognize this were simply not worthy of support. The army was the nation; it was the state; it was a microcosm of society; its mission was to be the permanent manifestation of each. In his essay "Étude sur la discipline" of 1904,[1] Captain Couderc de Fonlongue, it will be recalled, viewed the army as a "filter" through which passed generation upon generation of Frenchmen, and his analogy is as descriptive as most of the sustained perception of the officer-army-citizen relationship.

That thought and self-perception changed little in content or standpoint over the years leads to a second significant conclusion. Army officers relied heavily on precedent and established authority when putting their ideas down on paper for publication in an official organ. On all but technological matters they scrupulously cited great figures—the likes of Vigny and Clausewitz, Goltz and Lyautey, De Gaulle and Seeckt, as well as their own professional forbears. On numerous occasions they merely paraphrased. Sometimes they repeated word for word. Plagiarism was no sin to these essayists. Reliance on the past induced officers to show a selective disdain for the present.

They were well aware of the international scene and of technical advances in military science and allied fields. They believed themselves to be the technological vanguard in South America—and they were most probably correct—and at the very least up-to-date with Europe. One need only think of the sharp contrasts in the German army of the late 1930s between modern armor and horse-drawn supply wagons to realize just what the technological vanguard actually was. Officers argued in every way possible for a socioeconomic structure capable of providing for national defense and domestic progress—and stability. European officers were well aware of the domestic political scene. So were South Americans, but they realized full well that their countries were modern. Both participated in various ways in political decision-making, South Americans far more than their mentors.

For this reason, South American professionals had occasion to reject much of their own national, military, and political tradition and to adopt the military professionalism of France and Germany. In so doing, they adopted the search for the idealized past—a past idealized in Europe but never known in South America. Officers in Argentina, Brazil, Chile, and Peru came to perceive the profession as bridging the gulf between old and new, making as compatible as humanly possible sociocultural phenomena of a patrimonial, organic, and authoritarian nature with those more individualistic and egalitarian. They fancied themselves more capable than any civilian institution of reconciling the spiritual with the material, the personalistic with the impersonal and bureaucratic. They stated ad nauseam that the army was the most democratic of all social institutions. South Americans as well as Europeans were convinced that the profession embodied those ideals and values most suited to the total mobilization of social, economic, and administrative energies in a harmonious and reliable way in peacetime as well as in war. Anyone familiar with military institutions and how they can operate internally knows all this to be a grandiose delusion.

South Americans showed in print that they aspired to a status enjoyed by Prusso-Germans and to a role ostensibly played by French officers. They yearned for both *Rittertum* and the *rôle social*. A principal appeal of authoritarianism in South America was that it appeared to be the way professional officers could achieve both. Their advocacy of solutions for cultural, educational, and social ills read very much like the

Nazi party project of 1932 for a program of curricular revision to provide extensive courses of a practical nature, more classes in citizenship, civic thought, and mandatory gymnastics and sports, in order to produce healthy, indoctrinated minds in sound, disciplined bodies. Corporatism in its various forms meshed neatly with officer-corps thought and self-perception.

There was concurrence of thought and self-perception to a point in the 1930s, when, as I have noted, South Americans sounded as much like traditional Europeans as did their transatlantic contemporaries. They were truly representative of European military tradition, as outmoded as it may have been. The South American blend of idealized past and troublous present, of tradition and reality, produced professional militarism. The officers who took part (whether sincerely or hypocritically) in the blending process consequently searched vainly for the past and looked to the future concomitantly, hoping to improve the present.

Just over midway through the period an anonymous general wrote to his son, in one of those classic bits of military prose, that, the moment he became an officer, "your time, your brain, your life are now no longer your own, but the state's." He instructed him in etiquette, discipline, temperance, and responsibility to his peers and his men: "Be a good fellow," he told him. He warned him against vices (especially *cocottes* and drink), against any and all people "whose women paint themselves and who delight in music halls and fashionable Charlie Chaplin films." He decried the self-indulgence of civilians, their indiscipline, their materialistic pursuits. His views were those of his coevals, but he was neither a socially-conscious French officer, nor a worried *Junker*, nor an aspiring South American, he was a British general.[2] The similarity of thought and self-perception should come as no surprise. European military professionalism in South America was very much a phenomenon of the times: a *mentalité*, a *Weltanschauung*, and British officers were as mired in the past as were their contemporaries.

The foregoing conclusions indicate a potential for political involvement, at least a drawing of lines between civilian and military worlds. The persistent interest shown by Frenchmen and Germans in political affairs translated easily into Portugese and Spanish, with involvement dependent always on the specific nature of a political system. There are a number of examples in the foregoing chapters of South Americans applying a military ethos to a plethora of *grandes problemas.* Argentines, Brazilians, Chileans, and Peruvians worried about liberal democracy and what it truly meant in the same ways French and German officers did. They were perpetually concerned with bourgeois politics and political behavior. They worried about the failure of democracy to result in marked socioeconomic and cultural change; their concerns were similar to those of French officers who believed that parliamentary democracy was France's downfall. Brazilians and Peruvians adapted French colonial strategies in order to penetrate their own country's interior, to colonize, civilize, and develop. Argentines and Chileans took an elitist, Germanic stand on politicians, parties, elections, and civilians meddling. Most of these conclusions are interchangeable in South America.

Applications of professional ideals and values to the South American domestic scene became more clearly defined by 1940—but were obviously not in short supply in the preceding decades. The political thought of the 1930s envisioned an expanded state role in all spheres, for that was in vogue in European military circles. A military-conceived expanded state role in countries where societies are retrograde, where democracy is merely a veneer, and where economies are basically neo-colonial has clear consequences for politics, society, and economic policy. The fact that the state, in both monarchic and republican forms, has been a dominating influence throughout Latin American history simply reinforces the attraction of solutions based on a military ethos, for the army was, after all, "the purest image of the state." Justification of an expanded military role was an important component of thought and self-perception.

Edgardo Mercado Jarrín, one of the most influential leaders of the 1968 Peruvian military movement, wrote that "revolutionary changes in general staff organization and action carried out through a historical process made the army an efficient and modern institution at all levels long before the country began the process of modernization."[3] Mercado belonged to a select core of the Peruvian general staff and to a select group of authors and editors whose works influenced the thought and self-perception of their contemporaries. He believed that years of highly specialized education and training had advanced the profession beyond contemporary groups in the civilian sector and had made it in most ways superior to civilian society. His words bring two other conclusions to mind.

First, only a few Europeans or South Americans ever published; therefore, just how representative were they? How could so few be representative of so many? They were representative because their essays were selected by editorial boards composed of officers who wanted certain things in print. They were no less representative because the majority of officers simply did not write; the structure of the officer corps dictated who wrote and who simply read. Officers read from the works cited in the preceding pages, for it was wise professionally to do so. We have no way of estimating readership, but we certainly do know what was available to aspiring, ambitious professionals of the early twentieth century, to their successors, and to officers of the late twentieth century. The elitist, hierarchical, authoritarian nature of the military profession dictates that officers absorb ideas and values prescribed for them, if only to mouth them at the opportune time. Colonel (at the time) Mercado wrote nearly a quarter-century after the French had left Peru, but his initial intellectual formation and his advanced and specialized training were based on French models, and inspirations. The Escuela Militar, the Escuela Superior de Guerra, and the Centro de Altos Estudios Militares are direct outgrowths, in organizational and curricular terms, of French military presence.

World War II did indeed interrupt the process of professionalization, and in ways that World War I did not. It inserted a new and hitherto marginally considered military model into the South American environment. It set the stage for domestic variations of the Cold War ideological confrontation that have affected politics since 1945. The war temporarily altered the course of rising military professionals who had entered the senior ranks just prior to the outbreak of hostilities. The post-1945 decades have seen ideological confrontations played out in each of the countries dealt with here. The elaboration and application of counter-insurgency strategies, of military ideologies based on the internal security-socioeconomic development linkage, sometimes expressed through what has been called bureaucratic authoritarianism, are the results of military professionalism become professional militarism. It may be that such elaborations and applications would have occurred even if Europeans had never been involved in the professionalization process. But the essence of most of the ideas, doctrines, theories, and programs associated with an expanded military role stems from the 1890–1940 years. The generals involved in the institutional *golpes* of the 1964–73 years graduated from military schools in the 1930s or soon thereafter. They too are yesterday's soldiers. U.S. military influence has not erased the past, it has reinforced it and bolstered its appeal by perpetuating discontent with the present and hope for a better future. The United States is still considered something of an intruder in South American military circles.

Whatever else the *golpes* of 1964, 1966 (and 1976), 1968, and 1973 have represented in Brazil, Argentina, Peru, and Chile, they were the products of generations of thought and self-perception brought to bear on contemporary reality. Specific characteristics and past experiences, both political and professional, obviously influence governmental programs, but the underlying attitudes toward nation, state, and society are much the same. A perusal of the rhetoric and oratory of justification for recent military movements shows this to be true, more so than I once thought. It also renders rather useless the labeling of military movements as rightist or leftist on the basis of their specific achievements.[4] Examination of post-World War official military literature leads to the same conclusion.

There is no such thing as a monolithic officer corps. Neither in France nor in Germany nor in any of the client states did all officers subscribe to the very same ideals and values—ever. Furthermore, the changeover from military professional to professional militarist has never been an easy one; a military institution's inflexibility assures this. But this does not preclude a continued consensus of thought and self-perception among the elite of the corps over a fifty year-span of time, nor does it diminish the significance of that consensus. I believe that such a consensus persists. Whether such a consensus can be brought to bear in all spheres of military-political activity is another matter. I am convinced that social, economic, and cultural realities—but not thought and self perception—dictate otherwise.

In fine, the legacy of yesterday's soldiers, that which I term professional militarism, has not been dissipated. If anything, a search for the idealized past, motivated by pre-World War II reactions to the present and concerns for the future, and set forth in relevant terminology, still figures boldly in the South American professional military mind.

Notes

The following bibliographical citations make no pretence to being definitive. They do not represent every possible source of information. Secondary sources cited throughout the text contain ample bibliographies on all aspects of military-civilian relations and institutional history not treated herein. Since it has not been my purpose to duplicate existing studies of the military profession in South America or Europe, I have limited references to a degree consistent with sound scholarship and sufficient to indicate appropriate or alternative documentation. Omission of a work from the following notes is no indication of a negative qualitative evaluation on my part; it indicates that in my judgment further documentation is redundant, that the work is of such a nature that it does not apply sufficiently to the subject of this study, or that the work is cited in one of the principal secondary sources already mentioned.

In addition to abbreviations that are widely known, such as DSF for United States Department of State archival materials and MID for United States War Department, military intelligence papers, I have used abbreviations in the multiple citation of journals. The following list may aid the reader in identifying the most often cited official and semi-official European and South American journals. (Well-known scholarly and opinion journals are abbreviated as well in ongoing citations.)

ADN   *A Defeza Nacional* Brazil
BMEME   *Boletim Mensal do Estado Maior do Exército* Brazil
BMGM   *Boletín del Ministerio de Guerra y Marina* Peru
IRGAF   *Internationale Revue über Gesammten Armeen und Flotten* Germany

JSM/RMF   *Journal des Sciences Militaires/Revue Militaire*
               Française France
MECH   *Memorial del Ejército de Chile* Chile
MEMECH *Memorial del Estado Mayor del Ejército de Chile* Chile
MW   *Militär Wochenblatt* Germany
MR   *Militärwissenschaftliche Rundscahau* Germany
NMB   *Neue Militärische Blätter* Germany
RCMA   *Revista del Círculo Militar* Argentina
RCMP   *Revista del Círculo Militar* Peru
RI   *Revue d'Infanterie* France
RMA   *Revista Militar* Argentina
RMAE   *Revue Militaire des Armées Etrangères* France
RMB   *Revista Militar Brasileira* Brazil
RME   *Revue Militaire de l'Étranger* France
RMF   *Revue Militaire Française* France
RMF/JSM   *Revue Militaire Française/Journal des*
               Sciences Militaires
RMG   *Revue Militaire General* France
RMP   *Revista Militar del Perú* Peru

Introduction

1. Fritz K. Ringer, *Education and Society in Modern Europe* (Bloomington: Indiana University Press, 1979), p. 7.
2. Quentin Skinner, "Meaning and Understanding in the History of Ideas," *History and Theory* 8, no. 1 (1969): 9.

Chapter One

1. Frederick Jackson Turner, "The Significance of the Frontier in American History," *Proceedings of the State Historical Society of Wisconsin* (14 December 1893).
2. José Enrique Rodó, *Ariel* (first published, Montevideo, 1900); Manuel Ugarte, *El porvenir de la América Latina* (first published, Buenos Aires, 1923); and *El destino de un continente* (first published, Buenos Aires, 1923). Jean Franco's *The Modern Culture of Latin America: Society and the Artist*, rev. ed. (Baltimore: Penguin Books, 1970), pp. 52–81, contains a sophisticated discussion of the cultural nationalism of the early twentieth century.
3. On the development of South American armies during the nineteenth century see John J. Johnson, *The Military and Society*

in Latin America (Stanford: Stanford University Press, 1964), pp. 13–92, and Edwin Lieuwen, *Arms and Politics in Latin America*, rev. ed. (New York: Frederick A. Praeger, 1961), pp. 17–35. Both authors break their treatment at World War I.

4. *Revue des Deux Mondes* (15 March 1891): 443–59, hereafter cited as RDM. In the majority of cases herein I limit citations of periodical literature to title, journal, date, and pagination, for there are sufficient changes in series, volume numbers, publications dates, issues per volume, and volumes per series, along with errors in numeration, to make further identification virtually counterproductive, indeed downright confusing in some cases.

5. On French military-civilian relations during the 1890–1914 years see John Steward Ambler, *Soldiers against the State: The French Army in Politics* (Garden City, N.Y.: Anchor Books, 1968), esp. pp. 3–33, and David Ralston, *The Army of the Republic: The Place of the Military in the Political Evolution of France, 1871–1914* (Cambridge, Mass.: MIT Press, 1967).

6. Gordon A. Craig's *The Politics of the Prussian Army, 1640–1945* (New York: Oxford University Press, 1964) is a very informative work on pre-World War I German military-civilian relations. See esp. chap. 6, "The State Within the State," pp. 216–54. Indispensable to the study of the modern European military mind are essays in Edward Mead Earle, ed., *Makers of Modern Strategy: Military Thought from Macchiavelli to Hitler* (New York: Athenaeum, 1966).

7. See Samuel P. Huntington, *The Soldier and the State: The Theory and Politics of Civil-Military Relations* (Cambridge: Harvard University Press, 1957), 8–18.

8. In his unique *The "Fuero Militar" in New Spain, 1764–1800* (Gainesville: University of Florida Press, 1957), Lyle N. McAlister made a good case for the Bourbon reform program of the second half of the eighteenth century as a historical breaking-point in military-civilian relations. Works by Christon Archer, Leon G. Campbell, and Alan J. Kuethe (the second two are former McAlister students) make it clear that some earlier assumptions and conclusions were incorrect. See Archer's *The Army in Bourbon Mexico, 1760–1810* (Albuquerque: University of New Mexico Press, 1977); Campbell's *The Military and Society in Colonial Peru, 1750–1810* (Philadelphia: American Philosophical Society, 1978); and Kuethe's *Military Reform and Society in New Granada, 1773–1808* (Austin: University of Texas Press, 1979).

9. See Pike, *Spanish America, 1900–1970* (New York: Norton, 1973), esp. pp. 9–41.

10. *El gaucho Martín Fierro* (first published, Buenos Aires, 1872). In a touching stanza Hernández rendered the symbolic passing of the gaucho as a true folk type, personified by the eponymous Fierro and his crony thus:

> Cruz and Fierro rounded up
> a string of horses from a ranch;
> they drove them in front of them
> as wise criollos know how,
> and soon, without being noticed,
> they crossed over the frontier.
> Canto XIII, stanza 2295

11. Samuel Putnam introduced and translated *Os Sertões* (first published, São Paulo, 1902) as *Rebellion in the Backlands*, 1st ed. (Chicago: University of Chicago Press, 1944). Cunha's study is one of the most informative and incisive books ever produced in Latin America.

12. But they knew they were far from it. See, for example, Florentino Abarca, *La decadencia de Chile* (first published, Santiago, 1904), and Alejandro Venegas, *Sinceridad: Chile íntima en 1910* (first published, Santiago, 1910).

13. The development of predominant views and introspective vantage points can be ascertained by reading (in sequence) Ricardo Palma, *Tradiciones peruanas*, 10 vols. (Lima, 1872–1910); Manuel González Prada, "Discurso en el Politeama" (1884) and *Páginas libres* (first published, Paris, 1894); and José Carlos Mariátegui, *Seven Interpretive Essays on Peruvian Reality*, tr. Marjory Urquidi (Austin: University of Texas Press, 1971). This last work first appeared in Lima in 1928.

14. See Fernand Braudel, *The Mediterranean and the Mediterranean World in the Age of Phillip II*, tr. Sian Reynolds, 2 vols. (New York: Harper and Row, 1972), and Emmanuel Le Roy Ladurie, "Motionless History," tr. John Day, *Social Science History* 1 (1977): 115–36.

15. See Pike, *Hispanismo, 1898–1936: Spanish Conservatives and Liberals and Their Relations with Spanish America* (Notre Dame: University of Notre Dame Press, 1971).

16. *Das Volk in Waffen: Ein Buch über Heerwessen und Kriegsführung unserer zeit* (first published, Berlin, 1883). The English translation by Phillip A. Ashworth of the fifth edition (1898)

appeared as *The Nation in Arms: A Treatise on Modern Military Systems and the Conduct of War* (London: Hugh Rees, Ltd., 1913). The first Spanish-language edition appeared in Spain as *La nación en armas* (Toldeo: n.p., 1897).

17. The first edition (Paris: *Publications de la Revue des Deux Mondes*, 1835) appeared as a collection of three of Vigny's short stories previously published in the RDM. It was later rendered into English by Humphrey Hare as *The Military Necessity* (London: The Cresset Press, 1953). Unless otherwise noted I have consulted first editions of nineteenth- and twentieth-century European and South American works on the military.

18. See Craig, *The Politics of the Prussian Army*, p. 232–37.

19. Paul Marie de la Gorce's *The French Army: A Military-Political History*, tr. Kenneth Douglas (London: Weidenfeld and Nicolson, 1963) contains a comparatively optimistic appraisal of French military-civilian relations in the wake of the Franco-Prussian War. See esp. pp. 6–17. Allan Mitchell's "A Situation of Inferiority: French Military Reorganization after the Defeat of 1870," *American Historical Review* 86, no. 1 (February 1981): 49–62, is a more circumspect appraisal of military-civilian mutual hostility and French emulation of German military organization.

20. See Alan Scham, *Lyautey in Morocco: Protectorate/Administration, 1912–1925*, Berkeley and Los Angeles: University of · California Press, 1970), esp. pp. 3–48; Jacques Gabriel Paul Michel Benoist-Mechin, *Lyautey l'africain ou le rêve immole* (Lausanne: Clairfontaine, 1966), pp. 11–32; and André Maurois, *Lyautey*, 2nd ed. (Paris: Plon, 1964), pp. 11–42, for a discussion of Lyautey's early career and the intellectual influences on him.

21. RDM (1 January 1900): 308–29.

22. The standard source on French and German military missions in Japan is Ernst Presseisen, *Before Aggression: Europeans Prepare the Japanese Army* (Tucson: University of Arizona Press, 1965). See also Robert E. Ward and Dankwart Rustow, eds., *Political Modernization in Japan and Turkey* (Princeton: Princeton University Press, 1964) esp. chap. 8, pp. 283–327, "The Military: Japan," by Roger F. Hackett, and "The Military: Turkey," by Rustow.

23. For information on German military influence in the Turkish officer corps see Feroz Ahmad, *The Young Turks: The Committee of Union and Progress in Turkish Politics, 1908–1914* (Oxford: Oxford University Press, 1969), and Ulrich Trumpener, *Germany*

and the Ottoman Empire, 1914–1918 (Princeton: Princeton University Press, 1968).

24. See Felix Gilbert, *The End of the European Era, 1890 to the Present* (New York: W. W. Norton, 1970), esp. pp. 129–44.

25. Good for material on Argentina between 1890 and 1940 are James R. Scobie's *Argentina: A City and a Nation*, 2nd ed. (New York: Oxford University Press, 1971), esp. chaps. 5–8, pp. 112–216, and *Buenos Aires: Plaza to Suburb, 1870–1910* (New York: Oxford University Press, 1974). Scobie's bibliographies are abundant with material on the period in question.

26. I concur with Arthur P. Whitaker, who noted in his *Argentina* (Englewood Cliffs, N.J.: Prentice-Hall, 1964) that "The name is usually written Sáenz, but the accent was omitted by [Saenz himself]." Despite the appearance of negligence in things diacritical, Saenz shall remain Saenz.

   During Saenz Peña's state visit to Europe in 1910 the American minister in Berne referred to him as phlegmatic for a Latin, cosmopolitan, able, fair, and noble-minded, "suaviter in modo, fortiter in re." Lauritz S. Swenson to Philander C. Knox, United States Department of State Files 835.00/89 (formerly 4519/89), 15 July 1910, hereafter cited as DSF. On this trip don Roque became convinced that Germany favored Brazil because of Marshal Hermes's immense popularity there. See C. H. Sherril to Knox, DSF 835.00/95, 20 July 1910. President Pedro Montt of Chile also traveled in Germany that year; one of his companions was Emil Körner.

27. "El Peludo" refers to Yrigoyen's "eremitelike" and puzzling behavior. A *peludo* is a variety of armadillo that, when attacked, rolls itself into a ball, sealing off the vulnerable parts of its little body. Members of the foreign diplomatic corps knew Yrigoyen as such. D. Rankin White to Charles Evans Hughes, DSF 834.20/266, 16 December 1921. White drew attention to Yrigoyen's poor education, his "anacoluthic style" of writing and speaking, his misanthropic ways, his attraction to flattery and sycophants, and his belief that he was endowed with "supernal powers which make him the superman chosen to rule the country." This was an altogether hostile appraisal of the controversial Argentine.

28. On issues affecting the military in Brazil at this time see June E. Hahner, *Civilian-Military Relations in Brazil, 1889–1898* (Columbia, S.C.: University of South Carolina Press, 1969); Charles W. Simmons, *Marshal Deodoro and the Fall of Pedro II* (Durham, N.C.: Duke University Press, 1967); and William S.

Dudley, "Professionalization and Politicization as Motivational Factors in the Brazilian Army Coup of 15 November 1889," *Journal of Latin American Studies* 8, no. 1 (May 1976): 101–125, hereafter cited as JLAS; and "Institutional Sources of Discontent in the Brazilian Army, 1870–80," *Hispanic American Historical Review* 55, no. 1 (February 1975): 44–65, hereafter cited as HAHR.

29. Information on this episode can be found in Robert Nachman, "Positivism and Revolution in Brazil's First Republic: The 1904 Revolt," *The Americas* 34, no. 1 (July 1977): 20–39, hereafter cited as TAm.

30. "The State of St. Paul is justly proud of an armed force which it owes to French instructors. I need not criticize the Federal Army, which is officered by men of fine public spirit, but all agree that the force needs reorganizing." Georges Clemenceau, *South America Today* (London: T. Fisher Unwin, 1911), p. 243.

31. Harold Blakemore's *British Nitrates and Chilean Politics, 1886–1896: Balmaceda and North* (London: The Athlone Press, 1974), and "The Chilean Revolution of 1891 and its Historiography," HAHR 45, no. 3 (August 1965): 393–421, remain the most enlightening works on this period in Chilean history. A broader scholarly treatment can be found in Pike's *Chile and the United States, 1880–1962: The Emergence of Chile's Social Crisis and the Challenge to United States Diplomacy* (Notre Dame: University of Notre Dame Press, 1963), pp. 31–46. On military-civilian relations, see Frederick M. Nunn, *The Military in Chilean History: Essays on Civil-Military Relations, 1810–1973* (Albuquerque: University of New Mexico Press, 1976), pp. 83–106.

32. Alberto Edwards Vives used the term *la fronda aristocrática* as the title of the book (1st ed., Santiago: Editorial del Pacífico, 1927) in which he analyzed the Basque-Castilian aristocracy's opposition to strong centralized government. The term originated in France, and applied to *La Fronde*, the noble-parliamentary group that opposed the centralizing ambitions and administrative autocracy of Prime Minister Jules Cardinal Mazarin (Giulio Mazarini) prior to the majority of Louis XIV.

33. Federico Errázuriz Echaurren (1896–1901), son of Federico Errázuriz Zañartu (1871–76), turned over the government to German Riesco Errázuriz (1901–06); Riesco in turn gave way to

Pedro Montt Montt (1906–10), son of Manuel Montt Torres (1851–61).

34. The best standard sources treating aspects of this period are Pike, *The United States and the Andean Republics: Peru, Bolivia and Ecuador* (Cambridge, Mass.: Harvard University Press, 1977), esp. pp. 118–39, 143–73; and *The Modern History of Peru* (New York: Frederick A. Praeger, 1967); and Víctor Villanueva, *Cien años del ejército peruano: Frustraciones y cambios* (Lima: Juan Mejía Baca, 1972).

35. Grandfather of Division General Francisco Morales Bermúdez, president from 1975 to 1980.

36. Paul Clément, "Memorandum que eleva el general Paul Clément, jefe de la misión militar francesa, a s.e. el presidente de la república, el 24 de agosto de 1899," in Centro de Estudios Histórico-Militares del Perú, *Documentos donados al CEHMP por el r.p. Rubén Vargas Ugarte, S.J.*

37. See Scham, *Lyautey in Morocco*, pp. 144–62.

38. As Thomas M. Davies, Jr., remarked in the introduction to his study *Indian Integration in Peru: A Half Century of Experience, 1900–1948* (Lincoln: University of Nebraska Press, 1974): "*Soroche* is easy to describe and extremely unpleasant to experience. No amount of clothing keeps out the penetrating cold, and it is difficult to breath even while seated in a car. Minimal exercise is difficult and normal activity is almost impossible. The head begins to throb, accompanied by recurrent waves of nausea....On the train between Arequipa and Puno, I looked out the window and saw an Indian pedaling a bicycle at high speed. I have also seen soccer games at altitudes of 15,000 feet which made me feel even more of an outsider in an alien, hostile world." Identical confrontations with that physiological confirmation of Peruvian regional-topographical disunity convince me that Davies's description can be matched by few.

39. The subject is treated admirably in Davies, *Indian Integration in Peru*, passim.

40. A mission commanded by Captain (Colonel, in Bolivian rank) Hans Kundt, consisting of five officers and thirteen non-coms, began work in La Paz in 1910 at the request of President Ismael Montes. The Germano-Bolivian tie has been thoroughly treated in Jürgen Schaefer's exhaustive *Deutsche Militärhilfe an Südamerika: Militär und Rüstungsinteressen in Argentinien, Bolivien, Chile vor 1914* (Düsseldorf: Bertelsmann Universitätsverlag, 1974). Owing to the domestic sociopolitical turbulence of the altiplano

republic, German military missions in Bolivia would never achieve the results they did in Argentina and Chile. The mission was first discussed seriously as something of possible significance to U.S. interests in South America by Captain Constant Cordier, the U.S. military attaché in La Paz, two years after Kundt agreed to serve there. See Cordier's informative memorandum entitled "The German Military Mission in Bolivia," included in United States Archives, Military Intelligence Division, 6370-14, 15 October, 1912, hereafter cited as MID. Both Cordier and the U.S. minister, Harold Knowles, correctly pointed out the commercial and diplomatic significance of the German military presence in mineral-rich Bolivia. They both overestimated the ability of Germans to train the Bolivian army and modernize it. See Knowles to Knox, DSF 824.20/3, 24 January 1913.

Chapter Two

1. See Walter Goerlitz, *History of the German General Staff, 1657–1945*, tr. Brian Battershaw (New York: Frederick A. Prager, 1965), p. 97.
2. Augusto A. Maligne, *Historia militar de la república argentina durante el siglo 1810 a 1910* (Buenos Aires: La Nación, 1910), p. 154; República Argentina, *Reseña histórica del colegio militar, 1810–1910* (Buenos Aires: Imprenta del Colegio Militar, 1927), pp. 9–13.
3. See Ramón J. Carcano, *Guerra del Paraguay*, 3 vols. (Buenos Aires, n.p. 1939–41), for a detailed treatment of Argentina's involvement in the war. Charles J. Kolinski's *Independence or Death: The Story of the Paraguayan War* (Gainesville: University of Florida Press, 1965) presents the Paraguyan point of view. Pelham Box, *The Origins of the Paraguayan War* (Urbana: University of Illinois Press, 1929), is also valuable, especially for treatment of Brazilian motives.
4. See J. del Viso, "La conquista del desierto," *Revista Militar* (May 1934), pp. 917–57, hereafter cited as RMA.
5. República Argentina, *Memorial del departamento de guerra presentado al honorable congreso nacional correspondiente al año 1925–1926* (Buenos Aires: Departamento de Guerra, 1926), pp. xi–xxii.
6. República Argentina, *Monografía histórica del estado mayor del ejercito argentino* (Buenos Aires: Estado Major General del Ejército), pp. 53–128, passim.

7. *Reseña histórica del colegio militar*, p. 13.

8. Ibid., p. 23.

9. See Augusto G. Rodríguez, *Reseña histórica del ejército argentino (1862–1930)* (Buenos Aires: Secretaría de Guerra, 1964), p. 95.

10. See Nunn, *The Military in Chilean History*, pp. 53–59.

11. The best examples are: Comité de Historia del Estado Mayor del Ejército de Chile, *Historia militar de Chile*, 3 vols. (Santiago: Estado Mayor General del Ejército, 1969), I, 7–86; Alberto Polloni, *Las fuerzas armadas de Chile en la vida nacional: Compendio cívico-militar* (Santiago: Editorial Andrés Bello, 1972), passim; Agustín Toro Dávila, *Síntesis histórico-militar de Chile* (Santiago: Editorial Universitaria, 1976), pp. 2–48; Indalicio Téllez Cárcamo, *Historia militar de Chile* (Santiago: Instituo Geográfico Militar, 1925), passim; and José M. Barceló Lira, "La evolución del ejército desde la ocupación del territorio araucano (1859–1879) hasta nuestros días," *Memorial del Ejército de Chile* (March-April 1935): 199–218, hereafter cited as MECH. Needless to say, these works are all by army officers. See also Gerardo Zúñiga Montúfar's *El ejército de Chile: Impresiones y apuntes* (Santiago: Imprenta Universo, 1904). This is a perceptive appraisal by a Costa Rican major studying in Chile.

12. See Nelson Werneck Sodré, *História Militar do Brasil* 2nd ed. (Rio de Janeiro: Civilização Brasileira, 1968), pp. 33–45.

13. For example:
    Chile my scene; a fertile land remote,
    Hard by the border of antarctic seas,
    Home of a stiff-necked people, wed to arms.
    Renowned in war, by neighbor nations feared;
    Whose hot distempered blood alike rebels
    At rule domestic and at stranger yoke.
    No king among themselves they own, nor e'er
    Have bowed the knee to foreign conqueror.
    La araucana (1569), canto I, stanza 6

14. See Presseisen, *Before Aggression*, passim.

15. Nunn, *The Military in Chilean History*, 70–71.

16. For example, consult Carlos Ríos Pagaza, *Historia de la escuela militar* (Lima: Centro de Instrucción Militar, 1962), passim; Estado Mayor General del Ejército del Perú, 5a Sección, *Monografía histórica del ejército peruano* (Lima: Estado Mayor General del Ejército, 1930); and Carlos Dellepiane, *Historia militar del Perú*, 2 vols. (Buenos Aires: Círculo Militar, 1941).

Vol. 1 of the last-cited work deals with the pre-independence period and the decades up to 1879. José Zárate Lescano, in his "Consideraciones sobre la historia integral del ejército peruano," *Revista Militar del Perú* (January–February 1969), pp. 48–57, argued that a Peruvian military spirit can be traced to ca. 900 A.D.; hereafter cited as RMP.

17. This is treated in Campbell's *The Military and Society in Colonial Peru.*

18. The most useful material on early military education in Peru can be found in Ríos Pagaza, *Historia de la escuela militar;* Felipe de la Barra, *La escuela militar y su papel profesional y social* (Chorrillos: Imprenta de la Escuela Militar, 1939); Paul Clément, ed., *La escuela militar en el xxv aniversario de su fundación, 1898–1923* (Lima: Empresa Tipográfica La Unión, 1924); and, in English, Lyle N. McAlister, "Peru," in McAlister, Anthony P. Maingot, and Robert A. Potash, *The Military in Latin American Socio-Political Evolution* (Washington: American Institutes for Research, 1970), pp. 21–83. This last is an indispensable source for the comparative study of institutional development of the armies of Argentina (by Potash), Colombia (by Maingot), and Peru and Mexico (by McAlister), emphasizing the late nineteenth and the twentieth centuries.

19. Edgardo Mercado Jarrín emphasized that this is especially true of post-1940 graduating classes (*promociones*) in his seminal "El ejército de hoy y su proyección en nuestra sociedad en período de transición (1940–1965)," RMP (November–December 1964), pp. 1–21. See the discussion of this essay and other important Peruvian military literature in Nunn, "Professional Militarism in Twentieth Century Peru: Historical and Theoretical Background to the *Golpe de Estado* of 1968," HAHR 59, no. 3 (August 1979): 391–417. The theory that the officer corps had spoken for the middle classes and selected regional interests was advanced by James Petras and Nelson Rimensnyder in "The Military and the Modernization of Peru," in Petras, ed., *Politics and Social Structure in Latin America* (New York: Fawcett Books, 1970), pp. 130–158.

20. Carlos A. Miñano M., *Las misiones militares francesas en el Perú* (Lima: n.p., 1959), p. 5; Clément, *La escuela militar,* p. 15. Jehoval Motta, in his *Formação do Oficial do Exército: Currículos e Regimes na Académia Militar, 1810–1944* (Rio de Janeiro: Editôra Artes Gráficas, 1976), makes the same point for Brazil.

21. Clément, *La escuela militar,* p. 17.

22. Ibid., p. 18.

23. Celso Zuleta, "Historia militar del Perú," *Boletín del Ministerio de Guerra y Marina* (15 January 1905): 167–74, hereafter cited as BMGM. This was the forerunner to the *Revista Militar del Perú.* See as well the editorial, "Breve reseña histórica del ejército peruano," RMP (March–April 1967): 32–41.

24. *Annuário da Escola Militar, 1914* (Praia Vermelha: Escola Militar, 1915), pp. 9–58, contains information on nineteenth-century Brazilian military education.

25. See "A Escola Militar: Síntese Histórica da sua Fundação e Evolução," *Revista Militar Brasileira* (January–March 1942): 13–70, hereafter cited as RMB. The entire issue was devoted to the Escola Militar.

26. A good deal of the following discussion is based on information in João Baptista Magalhães, *A Evolução Militar do Brasil: Anotações para a História* (Rio de Janeiro: Biblioteca do Exército, 1958); Francisco de Paula Ciadade, "Da Missão Militar Franceza ãos Nossos Dias," RMB (July–December 1954): 131–86; and Sodré's *História Militar.* See also the Sodré's useful essay, "História Militar Brasileira," RMB (June–December 1944): 355–66.

27. See Robert Nachman's "Positivism and Revolution in Brazil's First Republic."

28. Benjamin Constant Botelho de Magalhães, cited in Heitor Lyra, *História da Queda do Império,* 2 vols. (São Paulo: Companhia Editôra Nacional, 1964). See esp. I, 75–79, 414–18.

29. See Theodorico Lopes and Gentil Torres, *Ministros de guerra do Brasil, 1808–1850,* 4th ed. (Rio de Janeiro: Borsoi, 1946), for data on Caxias. William S. Dudley's "Professionalization and Politicization" and "Institutional Sources of Discontent" are invaluable for information on politics and the army in the latter stages of the Empire.

30. Documented conclusions on this issue can be found in Lyra, *Historia de Queda do Império,* pp. 77–94; Magalhães, *A Evolução Militar,* esp. pp. 310–35; and Sodré, *História Militar do Brasil,* pp. 130–62.

31. Paula Cidade, "Da Missão Militar Franceza ãos Nossos Dias," pp. 319.

32. Cunha's *Rebellion in the Backlands* remains the best, most readable account of the Canudos campaign. It was Caxias himself who said: "Let us march shoulder to shoulder, not chest to chest." Cited in L. Correia Lima, "Pela pátria, pelo exército," *A Defeza Nacional* (April 1970): 148, hereafter cited as ADN.

33. Magalhães, *A Evolução Militar,* 312.

34. Robert N. Burr, *By Reason or Force: Chile and the Balancing of Power in South America, 1830–1905* (Berkeley and Los Angeles: University of California Press, 1965), pp. 1–11.

35. Th. Mannequin, ed. and tr., *Antagonisme et solidarité des états orientaux et des états occidentaux de l'Amérique du Sud* (Paris: Dentú, 1866), passim. Nearly forty years later, comments made by C. H. Sherril of the U.S. mission in Buenos Aires confirmed the outside world's convictions about Argentina's pacific ways and Brazil's aggressive policy of territorial aggrandizement at the expense of limitrophe states. Sherril to Knox, DSF, 835.00/95, 20 July 1910.

36. Friedrich von Bernhardi, *Kriegsbuch (The Customs of War)* tr. J. Ellis Barker (London: Wm. Dawson and Sons, Ltd., 1914), pp. 33–34. The English edition bore the subtitle cited herein on its cover. "General A.," in *Les Reforms dans l'armée française: Comparison entre cette armée et l'armée allemande* (Paris: Libraire Militaire de L. Baudoin et Cie., 1897), made it clear that any army unable to withstand a campaign during a European winter, or similar conditions, did not merit consideration as a true army.

37. Guglielmo Ferrero, *Militarism (Il Militarism)* (London: Wardlock and Co., Ltd., 1902), p. 223.

38. Jaillet, *Essai historique et critique sur le colonisation militaire* (Paris: V. Giard et E. Briere, 1903), p. 17.

39. Joffre wrote that a newly-formed army, a "young army" in his words, naturally favored offensive doctrines. It succumbed to what he called the "mystique of the offensive." *Memoirs,* tr. T. Bentley Mott, 2 vols. (London: Geoffrey Bees, 1932).

40. H. D'Ildeville, *Memoirs of Marshal Bugeaud: From His Private Correspondence and Memoirs,* tr. Charlotte M. Yonge, 2 vols. (London: Hurst and Blackett, 1884), I, 322.

41. Goltz, *The Conduct of War: A Short Treatise on its Most Important Branches and Guiding Rules,* tr. F. G. Leverson (London: Kegan Paul, 1899), pp. 2–43.

42. E. K. [Emil Körner], "Militärische Nachrichten aus Chile," *Militär Wochenblatt* (11 January 1890): 117–19, hereafter cited as MW.

43. "La Dernier campagne au Chile," *Revue Militaire de l'Étranger* (April 1982): 304–30, hereafter cited as RME. This journal became the *Revue Militaire des Armées Étrangères* in 1895, and will be cited RMAE in notes for issues subsequent to that date.

44. "Die deutschen Offiziere in Chile," *Internationale Revue über die Gesammten Armeen und Flotten* (March 1897): 491–97, hereafter cited as IRGAF.

45. "Der Krieg in Chile," *Neue Militärische Blätter* (March 1893): 215–25, hereafter cited as NMB.

46. "Die Revolution in Buenos Aires," MW (18 November 1890): 2836–31.

47. "Vier fremde Militärkommissionen," MW (19 August 1899): 1842.

48. "L'Armée brasilienne" RME (March 1893): 278–79.

Chapter Three

1. Vegetius (Flavius Vegetius Renatus), c. 375, *De Rei Militari*. The original Latin is *Qui desiderat pacem, praeparet bellum*.

2. See Burr, *By Reason or Force*, passim, esp. pp. 33–57, 73–96, 138–66, 245–59.

3. Gaetano Mosca, *The Ruling Class*, tr. Hannah D. Kahn (New York: McGraw Hill, 1939), p. 468.

4. Vilfredo Pareto, *Sociological Writings*, ed. S. E. Finer (London: Pall Mall Press, 1966), pp. 51–59.

5. Ferrero, *Militarism*, pp. 201–37, 275–79.

6. Ambler, *Soldiers against the State*, p. 23. See also La Gorce, *The French Army*, pp. 31–92, on French military-civilian relations, 1890–1914.

7. Lyautey, *Lettres du Tonkin et de Madagascar*, 2nd ed. (Paris: Colin, 1921), p. 479.

8. Alfred de Vigny, *The Military Necessity*, p. 17; La Gorce, *The French Army*, p. 1. In the Iberian languages *la grande muette* was frequently rendered in the masculine form *le grand muet*, then translated as either *el gran mudo* or *o grande mudo*, owing to the fact that *ejército* and *exército* are masculine in gender.

9. La Gorce, *The French Army*, p. 87. Concomitantly there was a revival of French nationalism and pro-army sentiment. See Eugen Weber, *The Nationalist Revival in France, 1905–14* (Berkeley and Los Angeles: University of California Press, 1968).

10. Vigny, *The Military Necessity*, p. 16; Bugeaud, *Memoirs*, p. 322.

11. This was the Dreyfusard line, as presented in Urbain Gouhier, *L'Armée contre la nation* (Paris: Éditions de la *Revue Blanche*, 1899), p. 16. On Action Française, see Weber, *Action Francaise, Royalism and Reaction in Twentieth Century France* (Stanford: Stanford University Press, 1962); Edward R. Tannenbaum, *The*

Action Française: Die-Hard Reactionaires in Twentieth Century France (New York: John Wiley, 1962); and Gaston Moch, *L'Armée d'une democratie* (Paris: Éditions de la *Revue Blanche*, 1900), pp. 17–23.

12. Marc Sangnier, *L'Armée et la république: Discours prononcée aux sociétés savantes le 3 de October 1912, suivi des résponses aux contradicteurs* (Paris: Édition de la Democratie, 1912), pp. 4–9.

13. La Gorce, *The French Army*, p. 50; Paul Gabillard, "Le Proletariat dans l'armée," in Henri Berenger et al., *Le Proletariat intellectual en France* (Paris: Éditions de la Revue, 1901), p. 184. During extended visits to Argentina, Brazil, Chile, and Peru in 1962, 1969, 1972, 1975, and 1978, I repeatedly heard this from officers who compared the salaries of captain and lieutenants with those of miners, oil field workers, and skilled workers as well as laborers.

14. Henri Felix Theodore Iung, *La République et l'armée* (Paris: Bibliotheque Charpentier, 1892), pp. 3–29. The quotation appears on p. 29.

15. Henri Jougla, *La Demilitarisation de la France* (Toulouse: Edouard, 1900), p. 9.

16. General Duchemin, *Les Troupes coloniales et la défense des colonies* (Paris: Libraire Militaire R. Chapelot et cie., 1905), p. 230.

17. Lyautey, "Du Rôle colonial de l'armée," pp. 309–310.

18. Treitschke, *Politics*, 2 vols., trs. Blanche Dugdale and Torben de Bille (London: Constable and Co., 1916), II, 390. On professional views of veterans' organizations see "Kriegervereine gegen Sozialdemokratie: Ein Mahnwort an die gebilden Stande," MW (8 March 1899): 537–40, and "Noblesse Oblige," NW (15 February 1899): 376–77. The essential crown–officer corps relationship is discussed in "Der Offizier und das dynastische Prinzip," MW (12 July, 1889): 1311–26.

19. Treitschke, *Politics*, II, 389–448.

20. Ibid., p. 292.

21. Helmuth von Moltke, *Essays, Speeches and Memoirs*, trs. Charles Flint McClumpha, C. Barter, and Mary Herms, 2 vols. (London: James R. Osgood, 1893), II, 57. See as well H. Petermann, "Über die Erziehung und die Erzieher des Soldaten," NMB (November 1892): 399–405.

22. See Emil Dangelmaier, "Der Zeitgeist, die Gegenwart und das Heer," NMB (June 1898): 481–96. The quotation is from

pp. 486–87. Other pieces written in this vein that merit mention are Anon, "Gefahren für die Disziplin," MW (10 April 1895): 835–39; "Heer und Sozialdemokratie," NMB (15 April 1901): 354–74; and "Das Heer und die Sozialdemokratie," NMB (15 September 1906): 466–67.

23. See Craig, *The Politics of the Prussian Army*, pp. 232–38. On all aspects of military-civilian relations in pre-World War I Germany, see as well Roger Chickering, *Imperial Germany and a World without War: The Peace Movement and German Society, 1892–1914* (Princeton: Princeton University Press, 1975); Karl Demeter, *The German Officer Corps in Society and State, 1650–1945*, tr. Angus Malcolm (London: Weidenfeld and Nicolson, 1965), esp. pp. 3–46, 63–102, 111–46, 157–85, and 217–47; and Holger Herwig, *The German Naval Officer Corps, 1890–1914* (Oxford: Oxford University Press, 1968).

24. Goltz, *The Nation in Arms*, pp. 8–11. The quotation appears on p. 11.

25. Ibid., p. 22.

26. These statements appear on the English translation's cover and in the translator's introduction, p. 6.

27. Bernhardi, *Kriegsbuch*, pp. 14–17.

28. Ibid., p. 72.

29. From *The German War Book: Being the Usages of War on Land*, tr., J. H. Morgan (London: John Murray, 1915), p. 43.

30. See Treitschke, *Politics*, II, 390.

31. K. Isenburg, *Die Disziplin, ihre Bedingungen und ihre Pflege* (Berlin: Ernst Siegfried Mittler und Sohn, 1885), p. 7 ff.; "Einem alten Offizier," in *Individualismus und Schablone im deutschen Heere* (Berlin: Verlag von Friedrich Luckhardt, 1894), pp. 1–59, passim. See also Anon., "Der junge Offiziere als Erzieher," NMB (November 1892): 3066–68; "Die Erziehung des Soldaten," NMB (April 1892): 289–92; and "Die Erziehung des Offizierkorps," NMB (October 1901): 312–25.

32. General von Hertzberg, "Charakter," MW (13 December 1913): 3817–22. As representative of consistency in argumentation across the decades, compare "Charakter" with General von Blume, "Les bases de la force militaire de l'Allemagne," IRGAF *Supplement* (December 1899): 189–93, and Anon., "L'Instruction militaire du soldat allemand," IRGAF *Supplement* (April 1907): 222–24. Cf. the earlier Gustav Jaeger, "Die Wehrpflicht und Volkserziehung," NMB (April 1893): 301–02. Jaeger employed the

English aphorism "Time is money" in advocating more efficient utilization of officers' and conscripts' time. He disdained the application of psychology to military training.

33. Goltz, *The Nation in Arms*, p. 21.

   In "Die Vorbildung unseres Offizierkorps," NMB (July 1899): 1–20, an anonymous contemporary of Goltz warned against changing the corps into a heterogeneous, technological institution, for fear it would cease to be a "spiritual bridge between army and nation."

34. Bernhardi, *Kriegsbuch*, pp. 74–75.

35. Lyautey, "Du Rôle social," p. 455.

36. For example see Anon., "Éducation du soldat," *Journal des Sciences Militaires/Revue Militaire Française* (February 1892): 302–15, (June 1892): 437–58, (October 1892): 51–67, and (December 1892): 430–48. Issues cited prior to the title change of 1908 cited JSM/RMF. See also General Cosseron de Villenoisy, "La Force militaire de la France," JSM/RMF (April 1890): 369; Anon., "Le Capitaine," JSM/RMF (November 1893): 235–47; C. Riet, "L'Armée moralisatrice," JSM/ RMF (May 1896): 255–74; Anon., "Le Recrutement des officiers en France et à l'étranger," JSM/RMF (September 1901): 396–410, (November 1901): 219–48, and (December 1901): 386–92; F. R., "Le Recrutement des officiers," *Revue Militaire Française/Journal des Sciences Militaires* (15 October 1913): 403–34. Issues subsequent to title change of 1908 cited RMF/JSM. Lieutenant Haffemayer, "Condition social de l'officier en France, en Allemagne et en Russie," JSM/RMF (March 1902): 432–40; Capitaine Bourget, "Du Relèvement intellectuel des sous-officiers au regiment," JSM/RMF (December 1906): 399–4051; and Lieutenant Jacquot, L'Éducation physique," RMF/JSM (15 November 1908): 195–210. Cf. the prototype counter-argument in "Un Officier Superieur," "La Vérité sur le rôle social de l'officier," JSM/RMF (December, 1894): 358–78. This is the reponse of an obvious Freemason to literature on the military-clerical *rôle social.*

37. Charles De Gaulle, *France and Her Army*, tr. F. L. Dash (London: Hutchinson and Co., 1940), p. 77. Cf. Eugen Weber's *Peasants into Frenchmen: The Modernization of Rural France, 1870–1914* (Stanford: Stanford University Press, 1976), which ably deals with obligatory service as a stimulus to national moral and cultural unity and an eradicator of local dialects, illiteracy, and isolation. See esp. pp. 292–302.

38. A. Garçon, *L'Éducation militaire à l'école* (Paris: Henri Charles–La Vouzelle, 1899), pp. 9–20, and Iung, *La République et l'armée*, p. 94.

39. Georges M. Duruy, "L'Officier éducateur," JSM/RMF (March 1904): 360–68; the quotation is from p. 361. See Couderc de Fonlongue, "Étude sur la discipline," JSM/RMF (October 1904): 78–97, and (November, 1904): 248–57.

40. See L'Abbé Lucas Championnierre's pamphlet *La Vie militaire* (Paris: Bureau Central des Oeuvres, 1893).

41. Le Père Didon, *L'Esprit militaire dans une nation: Discours prononcée a la distribution des prix des écoles Albert-Le-Grand et La Place* (Paris: J. Mersch Imprimeurs, 1898), p. 4; and R. P. Caruel, S. J., *L'Éducation nationale et l'armée: Discours prononcée a la distribution solenelle des prix de l'école libre Saint-Joseph de Reims* (Reims: Imprimeurie de l'Archevêché, 1898), pp. 4–11.

42. Gaston Moch, *L'Armée d'une democratie*, pp. 22–23. See also Lieutenant Ricq, "L'Idée de patrie," JSM/RMF (August 1898): 265–76, and Capitaine Gerard, "Instruction et éducation militaires," JSM/RMF (February 1903): 250–68.

43. See Marcel Demongeot, "L'Éducation de la solidaritée dans l'armée," RMF/JSM (15 February 1910): 272–86, and the earlier monograph *Citoyen et soldat: Étude sur l'armée nationale* (Paris: Ernest Flammarion, Editeur, 1903).

44. Demongeot, *Citoyen et soldat*, pp. 41–61; "L'Éducation de la solidaritée," passim. See also Colonel Gory, "Autorité, subordination et moyens de discipline," RMF/JSM (15 June 1911): 401–17, (1 July 1911): 35–58, (1 August 1911): 280–307, (15 August 1911): 443–59, (1 September 1911): 65–89, and (15 September 1911): 186–200; his "L'Exercise du commandant," RMF/JSM (1 March 1913): 5–25, (15 March 1913): 105–27, and (1 April 1913): 278–88; and F. R., "Le Recrutement des officiers," RMF/JSM (15 October 1913): 403–34.

45. Demogeot, *Citoyen et soldat*, p. 260.

46. Bernard Serrigny, *Les Conséquences économiques de la prochaine guerre d'après enseignments des campagnes de 1870–1871 et de 1904–1905* (Paris: V. Giard et E. Briere, 1909), pp. 19–20.

47. Ibid., p. 24.

48. Sangnier, *L'Armée et la république*, p. 6.

49. Jaurès, *Organisation socialiste de la France* (Paris: Publications Jules Rouff, 1911), pp. 675–85. Compare Jaurès's moderation with the aforementioned Dreyfusard Gouhier's scathing attack.

Gouhier called that supposed "home away from home," the barracks, "a school of all the vices of excess: laziness, lying, infamy, lewdness, debauchery, moral corruption, and drunkeness."

50. Leonard Wood's *The Military Obligation of Citizenship* (Princeton: Princeton University Press, 1915) stands as evidence of concurrence of professional views on obligatory military service in the Atlantic world prior to World War I. Wood's considerable rhetorical skills were equal in every way to those of his French and German counterparts.

51. Lieutenant Haffemayer, "Condition social de l'officier en France," pp. 432–34. See also Anon., "Le Recrutement des officiers en France et à l'étranger," (November 1901): 219–24, and (December 1901): 391.

52. Richard Theiss, *Die Wehrpolitik des deutschen Reiches unter Reichskanzler Graf Caprivi und Fürst Hohenloe* (Heidelberg: Buchdruckerei Heinrich Fahrer, 1938).

53. War-time potential estimates for the mid-1880s were app. 2,400,000 for France and 2,100,000 for Germany. See *Foreign Armies: Their Formation, Organization and Strength* (London: William Clawes and Sons, 1886); Charles Jerram, *The Armies of the World* (London: Lawrence and Bullen, Ltd., 1899). Brazil, Chile, and Mexico were the only Latin American countries included in Jerram's work.

54. See N. W. Barnardson, *Handbook of the French Army* (London: H.M.S.O., 1901).

55. A. Garçon, *Armées étrangères contemporaines*, 2 vols. (Paris: Henri Charles La Vouzelle, 1909), I, 24. Argentina, Brazil, Chile, Peru, Bolivia, Mexico, Paraguay, the United States, China, and Japan were the non-continental countries included.

56. Jerram, *The Armies of the World*, p. 105.

57. H. Albertall, "Die Waffen nieder," IRGAF (October 1890): 217.

58. Goltz, *The Nation in Arms*, pp. 53–54. See Moltke, *Essays, Speeches, and Memoirs*, II, 96–106.

59. Blume, "Les Bases de la force militaire de l'Allemagne," passim.

60. Karl von Bruchhausen, *Der Kommende Krieg: Eine Studie über die militärische Lage Deutschlands* (Berlin: Pan Verlag, 1906), pp.8–55. See also "Die heutige Französische Armee," *Beiheft zur/IRGAF* (July 1902): 24–25.

61. Friedrich von Bernhardi, *Britain as Germany's Vassal* (London: William Dawson and Sons, Ltd., 1914), pp. 37–38.

62. MacMahon, cited in De Gaulle, *France and Her Army*, p. 78.

63. See "General A.," *Les Réformes dans l'armée française: Comparison entre cette armée et l'armée allemande* (Paris: Libraire Militaire de L. Baudoin et Cie., 1887); "Une Prophetie militaire," JSM/RMF (April 1892): 58–82; Charles Roche, "L'Avancement de l'avenir et le rajeuissement des cadres de l'armée," *JSM/RMF (March 1899): 419*–34, (April 1899): 95–123, (July 1899): 129–51, and (June 1900): 147–53; and General X., "L'avancement dans l'armée," JSM/RMF (May 1899): 191–203.

64. General de Trentinian, "La Fusion des officiers de l'armée metropolitane et de l'armée coloniale," RMF/JSM (1 January 1911): 519.

65. See Anon., *Les Officiers d'aujourd'hui: Étude sur la position social des officiers européens* (Fribourg: Libraire de l'Université, 1889), pp. 9–12, and Captaine Verbier, *L'Esprit militaire*, 2 vols. (Paris: n.p., 1896), II, 325.

66. Capitaine Jibé, *L'Armée nouvelle: Ce qu'elle pense, ce qu'elle veut* (Paris: Plon, 1905), p. xii; Capitaine Spero, *La Défense nationale sous la république* (Paris: Libraire Felix Juven, 1906), pp. 4–32; and Paul Fontin, *Guerre et marine: Essai sur l'unité de la défense nationale* (Paris: Berger-Levrault et Cie., 1906), pp. 41–13.

67. Bernard Serrigny, *Les Conséquences économiques de la prochaine guerre*, pp. 37–70.

68. Ferdinand Foch, *Precepts and Judgments*, tr. Hilaire Belloc (London: Chapman and Hall, 1919), p. 150.

69. Victor Leuliette, *The Spirit of History Teaching: Attitudes of the Teacher towards War* (London: School Peace League, 1910), p. 7.

70. See the rendition of Kropotkin's classic published as *La Guerre* (Paris: Temps Nouveaux, 1912), p. 22.

71. George Herbert Perres, *The War Traders: An Exposure* (London: National Peace Council, 1913).

72. See Charles R. Ogden, *Militarism versus Feminism: An Enquiry and a Policy Demonstrating That Militarism Involves the Subjection of Women* (London: George Allen and Unwin, Ltd., 1915).

Chapter Four

1. Jürgen Schaefer's *Deutsche Militärhilfe an Südamerika* is indispensable for details on the activities of German military missions and their ties to German commercial and diplomatic

interests. A Marxist view of Germany's "imperialistic" relationship with Chile's army, government, and commercial institutions is Jürgen Hell, "Deutschland und Chile von 1871–1918," *Wissenschaftliche Zeitschrift der Universität Rostock* 14 (1965): 81–105. For details on all European missions in South America prior to 1940, see Fritz Epstein, "European Military Influence in Latin America," (unpublished ms., Library of Congress, 1941).

Much of the following material is drawn from Frederick M. Nunn, "Emil Körner and the Prussianization of the Chilean Army: Origins, Process and Consequences, 1885–1920," HAHR 50, no. 2 (May 1970): 300–322, and *The Military in Chilean History*, pp. 7–70.

2. Cited by Armando Donoso in *Recuerdos de cincuenta años* (Santiago: Editorial Nascimento, 1947), p. 372.

3. Francisco Javier Díaz Valderrama, *Cuarenta años de instrucción militar alemán en Chile* (Santiago: Imprenta Jeneral Díaz, 1926), pp. 10–12.

4. See *Memoria del ministerio de guerra presentada el congreso nacional en 1899* (Santiago: Ministerio de Guerra, 1900), hereafter cited as *Memoria*, followed by the appropriate date.

5. Díaz Valderrama, *Cuarenta años*, p. 18. The most accurate listing of German officers serving in South America is in the index to Schaefer's *Deutsche Militärhilfe an Südamerika*. Names of those South Americans who studied in Europe appear there as well.

6. As defined in Goltz, *The Nation in Arms*, pp. 51–52. Goltz emphasized equality, common interests and obligations, corporate responsibility. He compared the officer corps to a "brotherhood of knights" similar to the Orders in the heyday of their existence.

7. Tobías Barros Merino, *La vida militar en Alemania* (Santiago: n.p., 1890); Gustavo Walker Martínez, *Estudios militares* (Santiago: Imprenta Barcelona, 1901). Of the two, Walker's work provides more details on the Germano-Chilean experience.

8. See Indalicio Téllez Cárcamo, *Recuerdos militares* (Santiago: Instituto Geográfico Militar, 1945), pp. 48–49.

9. *Memoria*, 1895–96, pp. 13–14.

10. *Memoria*, 1896–97, pp. vi.

11. *Memoria*, 1899, pp. 11–17.

12. *Memoria*, 1903, p. 23.

13. *Memoria*, 1906, p. 13. See also Nunn, "Emil Körner and the Prussianization of the Chilean Army," pp. 311–12.

14. *Memoria*, 1905, passim.

15. Körner, "Memorial de la inspección general del ejército," *Memoria*, 1908.

16. *Memoria*, 1907, p. 10.

17. *Memoria*, 1908, p. 46.

18. Téllez, *Recuerdos*, 29; Carlos Sáez Morales, *Recuerdos de un soldado*, vol. 1, *El ejército y la política* (Santiago: Editorial Ercilla, 1933), p. 29; *Memoria*, 1909, p. 41.

19. *Memoria*, 1909, p. 5–6.

20. See Nunn, "Emil Körner and the Prussianization of the Chilean Army," pp. 314–18.

21. See Luis Correa Prieto, *El presidente Ibáñez, la política y los políticos: Apuntes para la historia* (Santiago: Editorial Orbe, 1962), pp. 45–52, for information on the Salvadoran mission. Pedro Zamora Castellanos, *Vida militar de Centro América*, 2 vols. (Guatemala City: Tipografía Nacional, 1924), II, 334–80, provides a general and anecdotal history of early twentieth-century Central American military affairs. On Ecuador see Luis Cabrera, Ernesto Medina, Luis Bravo, and Julio Franzani, *Misión militar chilena en el Ecuador* (Quito: Imprenta del Ejército, 1902), and Julio H. Muñoz, *Doctrinas militares aplicadas en el Ecuador* (Quito: Estado Mayor General, 1949), pp. 175–89.

22. On the Chilean pre-World War I missions to Colombia see *1907–1957: 50 años de la escuela militar* (Bogotá: Imprenta de la Escuela Militar, 1957); the Chilean Pedro Charpín's "La reforma militar y sus pugnadores," *Memorial del Estado Mayor del Ejército de Colombia* (March 1911): 91–97; and the Colombian Gonzalo Canal Ramírez's "Sesenta años después: La escuela militar de cadetes marca el final de las guerras civiles y el principio del civilismo," *Revista del Ejército* (June 1967), 236–66.

23. Miñano, *Las misiones militares francesas*, pp. xi–xii, 6–13.

24. Ibid.

25. Clément, *Memorandum*, pp. 2–4. This document constitutes one of the most valuable single sources on military missions in South America.

26. Ibid., pp. 14–15.

27. Ibid., pp. 63–64, 66.

28. Miñano, passim, and César A. Pando Enríquez, "Las misiones militares francesas en el Perú," RMP (November 1946), pagination inexact.

29. Sweepingly defined, the duties of each mission were to furnish "technical instruction and drill in the various arms...lectures to senior officers...and direction of exercises and maneuvers in order to provide the army with the best practical preparation." Pando Enríquez, "Las misiones militares francesas," passim.

30. Ejército del Perú, Cincuentenario de la escuela superior de guerra del Perú (Lima: Escuela Superior de Guerra), 1954).

31. Benavides, Ponce, Luna, and Montagne all appeared on a list of officers judged according to U.S. standards as "the most efficient" by military attaché Colonel Elwood M. C. Steward in his G-2 Report No. 32602, MID 2033-100/4, 1 October 1926. On historical links between ESG and CAEM see both Víctor Villaneueva's *El caem y la revolución de la fuerza armada* (Lima: Instituto de Estudios Peruanos, 1972), pp. 220–27, and his *Ejército peruano: Del caudillaje anárquico al militarismo reformista* (Lima: Editorial Juan Mejía Baca, 1973), pp. 121–296, passim.

32. *Cincuentenario de la escuela superior de guerra*, pp. 57–64. By 1914 the ESG had amassed data on regional cross-sections of Peru (coast, *sierra*, *montaña*) from the northern frontier to the Chilean border. From World War I onward these were renewed and revised, so that by 1930 the army had the best collection of topographical and statistical data of any government agency.

33. Clément, ed., *La escuela militar*, p. 3.

34. Barra, *La escuela militar*, pp. 14–15.

35. Humberto Núñez, "Por la seguridad de la nación," *Revista del Círculo Militar* (February, 1924): 107–14, hereafter cited as RCMP.

36. Leonidas González H., "La enseñanza en la escuela militar," in Clément, ed., *La escuela militar*, pp. 37–58.

37. Ministerio de Guerra y Marina del Perú, *Ley de servicio militar obligatorio y dispociones para su cumplimiento* (Lima: Ministerio de Guerra y Marina, 1905), pp. 1–16.

38. Ernesto Montagne Markholtz, *Memorias* (Lima: n.p., 1962), p. 31; Pedro Pablo Martínez, *Paginas militares* (Lima, n.p., 1924), pp. 11–16.

39. See Schaefer, *Deutsche Militärhilfe an Südamerika*, pp. 77–79 ff.; Warren Schiff, "The Influence of the German Armed Forces and

War Industry on Argentina, 1880–1914," HAHR 52, no. 3 (August 1972): 440; and George Pope Atikins and Larry V. Thompson, "German Military Influence in Argentina, 1921–1940," JLAS 4, no. 2, (November 1972): 257–59.

40. Angel Silva Nieto, "El ejército argentino y la comunidad nacional: La escuela superior de guerra" (typescript, Escuela Superior de Guerra, 1965). I saw this and other mss. bearing the same main title in 1969. They were written as partial fulfillment of a colonel's course in the Escuela de Altos Estudios of the ESG.

41. Silva Nieto, "El ejército argentino"; Schiff, "The Influence of the German Armed Forces," pp. 440–41.

42. A. A. M. [Augusto A. Maligne], *El ejército chileno y la guerra de mañana* (Buenos Aires: n.p., 1898), p. 69.

43. See Schaefer, *Deutsche Militärhilfe an Südamerika*, pp. 124–30.

44. See Rodolfo Martínez Pita, *Riccheri* (Buenos Aires: Peúser, 1952), and Círculo Militar, *Teniente general d. Pablo Riccheri* (Buenos Aires: Círculo Militar, n.d.), for biographical information.

45. Johannes Dingskirchen, *Juicios militares: Observaciones sobre la disciplina e instrucción del ejército argentino a propósito de las maniobras y paradas de 1892* (Buenos Aires: Jacobo Peúser, 1892). The remark about Argentina's "Spanish background" appears on pp. 122–23.

46. See República Argentina, *Colección de leyes y decretos militares concernientes al ejército y armada de la república argentina, 1810–1895*, 6 vols. (Buenos Aires: Arsenal Principal de Guerra, 1898–1905), VI, 213–32; Rodríguez, *Reseña histórica*, pp. 107–110.

47. See Silva Nieto, "El ejército argentino," pp. 91–95, for biographical information.

48. See José Ricardo Luna, *Informe general sobre el estado militar de la república argentina* (Lima: Ministerio de Guerra, 1942, 1922), pp. 48–49, 102. Luna was a Peruvian military army attaché in Buenos Aires when he wrote this monograph.

49. Alfred Arent, *Ein Land der Zukunft: Ein Beitrag zur nahren Kenntnis Argentiniens* (Munich: Verlag von Südamerika, 1906), pp. 163–91.

50. Ibid., pp. 164–274, passim.

51. See the intensely nationalistic Ernst von Halle, *The Rise and Tendencies of German Transatlantic Enterprise* (London: P. S.

King and Sons, 1908). This was an address of 1907 to the British Association for the Advancement of Science. Germany's motives were confirmed in the Cordier memorandum of 1912, cited in n. 40, chapter one. See also MID, 6370-2, 16 December 1910 (unsigned memorandum on German activities prepared for the commandant, Army War College). An extensive article in the 16 May 1911 issue of the *Berliner Tageblatt und Handels-Zietung* entitled "Panamerika in der Praxis" made the motives of all "patriotic-minded" Germans clear: "Germany is the protector of the South American states against the designs of North America! And North America is helpless either to inspire or demand respect for her proposals, policies, and interest in any part of the world, in America itself, without military power. It cannot be repeated too often that the world rates a nation by its military power—extent of territory, number of people, wealth do not determine a country's place in the list of nations. Whether America shall be the China of the Western Hemisphere depends on the attitude of the people toward the military."

52. Rodríguez, *Reseña histórica*, p. 95.

53. Schiff, "The Influence of the German Armed Forces," pp. 438–40.

54. José F. B. Uriburu, "Explicaciones sobre los nuevos reglamentos," RMA (April 1899): 259–61; Schiff, "The Influence of the German Armed Forces," p. 442.

55. This sobriquet was applied by Francisco de Paula Cidade in his "Da Missão Militar Francesa ãos Nossos Dias," RMB (April–June 1927): 152–68. See also Tristão de Alencar Araripe's *Tasso Fragoso: Um Pouco da História do Nosso Exército* (Rio de Janeiro: Biblioteca do Exército, 1960), pp. 140–41; his "Alguns Passos da História do Colégio Militar do Rio de Janeiro," RMB (July–December 1960): 5–22, passim; and Hahner, *Civilian Military Relations in Brazil*, pp. 82–84.

56. Lyra, *História da Queda do Império*, I, 415.

57. There are numerous references to the difficulties in utilization of sophisticated artillery pieces in *Rebellion in the Backlands*, pp. 189–434, passim. See Alfredo d'Escragnolle, Viscount Taunay, *La retraite de Laguna* [*A Retirada de Laguna*], (Rio de Janeiro: n.p., 1871), for an epic account of the Paraguayan War. It has long been considered "required reading" for Brazilian cadets, and in 1943 the Biblioteca do Exército established a literary prize in Taunay's honor. Some Brazilian officers

generously compare *A Retirada de Laguna* to Xenophon's *Anabasis.*

58. I have called this "a form of Brazilian Bushido." See Frederick M. Nunn, "Military Professionalism and Professional Militarism in Brazil: Historical Perspectives and Political Implications," JLAS 4, no. 1 (May 1972): 33.

59. Estevão Leitão de Carvalho, *Dever militar e política partidária* (São Paulo: Imprensa Editôra Nacional, 1959), pp. 28–34.

60. See DSF, 835.00/95, Sherril to Knox, 20 July 1910.

61. (First issue, October 1913). The letter "z" was mistakenly set in *Defeza* by the typesetter and retained by the editors for sentiment's sake.

62. ADN (October 1913): 1–2.

63. See Nunn, "Military Professionalism and Professional Militarism in Brazil," p. 37.

64. French mission officers were just as guilty of arm-twisting as their German counterparts. For a summary of complaints made by Brazilians see MID, 2006-44/0, 12 February 1921–MID, 2006-44/17, 6 January 1931.

65. See Cordier, "The German Military Mission in Bolivia," and Schaefer, *Deutsche Militärhilfe an Südamerika*, pp. 103–112. A general treatment of pre-1940 military missions in the Bolivian army can be found in Julio Díaz Arguedas, *Historia del ejército de Bolivia* (La Paz: Imprenta Instituto Central del Ejército, 1940), pp. 756–76.

66. Ernesto Medina Franzani, *El problema militar de Chile* (Leipzig: C. C. Röder, 1912), p. 30.

67. Ibid., pp. 83–86.

68. Alberto Muñoz Figueroa, *El problema de neustra educación militar* (Santiago: Estado Mayor Jeneral, 1914). On the same subject see also Carlos Dinator, "Educación cívica en el ejército," *Memorial del Estado Mayor del Ejército del Chile* (April 1915): 28–99, hereafter cited as MEMECH; Domingo Terán, *Tema militar* (Santiago: Imprenta del Ministerio de Guerra, 1917); Manuel Moore Bravo, *Instrucciones para el desarrollo de las virtudes militares del cuerpo de oficiales de la iv división del ejército* (Valdivia: Imprenta Central E. Lampert, 1917); and Aníbal Riquelme, "Relación que debe existir entre la política de un estado i el alto comando del ejército," MEMECH (September 1914), 638–50.

69. This is the central thesis of Nunn, "Professional Militarism in Twentieth Century Peru."

70. Gabriel Velarde Alvarez, "Instrucción civil del soldado," BMGM (October 1904): 843–45.

71. J. C. Guerrero, "La educación e instrucción de la raza indígena en las escuelas civiles de tropa," BMGM (June 1910): 666–68. See also A. Escalona, "El kechua y su importancia para los oficiales peruanos," BMGM (December 1910): 1296–98.

72. David Fernandini, "Conveniente reglamentación del servicio militar obligatorio," BMGM (February 1911): 181–96, and "EL ciudadano y sus deberes para con la patria," BMGM (March 1911): 314–18; Nicanor Beúnza, "Servicio militar en el Perú," BMGM (March 1911): 255–63. The "brutalizing trinity" was extracted, of course, from Gonzalez Prada's "Discurso en el Politeama."

73. Fernandini, "Medio de desarrollar el amor a la patria," BMGM (May 1911): 564–70.

74. Carlos Echazú, "La disciplina militar," BMGM (December 1914): 1451–55.

75. Maligne, *Historia militar*, pp. 156–58.

76. See the sharply anti-Riccheri and Roca tract, Anon., *El ejército argentino por adentro: Estudio para contribuir al reestablecimiento de nuestras instituciones militares arruinadas* (Buenos Aires: n.p., 1904), pp. 6–34, passim.

77. Ibid., p. 26.

78. R. von Colditz, "La guerra hispano-americana," *Revista del Círculo Militar* (October 1900): 629–43, hereafter cited as RCMA.

79. "Militares bolivianos en Buenos Aires," RCMA (January 1901): 111–14.

80. Augusto A. Maligne, "1810–1910: Cien años después," RCMA (May 1910): 473–80. See also Gaspar Soria, "El oficial argentino: El ejército argentino debe sustentar los ideales del pueblo," RCMA (March 1917): 137–42.

81. See José Rodríguez, "La guerra," RCMA (July–August 1914): 100–3. The citation is from p. 103.

82. See, for example, Benjamín Rattenbach, *Sociología militar* (Buenos Aires: Círculo Militar, 1958).

83. José F. B. Uriburu, "Socialismo y defensa nacional," RCMA (October 1914): 213–27.

84. *Relatório Apresentado ão Presidente da República dos Estados Unidos do Brasil pelo Marechal Hermes Rodrigues da Fonseca,*

Ministro de Estado da Guerra, 1907–1908 (Rio de Janeiro: Ministério de Guerra, 1908), p. 3.

85. Heitor d'Araújo Mello, "O Brasil como Nação Armada, *Revista dos Militares* (May 1914): 193–205.

86. Ibid., pp. 193–94.

87. See Bernardo Reyes, "Exposición y proyecto de ley para establecer el servicio militar personal y obligatorio en la república mexicana" (typescript dated 30 January 1911); and "Cartas, 1909–1911" (a file of correspondence with interim War Minister Manuel González Cosío), Archivo Personal Bernardo Reyes, Mexico, D.F.; Reyes's *El ejército mexicano* (Mexico City: n.p., 1901) is the best published work on the army prior to the revolution.

88. "Les Institutions militaries du Perou," RMAE (December 1909): 465–71.

89. "Peru," IRGAF (March 1901): 106.

90. "Ausgaben für Heer und Flotte," IRGAF (June 1901): 234–35.

91. "Die französische Militär-Mission in Peru," IRGAF (July 1903): 267–68.

92. IRGAF (April 1900): 194, and (October 1900): 514.

93. IRGAF (January 1902): 1.

94. "La Situation de l'armée federal brasilienne en 1912," RMAE (May 1902): 349–63.

95. "Vier fremde Militarkommissionen," p. 1842, and MW (16 June 1900): 1110.

96. "Korrespondenz aus Argentinien," MW (8 February 1902): 359–61.

97. "Militärische Eindrucke aus Argentinien," MW (4 August 1910): 2243–56.

98. RMAE (30 September 1905): 491–4. See also RMAE (March 1911): 275–77, for equally scanty treatment of obligatory military service in Chile.

99. "Die allgemeine Militärpflicht," IRGAF (June 1901): 233.

100. "Die Militärischen Machmittel der Staaten von Südamerika," *Beiheft zur* IRGAF 126 (February 1911): 14–21.

101. See MW (15 August 1905): 2590.

102. "Vom chilenischen Heere," MW (12 October 1909): 2936–37. See also the praise given Körner and his creation, "composed of representatives of the best...families of the land," in "Neues vom chilenischen Heere," MW (20 June 1903): 154.

103. "Ein Triumph preussischen Drills in Südamerika," MW (21 July 1910): 2108–10.

104. "Die militärischen Machmittel der Staaten von Südamerika," p. 1.

105. Georges Clemenceau, *South America Today*, p. 243.

106. Ibid., p. 133.

107. Henri Lorin, "Impresion du Chile: Les chiliens et la France," RDM (1 January 1912): 192–215. The quotation is from p. 209.

108. Raymond Poincaré, in Francisco García Calderón, *Latin America: Its Rise and Progress* (London: T. Fisher Unwin, 1913), pp. 12–13.

Chapter Five

1. See Craig, *The Politics of the Prussian Army*; Demeter, *The German Officer Corps*; and Goerlitz, *The German General Staff*, for information on German military-civilian relations during the 1920s.

   On politics and the army see F. L. Carsten, *The Reichswehr and Politics, 1918–1933* (Oxford: Clarendon Press, 1966); Andreas Dorpalen, *Hindenburg and the Weimar Republic* (Princeton: Princeton University Press, 1964); and Harold J. Gordon, *The Reichswehr and the German Republic, 1919–1926* (Port Washington, N.Y.: Kennikat Press, 1972). A good source on both Weimar and Third Reich military-political issues is Sir John Wheeler-Bennett, *Nemesis of Power: The German Army and Politics, 1918–1945*, 2nd ed. (New York: St. Martin's Press, 1964). See also Robert J. O'Neil *The German Army and the Nazi Party, 1933–1939* (New York: James H. Heinemann, 1967).

   On French military-civilian relations in the inter-war years see Philip C. F. Bankwitz, *Maxime Weygand and Civil-Military Relations in Modern France* (Cambridge: Harvard University Press, 1967), and La Gorce, *The French Army*. Evidence of continuity of thought on politics and the Third Republic as voiced by the likes of Lyautey, De Gaulle, and Weygand appears in Ambler, *Soldiers Against the State*, pp. 33–34.

2. Robert A. Potash, *The Army and Politics in Argentina, 1928–1945: Yrigoyen to Perón* (Stanford: Stanford University Press, 1969), pp. 29–78, treats the 1920s and early 1930s very well. This work is particularly sensitive to conflicts of opinion on economic and political policy within the officer corps. Also

worth consulting on political interests of the army is Darío
Canton, *La política de los militares argentinos, 1900–1971*
(Buenos Aires: Siglo Veintiuno Editores, S.A., 1971). Marvin
Goldwert's *Democracy, Militarism and Nationalism in Argentina,
1930–1966: An Interpretation* (Austin: University of Texas Press,
1972) is another solid work treating the development of
professional militarism in Argentina during the inter-war era.
See esp. pp. 11–93. See also Goldwert's earlier "The Rise of the
Modern Military in Argentina," HAHR 48, no. 2 (May 1968):
189–205. Interest in supervision of economic development is
discussed in Luis Vicat, "El desarrollo industrial como empresa
militar," and Enrique Mosconi, "La defensa y el nacionalismo
petrolero," in Jean Cazeneuve, ed., *Ejército y revolución
industrial* (Buenos Aires: Jorge Alvarez Editor, 1964), pp. 25–44,
47–82. Carl Solberg's *Oil and Nationalism in Argentina: A
History* (Stanford: Stanford University Press, 1979) is excellent
on the origins of the state petroleum monopoly and General
Mosconi's role in managing it.

3. Still valuable for a description of the origins of *tenentismo* is
Robert Alexander's "Brazilian Tenentismo," HAHR 36, no. 2
(May 1956): 229–42.

4. The following works by army officers ought to be consulted for
their varying views on military-civilian relations during the
1920s and 1930s: Estevão Leitão de Carvalho, *Dever Militar* (an
argument against political involvement); Nelson Werneck Sodré,
Memórias de um Soldado (Rio de Janeiro: Civilização Brasileira,
1967), esp. pp. 1–95; and Araripe, *Tasso Fragoso*. Asdrubal
Gwyer de Azevedo's *Os Militares e a Política* (Barcelos:
Companhia Editôra do Minho, 1926) provides information on
tenenista views aired in the influential Club Militar. It plays
down any significant Franco-*tenenista* linkage.

On the role of the *tenentes* and other officers in the downfall
of the Old Republic, see John D. Wirth's, "*Tenentismo* in the
Brazilian Revolution of 1930," HAHR 44, no. 2 (May 1964):
161–79, and Jordan Young, "Military Aspects of the 1930
Brazilian Revolution," ibid., pp. 180–96. Young's *The Brazilian
Revolution and Its Aftermath* (New Brunswick, N.J.: Rutgers
University Press, 1967) offers detailed coverage of military,
economic, and political aspects of the *golpe de estado.*
Extremely valuable for documentary information on the *golpe* is
Hélio Silva, *1930: A Revolução Traida*, vol. 3 of *O Ciclo de
Vargas* (Rio de Janeiro: Civilização Brasileira, 1966).

5. This is discussed in Frederick M. Nunn, *Chilean Politics,*

1920–1931: The Honorable Mission of the Armed Forces
(Albuquerque: University of New Mexico Press, 1970), pp.
28–55. The most heavily documented, but hardly neutral,
source on this period is Ricardo Donoso's *Alessandri, agitador y
demoledor: Cincuenta años de historia política de Chile*, 2 vols.,
(Buenos Aires: Fondo de Cultura Económica, 1952–54), I,
216–372.

6. See Nunn's *Chilean Politics, 1920–1931*, pp. 55–77; and the same
author's "Military Rule in Chile: The Revolutions of September 5,
1924, and January 23, 1925," HAHR, 47, no. 1 (February 1967):
1–21; and "A Latin American State within the State: The
Politics of the Chilean Army, 1924–1927," TAm 27, no. 1 (July
1970): 40–55.

7. Information on military-civilian relations in Peru during the
1920s can be found in Víctor Villanuevas's *El militarismo en el
Perú* (Lima: T. Scheuch, S.A., 1962), pp. 51–78, and Nunn,
"Professional Militarism in Twentieth Century Peru," pp.
409–13. Allen Gerlach's "Civil-Military Relations in Peru,
1914–1945," (Ph.D. dissertation, University of New Mexico,
1973) is extremely valuable for the entire inter-war era.

8. David Rock's "Machine Politics and the Argentine Radical Party,
1912–1930," JLAS 4, no. 2 (November 1972): 233–55, reveals the
reality of Argentine Radicalism. So does his *Politics in Argentina,
1890–1930: The Rise and Fall of Radicalism* (Cambridge, Eng.:
Cambridge University Press, 1975). Whitaker's *Argentina*,
pp. 41–82, provides a perspective on the Radical era.

9. See Pike's *The Modern History of Peru* and *The United States and
the Andean Republics* for solid treatments of the *oncenio*. An
exceptional source on all aspects of recent Chilean history is
Pike's aforementioned *Chile and the United States, 1880–1962*,
esp. pp. 86–122, 170–215.

10. Owing to the presence of documents representing the flavor of
the time, Silva's *A Revolução Traida* is especially recommended.

11. This should not be taken for a "dependista" argument. The
recent exchange between D. C. M. Platt and Stanley and
Barbara Stein indicates current, representative viewpoints on
dependence theory. See Platt, "Dependency in Nineteenth
Century Latin America," "Comment" by the Steins, and Platt's
"Reply," *Latin American Research Review* 15, no. 1 (1980):
113–49.

12. Statistics on Argentina come primarily from Scobie, *Argentina*,
pp. 303–9; on Brazil, from Rollie Poppino, *Brazil: The Land and*

People 2nd ed. (New York: Oxford University Press, 1973), pp.
370–74; on Chile, from Brian Loveman, *Chile: The Legacy of
Hispanic Capitalism* (New York: Oxford University Press, 1979),
passim; and, on Peru, from Henry E. Dobyns and Paul Doughty,
Peru: A Cultural History (New York: Oxford University Press,
1976), pp. 289–309.

Population data for France and Germany are taken from
Gordon Wright, *Rural Revolution in France: The Peasants in the
Twentieth Century* (Stanford: Stanford University Press, 1964),
and the essays in Andrew and Lynn Lees, eds., *The
Urbanization of European Society in the Nineteenth Century*
(Lexington, Mass.: D. C. Heath, 1976).

13. Villanueva raises this point (unconvincingly) on several occasions
    in his numerous works.

14. See Nunn, *Chilean Politics, 1920–1931*, pp. 115–59.

15. Ibid., pp. 160–76. The bibliographical essay in this work
    discusses military literature in the 1920s.

16. On military-civilian relations in the 1930s see Nunn, *The Military
    in Chilean History*, pp. 175–236, passim. One of the best recent
    works on Chilean politics is Paul W. Drake, *Socialism and
    Populism in Chile, 1932–1952* (Champaign: University of Illinois
    Press, 1977).

17. Goldwert's *Democracy, Militarism and Nationalism*, pp. 31–93,
    deals with this. See also Potash, *The Army and Politics in
    Argentina, 1928–1945* pp. 55–140, and Whitaker, *Argentina*, pp.
    83–103, on the 1930s. Valuable Argentine works on the *golpe de
    estado* of 1930 are Juan V. Orona, *La logia militar que enfrentó a
    Hipólito Yrigoyen* (Buenos Aires: Editorial Leonardo 1965), and
    José María Sarobe, *Memorias sobre la revolución del 6 de
    Septiembre de 1930* (Buenos Aires: Ediciones Guré, 1957).

18. Mark Falcoff and Ronald H. Dolkart have assembled a
    representative group of essays on the 1930s in *Prologue to Perón:
    Argentina in Depression and War* (Berkeley and Los Angeles:
    University of California Press, 1975).

19. The history of the GOU can be found in Orona's *La logia militar
    que derrocó a Castillo* (Buenos Aires: Talleres Gráficos
    "Moderna," 1966).

20. Evidence of continuity of military thought in state, nation, and
    society in Brazil can be found in Alfred Stepan, ed.,
    Authoritarian Brazil: Origins, Policies and Future (New Haven
    and London: Yale University Press, 1973), esp. Stepan's own "The

New Professionalism of Internal Warfare and Military Role Expansion," pp. 47–65. For interesting perspectives on military–New State relations from the standpoint of foreign policy priorities, see Frank D. McCann, Jr., *The Brazilian-American Alliance, 1937–1945* (Princeton: Princeton University Press, 1973). McCann's, "Origins of the 'New Professionalism' of the Brazilian Army," *Journal of Interamerican Studies and World Affairs*, 21, 4 (November 1979): 505–22, provides convincing evidence of early army orientation towards an internal role. See also Michael Conniff, "The *Tenentes* in Power: A New Perspective on the Brazilian Revolution of 1930," *JLAS* 10, 1 (May 1978): 61–83; and José Murilo de Carvahlo's incisive "Armed Forces and Politics in Brazil, 1930–1945," *HAHR* 62, 2 (May 1982): 193–223.

21. McCann's *The Brazilian-American Alliance* is the best source on Brazilian-U.S. relations. Indicative of the clash of opinion on this subject is a recent exchange between McCann and Stanley Hilton: See McCann, "Critique of Stanley F. Hilton's, "Brazilian Diplomacy and the Washington-Rio de Janeiro Axis during the World War II Era," and Hilton's "Reply," HAHR 59, no. 4 (November 1979): 691–700. The Hilton article under discussion appeared in HAHR 59, no. 2 (May 1979): 201–31. Hilton's earlier "Military Influence on Brazilian Economic Policy, 1930–1945," HAHR 53, no. 1 (February 1973): 71–94, challenges traditional claims of military interest in rapid industrialization.

22. In addition to works by Villanueva see Nunn, "Professional Militarism in Twentieth Century Peru," pp. 339–406, for information on the emergence of professional militarism in the 1930s and the significance of the Benavides administration. This essay provoked an exchange of views on military-civilian relations and the translation of professional militarism into action. See José Z. García's critique, and Nunn's reply, HAHR 80, no. 2 (May 1980): 302–12.

23. Fredrick B. Pike's "Religious Collectivism and Infrahistory: The Peruvian Ideal of Dependence," JLAS 10, no. 2 (November 1978): 239–62, is a provocative essay placing Aprismo in the total Peruvian historical context.

24. David Scott Palmer's recent *Peru: The Authoritarian Tradition* (New York: Frederick A. Praeger, 1980), provides thoughtful perspectives on Aprismo and background for military-political involvement. This work contains an up-to-date bibliography of the best English-language monographic sources.

25. The epoch has been chronicled in narrative and timely photographs by Guillermo Thorndyke in *El año de la barbarie: Perú 1932* (Lima: Editorial Neuva América, S.A., 1969).

26. A good source on U.S. military policy in the Caribbean is Goldwert's *The Constabulary in the Dominican Republic and Nicaragua: Progeny and Legacy of U.S. Intervention* (Gainesville: University of Florida Press, 1962).

27. The May-June 1939 visit of General George C. Marshall and developing Brazilian-U.S. ties figure prominently in dispatches sent to State by Ambassador Jefferson Caffery and others between 20 April 1939 (DSF 832.20111/1), and 13 December 1939 (DSF 832.20111/43). The earlier unfortunate but unavoidable Díaz episode is discussed in Ralph H. Wooten to G-2, MID 2257-0-87/12, M.A. Report 351, 16 December 1929.

28. As late as 1941, specialists in Washington, D.C., considered European influence strong enough to prompt the elaboration of Epstein's "European Military-Influence in Latin America."

Chapter Six

1. See Miles Poindexter to Frank B. Kellogg, DSF 823.20/18, 18 December 1925. Velarde succeeded Clément, who had returned to Peru after the war not as a mission officer but as a Leguía appointee.

    Rather than weigh down these notes with too many repetitive citations of materials utilized in chapter four, I have decided to emphasize opinions and evaluations gleaned from U.S. archival sources. The increasing political, international, and intercontinental ramifications of military professionalism as well as its institutional significance make these archival sources particularly valuable. American military and diplomatic observers proved perceptive once their interest was aroused. The reader, however, should by all means consult the appropriate South American and European sources already cited in order to supplement the documentation presented here.

2. See William Miller Collier to Kellogg, DSF 825.427/0, 6 April 1927.

3. See Thomas A. Pace to G-2, MID 2257-0-87/1, 11 June 1929; through Wooten to G-2, MID 2257-0-87/12, 16 December 1929. Names of senders and receivers do not appear consistently on all MID and DSF documents. See also the memorandum by George

Messersmith, "German Officers' Attachment to Chilean Army," of 20 June 1930, included in Henry L. Stimson to Patrick J. Hurley, DSF 825.20/63, 21 August 1930.

4. This is discussed in Edwin G. Morgan to Robert Lansing, DSF 832.227/-, 20 March 1918.

5. *O Jornal do Brasil*, 18 December 1928.

6. Henrietta Livermore to Joshua Baxter Wright, DSF 832.20/102, 29 November 1923.

7. See Francis White to Charles Evans Hughes, DSF 832.30/108, 12 February 1924, and Edwin Carleton Wilson to White, DSF 802.30/109 (also filed as 839.51/240/2404), 27 February 1924.

8. See Cordier's memorandum, "The German Military Mission in Bolivia," in MID 6370-14, 15 October 1912, and Winfield Jones to William Jennings Bryan, DSF 834.20/-, 21 February 1914. From Ascunción, Paraguay, Jones advised of German military-commercial connections and encouraged State to look into the possibility of training armies in South America in order to preclude German commercial expansion there.

9. H. B. Grow to George Akeson, DSF 823.248/18, 24 December 1929.

10. Miles Poindexter to Hughes, DSF 823.20/10, 27 August 1924.

11. See Wooten to G-2, MID 2257-0-87/12, 16 December 1929.

12. See William Phillips to Joseph Shea, DSF 825.20/29, 13 January 1919.

13. Collier to Hughes, DSF 825.20/40, 12 December 1922.

14. Unsigned memorandum, DSF 3835.20/8, 12 December 1922.

15. See Peter A. Jay to Kellogg, DSF 835.20112/1, 15 May 1926. On the reformation of the Mexican army during the 1920s, see Edwin Lieuwen, *Mexican Militarism: The Political Rise and Fall of the Mexican Army* (Albuquerque: University of New Mexico Press, 1968).

16. See Atkins and Thompson, "German Military Influence in Argentina," and Maligne, "1810–1910," passim.

17. Hugh Barclay to G-2, MID 2006-90/2, 22 November 1926. Cf. Maurice Gamelin's scathing remarks on Brazilian military potential early in his tenure as discussed in Stanley E. Hilton's authoritative "Brazil and the Post-Versailles World: Elite Images and Foreign Policy Strategy," JLAS 12, no. 2 (November 1980): 341–64.

18. Full title: "A Missão Militar Estrangeira: Bemvinda Seja," ADN (April 1919): 225–28.

19. Francisco de Paula Cidade, "Um pouco de Historia da Missão Militar Franceza: O Major Dumé," RMB (July–December 1960): 23.

20. See Magalhães, *A Evolução Militar do Brasil*, pp. 349–52.

21. Lester Baker to G-2, MID 2006/44-11, 8 November 1927; Magalhães, *A Evolução Militar*, pp. 348–50; and Tristão de Alencar Araripe, "A Escola de Estado Maior em um [*sic*] Trecho de sua Evolução," RMB (January–June 1960): 6–8.

22. See Magalhães, *A Evolução Militar do Brasil*, pp. 352–61; João Pandiá Calógeras, in *Relatório* (1920), p. 35.

23. Francisco de Paula Cidade, "Da Missão Militar Franceza ãos Nossos Dias," RMB (July–December 1954), pp. 136–37.

24. Araripe, "A Escola de Estado Maior," p. 7.

25. On Rondón's accomplishments in the interior of Brazil, see the informative Commissão de Linhas Telegráphicas Estratégicas de Matto Grosso ão Amazonas, *Lectures Delivered by Colonel Candido Mariano da Silva Rondón on the 5th, 7th and 9th of October 1915 at the Phenix Theatre of Rio de Janeiro on the Roosevelt-Rondón Scientific Expedition and the Telegraph Line Commission*, trs. R. G. Reidy and Ed. Murry (New York: Greenwood Press, 1969).

26. Oscar de Barros Falcão, "A Revolução de 5 Julho de 1924," RMB (July–December 1961): 3–5.

27. Derougemont, "O Papel do Official Numa Democrácia Moderna," ADN (June 1922): 358–60.

28. "Uma Importante Palestra com o General Gamelin," ADM (March 1920): 263–65.

29. See Lawrence C. Mitchell to Cordell Hull, DSF 832.2920/132, 25 February 1937, for an estimate of seventy French officers serving at the high point of influence in 1927. Discussions of mission strength, personnel, and Franco-Brazilian relations can be found as well in MID 2006-44/0, 21 February 1921, through 2006-44/17, 6 January 1931.

30. See, for example, "A Política e o Exército," ADN (10 August 1921): 33–35. Some issues of ADN were dated by day as well as month.

31. Captain Luis Correia Lima repeated Caxias's lines in "Pela Pátria, Pelo Exército." See also "Unidade de Doutrina," ADN (September 1921): 66; "A Nova Organização do Exército," ADN (February 1922): 193–95; and Bentes Monteiro, "Os Themas da Missão," ADN (10 May 1923): 625–28.

32. Samuel Ramos, "Palestra Militar," ADN (August 1920): 7–11.

33. See Miñano, *Las misiones militares francesas*, pp. 6–14. The citation is from p. 13.

34. Jorge [Georges] Thomas, "La carta nacional del Perú," *Revista del Círculo Militar del Perú* (March 1924): 323–40, hereafter cited as RCMP.

35. Francisco [Francois] Pellegrin, "El c.a.e.m. de Francia," RCMP (March 1925): 229–40.

36. Serrigny, "La organización de la nación para el tiempo de guerra," RCMP (February 1924): 199–220, esp. 201–8.

37. This situation is most reminiscent of that in Bolivia, where, on his return, Kundt assumed command of the army. President Bautista Saavedra, a Republican who seized power in 1920, was convinced that there were too many Liberal party affiliates in the officer corps, hence that the opposition party might seek to oust him. Although Liberal presidents had sponsored and encouraged Kundt's activities before the war, he satisfied Saavedra that his continued control of the army was no threat to the Republicans. See Jesse Cottrell to Hughes, DSF 824.20/27, 19 May 1923, and Cottrell to Kellogg, DSF 324.20/31, 1 June 1925.

38. A complete and accurate translation was included in Poindexter to Hughes, DSF 823.20/7, 30 January 1924. See also MID 2257-C-88/7, 8 February 1924.

39. Elmore Steward to G-2, MID 2033-100/4, 1 October 1926.

40. Walter Edge to Stimson, DSF 710.11/1391 (also filed as 332.20/50), 14 January 1930.

41. Edwin V. Morgan to Stimson, DSF 832.20/51, 26 February 1930.

42. G-2 Current Events Report, DSF 832.20/53, 2 February 1931.

43. Cited in ibid.

44. Combat Information Digest, DSF 832.20/60, 27 February 1932.

45. G-2 Report, DSF 832.20/61, 25 January 1933.

46. William Sackville to Hull, DSF 832.20/63, 4 August 1933.

47. See Sackville to Hull, DSF 832.20/68, 20 December 1933.

48. See McCann, *The Brazilian-American Alliance*, for a sophisticated discussion of the Vargas-Aranha maneuvering and its ramifications for the military.

49. Pauline Nimkoff to Hull and Hull to Nimkoff, both filed as DSF 832.20/134, 16 and 27 November 1937.

50. MID 2257-123/31, 22 November 1938.

51. MID 2472-47/7, 30 November 1936.

52. The most exhaustive documented biography of Sánchez Cerro to date is Pedro Ugarteche, *Sánchez Cerro: Papeles y documentos de un presidente del Perú*, 4 vols. (Lima: Editorial Universitaria, 1969). This is a sympathetic treatment of the controversial officer-president.

53. C. J. Allen to Stimson, DSF 823.20/39, 26 November 1930.

54. Fred Morris Dearing to Stimson, DSF 823.20/60 (also filed as 721.23/483), 13 November 1932.

55. William C. Burdett to Stimson, DSF 823.20/52, 22 June 1932.

56. For information from Lima, see Louis G. Dreyfus, Jr., to Hull, DSF 823.29/29, 8 May 1935; and from Santiago, John A. Weeks to Hull, DSF 825.20194/1, 13 June 1934.

57. Dearing to Hull, DSF 832.20/64, 8 April 1935.

58. See the exchange of notes between Peruvian ambassador Manuel de Freyre y Santander and Hull, filed together in DSF 923.20/66, 29 April–7 May 1935.

59. For Benavides's remarks see Dreyfuss to Hull, DSF 823-20/78, 19 December 1939.

60. See Messersmith's memorandum, "German Officers' Attachment to the Chilean Army," DSF 825.20/63, 21 August 1930.

61. See John A. Weeks to Hull, DSF 825.20/79, 24 May 1934, and MID 2257-123/32, 23 November 1938.

62. Alexander W. Weddel to Hull, DSF 835.20/21, 28 April 1936.

63. Ibid.

64. Ibid.

65. Unsigned dispatch, DSF 835.20/24, 23 December 1937.

66. Caffery to Hull, DSF 835.20/27, 11 September 1939.

67. Caffery to Hull, DSF 835.248/98, 11 May 1938.

68. Hull to Caffery, DSF 835.248/98, 12 May 1938.

69. See Caffery to Hull, and Hull to Caffery, both filed in DSF 835.248/100, 18 and 20 May 1938.

70. Hull to Caffery, DSF 835.248/102, 24 May 1938.

71. This is briefly explained in Morgan to Lansing, DSF 832.20/116, 13 November 1917.

72. MID 2657-K-110/9, 4 December 1940.

73. MID 2257-C-104/8, 29 October 1940.

74. MID 2257-C-88/22, 16 December 1940.

75. MID 2257-C-88/21, 5 October 1940.

76. "A Política e o Exército," pp. 33–35; "Os Themas da Missão," pp. 625–28.

77. "A Renovação do Contrato da Missão Militar Franceza," ADN (March 1933): 133–55.
78. Biblioteca Militar, *Escola de Estado Maior, 1940: Encerramento dos Cursos* (Praia Vermelha: Biblioteca do Exército, 1940), passim.
79. V. Benício da Silva, "Novo Rumo," RMB (January–June 1941): 39–43; Magalhães, *Evolução Militar do Brasil*, pp. 348–50. See also Cidade, "Um Pouco de História da Missão Militar Franceza," passim.
80. Editorial, BMGM (August 1919): 929–31; Major Chouteau, "El oficial," RMP (January 1935): 5–18; General Gamelin, "Reflexiones sobre el jefe," RMP (November 1935): 2051–73.
81. For but one example see the remarks of General Nicolás Lindley López (Commandant of the Centro de Instrucción Militar, Chorrillos), "Homenaje al ejército de Francia," *Revista de la Escuela Militar de Chorrillos* (November–December, 1957): 521–23.
82. For examples of the perduration of French influence in Peru see Nunn, "Professional Militarism in Twentieth Century Peru," pp. 415–17. In 1946, on the occasion of the fiftieth anniversary of the first French mission and of the founding of the Escuela Superior de Guerra, there were outpourings of literature in all Peruvian journals on the debt to "el ejército de Francia."

Chapter Seven

1. Seeckt, *Thoughts of a Soldier*, tr. Gilbert Waterhouse (London: Ernest Benn, 1930).
2. See ibid., p. 80.
3. Ibid., pp. 74–75.
4. Seeckt, *The Future of the German Empire: Criticisms and Postulates*, tr. Oakley Williams (London: 1930), p. 9, 19. The contents of this book indicate that *Judgements and Challenges* might have been a more appropriate subtitle than *Criticisms and Postulates*.
5. Ibid., pp. 121, 139–40.
6. Ibid., pp. 171–72.
7. Seeckt, *Die Reichswehr* (Leipzig: R. Kittler Verlag, 1933), pp. 7–9.
8. Charles De Gaulle, *The Edge of the Sword*, tr. Gerard Hopkins (London: Faber and Faber, 1960), pp. 34–52.
9. Ibid., pp. 39, 42.

10. Ibid., pp. 108–9.

11. Ibid., pp. 52–73, passim. The citation is from pp. 52–53.

12. Ibid., p. 117.

13. Charles Maurras, *Le Quadrilatère* (Paris: Flammarion, 1931). In addition see the works on Foch cited infra, notes 17–19, and the following contemporary items on inter-war military figures: Paul Marie Vauthier, *Un Chef: General Mangin, 1866–1925* (Paris: Les Publications Coloniales, 1936); General Gamelin, *Servir*, 3 vols. (Paris: Plon, 1946); Émile Mayer, *Trois Maréchaux: Joffre, Gallieni, Foch* (Paris: Libraire Gallimard, 1928).

14. Maurras, *Le Quadrilatère*, passim.

15. Paul Gentizon, *L'armée allemande depuis la defaite* (Paris: Payot et Cie., 1920), pp. 93–108. *Officiersdämmerung* is French orthography.

16. Ibid., p. 96.

17. See Ferdinand Foch, *Precepts* and *Judgments*, passim. A friendly contemporary biography emphasizing Foch's views on military-civilian relations is Sir George Aston, *The Biography of the Late Marshal Foch* (London: Hutchinson and Co., Ltd., 1929).

18. Cited in Commandant Bugnet, *Foch Talks*, tr. Russel Green (London: Victor Gollancz, 1929), p. 108. Bugnet was Foch's aide, 1921–29.

19. See Jere C. King's *Foch versus Clemenceau: France and German Disarmament, 1918–1919* (Cambridge, Mass.: Harvard University Press, 1960) for a scholarly, balanced view of military and civilian points of view on post-war policy-making.

20. As cited in Raymond Recouly, *Marshal Foch: His Own Words on Many Subjects*, tr. Joyce Davis (London: Thornton Buttersworth, Ltd., 1929).

21. See Vauthier, *Un Chef*, pp. 27–35.

22. See Gamelin, *Servir*, II, 7–18.

23. Arthur Harrison Miller, *Leadership* (New York: G. P. Putnam's Sons, 1920), p. 56. For similar contemporary views on the perishing of tradition see F. C. Bartlett, *Psychology and the Soldier* (Cambridge, Eng.: Cambridge University Press, 1927); B. H. Liddel-Hart, *The Remaking of Modern Armies* (London: L. John Murry, 1927); William A. Mitchell, *Outlines of the World's Military History* (Washington, D.C.: National Service Publishing Co., 1931); J. F. C. Fuller, *Generalship: Its Diseases and Their Cause: A Study of the Personal Factor in Command* (London:

Faber and Faber, 1933). Fuller cited Goltz's *The Nation in Arms* extensively.

24. P. L. Federphil, *Nos vingt ans à St. Cyr* (Paris: Charles La Vauzelle et Cie., 1933), p. 23.

25. Ibid., pp. 56–65.

26. Maxime Weygand, *Comment élever nos fils* (Paris: Flammarion, 1937), pp. 5–6.

27. Ibid., pp. 8–9.

28. Ibid., p. 12.

29. Paul Reynaud, *Le Problème militaire français* (Paris: Flammarion, 1927), passim.

30. "Video," *L'Armée et la politique* (Paris: Libraire Action Française, 1937), pp. 8–14.

31. Tanant, *La Discipline dans les armées françaises* (Paris: Charles La Vauzelle et Cie., 1938), pp. 221–23, 291–303.

32. Pierre Poummeyrol, *L'Armée: Bien fait social* (Paris: Charles La Vauzelle et Cie., 1938). This book was based heavily on Lyautey's works. The author also made reference to the Lyauteyesque André Gavet, *L'Art de commander* (Paris: Editions Berger-Lebrault, 1899), a technical work well-known throughout the early twentieth century in South America. See for example the most recent edition, *El arte de mandar* (Santiago: Estado Mayor General del Ejército, 1973). The Gavet work was released just prior to the 1973 *golpe de estado* that resulted in the overthrow and death of Salvador Allende, and is still valued by Chilean military leaders for its insistence on authority, a military sociopolitical role, and glorification of the leadership function of the commander of men.

33. Poummeyrol, *L'Armée*, pp. 1–46, passim, esp. pp. 15–24.

34. Henri Phillippe Pétain, *Le Devoir des élites dans la défense nationale* (Paris: Editions Berger Levrault, 1939).

35. Ibid., pp. 1–3, 19.

36. This is the core of the argument presented most cogently in General Debeney, "Armée nationale ou armée du métier?" RDM (15 September 1929): 241–76. See also Debeney's "Hier et demain: L'Officier," ibid., (1 May 1920): 5–34, for a more immediate, post-war argument.

37. Freytagh Loringhoven, *Deductions from the World War* (London: Constable and Co., 1918), and *A Nation Trained in Arms or a Militia?* (London: Constable and Co., 1918).

38. Freytagh Loringhoven, *Deductions from the World War,* pp. 68–118.

39. Friedrich von Bernhardi, *The War of the Future in the Light of Lessons of the World War* (London: Hutchinson and Co., 1920), pp. 189–90.

40. Ibid., pp. 191–97.

41. Erich Ludendorff, *Kriegführung und Politik* (Berlin: E. G. Mittler & Sohn, 1922), pp. 340–42, passim.

42. Bernhard Kiesling, *Deutschlands Reichswehr der Zukunft* (Berlin: Bossische Buchhandling, 1919), pp. 8–11, 33.

43. Arno Voigt, *Der deutsche Offizier der Zukunft: Gedanken eines "Unmilitärischen"* (Stuttgart: Verlag von J. Engelhorns, 1919), p. 118.

44. Fritz von Rakenau, *Die alte Armee und die junge Generation: Kritische Betrachtungen* (Berlin: Mittler & Sohn, 1925), passim.

45. Information on the social composition of the German officer corps can be found in Carsten's *The Reichswehr and Politics*. His figures indicate a slight post-1918 decline in middle-sector membership and a distinct rise in the number of sons of officers and in noble cadets earning commissions soon after the war. Fully 95 percent were representative of pre-1914 "acceptable origins." Carsten stresses, nevertheless, that education and specialized training were more significant than social origins in the creation of officer-corps homogeneity, hence professional thought and self-perception. See also Demeter, *The German Officer Corps*, for remarks on the decline of noble influence in the army of the Third Reich.

46. Cited in Walter Frank, *Franz Ritter von Epp: Der Weg eines deutschen Soldaten* (Hamburg: Hanseatische Verlagsanstalt, 1934), p. 141.

47. Ewald Banse, *Germany: Prepare for War! (Raum und Volk im Weltkriege),* tr. Alan Harris (London: Lovat Dickson, Ltd., 1934).

48. Herman Gauer, *Von Bauerntum, Bürgertum und Arbeitertum in der Armee* (Heidelberg: Friedrich Schulze Embh, 1936), passim.

49. Kurt Hesse, *Soldatendienst im neuen Reich* (Berlin: Verlag Ullstein, 1935), p. 15.

50. Ibid., pp. 12–13.

51. Axel Freiherr von Maltzahn, *Der deutsche Soldat: Ein Rückblick und Ausblick* (Berlin: Kӱffhäuser Verlag, 1936), pp. 50–88, passim.

52. Reichskriegministerium, *Waffenträger der Nation: Ein Buch der*

deutschen Wehrmacht für das deutsche Volk (Berlin: Verlag für Vaterländische Literatur, 1935), frontispiece.

53. See Egon Hundeiker, *Rasse, Volk, Soldatentum* (Berlin: J. F. Lehmanns Verlag, 1937), passim. On the same theme see Ernst Rudolf Hüber, *Heer und Staat in der deutschen Geschichte* (Hamburg: Hanseatische Verlagsanstalt, 1938); Friedrich Kracke, *Wehrkraft Volk, einst und jetzt* (Berlin: Schlieffen Verlag, 1938); Alfred Weise, *Soldner und Soldaten: Der Weg zum Volksheer* (Berlin: Fundsberg Verlag, 1936); and Hans Roden, ed., *Deutsche Soldaten: Vom Frontheer und Freikorps über die Reichswehr zur neuen Wehrmacht* (Leipzig: Verlag von Britkof und Härtel, 1935).

54. Georg Wetzel, et al., *Die deutsche Wehrmacht, 1914-1939: Rückblick und Ausblick* (Berlin: E. S. Mittler & Sohn, 1939), p. 381. See also Valentin Beyer, ed., *Das neue Deutschland: Bausteine für den national politischen Unterricht an der Wehrmacht-Fachschulen* (Berlin: Kameradschaft Verlagsgesellschaft, 1935); Karl Schulz Luckau, *Soldatentum und Kameradschaft: Anderthalb Jahrhunderte deutscher Reichskriegerbund* (Berlin: Kÿffhäuser Verlag, 1936); and Bernhard von Volkmann-Leander, *Soldaten oder Militär? Ein Buch zum Nachdenken* (Berlin: J. S. Lehmanns Verlag, 1937).

55. See Mayer, "Notre organisation militaire," *Revue Militaire Française* (September 1921): 311–26, hereafter cited as RMF. The citation is from p. 323.

56. See Viotte, "Quelques mots sur la réorganisation de l'armée," RMF (January 1922), 48–68.

57. See Henri Michel, "Pour l'enseignement de l'organisation à l'école supérieure de guerre," RMF (February 1922): 196–220; and Dessoffy de Czernek, "La Psychologie du commandement," RMF (September 1924): 289–305.

58. See Grenier, "Officers allemands d'hier et d'aujourd'hui," RMF (October 1924): 27–44, and (November 1924): 174–98.

59. Data and conclusions in both William Serman's recent *Les Origins des officiers français, 1848–1870* (Paris: Publications de la Sorbonne, 1979) and the pioneer Raoul Girardet's *La Société militaire dans la France contemporaine, 1815–1939* (Paris: Plon, 1953) indicate that the French officer corps may have indeed resembled the pre-Republic corps in social composition. Increasing numbers of bourgeois officers made the corps more like that of the Second Empire, in which approximately 70 percent were commissioned from the ranks.

60. Damidaux, "L'Officier d'état major," RMF (October 1925): p. 94;

Lieutenant Colonel de Nerciat, "À propos de cinquentenaire de l'école supérieure de guerre," RMF (August 1926): 249.

61. Damidaux, "L'Officier d'état major," pp. 85–94.

62. Charles De Gaulle, "Mobilisation économique à l'étranger," RMF (January 1934): 62–88. The citation is from p. 88. See, as well, Jacques Maupas, "La Politique militaire de l'Allemagne," RDM (1 July 1933): 49–77; Lieutenant Ailleret, "La mobilisation industrielle," RMF (February 1936): 155–206; Henri Phillippe Pitain, "Défense nationale et commandement unique," RDM (1 May 1936), 5–17; Vice-Admiral Castex, "Les Hautes études de la défense nationale," *Revue Militaire Generale* (January 1937): 37–49, hereafter cited RMG; General Manginel, "Le Commandement unique," RMG (February 1937): 689–707; Raymond Tourle, "Imperieuse necesité du commandement unique," RMG (February 1937: 708–15; and General Debeney, "La Mystique de notre corps d'officiers," RMG (January 1937): 21–23.

63. The *Revue Militaire Generale* replaced RMF as journal of record at the urging of Castex, Debeney, Gamelin, and Pítain. It was designed by officers affiliated with the College des Hautes Études de la Défense Nationale to serve as a forum for ideas on combined land, air, and sea defense and on military-civilian joint administration. The board of editors reflected this, made up as it was of representatives of all services. Essays published in 1937–38 dealt with staff organization, planning, unity of command, natural resources, energy policy, national security, Argentina's relations with Germany, Gamelin's work in Brazil, and high-level, specialized courses for staff officers. It carried far more coverage of foreign affairs than any European journal of the time.

64. See M. J. Le Clerc, "Commandement unique et la défense nationale," RMG (June 1938): 695–708.

65. Le Guebe, "Esprit guerrier allemand et français," RMG (October 1937): 504–19.

66. See Emile Mayer, "Qui doit lire un officier," RMG (November 1937): 648–62; Hector Dassonville, "L'Officier dans la nation," RMG (January 1938): 89–102; and Maxime Weygand, "L'Armée d'aujourd'hui," RDM (15 May 1938): 325–36.

67. "Soll der deutsche Offizierbund Politik treiben?" MW (4 January 1919): 1411–14; "Die Parteipolitiker im Offizierbund," ibid., pp. 14–15; and Admiral Karl Hollweg, "Die Revolution, die Offiziere und die Nationalversammlung," MW (7 January 1919): 1425–32.

68. "Staat, Heer und Volk," MW (12 May 1920); 2037–42, and (15 May 1920): 2057–60. The citation is from p. 2060.

69. Cited in "General Major Wetzel: Die alte Armee und die junge Generation" (a review by General von Rakenau), MW (11 July 1925): 60.

70. Oberst von Notz, "Andere Gedanken zur Arbeitsdienstpflicht," MW (18 July 1925): 89–91.

71. See "Reichswehr und Kommunisten," MW (18 February 1930): 1210–11; "Offizier und Gesellschaft," MW (11 December 1929): 853–54.

72. "Offizier und Gesellschaft" and "Offizier und Ziviltragen," MW (4 February 1930): 1134–36.

73. Wolfgang Muss, "Die Bewegung der Jugend im Offizierkorps," MW (11 June 1930): 1801–5. See also "Neue Tradition," MW (25 March 1931): 1410–12, and (18 April 1931): 1532–33.

74. "Nationaler Sozialismus?" MW (11 August 1931): 215–18.

75. "Der Offizier als Erzieher," MW (25 June 1933): 1570–73; "Junge Generation des Heeres," MW (4 March 1933): 1089–91; and "Erziehung zur jungen Führerschaft des Heeres," MW (18 April 1933): 1283–86.

76. See "Die Wehrmacht in Staat und Volk," MW (18 June 1934): 1619–21; "Soldat und Volk," MW (11 June 1934): 1579–80. "Der Soldat und die National Revolution," MW (18 August 1933): 209–11; and "Wehrmacht und National Sozialismus," MW (4 February 1934): 947–48. Intricacies of party-army relations are treated well in the classic study by Telford Taylor, *Sword and Swastika: Generals and Nazis in the Third Reich* (Chicago: Quadrangle Books, 1969).

77. See "Gedanken über die Erziehung des heutigen deutschen Soldaten," MW (4 September 1935): 369–72.

78. See, for example, Otto Mossdorf, "Der Offizier," MW (7 May 1937): 2653–56.

79. See Gerhard Ritter, "Zum 150 Todestage Friedrichs des Grossen: Kriegführung und Politik in der Geschichte Friedrichs des Grossen," *Militärwissenschaftliche Rundschau* (17 August 1939): 555–64, hereafter cited as MR. See also Konstantine Hierl, "Die Idee der allgemeinen Arbeitsdienstpflicht und ihre Bewirklichung im Reichswehrdienst," MR (March–April 1936): 230.

80. "Soldaten," MW (1 January 1937).

81. "Die Berufung zum Offizier," MW (5 August 1938), 321–25. See

also "Erziehung des Soldaten zu Volkstum und Heimat," MW (18 February 1938): 2161–64.

Chapter Eight

1. Charles M. E. Mangin, *Avec le "Jules Michelet": Autour de continent latin* (Paris: Libraire Pierre Roger, 1925). Mangin's work appeared in Spanish translation as *En el Perú: En torno al continente latino con el "Jules Michelet"* (Paris: Libraire Pierre Roger, 1925). Important sources for all aspects of military-civilian relations during the inter-war years are Johnson's *The Military and Society*, pp. 93–173, and Lieuwen's *Arms and Politics*, pp. 36–58. Both authors carry their discussion well into the post-World War II era. Johnson's discussion of civilian attitudes toward the military (pp. 153–73) is especially antidotal to military views of civilian society. See also Roberto Calvo, *Le doctrina militar de la seguridad Nacional (Autoritarismo político y neoliberalismo en el Cono Sur)* (Caracas: Universidad Católica Andrés Bello, 1979), for background to contemporary problems in Argentina, Brazil, Chile, and Peru.

    Two members of civilian society whose views impressed army officers were the Brazilian Olavo Bilac and the Argentine Leopoldo Lugones. Both were recognized poets and skilled essayists and orators; both were ultra-nationalistic in their writing, speaking, and politics. Bilac lavished praise on the army as a nation-building institution in numerous speeches and in his *A Defesa Nacional* (Rio de Janeiro: Francisco Alves, 1917). Lugones did the same in various essays, most boldly in *Política revolucionaria* (Buenos Aires: Librería Anaconda, 1931), a defense of the 1930 *golpe de estado* and military-sponsored authoritarian rule.

2. Mangin, *En el Perú*, p. 13.

3. Ibid., pp. 20–180, passim.

4. Charles A. E. X. Maitrot, *La France et les républiques sud-americaines* (Paris: Berger Levrault, Editeurs, 1920), p. v.

5. Ibid., p. 9.

6. Ibid., pp. 12–13. See also Wilhelm Faupel, *Problemas de instrucción y organización del ejército* (Lima: Estado Mayor General del Ejército, 1930), pp. 10–15, 39.

7. Maitrot, *La France et les républiques sud-americaines*, pp. 317–23, passim. Hans von Kiesling concurred in his own

memoirs, *Soldat in drei Weltteilen* (Leipzig: Grehlein and Co. Nachf., 1935), 85–117.

8. República Argentina, *Memoria del departamento de guerra presentada al honorable congreso nacional correspondiente al año 1925—26* (Buenos Aires: Departamento de Guerra, 1926), pp. i–ii.

9. Miguel S. Gallardo, "Pedagogía militar," RMA (April 1925): 549–55. See also Enrique López Rivarola, "El instituto militar en el ejército francés y nuestra preparación militar superior," RMA (March 1925): 325–45.

10. Julio A. López, "¡Patria, ejército, bandera!" RMA (July 1924): 7–10.

11. "Serviço Militar," ADN (July–August 1925): 157–59.

12. João Pereira, "Pelo Tributo de Sangue," ADN (January–February 1926): 37. See also editorials in ADN (July 1926): 157–59, and (September 1926): 237–39.

13. For a lengthy paraphrase of Vigny, Lyautey, and Couderc de Fonlongue, see Gregório Fonseca, "Amor da Pátria, Culto à Bandeira, Exército," *Boletim Mensal do Estado Maior do Exército* (July–December 1919): 99–109, hereafter cited as BMEME.

14. Ibid., pp. 108–9.

15. Vicat, "Necesidad de una metalurgia propia como elemento indispensable para asegurar la defensa nacional," RMA (August 1925): p. 125.

16. See Molina, *La defensa nacional: Sus problemas fundamentales* (Buenos Aires: La Nación, 1926), passim; and Molina, "La defensa profesional," RMA (January 1927): 1–4.

17. See Luiz Lobo, "A Geografia Militar no Brasil," BMEME (January–June 1921): 33–45; Joaquim Marquês da Cunha, "O Papel das Estradas de Ferro nas Guerra Futuras," BMEME (October–December 1923): 507–11; and S. Sombra, "O Estado, o Exército e o Plano Nacional de Educação," RMB (April–June 1926): 179–80, which repeats the Lobo and Marques da Cunha arguments.

18. See, for example, RMA (9 July 1922): 101 for notes on Brazil's *Forças Públicas*; and RMA (January 1923): passim for information on the U.S. naval mission in Brazil. Articles on Brazil, Chile, and Peru begin appearing regularly from October 1922 forward.

19. "A Defesa Nacional," ADN (May–June 1926): 123–30; (July 1926): 205–10; (August 1926): 205–10; and (September 1926): 247–51.

20. See "A Organização da Defesa Nacional," ADN (September 1926), 237–39, and other editorials appearing during the remainder of 1926 and 1927.

21. Leitão de Carvalho, "A Questão dos Armamentos na América do Sul," RMB (April–June 1927): 152–68, and Magalhães, "Meditações sobre a Política Militar Sul-Americana," RMB (October 1929): 20–24.

22. Mayor Diana, "Las cuestiones militares en la honorable cámara de diputados," RCMA (January 1917): 21–24, and Soria, "El oficial: El ejército debe sustentar los ideales del pueblo," passim.

23. See "A Política e o Exército," pp. 33–34. The citation appears in "O Papel do Official numa Democrácia Moderna," p. 358.

24. In "Serviço Militar," ADN (July–August 1935): 157–59.

25. "Deve se Reeducar o Espírito Militar da Nação," ADN (July 1926): 157–59.

26. Parga Rodrigues, "A Missão do Exército Brasileiro na Actual Phase da Nossa Evolução," ADN (October 1929): 25–27.

27. See Carlos A. Gómez, "La guerra y la economía nacional," RMA (March 1938): 589–93; Juan Carlos Sanguinetti, "La decadencia del comunismo," RMA (November 1938): 1167–74; Gómez, "La nueva política mundial y la situación de la Argentina," RMA (November 1938): 1175–80; Jorge B. Crespo, "La defensa militar de los estados ante los últimos acontecimientos europeos," RMA (December 1938): 1403–8; Juan Ferrari, "El comunismo: Su prédica contra la moral de neustra civilización," RMA (December 1938): 1409–15; Gómez, "La movilización antes y ahora," RMA (December 1938): 1417–22; and Sanguinetti, "La situación internacional europea," RMA (March 1939): 479–83.

28. Jorge A. Giovanelli, "La guerra moral: Sus principios," RMA (July 1940), 3–6.

29. Enrique Rottjer, "La revolución del 6 de septiembre desde el punto de vista militar," RMA (October 1930): 575–90. The quotation is from p. 577.

30. Juan Vacarezza, "Etica militar y cumplimiento del deber," RMA (July 1932): 1–6. The quotation is from p. 4.

31. See Arturo Rawson, "Reflexiones sobre la movilización y la estadística," RMA (March 1931): 465–99; Francisco Fasola

Castaño, "Argentina para los argentinos," RMA (July 1935): 3–7; and José María Sarobe, "Los problemas de la educación popular en la Argentina, país agrario," RMA (November 1940): 951–68. See also Alberto Baldrich, "Interpretación de la actual situación internacional europea," RMA (9 April 1939): 789–96.

32. Juan Ramón Beltrán, "Misión del oficial frente a los problemas sociales contemporáneos," RMA (September 1936): 499–513.

33. Besides works cited in notes 27 and 31, see Atilio Cattaneso, "Organización: Los ascensos en el ejército," RMA (January 1930): 1–16; Oscar Uriondo, "Reflexiones profesionales: Educación militar," RMA (August 1931): 239–46; Enrique López Rivarola, "El desarme y el potencial de guerra," RMA (June 1932): 427–32; and Ricardo Miró, "¡Fuerza moral, fuerza moral!" RMA (June 1935): 1103–6.

34. Hernández, "Nuestro militar profesional," RMA (June 1935): 1042–47.

35. See Jorge B. Crespo, "Colaboración orgánica fundamental," RMA (February–October 1936): 235–42, (March 1936): 495–507, (April 1936): 789–811, (May 1936): 991–1003, (June 1936): 1287–1305, (July 1936): 41–59, (August 1936): 257–79, (September 1936): 515–40, and (October 1936): 767–803; Alberto Baldrich, "La ascendencia espiritual del ejército argentino," RMA (August 1940): 321–51; and Sarobe, "Los problemas de la educación popular," passim.

36. Baldrich, "La ascendencia espiritual del ejército argentino," pp. 350–51.

37. In a speech to the Infantry School of 15 December 1930. It is enlightening to compare Argentine attitudes of the 1930s with the varying post-World War II authoritarian approaches to sociopolitical and economic problems, as discussed, for example, in Robert A. Potash, *The Army and Politics in Argentina, 1945–1962: Perón to Frondizi* (Stanford: Stanford University Press, 1980).

38. Anon., "Aspectos presumibles de la guerra futura," RMA (July 1930): 111–35.

39. Julio A. López, "Influencia del paludismo asociado al alcoholismo en la vida psíquica en el noroeste argentino," RMA (9 January 1931): 95–109. See also Alberto Levene, "La función social de la sanidad," RMA (9 December 1933): 1107–10. In the Andean countries at this time there was great concern about coca addiction as a hindrance to "national well-being," i.e. military service.

40. See Fasola Castaño, "La cuestión de los efectos de paz del ejército," RMA (9 November 1934): 1017–35, and (December 1935): 1225–34; J. del Viso, "La conquista del desierto," RMA (May 1934): 917–57; and Conrado Sztryle, "La Patagonia y su progreso integral," RMA (September 1935): 489–92.

41. See also Beltrán, "Misión del oficial frente a los problemas sociales contemporáneos," passim.

42. Ricardo Marambio, "Industrias argentinas y tecnocracia," RMA (December 1936): 1261–81, (January 1937): 109–43, (February 1937): 333–65, (March 1937): 591–607, and (April 1937): 808–23; and his "Movilización industrial," RMA (June 1937): 1325–34. Argentine preoccupation with geo-economic issues can still be noted in the pages of the widely-circulated Argentine journal *Estrategia* (May–June 1969 and later issues).

43. See Alvaro Alsogaray, "Defensa nacional y commando único," RMA (September 1937): 675–91; Carlos A. Gómez, "La guerra y la economia nacional"; and Jorge B. Crespo, "Si vis pacem, para bellum," RMA (June 1939): 1223–26.

44. Chief of Staff Góis Monteiro delivered a sharp attack against the Old Republic and its politics in the 1934 *Relatório*, pp. 3–48, passim. See also the pro-fascist essay by João Baptista Magalhães, "Hitlerismo, Fascismo, Bolshevismo," ADN (November 1933): 583–88. This essay is alarmingly similar in tone to the "Reichswehr und Kommunisten" and "Nationaler Sozialismus" cited in chapter seven.

45. See "Exércitos Modernos," ADN (February 1933): 57–60. The quotation is from pp. 57–58.

46. "A Futura Constituição e a Defesa Nacional," ADN (November 1933): 551–55. The quotation is from p. 555.

47. "O Exército e a Política," ADN (May 1934): 280–81. See also "O Exército no Estado," ADN (February 1934): 104–5.

48. João Ribeiro Pinheiro, "O Exército e um Grave Problema," ADN (July 1935): 810–11.

49. See War Minister Dutra's introduction to the 1936 *Relatório*, pp. 5–9.

50. "A Renovação do Contrato da Missão Militar Franceza," pp. 133–35, and Magalhães, "Hitlerismo, Fascismo, Bolschevismo," passim.

51. See Benício da Silva, "Novo Rumo," pp. 39–43, and "Momento de Acção," RMB (July–September 1941): 163–66.

52. Góis Monteiro in the 1934 *Relatório*, pp. 5–10, passim, and Ribeiro Pinheiro in the 1935 *Relatório*, pp. 6–7.

53. Fernando Magalhães, "Patriotismo Militar," RMB (October–December 1936): 249–58. In 1936 the *Revista Militar Brasileira* inaugurated a new section devoted to "Educação e Civismo." See also Góis Monteiro, "Um programa de Trabalho," RMB (January–December 1937), 13–19.

54. See the descriptive essay "A Escola Militar: Síntese Histórica da sua Fundação e Evolução," RMB (January–March 1942): 13–70.

55. Aloysio Miranda Mendes, "A Disciplina, as Virtudes e a Profissão Militares," ADN (January 1936): 80–90. See also "Acção Social do Exército," RMB (January–March 1936): 37–46, which stressed military colonization of the interior as something just as valuable as barracks life and routine active duty in the molding of good citizens. Indicative of the perduration of officer-corps views that the army was a cultural institution and a legitimate participant in social, political, and economic affairs are Umberto Peregrino, *História e Projeção dos Instituições Culturais do Exército* (Rio de Janeiro; Biblioteca do Exército, 1967), and Estado Maior do Exército, *História do Exército Brasileiro: Perfil Militar de um Povo*, 3 vols. (Brasília: Estado Maior do Exército, 1972).

56. M. Paulo Filho, "Quartel: Escola de Civismo," ADN (October 1936): 425–33; Sombra, "O Estado, O Exército." See also Magalhães, "Patriotismo Militar" and "Reclutamento para o Officialato," ADN (June 1937), 603–8.

57. Tobías Barros Ortiz, *Vigilia de armas: Charlas sobre la vida militar destinadas a un joven teniente* (Santiago: Estado Mayor General del Ejército, 1920).

58. Ibid., pp. 10, 11–12, 20–27.

59. Ibid., pp. 21–22, 61–62.

60. Ibid., p. 39.

61. Ibid., pp. 41–43, 127.

62. See Nunn, *The Military in Chilean History*, pp. 9–27, 107–50.

63. "Misión militar francesa en el Perú," MEMECH (April 1924): 367–97.

64. Javier Palacios, "Argentina y sus progresos en 1923," MEMECH (April 1924): 367–97.

65. Clodomiro Eurípides Márquez, "El ejército colombiano y la obra realizada en él por las misiones militares chilenas," MEMECH (August 1926): 682–92.

66. Jorge Carmona, "Escuela francesa o escuela alemana," MEMECH (December 1929): 1073–74.

67. René Montero Mareno, *Orígenes del problema social en Chile: Tema de invierno* (Santiago: N. Avaría, 1926); see also Carlos Dinator, "La educación cívica en el ejército," MEMECH (April 1925): 288–99.

68. Ernesto Würth Rojas, *Ibáñez: Caudillo enigmático* (Santiago: Editorial del Pacífico, 1958), passim.

69. Arturo Ahumada Bascuñán, *El ejército y la revolución del 5 de septiembre: Reminiscencias* (Santiago: Imprenta La Tracción, 1931), p. 39.

70. Carlos Sáez Morales, *Recuerdos de un soldado*, I, 33–35.

71. Carlos Ibáñez del Campo, in an address of July 20, 1927, quoted in *El Mercurio*, July 21 1927.

72. Víctor Molina, "El ejército y su función social de acuerdo con la necesidad de capacitar el individuo en un oficio que le permita desempeñarse en forma más eficiente al ser restituido a la sociedad civil," MECH (September–October 1935): 835. Emphasis mine.

73. Sáez Morales, *Y así vamos: Ensayo crítico* (Santiago: Ediciones Ercilla, 1938), pp. 39–41.

74. Angel Varela, "La instrucción escolar en el ejército," MECH (May–June 1935): 397.

75. Barros Ortiz, "Apuntes y notas sobre la formación del oficial de hoy," MECH (January–February 1937): 1–28, passim.

76. Tomás Sánchez Hernández, "La cultura militar francesa y su difusión mundial," MECH (January–February 1938): 121–36; Weygand, "Como educar a nuestra juventud," MECH (May–June 1938): 453–76, and (July–August 1938): 585–602; and Lyautey, "La función social del oficial," MECH (November–December 1939): 851–67.

77. On the army's earlier advocacy of an educative role see also "Reclutador," La educación militar del país," MECH (January 1932): 39–44, and Ramón Cañas Montalva, "Fuerzas morales," MECH (October 1932): 369–74. On physical education and training see Ramón Venegas O., "Ejercicios físicos desde el punto de vista militar," MECH (January 1931): 33–43; Daniel Sánchez A., "¿Convendría introducir alguna reforma en el sistema de educación física que actualmente emplea el ejército?" MECH (February 1931): 131–42; Cañas Montalva, "Escuela activa: Nuestra reforma educacional y el ejército," MECH (April 1931): 419–23; Jorge Carmona, "¡Hacia la economía! La racionalización de neustra instrucción militar,"

MECH (November 1931): 587–93; and Electo Pereda L.,
"Cultura física en el ejército: Sus proyecciones sociales," MECH
(September–October 1940: 665–86.

78. Guillermo Aldona, "El ejército: Escuela de civilismo e
    institución de equilibrio social," MECH (September–October
    1940): 687–709.

79. Indalicio Téllez, "La profesión militar," MECH (March–April
    1942): 1135–40, passim.

80. Ibid., p. 1138.

81. José Maravá, "El ejército y la armada y la cultura nacional,"
    BMGM (June–July 1919): 799–817.

82. BMGM (August 1919): p. 927–29.

83. Serrigny, "La organización de la nación para el tiempo de
    guerre." The article appeared originally as "L'Organisation de la
    nation pour le temps de guerre," RDM (1 December 1923):
    583–602.

84. Andrés Escalona, "Los conscriptos," RCMP (February 1925):
    130–4.

85. Vidal Panizo, "La ley de conscripción vial y la defensa del país,"
    RCMP (April 1926): 339–41. See also the earlier, modest article
    by Ernesto Montagne Markholtz, "Un camino de interés
    nacional," RCMP (Arpil 1925): 336–40.

86. Paz García, "El cuartel y la redención del indio," RCMP (April
    1926): 385–94.

87. Panizo, "La disciplina es el alma del ejército," RCMP (December
    1926): 1409–17.

88. Genaro Muro, "Colonización de nuestros ríos fronterizos de
    oriente," RCMP (October 1927): 33–38.

89. Valdivia, "Conscripción vial," RCMP (December 1927): 249–54.

90. Federico Gómez, "Datos estadísticos," RCMP (June 1930):
    187–96.

91. Manuel Morla Concha, "Función social del ejército en la
    organización de la nacionalidad," RMP (October 1933): 843–72.
    See Nunn, "Professional Militarism in Twentieth Century Peru,"
    for information on Morla's influence on post-World War II
    Peruvian writers.

92. Morla Concha, "Función social del ejército," pp. 854–64, passim.

93. Isaac Portugal, "Las vías de comunicación desde el punto de
    vista del comercio y de los problemas militares," RMP (August
    1933): 659–64.

94. Mauricio Barbis, "El ejército y la colonización de la montaña," RMP (December 1933): 1239–42; and Jorge Vargas, "Charla sobre el ejército," RMP (January 1934): 103–10.

95. See Luis Velarde, "¡Superación, superación!" RMP (January 1935): 105–11, and "La instrucción civil en el ejército," RMP (November 1935): 2119–21. Lyautey's "Du Rôle social," translated by Colonel J. M. Pérez Manzanares, appeared in Peru as "Papel social del oficial," RMP (March 1934): 285–309.

96. Alejandro Aliaga, "Papel social del ejército en tiempo de paz," RMP (December 1935): 2309–15.

97. Enrique Barreto, "Rol de los estados mayores en tiempo de paz," RMP (August 1936): 1381–98.

98. "La política interna y el ejército," RMP (September 1936), 1566–81. Cf. Vigny, "The army is a nation within the nation," and Seeckt, "The army should become a state within the state."

99. Federico Hurtado, "El ministro de guerra se dirige a la cuidadanía," RMP (March 1938): i–xxii.

100. Oscar Benavides, "Discurso del presidente de la república en la ceremonia de clausura del año académico de la escuela militar," RMP (January 1939): i–vi.

101. Manuel Prado y Ugarteche, "Discurso en la clausura del año académico de la escuela militar," RMP (January 1940): i–vi.

Postscript

1. Couderc de Fonlongue, "Étude sur la discipline."

2. Anon., *A General's Letters to His Son on Obtaining His Commission* (London: Cassell and Co., Ltd., 1917), pp. 2, 19–42, passim.

3. Mercado Jarrín, "El ejército de hoy," p. 6.

4. A handy, authoritative source for such a comparative perusal is Brian Lovemen and Thomas M. Davies, Jr., eds., *The Politics of Antipolitics: The Military in Latin America* (Lincoln: University of Nebraska Press, 1978), pp. 173–219, wherein are found excerpts from the speeches and proclamations of the following generals: Argentines Juan Carlos Onganía and Jorge Rafael Videla, Brazilians Humberto Castello Branco and Ernesto Geisel, the Chilean Augusto Pinochet Ugarte, and Peruvians Juan Velasco Alvarado and Francisco Morales Bermúdez Cerruti.

Index

Academia de Guerra (Chile), 35, 101–12, 118, 127
Académia Real Militar (Brazil), 57
Action Française, 77, 159, 176, 225, 251
Afrancesados, 42; in Brazil, 132, 146, 178, 194, 203, 206–7, 218, 220, 286–89; in Peru, 56, 112–22, 178, 210–11, 220–21, 288–96
Africa: French in, 26, 66, 79–80, 200, 252, 279; Germans in, 66
Aguirre, Manuel, 112
Aguirre Cerda, Pedro, 170, 255
Ahumada Bascuñán, Arturo, 111, 112
Akeson, George, 188
Aldona, Guillermo, 275–76
Alem, Leandro, 27, 49, 52
Alessandri Palma, Arturo, 163, 165, 170–71, 181, 190, 211, 255, 271
Aliaga, Alejandro, 281–82
Alsace-Lorraine conflict, 87, 94
Alsina, Adolfo, 46
Alsogaray, Alvaro, 264
Alvear, Marcelo de, 162, 184
Alvensleven, Constantine von, 105
Alves, Francisco de Rodrigues, 31

Anti-Communism: in Argentina, 145, 176, 260; in Brazil, 266–67; in Chile, 170, 274; in France, 160; in Germany, 160, 238, 245, 246, 248; in Peru, 282
Anti-European opinions, 99–153, 249–86; in Argentina, 123–24, 230; in Brazil, 205–6; in Chile, 272; in Peru, 201–2
Anti-militarism: in Europe, 97–98, 238–89; in South America, 182–221, 249–96
APRA (Alianza Popular Revolucionaria Americana, Peru), 174–75, 176, 254, 280–83
Aranha, Oswaldo, 177, 208, 216–17
Araucanians, 50, 306 n. 13
Arent, Alfred, 68, 122–30
Argentina, 13–42, 43–69, 99–153, 157–81, 182–221; army of, 6, 13–42, 43–69, 99–153, 182–221, 249–96; German missions to, 122–31; military-civilian relations in, 2–4, 18–22, 26–29, 61–64, 122–31, 162–65, 170–72, 175–79, 211–15, 249–96; military history and tradition of, 45–49; military literature of,

142–45, 249–96; military professionalism in, 45–49, 122–31, 182–221, 249–96; officer corps thought and self-perception in, 8, 41–42, 122–31, 249–96; professional militarism in, 17, 249–96. *See also* Diplomatic relations; Geopolitics; Government and politics
Argentinidad, 21
Aristocracy: in Europe, 74–75, 82; in South America, 26–27, 29–30, 36–37, 49–50
Army. *See names of individual countries*
Army Society for Regeneration (Chile), 271
Army War College (U.S.), 190
Authoritarianism, appeal of to officers, 71–98; 222–48, 250–96
Authority, as military ideal, 70–98, 100–153, 222–48, 249–86
Avellaneda, Nicolás, 46
Azan, Paul, 244

Baldrich, Alberto, 262
Baley de Langlade, Roger, 118
Balmaceda, José Manuel, 34, 52, 67, 103, 163
Banse, Ewald, 240
Banza, Edward, 105
Barat, Albert, 193
Barber, Lester, 204
Barbis, Mauricio, 281
Barbosa, Rui, 32
Barceló Lira, José María, 106
Barclay, Hugh, 192, 194
Barnardston, N. W., 92
Barracks life, as civilizing experience, 70–98, 100–153, 249–86

Barrand, Gabriel, 193
Barreto, Enrique, 282
Barros Merino, Tobías, 106–269
Barros Ortiz, Mario, 269
Barros Ortiz, Tobías, 262, 269–71, 275–76
Basque-Castillian aristocracy (Chile), 36, 49
Baudiez, Jules, 198
Baudoin, Colonel, 206
Below, Günther von, 105
Below, Hans von, 123
Benavides, Oscar, 40, 119, 168, 169, 174–75, 203, 210–11, 255, 282–83
Bennett Argandoña, Juan Pablo, 106, 111, 112
Bentes Monteiro, Captain, 220
Beretron, Paul, 117
Bernardes, Arthur, 205
Bernhardi, Friedrich von, 66, 83, 84–85, 94, 96, 97, 144, 237–38
Berthon, Pierre, 117
Bertling, Hans, 105
Betzhold, Major, 102
Beúnza, Nicanor, 141
Bieberstein, Herman von, 105
Bilac, Olavo, 265
Billinghurst, Guillermo, 40
Bismarck, Otto von, 78
Blanche Espejo, Bartolomé, 29, 112, 164
Blume, General von, 94
Bolivia, 33, 44, 52, 133, 136, 143, 147, 180, 191, 215
Boonen Rivera, Jorge, 101
Borderies, René des, 198
Borgoño, Justiniano, 55
Bourgeoisie, as source of officer corps recruitment, 72, 74–75, 82, 96, 101–53, 224, 240, 243
Bourget, Samuel, 118, 119
Bourgueil, Emile, 118

Bourgignon, Louis, 198
Bravo, Luis, 111
Brazil, 6–7, 13–42, 43–69, 99–153, 157–81, 182–221, 249–96; army of, 6, 14–16, 43–69, 99–153, 182–221, 249–96; French missions to, 146–47, 162, 183–87, 192–98, 219–20; German military influence in, 131–36; military-civilian relations in, 2–4, 18–22, 29–33, 61–64, 131–36, 162–65, 172–74, 175–79, 203–8, 215–18, 249–96; military history and traditions of, 56–61; military literature of, 8, 131–36, 249–96; military professionalism in, 56–61, 131–36, 182–221, 249–96; officer corps thought and self-perception in, 41–42, 131–36, 249–96; professional militarism in, 17, 249–96. *See also* Diplomatic relations; Geopolitics; Government and politics
Brenaud, Abel, 198
Bresard, Pierre, 193
Briand, Aristide, 231
Brockderfallfeld, Thilo, Graf von, 104
Brooklyn Women's Anti-Fascist League, 207
Bruchhausen, Karl von, 94, 97
Bruyère, Emile, 198
Buchalet, Louis, 193
Bugeaud de la Piconnerie, Thomas Robert, 67, 77, 78
Bulnes, Manuel, 106

Caballeros de San Martín, Order of (Argentina), 262
Cabrera, Luis, 111
Cáceres, Andrés, 54

Cáceres, Ricardo, 114
Cafferey, Jefferson, 215–17
Cagoulle, 160, 225, 254
Calmel, Jean, 118
Calógeras, João Pandiá, 194
Caminade, Etienne, 199, 211
Campos, Manuel J., 49
Canevaro, José F., 112
Canto, Estanislao del, 103
Canto Toske, Julio César del, 106
Canudos, 61, 132, 133, 184
Carpentier, Major, 206
Caruel, Père, S. J., 87
Casamatia, Charles, 118
Casement, Roger, 40
Castex, Admiral, 244
Castilla, Ramón, 51
Cattaneso, Atilio, 262
Caxias, Duke of. *See* Lima e Silva, Luis Alves de
Centre des Hautes Études Militaires (France), 232
Centro de Altos Estudios Militares (CAEM) (Peru), 119, 199, 233, 277
Chabrier, Albert, 198
Chadebec de Lavalade, Major General, 207, 219
Championière, Abbé H. Lucas, 87
Character, as military virtue, 70–98, 99–153, 182–221, 222–48, 249–86
Charlottenburg, 100, 106
Charpín Rivel, Pedro, 106, 111
Chaumeton, René, 117
Chevalerie, 289
Chevalier, Joseph, 198
Chile, 6–7, 13–42, 43–69, 99–153, 157–81, 182–221, 249–96; army of, 6, 14–16, 43–69, 101–12, 182–221, 249–96; German missions to,

101–12; military-civilian relations in, 2–4, 18–22, 33–37, 49–52, 61–64, 101–12, 162–65, 169–70, 175–79, 211–13, 249–96; military history and tradition of, 49–52; military literature, 8, 138–40, 249–96; military professionalism in, 49–52, 101–12, 182–221, 249–96; officer class thought and self-perception in, 41–42, 101–12, 138–40, 249–96; professional militarism in, 17, 249–96. *See also* Diplomatic relations; Geopolitics; Government and politics

Chilenidad, 21

Cisplatine Province. *See* Uruguay

Civic education, as result of military service, 70–98, 99–153, 222–48, 249–86

Civilista Party (Peru), 38–39, 41, 54, 56, 65, 174

Civilizing mission, 71–98, 101–53, 250–96

Civil War of 1891 (Chile), 34–35, 62, 100–13

Clausewitz, Carl Maria von, 23, 78, 93, 228, 230, 240, 290

Clemenceau, Georges, 151, 231

Clément, Paul, 38, 55, 62, 66, 79, 112–22, 123, 124, 126, 152, 163, 199, 223

Cochrane, Thomas, 56

Coffec, Frederic Mathieu Marie, 196

Colditz, Ricardo von, 143

Cold War, 295

Colegio Militar (Argentina), 45, 47, 122–31, 144, 190

College des Hautes Études, de la Défense Nationale (France), 244, 340 n. 63

Colombia, 111–12, 136, 147, 180, 191

Communism, 176, 238, 245, 248. *See also* Anti-Communism

Concordancia, La (Argentina), 254

Cono Sur (Southern Cone), 191

Conduret, Louis, 198

Conscripción vial (Peru), 278

Constant, Benjamin. *See* Magalhães, Benjamin Constant Botelho de

Corbé, Colonel, 206

Cordier, Constant, 188, 304–5 n. 40

Córdoba Clique (Argentina), 27, 52, 165

Corporatism. *See* Fascism

Correia Lima, Luis, 197

Couderc de Fonlongue, Captain, 87, 290

Cousin, Pierre, 198

Crespo, Jorge, 264

Croix de Feu, 160, 225

Cunha, Euclydes Da, 19, 30, 132

Dalmassy, Chavanne de, 193

Damidaux, Captain, 243

D'André, Felix, 117, 119

Dangelmaier, Emil, 81

Danudoux, Émile, 198

D'Araújo Mello, Heitor, 145–46

D'Arnoux Armand, 207

Dartnell Encina, Pedro Pablo, 106

Dassonville, Hector, 199, 211, 219

Dearing, Fred Morris, 209

Debeney, General, 244

Deinert, Felix, 105

Dellepiane, Jorge, 219

Democracy. *See* Government and politics

Democratic Party (Peru), 40, 56

Demongeot, Marcel, 88–89, 141
Demoreulle, Pierre, 199, 209,
   211, 219
Department of State (U.S.), 184,
   221
Derougemont, Louis, 193,
   195–96, 197
Dessofy de Czernek, Colonel, 243
Desvoyes, Marcel, 118
Devine, M. A., Jr., 219
Diana, Major, 258–59
Dianderas, Antonio, 119
Díaz Valderrama, Francisco Jav-
   ier, 106, 111, 112, 177, 189,
   272
Didon, Père, 87, 88, 97
Dieloulard, Paul, 193
Dingskirchen, Johannes. *See* Ric-
   cheri, Pablo
Diplomatic relations: European,
   70–98, 160–61, 231–48; Euro-
   pean–South American, 99–153,
   182–221; South American,
   45–46, 52–53, 64–65, 142,
   249–86; U.S.–South American,
   183–221, 249–86
Discipline, as military virtue,
   71–98, 99–153, 222–48,
   249–96
Diserre, Alphonse, 123
Dogny, Edouard, 112–14, 117,
   122
Dorroux, Pierre, 118
Dreyfus Affair, 15, 25, 71, 76–77
Ducep, André, 198
Dumas, Raymond, 193
Duran de Marevil, Robert, 193
Durandin, Eugene, 193
Duruy, Georges, 87
Dutra, Gaspar Eurico, 173, 218,
   266

Echazú, Carlos, 142, 277

Ecole Polytechnique (France), 75,
   91, 112–20
Economic and demographic sta-
   tistics: Argentina, 29, 166–67;
   Brazil, 33, 167; Chile, 37,
   167–68; Peru, 41, 168
Economic development, in South
   America, 13–42, 157–81,
   249–86
Ecuador, 111, 136, 147, 180, 191
Edge, Walter, 203–4
Education, military views on,
   47–48, 49, 101–53, 234–35,
   239–40, 274–75. *See also* Mili-
   tary schools
Egalitarianism, as military vir-
   tue, 71–98, 222–48, 249–86
Ekdahl, Wilhelm, 104
Elitism, as military characteris-
   tic, 71–98, 222–48, 249–86
El Salvador, 111, 136
England, 144, 248
Epp, Franz Ritter von, 239
Erbert, Friedrich von, 105
Escalona, A., 141, 277
Escalona, Andrés, 277
Escola de Aperfeiçoamento (Bra-
   zil), 193
Escola do Estado Maior de Exér-
   cito (Brazil), 58, 193
Escola Militar-Praia Vermelha
   (Brazil), 58, 193
Escolas de Aplicação (Brazil),
   57, 58
Escuela de Artes y Oficios (Ar-
   gentina), 45
Escuela de Clases (Chile), 105
Escuela de Matemáticas (Argen-
   tina), 45
Escuela Militar (Chile), 49, 51,
   101–12, 190, 269
Escuela Militar (Colombia), 111
Escuela Militar (Peru), 53–54,

112–22
Escuelas de Aplicación (Chile),
    101–12
Escuela Superior de Guerra (Argentina), 47, 68, 118, 122–31
Escuela Superior de Guerra
    (Peru), 114–22
Estado Novo (Brazil), 172, 174,
    206, 218, 254, 266, 267–68

Fascism: in Europe, 222–48; in
    South America, 250–96. *See
    also* Authoritarianism
Faupel, Wilhelm, 185, 189, 191,
    202, 209, 211, 223
Fay, Major, 206
Federphil, Lieutenant, 234
Feminism, 98
Fernández Pradel, Carlos, 106
Fernandini, David, 141–42, 277
Fievet, Georges, 117
Figueroa, Andrés, 191
Foch, Ferdinand, 97, 193, 231,
    232–33, 236
Fonseca, Deodoro da, 30, 34, 59,
    60, 61, 132, 195
Fonseca, Hermes da, 32, 58, 111,
    132, 133
Fontin, Paul, 96
Força Pública (Brazil), 32, 61,
    131–36, 267
France: army of, 16, 25–26,
    70–98, 222–48; military civilian relations in, 70–98, 147,
    158–62, 222–48; military history and tradition of, 70–98,
    222–48; military literature of,
    70–98, 147–51, 222–48; military missions to Brazil,
    146–47, 162, 183–87, 192–98,
    219–20; military missions to
    Peru, 38–39, 112–20, 163–64,
    183–90, 198–203, 251–52; mil-

itary professionalism in,
    70–98, 163, 220–21, 222–48;
    officer corps thought and self-perception in, 70–98, 222–48.
    See also Diplomatic relations;
    Government and politics
Franco-Prussian War, 24
Franzani, Julio, 111
Frederick the Great, 124
Free France, 218
Freye, Wilhelm, 189
Freytagh, Loringhoven, Graf von,
    237, 243
Fritzsch, Eugen von, 105

Gallardo, Miguel, 255
Gallieni, Joseph Simon, 147, 231,
    233
Gamarra, Agustín, 53, 55
Gamelin, Maurice, 61, 146, 162,
    193, 195–97, 221, 223, 233,
    244
García Calderón, Francisco, 152
García Huidobro, Estanislao, 111
García Godos, Aurelio, 203
Garçon, A., 87, 92
Gaston, Alfredo, 114
Gauer, Herman, 240
Gaulle, Charles de, 86, 158, 161,
    175, 218, 225–26, 228–31, 244,
    290
General Staff organization: in Argentina, 122–31; in Brazil,
    135–36; in Chile, 101–12; in
    Peru, 112–21
Gentizon, Paul, 232
Geopolitics, 249–96
German Empire, 16, 70–98, 158
Germanófilos, 32, 42, 62, 101–12,
    122–37, 162, 178, 194, 217,
    218, 224, 252, 260, 272,
    288–96
Germany: army of, 15, 25–26,

71–98, 222–48; military-civilian relations in, 70–98, 147, 158, 222–48; military history and traditions of, 70–98, 222–48; military influence in Brazil, 131–36; military literature of, 71–98, 222–48; military missions to Argentina, 27, 122–31, 190–92; military missions to Chile, 101–12, 190–92; military professionalism in, 71–98, 222–48; officer corps thought and self-perception in, 70–98, 222–48; post–World War I influence of, 183–213. *See also* Diplomatic relations; Government and politics; Prussia

Góis Monteiro, Pedro Aurélio de, 173, 215, 218, 266, 267

Goltz, Colmar Freiherr von der, 23, 28, 44, 65, 78, 82–83, 85, 89, 93, 97, 130, 138, 143, 146, 152, 224, 228, 230, 262, 269, 290

Goltz, Friedrich, 123

Gomes, Eduardo, 173

Gómez, Carlos, 262, 264

Gómez, Federico, 279

González, Enrique, 114

González Prada, Manuel, 19, 39

Good Neighbor Policy, 216–17

GOU (Grupo de Oficiales Unidos, Argentina), 172, 174, 264

Goubeaux, Ferdinand, 117, 119

Goubeaux, Paul, 198

Gouhier, Urbain, 77

Government and politics, 13–42, 70–98, 158–81, 182–221, 222–48, 249–96; Argentina, 26–29, 48–49, 162–65, 170–72, 175–79, 249–96; Brazil, 29–33, 162–65, 172–74, 175–79, 249–96; Chile, 33–37, 101–12, 162–65, 169–70, 175–79, 249–96; France, 70–98, 158–62, 222–48; Germany, 70–98, 158–62, 222–48; Peru, 33–34, 37–41, 162–65, 174–75, 176–77, 249–96

Grace, Michael, 38

Grace, W. R., 38

Grausot, Pierre, 207

Grenier, Major, 243

Grove Vallejo, Marmaduke, 112, 164

Grow, H. B., 188–89

Gueriot, Jean, 193

Guerrero, J. C., 141

Guillén, Diego, 111

Guttich, Fritz, 105

Haard, Herman, 105

Haffemeyer, Lieutenant, 91

Halbfuss, Colonel, 213

Haya de la Torre, Víctor Raúl, 254

Hébert, Gaston, 117, 118, 198

Hegel, Georg Wilhelm Friedrich, 93

Hermann, Erich, 105

Hernández, Jacinto, 262

Herzbruch, Werner, 105

Hesse, Kurt, 240

Hindenburg, Paul von, 100, 158, 159, 255

Hitler, Adolf, 158, 160, 247, 255

Hoover, Herbert, 188

Horm, Robert, 105

Houdelot, Camille, 198

Hull, Cordell, 207, 216–17

Hundeiker, Egon, 241

Huntziger, Charles, 61, 205–6

Hurtado, Federico, 283

Ibáñez del Campo, Carlos, 35,

111, 112, 163, 164, 169, 170,
186, 189, 190, 212, 254, 272,
273–74
Ibañismo (Chile), 176
Idealized past, as aspect of officer corps thought and self-perception, 3–4, 8, 137–38,
176–77, 180–81, 223–25,
240–48, 249–96
Indians. *See* Race
Indo-China, French in, 26
Industralization, military advocacy of, 249–86
Inman, Samuel Guy, 187
Institutional *golpes de estado*,
295
Integralistas (Brazil), 176
Intra-military relations: in Argentina, 99–153, 249–86; in
Brazil, 99–153, 249–86; in
Chile, 99–153, 249–86; in
Peru, 99–153, 249–86
Isenburg, K., 84
Iung, Henri, 87

Januskowski, Captain, 102
Japan: armaments mission to
Peru, 210; European military
influence in, 44–45
Jaurès, Jean, 71, 90, 97
Jews, military attitudes toward,
24–25, 238, 248
Jibé, Captain, 96
Jiménez, Julio, 114
João VI, 57
Joeden, Alexander von, 105
Joffre, Joseph, 76, 231, 233
Jones, Winfield, 188
Jougla, Henri, 79
Jovens Turcos (Young Turks, Brazil), 193, 259
Juárez Celman, Miguel, 27–28
Junkertum, 24, 75, 80, 230, 243

Justo, Agustín, 162, 164, 169,
171, 174, 184, 191, 211, 214,
254, 260, 271

Kameradschaft, 243
Kellermeister von der Lund, Alfred, 105
Kellog-Briand Pact, 187, 250
Kiesling, Bernhard, 238
Kiesling, Hans von, 186, 190,
211, 212–13, 223
King, William Henry (D-Utah),
187
Klinger, Bertholdo, 133, 134, 146
Königsmark, Wilhelm, Graf von,
105
Kornatski, Rollo von, 123
Körner, Emil, ix, x, 35, 37, 51,
62, 65, 100–112, 123, 124, 126,
128, 129, 130, 131, 150, 152
Kramer, General von, 213
Kretzschmar, Johannes, 191, 192,
211
Kriegsakadamie (Germany), 35,
67, 72, 101, 118, 127
Kropotkin, Peter, 98
Kundt, Hans, 103, 128, 136, 147,
224, 304–5 n. 40, 333 n. 37

Lagreze, Francisco, 106, 111
Lama, Miguel de la, 114
Lanfranco, Leoncio, 114
Larregain, Leoncio, 117
Laurent, Raymond, 199, 209, 211
League of Nations, 180
Lebensphilosophie, 85
Leguía, Augusto B., 40, 56, 163,
164–65, 174, 177, 181, 185,
189, 201–202, 203, 205, 208,
254, 277
Leguiismo, 209
Leitão de Carvalho, Estevão, 132,
135, 146, 258

Lelong, Lucien, 193
Le Mehaute, François, 193
Leroy, Major, 207
Leuliette, Victor, 97
Liebknecht, Karl, 71, 90, 98
Liga Militar (Chile), 271
Liga Naval (Chile), 271
Lima e Silva, Luis Alves de, Duke
   of Caxias, 59, 132, 169
Lindholm, Victor, 105
Livermore, Henrietta, 187
Llanos Calderón, Armando, 111
López, Julio, 256
López de Romaña, Eduardo, 40
López Rivarola, Enrique, 262
Lorin, Henri, 152
Ludendorf, Erich, 237
Lugones, Leopoldo, 262
Luna, José R., 119, 122, 203
Luther, Martin, 93
Lyautey, Louis Hubert Gonzalve,
   23–25, 75, 79–80, 86, 97, 140,
   147, 186, 224, 228, 230, 269,
   275, 280, 290

MacMahon, Marie Edme Patrice
   Maurice de, 95
Madrazo, Paulino, 191
Magalhães, Benjamin Constant
   Botelho de, 59, 61, 131–32
Magalhães, Fernando, 267
Magalhães, João Baptista, 22, 258
Maitroit, Charles, 252–53
Maligne, Augusto, 143–44, 192
Maltzahn, Axel Freiherr von, 241
Mangin, Charles, 197, 231, 233,
   251, 253
Manpower, 99–153, 249–86, 315
   n. 53; of Argentina, 47, 92,
   142, 191; of Brazil, 56, 61, 92,
   192; of Chile, 51, 92, 101–12,
   190, 213; of France, 66, 92; of
   Germany, 66, 92; of Peru, 55,

92, 209
Marambio, Ricardo, 264
Maravá, José, 276
Marcard, Henry, 105
Marcel, Georges, 198
Mariátegui, José Carlos, 19
Marlanger, Henri, 193
Marshall, George C., 177, 218
Martínez, Pedro Pablo, 122, 203
Marxism, 20, 145, 159, 168, 176,
   238, 241, 245, 246, 248. *See
   also* Anti-Communism;
   Communism
Mascarel, René, 198
Materialism, military criticism
   of, 70–98, 222–48, 249–96
Matta, Guillermo, 51
Maurras, Charles, 231, 251
Mayer, Emile, 242
Meckel, Jacob Clemens, 51, 65,
   100–101
Medina Franzani, Ernesto, 106,
   111, 138–39, 269
Melot, André, 118
Melot, Henri, 118, 119
Menu, Charles, 198
Mercado Jarrín, Edgardo, 294,
   307 n. 19
Messersmith, George, 212
Mexico, 145, 147, 190, 191
Michel, Henri, 243
Middle sectors. *See* Bourgeoisie
Military: as civilizing force,
   22–23, 63, 70–98, 99–153,
   222–48, 249–96; as educating
   force, 70–98, 99–153, 222–48,
   249–96; as integrative force,
   70–98, 99–153, 222–48,
   249–96; peacetime role of,
   70–98, 99–153, 222–48,
   249–96; political activities of,
   158–81, 183–221, 222–96. *See
   also* Officer Corps

Military-civilian collaboration, as
officer corps priority, 99–153,
222–48, 249–96
Military-civilian relations. *See
names of individual countries*
Military elitism, 99–153, 222–48,
249–96
Military ethos, 99–153, 222–48,
249–96
Military families, 4, 60
Military history and tradition.
*See names of individual
countries*
Military ideals and values (officer corps thought and self-
perception), 4–5, 62, 70–98,
99–153, 176–81, 222–48,
249–96
Military ideology, 249–96
Military legislation, 99–153
Military literature, 70–98,
99–153, 222–48, 249–96
Military lore, 62, 70–98, 99–153,
222–48, 249–96
Military missions. *See names of
individual countries*
Military modernization, 63,
99–153, 183–221, 222–48,
249–96; in Argentina, 122–31,
255–64; in Brazil, 60, 131–36,
255–60, 265–68; in Chile,
101–12, 268–76; in Peru,
112–22, 276–85
Military personnel and recruitment, 99–153, 249–96; in
Argentina, 45–49, 99–153,
255–64; in Brazil, 56–61,
99–153, 255–60, 265–68; in
Chile, 49–52, 101–12, 268–76;
in France, 70–98, 222–49; in
Germany, 70–98, 222–49; in
Peru, 53–56, 112–22, 276–85.
See also Obligatory military
service

Military professionalism. *See
names of individual countries;*
Professional militarism
Military professionalization,
45–64, 99–153, 222–48
Military schools: of Argentina,
45–49, 122–31, 255–64; of Bra-
zil, 56–61, 131–36, 255–60,
265–68; of Chile, 49–52,
101–12, 268–70; of Peru,
53–56, 112–22, 276–85. *See
also* Ecole Polytechnique;
Kriegsakademie; St. Cyr
Millerand, Alexandre, 251
Miranda Mendes, Aloysio, 268
Miró, Ricardo, 262
Misión civilizadora (Peru),
140–42, 185, 200, 249–96
Missão indígena (Brazil),
134–35, 193, 195, 265
Mission civilizatrice (France), 79
Mitre, Bartolomé, 45, 47–48
Mobilization, military opinion
on, 249–96
Mobilization of 1920 (Chile), 271
Moch, Gaston, 77, 88
Modernization, military ad-
vocacy of, 99–153, 182–221,
249–96
Mohr, Guillermo, 215–16
Molina, Ramón, 257–58, 272
Molina, Víctor, 274
Moltke, Helmuth von, 81, 93, 97,
239
Monroe Doctrine, 189
Montagne Markholtz, Ernesto,
119, 122, 163, 203, 252, 279
Montecinos, Arturo, 111
Montero, Washington, 106, 111
Montero Moreno, René, 272–73
Montes, Ismael, 208
Montt, Jorge, 103
Montt, Manuel, 34
Moore Bravo, Manuel, 139

Morales Bermúdez, Remigio, 38
Morality, as result of military service, 70–98, 222–48, 249–86
Morgan, Edwin V., 204
Morla Concha, Manuel, 280–81
Mosconi, Enrique, 255
Muñoz Figueroa, Alberto, 139
Muro, Genaro, 279

Nación en Armas (Nation in Arms, *Volk in Waffen*), 82–83, 224. *See also* Civilizing mission; *Missão indígena*; *Nation armée*
Nacis (Chile), 176, 274
Nalot, Samuel, 207
National Autonomist Party (Argentina), 28
National defense, 70–98, 99–153, 182–221, 222–48, 249–96
Nationalism, and military, 70–98, 99–153, 182–221, 222–48, 249–96
National security, 70–98, 99–153, 182–221, 222–48, 249–96
Nation armée, 237
Natural resources, military views on, 249–96
Naulin, Stanislaus, 117, 119
Nazi Party (NSDAP, Germany), 161, 176, 225, 239–42, 245–47, 251
Negrete, Luis, 111
New State. *See* Estado Novo
Niederfuhr, Günther, 218
Nimkoff, Pauline, 207
Noel, Paul, 207–19
Notz, Colonel von, 245
Nunk, Friedrich, 105

Obligatory labor service, 245–46. *See also Conscripción vial*
Obligatory military service: in Argentina, 122–31, 249–86; in

Brazil, 136, 145, 249–86; in Chile, 107–12, 249–86; in France, 70–98, 234–37, 242–45; in Germany, 70–98, 237–42, 245–47; in Peru, 120–21, 249–96
Officer corps: of Argentina, 43–69, 99–153, 182–221, 249–96; of Brazil, 43–69, 99–153, 182–221, 249–96; of Chile, 43–69, 99–153, 182–221, 249–96; of France, 70–98, 222–48; of Germany, 70–98, 222–48; of Peru, 43–69, 99–153, 182–221, 249–96. *See also* Military personnel and recruitment; Obligatory military service
Officiersdämmerung (*Offiziersdämmerung*), 232, 239
Offizierbund, 243, 245
Ogden, Charles, 98
O'Grady, Gilbert, 104
O'Higgins, Bernardo, 49
Old Republic (Brazil), 30–33, 162, 164, 165, 181, 195, 203, 267
Oncenio (Peru), 163–64
Opportunitätspolitik, 245
Ortiz, Roberto, 172, 260
Osma, Javier de, 55
Oven, Georg von, 105

Pacifism, 97–98
Palacios, Javier, 271
Pando, José, 143
Panizo, Alberto, 114
Panizo, Vidal C., 278, 279
Paraguay, 45, 147, 180, 191
Pardo, José, 40, 200
Parga Rodrigues, Colonel, 259
Paris, Georges, 199, 209
Parliamentary Republic (Chile), 34–37, 139–40, 162, 164

Partie Communiste (France), 176
Pascal, Ferdinand, 193
Patart, Paul, 118
Paté, Edouard, 118
Paucheu, Omar, 198
Pauli, Karl, 54
Paulo Filho, M., 268
Pax Americana, 217
Paz García, Lieutenant, 278
Pedro I, 57
Pedro II, 29, 57, 59, 103
Peixoto, Floriano, 30, 132
Pellegrin, François, 198, 199–200, 202, 277
Pellegrini, Carlos, 28
Pelotas, Viscount, 59, 132
Penna, Affonso, 31
Pérez Manzanares, José C., 199, 200, 277
Perón, Juan, 174
Perres, George, 98
Perrot, Ernest Claude, 112–14, 117
Pertiné, Basilio, 190, 214
Peru, 13–42, 43–69, 99–153, 157–81, 182–221, 249–96; army of, 6–7, 13–42, 43–69, 99–153, 182–221, 249–96; French missions to, 38–39, 112–22, 163–64, 183–87, 192–98, 219–20; military-civilian relations in, 204, 18–22, 33–41, 53–56, 61–64, 112–22, 162–65, 174–75, 176–79, 203, 208–11, 249–96; military history and tradition of, 53–56; military literature of, 8, 112–22, 140–42, 249–96; military professionalism in, 53–56, 112–22, 182–221, 249–96; officer corps thought and self-perception in, 41–42, 112–221, 140–42, 182–221, 249–96; professional militarism in, 17,

249–96. *See also* Diplomatic relations; Geopolitics; Government and politics
Peruanidad, 21
Peruvian Corporation of London, 38
Pétain, Henri Philippe, 160, 161, 218, 234, 236, 244
Petibon, Jean, 193
Pettier, Major, 207
Philbois, Gaston, 118
Piérola, Nicolás de, 37, 40, 54, 55–56, 113
Pillegrand, August, 199, 209, 211, 219
Pilot, Marcel, 199
Pilot, Louis Emmanuel, 211
Pirsher, Friedrich, 105
Poder moderador (moderative power, Brazil), 60
Poincaré, Raymond, 152, 231, 254
Poindexter, Miles, 189
Politicians and politics. *See* Government and politics; Military-civilian relations
Ponce, Manuel Maria, 119, 203
Popular Front (Chile), 170, 205
Population. *See* Economic and demographic statistics
Portales, Diego, 34, 49
Portugal, Issac, 281
Positivism, 29–31
Prado y Ugarteche, Manuel, 174, 283–84
Prestes, Júlio, 254
Prestes, Luis Carlos, 126, 259
Prieto, Joaquín, 49
Prioux, René, 198
Professional militarism, 170–171, 220–21, 249–96
Protestantism, 76, 88
Prussia, military tradition of, 237–42, 245–47

Prussianization, 99–153
Psichari, Ernest, 228, 262

Race, in military life, 54–55, 60,
    66, 94, 140–42, 151–52, 241,
    278, 280–81
Radical Era (Argentina), 162,
    164, 181, 254
Radical Party (Argentina),
    26–28, 34, 49, 62, 127, 170,
    172, 176
Rakenau, Fritz von, 239
Ramírez, Pablo, 169
Rattenbach, Benjamin, 144
Reyes, Bernardo, 147
Reyes, Rafael, 27, 111
Reynal, Luis, 114, 236
Reynaud, Paul, 235
Riberão Filho, João Gomes, 267
Riccheri, Pablo, 27, 49, 123, 124,
    125–26, 129, 130, 133, 142,
    143, 150
Richon, Paul, 193
Rio Branco, Baron of, 31, 132,
    133
Ríos Gallardo, Conrado, 190
Riquelme, Aníbal, 139
Ritterlichkeit, 246
Rittertum, 24, 80, 144, 145, 230,
    243, 269, 285, 291
Riva Agüero, José María, 53
Roca, Julio Argentino, 27, 46,
    48–49, 52, 61, 111, 123, 126,
    128, 129, 130, 133, 142, 144,
    150
Rochère, Dutheil de la, 118
Rodríguez, José, 144
Rojister, Friedrich von, 105
Rôle social, 70–98, 236–37, 285,
    291
Roman Catholicism, 25–26, 76,
    87–88
Romieux, Jacques, 117

Rondon, Cándido Mariano da
    Silva, 195
Rosas, Juan Manual de, 27, 45,
    48
Rose, Otto, 47
Roth, Ernst, 105
Rotos (Chile), 270
Rottjer, Enrique, 261, 262
Russia, 144, 159, 238, 245

Sackville, William, 206
Sáez Morales, Carlos, 112, 274
Saenz Peña, Roque, 28–29, 302
    n. 26
St. Cyr (France), 45, 47, 75, 91,
    120, 233, 234
Salatz, Louis, 117
Salinas, Julio, 111
Salles, Manuel de Campos, 31
Saly, Sebastian, 193
Sánchez Cerro, Luis María,
    40–41, 164, 168, 174, 203,
    208–9, 254
Sánchez Hernández, Tomás, 275
Sanders, Carl, 104
Sanders, Liman von, 44
Santa Cruz, Andrés de, 53
Santa María, Domingo, 51
Sarmiento, Domingo, 45, 47, 48
Scharnhorst, Gerhard Johann
    David von, 240
Schellendorf, Wilhelm Bronsart
    von, 105
Schliecher, Kurt von, 246
Schlieffen, Alfred, Graf von, 239
Schnevoigt, Hugo, 105
Schönmayer, Alfred, 105
Schulenburg, Hans, Graf von,
    105
Schunk, Bertram, 123
Schwartz, Jean, 207
Seeber, Ricardo, 123
Seeckt, Hans von, 158, 225–28,
    230–31, 239, 275, 282, 290

Seneca, 95
Serrigny, Bernard, 89, 96–97, 200, 277
Silva, Benício da, 220
Sipman, Friedrich, 105
Slavery, 36
Social Darwinism, 20
Social Democrats (Germany), 15, 80, 160, 245
Socialism. *See* Marxism
Sofer, Emilio, 120
Soria, Gaspar, 259
Soroche (altitude sickness), 304 n. 38
Sombra, S., 268
South America, in European military literature, 65–68, 147–51. *See also* Diplomatic relations
Souza, Washington Luis Pereira de, 165, 203, 254
Spartacists (Germany), 176
Spero, Captain, 96
Spire, Joseph, 196, 197
Steward, Elmore, 203
Stimson, Henry, 203, 209

Tacna-Arica dispute, 33, 53
Tanant, General, 235
Téllez Indalicio, 276
Tenentes, 162–63
Tenentismo, 163, 176, 195, 196
Terán, Domingo, 139
Termé, Christian, 118
Theiss, Richard, 92
Thiebert, Louis, 193
Third Reich, 16, 214, 248
Third Republic, 16–17, 71–98, 158, 225–48
Thomas, Georges, 198, 199
Thorndyke, Guillermo, 209
Tisseyre, Raymond, 118, 119
Totalitarianism, and the military, 239–42, 245–47

Treitschke, Heinrich von, 80–81, 84
Trentinian, General de, 95
Turkey, Germans in, 26, 44

Unicato (Argentina), 165
Unión Cívica de la Juventud (Argentina). *See* Radical Party
Unión Patriótica (Peru), 176
United States, 5, 7–8, 14, 177, 248; army of, 144; military relations with Argentina, 177–79, 182–221, 249–96; military relations with Brazil, 173, 177–79, 182–221, 249–96; military relations with Chile, 177–79, 182–221, 249–96; military relations with Peru, 177–79, 182–221, 249–96
Urcullo, Félix, 106
Uriburu, José Evaristo, 126
Uriburu, José F. B., 125, 126–27, 130, 133, 145, 164, 171, 184, 191, 211, 254, 263
Uriondo, Oscar, 262
Uruguay, 45, 57, 147, 191

Vacarezza, Juan, 261, 262
Valdez, Renato, 106
Valdivia, Francisco, 279
Vallaume, August, 193
Vallejo, César, 251
Varela, Angel, 114, 275
Vargas, Getúlio, 172, 174, 203–8, 254, 267
Vargas, Jorge, 281
Vassal, Bonaventure, 198
Vauvineux, Armand Pottin, Comte, 112–14, 117
Velarde, César, 281
Velarde Alvarez, Gabriel, 140, 185, 202, 277
Venezuela, 191

Verdy, Bernard, 198, 199
Versailles, Treaty of, 190, 192, 221
Vicat, Luis, 256–57
Vichy regime, 211, 218–19
"Video," 236
Vignola, Pedro, 112
Vignon, Major, 206
Vigny, Alfred, Comte de, 23, 75, 77, 78, 228, 230, 262, 266, 282, 290
Viotte, Colonel, 242
Voigt, Arno, 238–39

Walker Martínez, Gustavo, 106
War Department (U.S.), 184–221
War of the Desert (Argentina), 27
War of the Pacific, 28, 33, 41, 49, 50–51, 54, 55, 62–63
War of the Triple Alliance, 45, 56, 62
Weddel, Alexander W., 214, 215

Weimar Republic, 16–17, 222–48
Weller, Joseph, 199, 209, 211
Wetzel, Georg, 240–41
Weygand, Maxime, 234–35, 275
Wilhelm II, 103, 130
Wood, Leonard, 90–91
Wooten, Ralph, 189
Wrangel, Fritz von, 105
Wright, Joshua Baxter, 187
Wulffen, Egon von, 105
Würth Rojas, Ernesto, 273

Yacimientos Petrolíferos Fiscales (YPF, Argentina), 255
Yáñez, Germán, 119, 203
Yrigoyen, Hipólito, 28–29, 162, 165, 170, 171, 184, 254, 260, 302 n. 27

Zapater, Issac, 119
Zimmerman, Carl, 105
Zola, Emile, 25, 71
Zuleta, Celso, 114